Praise for
NECESSARY TROUBLE

"*Necessary Trouble* is American history at its freshest and most compelling. Sarah Jaffe traces the many ways—from left to right—that Americans have risen up in response to the country's ongoing takeover by the obscenely rich. Sometimes we have to make trouble, and, as Jaffe reports, we're pretty damn good at it!"

—BARBARA EHRENREICH, author of *Nickel and Dimed*

"History is filled with stories of rebellion—and not just history, as Sarah Jaffe shows. What we've too often lacked are reporters willing and able to weave one-day stories into meaningful fabric. Jaffe does just that, with depth and breadth and eloquence. *Necessary Trouble* is necessary reading, and Jaffe's arrival is something to celebrate."

—LAURA FLANDERS,
host and founder of *The Laura Flanders Show*

"Like Boadicea leading the Celts against the Romans or Joan of Arc breaking the siege of Orleans, Sarah Jaffe marches into the class war, fighting the good fight with a pen as sharp as any sword."

—BILL MOYERS

"The political activism and beliefs of ordinary Americans are as ignored as they are consequential. Sarah Jaffe is one of the few American journalists who has meaningfully covered this vital, growing force—invariably with passion, empathy, and unflinching insight. Her new book is indispensable for understanding how marginalized and resource-deprived communities are politically empowering themselves in ways that will fundamentally shape America's future."

—GLENN GREENWALD, author of *No Place to Hide*

"Declarations of democracy's demise are greatly exaggerated. Democracy has been in bloom since the 2008 economic crisis, flowering in the Occupy movement, in the South's Moral Mondays, in the BlackLivesMatter movement and the Fight for $15, in the streets and halls of government in Chicago and Detroit, Seattle and St. Louis. While commercial media can't seem to turn away from the Trump circus or Hillary's e-mails, Sarah Jaffe follows America's new radicals. And in doing so, tells a far more consequential story—one that reveals our recent past and an alternative future. The most compelling social and political portrait of our age, *Necessary Trouble* should be mandatory for anyone who thinks justice is necessary."

—ROBIN D. G. KELLEY, author of *Freedom Dreams: The Black Radical Imagination*

"Sarah Jaffe has written a wise and eloquent book about the surging movements against inequality that are giving the one percent a run for its money. If you want to understand the present and future of the American left, you must read *Necessary Trouble*."

—MICHAEL KAZIN, coeditor of *Dissent* and author of *War Against War: The American Fight for Peace, 1914–1918*

"Sarah Jaffe draws on her journalistic experience and talent to give us a vivid portrait of the contemporary protest movements that just may transform America."

—FRANCES FOX PIVEN, author of *Challenging Authority*

"Sarah Jaffe's book tells the story of the giant step made by America's networked young people off the sidelines of progressive politics and into the foreground. It weaves together the story of radicalized labor activism, black protests against police violence, and the horizontalist movements. These are the stories the millennial generation will tell their grandchildren—about how they reversed the balance between the citizen and corporate power, and saved the planet."

—PAUL MASON, author of *Postcapitalism:*
A Guide to Our Future

"What kind of troublemaker is Sarah Jaffe? The Tom Paine, Frederick Douglass, Ida B. Wells, and Upton Sinclair muckraking, radical kind. She identifies the issues that must be addressed and then finds the rebels and rabble-rousers, agitators and change makers who are doing the addressing. She amplifies their voices with a power that demands an immediate response to the age-old question: Which side are you on? I'm ready with my answer: If Sarah Jaffe says it's time to fight, I'm in."

—JOHN NICHOLS, author of *People Get Ready*

"*Necessary Trouble* is an engaging and insightful guide to the new American radicalism that erupted in the wake of the Great Recession. Jaffe deftly exposes the roots of anti-establishment activism across the political spectrum, from the Tea Party to Occupy Wall Street, the BlackLivesMatter movement, and the Fight for $15. A must-read for anyone interested in the nation's future."

—RUTH MILKMAN, president, American Sociological
Association, and author of *On Gender, Labor and Inequality*

"Americans can be a quiescent people. But for the past eight years, we have been in revolt—consider #BlackLivesMatter, Moral Mondays, the Fight for $15, Occupy, the Bernie Sanders campaign, fights to save the public sector in Wisconsin and Chicago, and many more insurgencies. Yet few journalists have properly chronicled this moment, much less explained how and why such efforts came about, or analyzed their relation to one another. In this whip-smart, informative, and inspiring book, Sarah Jaffe has done all that and much more: she has also summoned us to join in and make history. We must heed her!"

—LIZA FEATHERSTONE, author of *Selling Women Short: The Landmark Battle for Workers Rights at Walmart*

"Without a doubt, Sarah Jaffe is the preeminent social movement chronicler of her generation. Cutting through the hype, she finds the unsung heroes and tells the real story of how change happens. Mixing razor-sharp analysis with moving reports from the front lines, *Necessary Trouble* reveals the interconnections, complexities, and possibilities of nearly a decade of radical uprisings. Read this book now—and then join the revolt."

—ASTRA TAYLOR, author of *The People's Platform* and cofounder of The Debt Collective

"Sarah paints a clear picture of the very real inequalities facing working people today, as well as the anger, energy, and optimism that is fueling movements and activism across the county. From Occupy Wall Street to BlackLivesMatter, this book proves that there is incredible power when people come together to take back the power that belongs to them and change the rules so everyday people can win."

—SARITA GUPTA, Jobs with Justice

NECESSARY
TROUBLE

NECESSARY TROUBLE

Americans in Revolt

Sarah Jaffe

NATION BOOKS
NEW YORK

Books published by Nation Books are available at special discounts for
bulk purchases in the United States by corporations, institutions, and
other organizations. For more information, please contact the Special
Markets Department at the Perseus Books Group, 2300 Chestnut
Street, Suite 200, Philadelphia, PA 19103, or call (800) 810-4145,
ext. 5000, or e-mail special.markets@perseusbooks.com.

Designed by Linda Mark

Library of Congress Cataloging-in-Publication Data
Names: Jaffe, Sarah, 1980– author.
Title: Necessary trouble : Americans in revolt / Sarah Jaffe.
Description: New York : Nation Books, [2016] | Includes
bibliographical references and index.
Identifiers: LCCN 2016017890| ISBN 9781568585369 (hardcover) |
ISBN 9781568585376 (ebook)
Subjects: LCSH: Protest movements–United States. | Political
    participation–United States. | Political activists–United States. |
    Social movements–United States. | United States–Politics and
    government—2009–
Classification: LCC HN59.2 .J34 2016 | DDC 303.48/40973–dc23 LC
record available at https://lccn.loc.gov/2016017890

10 9 8 7 6 5 4 3 2

For my parents

This is the way another generation did it, and you too can follow that path, studying the way of peace, love and nonviolence, and finding a way to get in the way. Finding a way to get in trouble, good trouble, necessary trouble.

—Rep. John Lewis, US Congress (D-GA)

CONTENTS

INTRODUCTION	No Future Shock	1
ONE	Banks Got Bailed Out, We Got Sold Out	13
TWO	Middle-Class Meltdown and the Debt Trap	45
THREE	Walmart, Walmart, You Can't Hide, We Can See Your Greedy Side	71
FOUR	Challenging the Austeritarians	99
FIVE	Race to the Bottom	129
SIX	A Moral Movement	159
SEVEN	Red Scares and Radical Imagination	189
EIGHT	The Militarization of Everything	215
NINE	Change Is Gonna Come	249
CONCLUSION	Our Future Is Not Yours to Leverage	277
	Acknowledgments	289
	Notes	293
	Index	325

NO FUTURE SHOCK

T HE MAN ON THE SCREEN HAS A RICH SOUTHERN ACCENT, AND he speaks with pride of his hometown. Ripley, Mississippi, to hear J. D. Meadows tell it, is a great place to live.

It's just that the economy has gone to hell. "My uncle lost his job up here at Bench Craft, and so did my aunt. Their company shut down and moved to China," he says to the filmmakers who have come down to Ripley to talk to him and other members of the then burgeoning Tea Party movement.

It's January 2010. I'm sitting in a TV studio in New York, a long way from Ripley, listening to my boss, Laura Flanders, interview Meadows about the Tea Party and why he has decided to join. The economy collapsed while I was finishing journalism school, and though I was tempted to stay in school, get another degree, and hope that the job market would be better by the time I finished, or at least before I racked up too much more debt, I rolled the dice and got lucky. I found a job during the worst economic crisis since the Great Depression, working on a small independent TV program, GRITtv.

After Bench Craft left, Meadows is saying, his town's industrial park started to dry up. "A lot of it has to do with Wall Street," he tells Laura. "I've had a lot of family lose jobs." He's a small business owner, a computer repairman, and the loss of jobs in town has hurt his business. "The number one issue right now," he says, "is the economy."

Meadows is on today's show along with filmmaker Rick Rowley, who has coproduced a short documentary on the rise of the Tea Party, and Chip Berlet of Political Research Associates. Rowley met Meadows after he joined the Council of Conservative Citizens and helped organize a Tea Party event in Ripley. The Tea Party was easily caricatured, particularly by people on the left side of the political aisle, but Meadows's complaints sound like the ones my friends and I make to each other. He expresses distaste for both political parties and their connections to wealthy elites. It's a refrain I will hear over and over again in the next several years.

Nearly two years later, I walk through Zuccotti Park in Lower Manhattan. It has been renamed Liberty Plaza by its new "occupants," and it is ringed with handmade cardboard protest signs. In front, a young woman holds a sign that says "Too Big to Fail? Corruption is Bleeding Our Wealth!" A young man beside her has one that reads "Take Back America . . . Reclaim Democracy!" Meadows's complaints would not have seemed out of place carefully lettered on cardboard at Occupy Wall Street.

It started on a Saturday in September 2011—the 17th—when a band of activists who'd answered the call from the magazine *Adbusters* was blocked from taking up residence on Wall Street itself and headed for a park around the corner, where they camped out. I had shrugged the movement off at first; I'd seen a lot of protests since the 2008 crisis, but none of them had seemed to achieve much. The occupation of the Wisconsin State Capitol a few months earlier had been a spark, but that energy had faded, at least for those of us not in Madison, and I was faced with a constant grind of depressing news coming out of Washington, where a government shutdown was looming that I was required, as a staff reporter at the independent online news outlet AlterNet, to cover.

But on Day 5, I decide to give Occupy a chance anyway. Walking through the park, I begin to see what has people excited. The "occupiers" are mostly, but not exclusively, young, and there is already a rudimentary infrastructure in the park, including the famous library. The comfort station is stacked with blankets, there for the asking. The kitchen is handing out food, which I don't take at first. There are guitarists, drummers, dancers. An American flag flies over the information station, which offers a Daily Schedule. "Wall Street is Our Street," reads a sign leaning against a garbage can.

The movement is spreading across the country; in the course of my reporting on Occupy over the next year, I talk to activists from Kentucky, Ohio, California, Connecticut, and many, many more places. "We are the 99 percent," is the rallying cry, and people who don't have a park near their home to occupy—or who can't take time away from the never-ending hustle to make enough money to pay the bills—take to the Internet. On a Tumblr blog, they begin posting photos of themselves holding up posters or sheets of notebook paper, some handwritten, some typed, telling their stories of economic distress. They write letters to bank CEOs on a website called Occupy the Boardroom. They briefly dominate the news cycle—any story that I write about Occupy gets hundreds of thousands of clicks.

I sometimes think of Meadows while walking through Zuccotti Park. For some reason, his story sticks with me, along with something that Rick Rowley said: that people like Meadows were looking for someone with an answer to why they were so screwed. There was no party, no organization, that had answers to our problems that went beyond the level of the individual. Work hard, roll the dice, like I had, and hope to find a decent job that pays the bills. The Tea Party had given people a place to express their anger, but years later, things are still not getting better, and Americans still have so much to be angry about.

People like Meadows, and like the people I met in the park, are still struggling. The "recovery" hasn't brought about fundamental change in the way society functions (or even in the way banks are regulated); instead, it has made things worse for the majority of Americans. It has accelerated the decline of wages, spurred the movement of jobs overseas, and increased the concentration of wealth in a few hands.

The Tea Party and Occupy were some of the earliest and most prominent movements to register frustration; they helped usher in a new era of protest and activism that has had a dramatic effect on the way Americans understand their power to disrupt the status quo, to challenge lingering inequality wherever it is found. I was hired at AlterNet to be the labor editor, but these movements quickly become my beat: the troublemakers who are marching through the financial district, occupying bank lobbies, locking arms and refusing to leave a foreclosed home, blocking streets, rising up. The seeds have been planted by a thousand outrages, and that they would sprout has always been a question of when, not if.

THE FINANCIAL CRISIS WAS THE SPARK, THE MOMENT THAT CRYSTALlized for people around the country that something was wrong, something that one election couldn't possibly fix. All of the trends—the slow disappearance of good jobs, the endless cuts to public institutions, the concentration of wealth at the top—that had been underway since at least the Nixon era suddenly seemed to go into hyperspeed. The mechanisms by which the world ran became visible, and it suddenly seemed possible, not that someone would overthrow capitalism, but that it would self-destruct.

In 2008, though, we weren't ready. Nobody was ready. As the stock market plummeted in the fall of 2008, high-ranking executives who hadn't shown their faces on the trading floor in years came down to stand and watch a giant screen as the numbers plummeted. The masters of the universe that we had been assured had everything under control had nothing of the sort, but bipartisan consensus had long ago coalesced around the idea that Wall Street was equivalent to the economy itself, that markets were not only the best but the only possible way to arrange things, and there was almost no one left who had access to a microphone of any size offering up answers. Instead, we got shock.

Americans had been losing faith in our elites for some time. The steady erosion that began perhaps with Vietnam had sped up during what political commentator Christopher Hayes called the "fail decade" of the 2000s. The attacks of September 11, 2001, the wars in Afghanistan and Iraq that spun out of control, and the devastation of the Gulf Coast after Katrina all culminated in the crisis of 2008, and the powerful failed to protect us. After the collapse, we expected someone to have a solution, but none was forthcoming. Instead, we got unemployment that spiked to 10 percent in 2009 and foreclosures that spiraled above 5 million. As the protest chant went, "Banks got bailed out, we got sold out." We remain, in one estimate, about 3.5 million full-time jobs short of where we need to be. Everywhere I heard a profound dissatisfaction with the way things were, coupled in most people with resignation. Or perhaps it was simply a matter of priorities—everyone was working too hard to stay afloat to have time to think about rebellion. Congress regularly polled below cockroaches, witches, and Nickelback. That dissatisfaction manifested itself in rock-bottom voter turnout rates—falling from 2008's 62.2 percent to 2014's 36.7 percent, the lowest since World War II—and rapid electoral swings from party to party among the voters who bothered at all.[1]

American politics, people realized, had been bought and paid for, and the bank bailouts were just the biggest indication of, by, and for whom. Powerful interests, as political scientists Thomas Ferguson, Martin Gilens, Benjamin Page, and others have been telling us for years, are the ones who pay for elections, and they are the ones whose preferred policies get enacted. The 2012 election was estimated to cost $10 billion—nearly double what was spent on the 2008 race—and 2016 is shaping up to double again. The idea that the United States has a functioning democracy has come to seem, to most people who are not personally invested in the system, laughable.[2]

We needed something beyond the ballot box, but in 2008 and 2009, it wasn't clear what that something would be. Slowly, Americans began to find other ways to express their power; the rapid response of a rattled Republican Party to the first actions of the Tea Party showed that disruptive action could have an effect on policy, could drive politicians to court movements. When Occupy Wall Street first took Zuccotti Park, it was laughed off even by those who might have been expected to be supportive—until it began to spread across the country, holding spaces for people to come together and discuss the deep-rooted problems that had created the crisis they still felt, despite all the politicians' promises of recovery. By the time Black Lives Matter seized the stage, it became clear that something was fundamentally changing. Americans, in short, were getting radical.

The issue of inequality came roaring back onto the scene with Occupy Wall Street. It was not simply that so many people just didn't have enough to get by, from autoworkers who had taken a pay cut to keep their companies afloat to retirees who had seen their savings evaporate, teachers who found themselves blamed for state budget gaps, college graduates serving lattes at Starbucks, and single mothers stringing

together two fast-food jobs to feed the kids. It was that there for all to
see were the people who had too much. The wealthy recognized it, too:
newspaper stories occasionally appeared about $230,000 guard dogs,
armored yachts, and luxury bomb shelters to protect the rich from an
imagined assault from below. It was no longer a question, for many
people, of left or right, of Democrat or Republican, but of powerful
and powerless. The two parties, as the Reverend William J. Barber II of
Moral Mondays said, offered a choice too puny for this moment.[3]

It is not just inequality in income or wealth that is setting off protests
in the streets, either; it's the whole set of other inequalities that come
alongside them. It's the way a police officer who shoots or chokes a black
man to death can walk away with paid leave, while the man who video-
taped the killing winds up in jail on petty charges. It's the way multibil-
lionaires (or talk-show hosts pretending to be them) can get a personal
phone call from the governor of a state, while ordinary citizens seeking
redress from him are likened to terrorists. It's how decisions are made
about where to locate a new coal-fired power plant. As South Bronx activist Mychal Johnson told me, it's the air we breathe: it's about power, it's
about inclusion, it's about access, and it's about who counts as a person.[4]

Concentrated economic power leads to concentrated political power.
Those with the money can buy not just an election, but all the legislating
that comes in between; the rich see their policy preferences enacted,
and the rest of us see that happen only when our desires align with those
of the rich and powerful. As wealth becomes concentrated in the hands
of a smaller and smaller group, it is easier and easier for that group to
shape policy, and harder for the rest of us to have any influence. And so
Americans are searching for other ways to exercise power, to have their
own voices heard. Anger continues to simmer just under the surface,
and occasionally, when enough people are angry enough to overcome
their reasons for holding back, it explodes.

In writing this book, I wanted to find out what people were angry
about, and what they were doing to take their power back. I traveled the
country, building on the years of reporting I'd already done by meeting
activists where they lived and worked and organized. I attended a people's assembly in a church gymnasium in Ferguson, Missouri; walked
a picket line at an Atlanta Burger King at 6 a.m.; rode a bus from New
York to Ohio with student organizers; and sat with airport and home

care workers in Seattle as they told stories about their jobs. I danced at a fundraiser for Occupy Homes Minnesota, and I went door to door in Far Rockaway, Queens, days after Hurricane Sandy. I met people who were struggling but were finding ways to make change.

I wanted, too, to provide some historical context for what I was seeing and hearing, to dig into the stories of America's past rebels and rabble-rousers. My aim was not to weigh and measure today's troublemakers against their ancestors but to help us understand the threads that these movements picked up and the ones they discarded, the ways they have learned from the past and the bits of the past that many people have forgotten or never knew. The words of abolitionists, populists, teachers, miners, and steelworkers who struggled against the powerful are echoed by the troublemakers of what some are calling the New Gilded Age.

Across the country, people from vastly different backgrounds were coming together to make trouble. People who were often considered— and had considered themselves—on opposite sides of the political spectrum have joined forces to shake up the powerful. Many others who had never considered political action at all have come forward, too, activated by fighting foreclosure or fracking in their communities, or by the difficulty of trying to win a raise in the workplace. From localized, individual fights, they progressed into something else, into engaging in civil disobedience at the Justice Department, or blocking a highway to demand justice for a victim of police violence. Many of the movements discussed in this book come from what would have been considered the political left—but for the people taking part in them, it is not a question of left or right, but of the powerless against the powerful.

It is often assumed that activism is powered by young people, and I did find many uprisings powered by those much-maligned "millennials," the people British journalist Paul Mason called "graduates with no future," and who Trish Kahle, historian, labor activist, and member of that generation, deemed "the Left Out generation." But I also met quite a few older people, those retired or near retirement whose savings had been wiped out in 2008, or grandparents worried about the world they were leaving their grandchildren. I met Barbara Smalley-McMahan in Raleigh, North Carolina, who gave up her pastoral counseling practice of thirty years in order to become a full-time activist, and who told me about the "theology of disrespect" that she'd learned from young people in St. Louis. I met Martha Sellers, who by age fifty-seven had spent twelve years working at Walmart in Paramount, California, and who after the death of her husband had decided she'd had enough.[5]

The movements I cover in this book are often figured as discrete phenomena, analyzed as if they had each happened in a vacuum. But in fact, as I followed them through the years, I would find similar patterns and even direct connections between them. They were all, in one way or another, responding to elite failure and inequality; they were powered by and shaped by social media and the network—both technological and human communication networks—but relied on public space to make their impact felt. They went "viral," spreading horizontally across the country, rather than being led by a single person or even a single organization, which made them hard to corral and sometimes hard to decipher, for a media and a country used to power structured in hierarchies. They embraced the power of disruption. And especially as they began to overlap and to connect, they became intersectional movements, wrapping up issues as seemingly disparate as mortgage debt and climate change into one.

"Intersectionality" is a term coined by legal theorist Kimberlé Crenshaw to explain the way that social inequality has many layers that overlap—intersect—with one another and shape the way different people experience oppression. To Diamond Latchison, from the Ferguson movement, this meant that she could not separate the fact that she was black from the fact that she was a woman and that she was queer, and that the abuses she faced in her life were often not because of one or the other facets of her identity, but of multiple facets at once.

The technologies that the movements used influenced how they were structured: a movement spreading virally across the country has less need for the charismatic leadership that Americans seem to expect from social movements. No one had to wait for permission, which made the movements harder to stamp out. One individual, or one group, could fail and others continue without them; the eviction of one occupation, or one protest called where no one showed up, was not the end of anything. This "horizontal" structure seems to suit something about the twenty-first century and about the particular set of outrages, frustrations, and grievances that brought people together, but it also tells us something about the values of the movements. The ability to be heard is deeply important to many people today. We are in a world that feels like it is powered by elites who pay little attention to the rest of us. So in movements that are responding to the failure of elite leadership, it makes sense that there is resistance to the idea of a "movement elite," even as leaders emerge and fade.

Horizontal structures also recognize that the power of these movements stem from their broad base; while the vast majority of Americans, of course, are not becoming activists, these movements rely on the power of many people to break through the walls that hold individuals back. When people talk to one another about their problems, and come to the realization that their struggles are not their fault, they become more likely to take action. People are drawn to movements that appear to already have support, in part because they are simply more visible, and in part because they feel like they can win. Solidarity—a value that, in recent decades, had fallen out of favor in the face of the glamour of the free market and the promise that, individually, we could all get rich—has come back in these movements, often in surprising ways.

The ideal of horizontalism is connected to the sense that democracy, in this country, is failing, or perhaps, as some are coming to believe, that it never really worked. The general assemblies of the Occupy movement were perhaps the most obvious experiment with other forms of democracy, flawed but fascinating in their particular procedures: the twinkling fingers of assent, the voices repeating one another through the "people's mic." At the same time, these movements have fraught and complicated relationships with electoral politics. Many of the troublemakers write off voting as irrelevant, impossible; others aim to influence the political process through action and have had some success, converting politicians like New York governor Andrew Cuomo from opponents to proponents of their cause in the space of a year. Collective action is seen as a way to influence politicians who might otherwise simply listen to their well-heeled donors, a way to build change that goes beyond what happens at the ballot box.

Today's movements might be spawned on the Internet, but they come together in public space. They challenge contested political locations—Tea Partiers gathered at congressional "town hall" meetings, Moral Mondays committing civil disobedience at the state assembly— and they hold symbolic spaces, like occupying Zuccotti Park or holding a sit-down strike at Walmart in California. Instead of quietly voting and going home to shout at the television, people who seemed to have very little in common are coming together in such spaces to reclaim the power of public protest, of communicating directly with one another, of being together.

Most importantly, today's activists have discovered the power of making trouble, of causing disruption. Disrupting things, says longtime labor organizer Stephen Lerner, is the best way for regular people to exercise some power. It isn't about winning everyone over to one's side; it is, instead, about finding a way to disrupt the day-to-day existence of those who do have power, to make them feel the crisis that they have inflicted on millions of people. Disruption, whether it be blocking a street, going on strike, or occupying a space, is a way to ensure that the message—that something has got to give—gets across.

It is not due to tactics, though, that I refer to today's troublemakers as "radicals." I use the word here to mean those who seek to understand and change problems at their root. As civil rights icon and organizer Ella Baker put it, to think in radical terms "means facing a system that does not lend itself to your needs and devising means by which you change that system." For really changing a society where a small elite controls most of the power and resources will not be easy. There will be a lot of resistance, and tinkering at the surface is unlikely to last. It is that understanding that drives the people I spoke to for this book, and that gives me hope that they might have an effect.[6]

THE IDEA FOR THIS BOOK WAS PERCOLATING IN MY MIND FROM THE moment I heard J. D. Meadows speak, but it took shape over the course of the years of reporting that came afterward. Hundreds of conversations, interviews, and arguments—and a lot of shoe leather—brought me to a place where I thought I could write a book that sheds some light on why people from Oakland to Raleigh and from Miami to New York were willing to put their bodies on the line in order to insist that things are unfair and must change. In the midst of that work, I sat down with a former Student Nonviolent Coordinating Committee leader, Congressman John Lewis (D-GA), fresh from the publication of a rendition of his life told through comics, and asked him for advice for the Dream Defenders, who at that time were occupying Florida's Capitol building in protest after the death of Trayvon Martin. The words he spoke gave this book its title and epigraph.

I set out to put these movements in context—both in the context of one another and in the context of the history that laid the groundwork for them to emerge. This book necessarily omits some of that context— the United States was erupting in protests at the same time that countries around the world were, and organizers in the United States drew heavily from their overseas counterparts. In fact, one of the first people I met at Occupy Wall Street was a visitor from Spain, who had been part of the *indignados* protests there and came across the Atlantic to help Occupy set up. But other books have been written that explore those connections.

This is mostly not a book about electoral politics, with a few significant exceptions when candidates sprang directly from movements, rather than claiming the mantle of one or the other in order to capture press attention, as so many did when the Tea Party arose. Nor is it a book about cheap populism spouted by posturing elites. Rather, it is about the way people discover their power together. Other movements, in particular the vibrant immigrant rights struggle that reached its apex in the "Day Without an Immigrant" general strike on May Day 2006, fed into the ones I wrote about as well, and other moments besides the financial crisis no doubt contributed to the anger and momentum that launched the new radicals into the streets. But to cover every possible spark is beyond the scope of one book.

Few writers have explored the connections between the post-2008 movements within the United States. In fact, many people seem determined to pretend that there have been none, a fact that never ceases to surprise me, as the marches, demonstrations, and occupations of this decade have drawn more people, perhaps, than any other protest movement in this country's history. But as historian Robin D. G. Kelley reminded me, "having numbers in the streets is not an automatic measure of success." We have an image in our heads of what a movement looks like, and often nostalgia allows us to misunderstand both the past and the present. Getting people into the streets is simply a start; it matters what those people do once they are activated, how they manage to exert power—whether that is shutting down a shopping corridor on the busiest shopping day of the year, stopping the foreclosure on a home, or blockading a pipeline.

It matters to get this story right. It matters because, as Seattle City Council member Kshama Sawant told me, if we continue to assume that change happens because benevolent leaders at the top hand it down, then we will continue to ask nicely, and to be disappointed, frustrated, and disempowered when asking nicely does not do the trick.

This book is not about me, and yet I have to admit that reporting it and writing it changed me, that every person I spoke with, marched with, and stood with as they were arrested changed my understanding of how the world works. They also changed the world around them, forcing new political possibilities to exist when there were none and shaking up the comfort of the so-called "one percent."

I did my best to tell their story in their words. In many cases, I deliberately sought out those whose stories had not been told, whose voices had not been heard, because even in a "leaderless" movement, there will be those whose voices are louder, and there are social and political reasons why this is so. I could not hope to tell the entire story of any one movement or even any one event; there have been and will be books that will delve deeper and uncover stories that I did not find.

Instead, what I have tried to do is to bring you an understanding of today's new radicals, the troublemakers who refuse any longer to sit on the sidelines and wait for things to improve, for the electoral process to offer us up the lesser of two evils, and for the people who sign our paychecks to decide to grant us a raise. They are coming together and presenting a significant challenge to the status quo; indeed, they have already changed it.

CHAPTER ONE

BANKS GOT BAILED OUT,
WE GOT SOLD OUT

IT WAS DECEMBER 2, 2008, WHEN THE 240 PEOPLE WHO WORKED at the Republic Windows and Doors factory in Chicago got the notification that they were losing their jobs.

Months into the recession launched by the collapse of financial markets, the company, which made energy-efficient windows and doors ideal for the green retrofitting being touted by president-elect Barack Obama, was struggling. But the biggest problem, according to the workers themselves, was Bank of America. Despite a fresh infusion of taxpayer dollars being pumped into the bank's coffers—$25 billion, supposedly to reinvigorate its stalled lending in the wake of the financial crisis—the bank was apparently unwilling to continue extending credit to Republic.

There had been some indications that things were not going well for Republic, according to Leah Fried, an organizer with the United Electrical, Radio and Machine Workers of America (UE) Local 1110, the union representing the employees. But while the announcement came as a shock, the workers at Republic were not going to join the ranks of the 600,000 other manufacturing workers laid off that year without a fight. "If I don't fight, I know I lose," said Melvin "Ricky"

Maurice Maclin, vice president of Local 1110. "If I do fight, at least I stand a chance of winning."[1]

Two hundred or so of those window-and-door makers refused to leave, locking themselves into the factory in the first such occupation the United States had seen in decades. Their demands were simple: their legally required severance pay, called for under the Worker Adjustment and Retraining Notification (WARN) Act, which requires sixty days' notice before a mass layoff. Lalo Munoz, who had worked for Republic for thirty-four years, said, "They decided just to kick us into the streets, with no benefits or nothing, not even what we have already earned."[2]

The workers' willingness to resist surprised the organizers. "We proposed this idea of occupying the factory as a peaceful nonviolent civil disobedience," Fried told me. "What we didn't anticipate was everybody wanting to be a part of it." She'd expected fifty or so workers to stay in the factory, but over four times that number did. "We're here, and we're not going anywhere until we get what's fair and what's ours. They thought they would get rid of us easily, but if we have to be here for Christmas, it doesn't matter," said Silvia Mazon, a thirteen-year employee at Republic at her first protest.[3]

Their occupation tapped into a growing anger among Americans at the size of the bailout package extended to the world's biggest banks, the very people responsible for the crisis that had tossed so many out of work, shuttered so many small businesses, and evaporated billions in housing wealth. National media, long unused to covering labor struggles, poured in, speaking to workers through an open door. Rabble-rousing documentarian Michael Moore turned up. So did the local bishop of the Evangelical Catholic Church, James Wilkowski, the son of a steelworker, who administered Communion to the workers in the occupied factory. Jesse Sharkey, a local teacher who was also engaged in a fight over public schools turned up and spoke. Congresswoman Jan Schakowsky (D-IL) paid the workers a visit. And president-elect Barack Obama addressed the workers in a news conference, saying, "The workers who are asking for the benefits and payments that they have earned, I think they're absolutely right and understand that what's happening to them is reflective of what's happening across this economy."[4]

After six days of splashy media coverage and protests in front of Bank of America branches around the country in solidarity with the occupiers,

Republic and the bank agreed to the workers' demands. In February 2009, California company Serious Materials purchased the factory and agreed to hire back the old workforce.

After the victory, the workers took a "Republic victory tour" to inspire more people to fight back as they had. They told their listeners they didn't have to take concessions and accept the status quo. "I'd like to think that we helped kick off the next wave, and certainly the chant that we came up with, which was 'Banks Got Bailed Out, We Got Sold Out,' was adopted by a lot of people," Fried said.

While the Republic workers were trying to encourage others to stand up and fight, most of the country remained in shock. But shortly after Serious Materials bought the Republic factory, a group of Connecticut residents boarded a bus headed to prosperous Fairfield, median income over $78,000. They were headed to the home of Douglas L. Poling, executive vice president for energy and infrastructure investments at American International Group (AIG), technically an insurance company, but one with an investment bank grafted on top. This unwieldy beast had insured a slew of bad mortgages via credit-default swaps, which required AIG to pay out if the mortgages went into default. When those bad mortgages failed, so did AIG, and the US government stepped in and bailed it out, to the tune of over $170 billion.[5]

The bailout alone would have made people angry enough. Regular people, many of them suddenly unemployed or facing foreclosure, were already wondering why the big banks merited more than $700 billion and they got nothing. Congress rebelled at the idea that it should hand over that many taxpayer dollars without any strings attached, and made Treasury Secretary Henry Paulson, formerly of Goldman Sachs, go back and revise the main bailout during the last days of his tenure in the job. He promised to use the money to modify mortgages for homeowners facing foreclosure. But when AIG announced that it would be distributing $165 million in bonuses to executives who oversaw the same unit that had made the colossally bad decisions that nearly broke the company, at least one group had had enough.[6]

"I wanted to make T-shirts that said 'too small to fail,'" remembered Joe Dinkin of the Working Families Party (WFP), a political organization that at the time worked in Connecticut, New York, and Oregon alongside labor and community groups to put working people's concerns on politicians' radar. The idea played on the "Too Big to Fail" line already being passed around as justification for the bailouts, meaning that AIG, Bank of America, and other institutions were too systemically important to be allowed to go under.

The WFP decided to put together the daylong bus tour to "show who had actually been hurt by the collapse," Dinkin said. "It wasn't the trader who had made $3 million a year for the last five years; it was actually the people who had been foreclosed, the people who had lost their low-wage jobs, the people whose employers had gotten rid of their health-care coverage." Having chartered the bus, WFP gathered people like Asaad Jackson, a music teacher from Hartford who was paying down medical debt; Mary Huguley, a pastor whose sister-in-law was facing foreclosure; and Mark Dziubek, a steelworker who'd lost his job at a Bristol factory. The tour, nicknamed "Lifestyles of the Rich and Shameless," was eye-opening for the participants. "It's like comparing a rosy red apple to burnt toast, and that's not even the best metaphor," Jackson said of the difference between his neighborhood and that of AIG's Douglas Poling.

The WFP tour seemed to fit a niche that the media had been looking to fill. The press response, at least at first, was massive. Dinkin remembered, "People were portraying us like we were going to be there with flaming pitchforks."

There were no pitchforks on the day of the bus tour, March 21, 2009. In Fairfield, the participants climbed down from the bus and, backed by about fifty reporters, approached Poling's home. The single largest bonus check, a full $6.4 million, according to reports, had gone to Poling, which the company's government-appointed chairman justified by writing, "We cannot attract and retain the best and the brightest talent to lead and staff the A.I.G. businesses—which are now being operated principally on behalf of American taxpayers—if employees believe their compensation is subject to continued and arbitrary adjustment by the U.S. Treasury."[7]

Intent on inviting the wealthy executive to come visit their neighborhoods, the protesters were greeted by a private security guard instead. Jeff Meyer, a local dog-walker, stopped to join them. "Because the American taxpayer now owns 80 percent of AIG, they should have full access to anything and everything they own, including their country club memberships, their recreation facilities, their built-in swimming pools, but we'll do it on a schedule," he said. "America has stopped being a country that cares about its people. It's all about greed."[8]

At the time, the WFP's goal was fairly simple and localized, though it seemed to tap into something bigger. The organization aimed to draw attention to the budget struggle in Hartford and prevent cuts from going through that would hurt people like the ones who participated in the tour. And on that level, they were modestly successful: the Republican governor of Connecticut actually approved a small tax increase on high earners to make up for the revenue lost to the recession. "In our minds the small-bore goal was not to indict the system, though we thought the obvious screwed-up nature of the system was a pretty good hook," Dinkin said.

But the national press did not lavish attention on the Working Families tour or the Republic Windows and Doors because of severance checks of $7,000 per worker or the Connecticut budget wars. Reporters came because the crisis that was rocking the nation was unlike anything Americans had experienced before, and it was still unclear how the public was going to react to it. They came because if any moment seemed to call for people in the streets, it was this one.

Despite the WFP's attempts to be polite during the bus tour, AIG executives reacted as though they were being hunted by howling mobs. One, speaking anonymously, compared the protests to McCarthyism; AIG's CEO later argued that protests were "intended to stir public anger, to get everybody out there with their pitch forks and their hangman nooses, and all that—sort of like what we did in the Deep South [decades ago]. And I think it was just as bad and just as wrong." Private security companies reported a boom in the executive-protection business. Executives were going to react as though they were under assault no matter how polite the protesters were, but maybe something rowdy was exactly what the rest of the country was looking for.[9]

Most existing political organizations, particularly those aligned with the new president, seemed to be waiting for elected officials to take the lead, and they didn't appear to want to get rowdy. George Goehl, executive director of National People's Action (NPA), a coalition of community groups that at the time of the recession was concentrated mostly in the Midwest, said that one of NPA's goals was to produce public images of unrest, but he felt that the response did not live up to the goal. "The financial crisis was incredibly painful and hurtful for most Americans and, really dramatically, for certain communities. And we did not respond as a movement in the way that we could have and should have. At some level, capitalism was against the ropes gasping for air for a second, and we were working on health-care reform."

There was, in his view and that of longtime labor organizer Stephen Lerner, a failure by the Democratic Party and its allies—the ones now in power in Washington—to pivot away from the plan formed on the campaign trail and understand the fundamentally different moment over which they found themselves presiding. The organizations that had a history of making trouble specifically for the financial industry were in a weak position, the groups that had formed in the Bush era to protest the wars were unprepared for a massive economic meltdown, and the labor movement was focused on supporting the Obama administration's priorities. "We kind of watched for a minute and it was like, 'Wow. There is nobody in the streets,'" Goehl said. "'This is nuts.'"

THE CRISIS THAT RIPPLED ACROSS THE WORLD IN 2008 LEFT THE United States mostly in shock. It rattled presidential candidates and pundits alike, fundamentally changing the political debate as the election rolled toward its close. Alexis Goldstein, working at Merrill Lynch at the time, remembered executives coming down to the trading floor, staring at a sort of market scoreboard that hung there, arms folded, watching the numbers fall. "There was definitely a sense that the market had imploded," she said. "Everything spread to every market. There was absolutely no confidence that other banks were solvent, so it didn't matter that 'Oh, it is mortgage backed securities that are worthless.' You didn't know if the bank was going to be around tomorrow, so why would you trade with another bank?"

It still seems, as financial journalist Moe Tkacik wrote in 2010, that the story of 2008 is too big to tell, which goes some way toward explaining the fragmented nature of the immediate response. Most accounts get at part of it—at the bursting of a housing bubble filled with the hot air of speculators packaging and reselling mortgages into securities overrated by ratings agencies that were paid by the banks that hired them; at the fraud that happened at bank after bank in the rush to issue a mortgage to everyone who could afford one, and plenty of people who couldn't; at the predatory practices that shoved black and Latino homebuyers into "subprime" mortgages with higher interest rates, even if they qualified for a more traditional "prime" mortgage. There are stories of the collapse of investment firm Lehman Brothers and stories of the rescue of Bear Stearns or Washington Mutual or Countrywide, making the too-big-to-fail banks even bigger and less likely to be allowed to fail. There are stories of the growing inequality in the country, the concentration of wealth in the hands of a small number of the ultra-wealthy, while real wages stagnated and fell, union membership declined, and entire companies decamped for other shores; and stories of how working people compensated for those falling wages with debt, using their homes as credit cards when actual credit cards wouldn't cut it, and how this was the last straw that made the whole broken edifice tumble down when those homes lost value, even the bad jobs disappeared, and we had no way to spend ourselves out of economic stagnation.[10]

What most of those stories leave out is how it felt in those moments in 2008 and 2009, when even the bankers were afraid their banks were about to be nationalized, and when the treasury secretary and Federal Reserve chairman shifted from their reassuring coos about a small recession to increasingly shrill warnings of imminent economic collapse. We were teetering on the brink of something that most people in the United States had a hard time imagining. As it happened, we remained on that brink, never quite crossing the line into a moment where the buses stopped running or the grocery-store shelves were empty. But it can be hard to remember that it felt like that moment was on its way. All we can do is rub our eyes, look around at the wreckage, and think about what has changed.

And much has changed. The biggest banks got not only the $700 billion authorized by Congress in the last days of the Bush administration, but also trillions—with a T—more from the Federal Reserve, an amount that equaled, according to financial journalists at Bloomberg, "more than half the value of everything produced in the U.S. that year." Economist Dean Baker argued that putting the Troubled Asset Relief Program up for a vote at all was simply "a way to get Congress's fingerprints on the policy of subsidizing the banks," to make it look like the giant safety net of taxpayer cash strung below giant multinational finance firms was democratically created.[11]

The "bailout" for the nonfinancial sector—leaving aside the bailout of the auto industry, which was mostly notable for the amount of strings attached to it, unlike the money handed to the banks—was the American Recovery and Reinvestment Act (ARRA), a stimulus bill that was more than half tax cuts and that may have been the kiss of death to bipartisanship in the US Congress. It totaled $787 billion when it was passed in February 2009, but many of its parts wouldn't take effect for years. That was not enough to make up for what Baker calculated would be a shortfall in annual demand more in the neighborhood of $1.3 trillion in 2009 and 2010.[12]

Some 8.7 million jobs were lost between the start of the recession in December 2007 and early 2010. The previous record had been 4.3 million lost at the end of World War II. And, as the protesters in Connecticut feared, cities slashed budgets, cutting public services to make up the shortfall in their finances.[13]

Yet much remains the same. Not a single banker went to jail for the ritualized fraud that had created the crisis. No major financial firm was forced to suffer a cut in the value of its assets. That there were effectively no consequences for these firms, largely because they were described as systemically important, simply encourages more risk-taking, with the expectation that they will be bailed out again. In fact, a 2012 analysis actually quantified the value to the biggest banks on the assumption that taxpayers will foot the bill for their crises. The subsidy provided by that assumption is worth about $76 billion a year to the biggest banks—more than the federal government spends on education.[14]

The financial sector had grown exponentially in the decades leading up to the crisis—to the point where it accounted for about 40 percent of all corporate profits in the early 2000s, and rebounded from the crash to around 30 percent. And yet it was not very good at doing what it was supposed to do, which is to direct capital toward the best possible investments. Stock trading had little to do with raising money to keep businesses flowing, and more to do with fattening the pockets of the already-wealthy at the expense of the rest of us. Keeping the stock price of a company high was more important to the people who ran it than keeping its factories producing or its workforce paid. A J. P. Morgan executive admitted in a 2011 letter to clients that "reductions in wages and benefits explain[ed] the majority" of the increase in profits.[15]

What Wall Street was very good at was concentrating wealth. Those laid-off workers, or the ones who kept their jobs but found their wages shrinking, had no choice but to rely on credit as a substitute for that lost income—credit, of course, lent from the very same banks, whether that be a shiny gold credit card with "CHASE" across the top or a home equity line of credit, a second mortgage mining your home for cash. Wall Street began to make more of its money from repackaging this debt into "innovative" securities for resale than it did from making loans the old-fashioned way. As the rich got richer, they needed outlets for their investments; as the members of the working class got poorer, they needed money, which they got not in increasing wages for their increasing productivity, but in loans. Growing inequality wasn't a side effect—it was the main effect.[16]

The complexity and power of Wall Street served as one more barrier to protest for working people. As financial observer Doug Henwood wrote, a sizable amount of the power wielded by the financial sector comes "from the sense of powerless awe [it inspires] among non-initiates." Those bonuses being paid to AIG executives who had just participated in a massive crash, and the inability of the banks to fire the people whose actions had led to the problem in the first place, were justified because, bankers said, no one else was qualified to un-create the complicated web of securities they'd created. The rest of us, again, simply could not possibly understand these "toxic" financial products. We could not even understand why these things had been created in the first place—the whole house of cards was meant to hedge against loss, to de-riskify risk, and it had simply increased risk for the rest of us.[17]

Just as the TARP vote worked to get Congress's imprimatur on public bailouts for the banks in 2008, the public's participation in the stock market gave ideological cover to whatever the stock market did: if "the people" supported it, it must be democratic and just. Yet the public's involvement with Wall Street, while it did grow, has always been overstated: stock ownership is concentrated at the top, with 81 percent of stocks owned by the top 10 percent, and 38 percent of stocks owned by the top 1 percent. Half of all households own no stock whatsoever. Mostly, their entanglement with finance is through debt.[18]

Sometime during the crisis, Goldstein remembered asking her boss, "How will the public ever forgive us?" His response surprised her. "He was like, 'The public is going to forget and then everything is going to go back to normal. The public forgot after the long-term capital management hedge funds imploded and the banks bailed them out. They forgot after the savings and loan crisis. It is going to be a little rocky for a while, but don't worry about it. Everything will go back to normal.'"

Wall Street's crisis was not simply adjacent to the economic system we live under, but a crisis of capitalism itself. We had been told that deregulating markets would allow markets to work more perfectly, that it would result in better allocation of capital to businesses that would then create jobs for the rest of us, yet the opposite had happened. Since the late 1980s and the collapse of the Soviet Union, capitalism had been triumphant, its cheerleaders sure they had prevailed because their system was just and right—and besides, it was the only option. British writer Mark Fisher called this attitude "capitalist realism"; it was the sense that it was now impossible even to imagine an alternative.[19]

And yet in the days of the crisis, even capitalism's biggest boosters admitted that it was in danger. Judge, legal scholar, and market devotee Richard Posner titled his book *A Failure of Capitalism*; financial journalist David Faber subtitled his *How Wall Street's Greed and Stupidity Brought Capitalism to Its Knees*. No less august a publication than *The Economist* ran a story called "Capitalism at Bay." These prominent voices and so many others discussing capitalism's flaws got people talking about the system itself, whether it would last, and whether it should. Capitalism had become visible as a manmade system, something that could have an end, something that in fact seemed to have self-destructed.[20]

A recession was one thing; a crisis that rattled the entire economic system was something very different. The story we'd been told about capitalism triumphant, democratic, and practical was obviously untrue, but political and economic elites seemed to simply have no answers. Capitalist realism was over. The question now was what would happen next.

"THE TEAPOT STARTED BOILING UNDER THE BUSH ADMINISTRATION" for Debbie Dooley, a lifelong conservative and resident of Atlanta, Georgia. "I just felt like the Republican Party lost its way and I had major issues with some of Bush's big government policy. Especially the Wall Street bailout. The Tea Party actually started under the Bush administration, we just didn't call it a Tea Party."

But on February 19, 2009, a commentator on CNBC, NBC's business-oriented cable channel, reporting from the floor of the Chicago Board of Trade, gave Dooley and people like her something to rally around. Rick Santelli, dressed in a suit and yellow tie with traders bustling on all sides of him, ranted about the government "subsidiz[ing] the losers' mortgages," to applause from the traders. "This is America!" he shouted, turning to the traders, who all booed. And then he made the call heard round the country: "We're thinking of having a Chicago Tea Party in July. All you capitalists that want to show up to Lake Michigan, I'm going to start organizing. . . . We're going to be dumping in some derivative securities, what do you think about that?"[21]

Santelli was responding to the demand for write-downs of mortgages that were "underwater" after the drop in housing values brought on by the crisis; "underwater" mortgages were ones where the homeowner owed more on their mortgage than the house was then worth. But beyond that, he was calling for a rebellion in defense of capitalism, in defense of the idea that the winners and losers had somehow earned what they had. His call resonated with Dooley. "We were still outraged over the Wall Street bailout and here come more bailouts," she said. "I heard his rant and I said 'We are going to hold a Tea Party.'"

She was one of twenty-two on the first call to plan for the Tea Party actions that followed. Word of Santelli's rant and the Tea Party idea spread through the social networking site Twitter and through conservative blogs. Loose networks formed around Twitter hashtags. The first round of Tea Party events came on February 27, 2009, but the one that stood out to Debbie Dooley was in Atlanta on Tax Day, April 15, 2009. "We had twenty thousand people," she said. "We had [Fox News host] Sean Hannity broadcast there."[22]

Though Fox's competitor, CNBC, had launched the idea of the Tea Party, conservative Fox hosts like Hannity and Glenn Beck quickly jumped into the fray, publicizing Tea Party events and even hosting their own. Dooley helped to plan a march on Washington sponsored by Beck on September 12, 2009, connected to Beck's "9/12 Project," which aimed to reclaim the sense of unity Americans felt after the attacks of

September 11, 2001. "When I flew into Reagan National the day before, I was overwhelmed," Dooley said. "You had people wearing Tea Party T-shirts and Tea Party flags that were getting off of planes, unfurling their flags, from all over the United States."

Dooley became the chairperson of the Atlanta Tea Party and joined the board of directors of Tea Party Patriots, a coordinating organization for the local Tea Party groups that quickly began to dot the country. A fast talker with a thick Georgia accent, she relished the idea of holding disruptive protests and challenging the political elites, expressing pride in the number of times she and the Atlanta group were able to pull together broad coalitions for political battles. She was a firm advocate for shaking up the people who had held power for too long, saying, "I firmly believe that the ruling elite in both the Democrat and Republican Party want to keep us separate. They don't want the grassroots to work together and discover that We the People have the real power and not these elected officials."

At the grassroots, the Tea Party became a loose network of local groups, often holding regular meetings to talk politics, plan campaigns, and sometimes hear guest lectures. One study counted approximately 1,000 local groups by the end of 2010. These activists went beyond simply talking to one another online—though the Internet remained central to their work—to engage in face-to-face organizing and action. Dramatic protests at town hall events punctuated the summer of 2009. These meetings, initially arranged by members of Congress during the recess to discuss the pending health-care reform bill, turned into raucous events where Tea Party members shouted at their representatives about the economy and "Obamacare." Disruption, it turned out, was fun as well as attention-grabbing.[23]

In the 2000s, online organizing mainly consisted of groups like MoveOn, a progressive organization that mobilized its members through email blasts, mostly to sign petitions, but occasionally to take offline action. Political blogs often had vibrant constituencies, but for the bloggers, the idea of going out and disrupting an event was mostly anathema. There had, of course, been massive marches against the war, but those were planned well in advance, and smaller protests were mostly ignored by the press.

The Tea Partiers used online tools to get together and work toward a political solution. Many were relieved to realize they weren't alone in their outrage. Where Joe Dinkin and the Working Families Party were cautious about expressing anger, the Tea Party wore that anger on its sleeve. Often, it was directed at the newly elected president, but it was also often aimed at local representatives who were not seen as being responsive enough, because they had acquiesced in the bailouts of the banks, the auto companies, and pretty much everyone who had a private jet to get to Washington and hold out their hands. Dooley called it "crony capitalism" and argued against the government "picking winners and losers."

Populist anger aimed at elites had once been a tool of the left, but in the post-crash moment it was conservatives who provided a space for that anger to be heard and validated. A president elected on promises of bringing both sides together, of making Washington a less rancorous place, allowed little space for outrage, and those who had supported him clung to the belief that he would help, in time. For someone like J. D. Meadows, angry at Wall Street, seeing only politicians willing to give more bailouts to corporations while jobs disappeared in his hometown in Mississippi, it made sense to join up. The anger that the Tea Party embraced was central to its appeal.

The Tea Party's skepticism of elites shaped its structures, keeping its organization loose and relatively nonhierarchical. Tea Partiers saw themselves as regular people working with their neighbors to take their country (and the Republican Party) back.

A growing sense that the government no longer served everyday people was crystallized by the financial crisis and the bailouts that followed, the impunity granted to those who had caused the economy to crash. Dooley said, "I think that there are some CEOs and presidents of these banks and large corporations, financial institutions, that should be sitting in a jail cell now. I believe if we did the same thing, the average person, we would be in jail."

The Tea Party blamed bad actors—the buyers of homes they couldn't afford as well as the bankers who came open-handed for bailouts—rather than capitalism itself, for the crisis. The particular confidence in free markets and deregulation that emanated from the Tea Party was deeply connected to the sense that government was no longer functioning as it should. If the state was incapable of punishing the people who broke the economy, it could at least have let the market do its job and let the banks fail. While that message dovetailed quite nicely with the one that had been promoted for years by groups like FreedomWorks and Americans for Prosperity, or indeed by Fox News, it was a mistake to write the Tea Party off as an "AstroTurf" movement created out of whole cloth from above. There was real outrage, and real fear, at its core.[24]

Yet it is undeniable that Fox News—and because of it, the rest of the mainstream media—helped the Tea Party grow. The attention initially showered on pockets of resistance, like the Republic Windows and Doors workers or the bus tour to bankers' homes, had been unexpected, but it was nothing compared to the sustained effort that Fox News put into helping the Tea Party grow. Media scholars have written for decades about the media's allergy to covering protest movements, particularly those that dare to disrupt the day-to-day theater of politics or business. Yet Fox's efforts to legitimize the Tea Party paid off in quantifiable ways. Fox coverage promoted events, made special occasions of the protests themselves, and allowed Fox viewers to feel connected to the movement. It described the movement using words like "grassroots," "independent," "mainstream," and "genuine," making those previously inexperienced with public protest feel comfortable joining up.[25]

By 2010, other news networks had joined in the fun. CNN even co-hosted a debate with the national conservative group Tea Party Express. The Tea Party was the new big thing in American politics, helped along by well-positioned, well-established organizations and elected officials, such as Congresswoman Michele Bachmann (R-MN), who had no problem speaking on behalf of a dispersed, nonhierarchical group of activists. Dooley expressed skepticism about some of these ventriloquists, from Wisconsin governor Scott Walker to the Koch brothers, the billionaires who fund Americans for Prosperity, but there is little doubt that their stars rose because they were able to hitch their brands to the actions of people like her.

Dooley credited the Tea Party with revitalizing protests on both the left and the right. "I think that the people were sleeping giants for years—I think that a lot of activists on the Left, many more became much more engaged than what they were in the past," she said, and it is hard to argue with her. Joe Dinkin of the Working Families Party remembered looking at Tea Partiers disrupting town hall meetings and wishing they'd had the tools to make their Fairfield County protest spread in the kind of "open-source" manner the Tea Party had. It didn't hurt that each time the Tea Party did something, Fox News was there to cover it and to tell its audience that this was the righteous anger of a people's uprising.

At least some Tea Party groups were willing to join with surprising allies in support of shared goals. In Georgia in the fall of 2011, when a state legislator proposed a bill that would criminalize picketing and other protest activities, Dooley and the Atlanta Tea Party teamed up with the Teamsters Union, Occupy Atlanta, the NAACP, the Sierra Club, and many other groups to defeat the bill and preserve their right to take political action. "They have a right to do what they want to do and we have a right, too," she said of the other groups. Not every Tea Party organization has been so willing to reach out to those not sharing their political views, but they have all affirmed the value of making some noise to affect the political process.

Surveys of the Tea Party—something of a loose term, since not all people who expressed support for the movement were activists, or even members of a local group—repeatedly found its members to be both older and better-off than the average American, as well as much more likely to be white. The Tea Party was a middle-class movement both in its actual makeup and in its politics: its members were not the most likely to have been hurt by the recession, but they were certainly psychologically affected by the crash. When the stock market plunged, so did retirement accounts, alongside the drop in home values caused by the bursting of the housing bubble, hitting Tea Partiers and other older Americans in what had seemed like safe investments.[26]

The middle-class Tea Partiers were responding to a particular set of fears. The middle class is characterized more and more by what writer Barbara Ehrenreich called the "fear of falling," the awareness that there is a class below, into which it is possible to slip, as well as a class above, where the real power is concentrated. In the post–World War II era, the booming economy, labor protections, and housing subsidies helped many more people climb into the middle class, but in recent years, many have slipped back out of it. The financial crisis made what had been a hazy awareness into a sharp realization. The rules of the game had changed, and hard work did not necessarily pay off.[27]

From that feeling emerged the most common refrain of the Tea Party faithful: "We need to take our country back," back to a time when things were better. This slogan implies, of course, a memory (or an imagined one) of that better time. In this view, our foundation is good, but somewhere along the way, something was broken, and it needs to be fixed. The call to "take our country back" or to "rebuild the American Dream" is a way of protesting social and economic inequalities without having to question the entire political and economic system. Others questioned whether the times the Tea Partiers were invoking were in fact better for everyone.

"Taking our country back" could also have nastier connotations, and surveys found that Tea Party participants, compared to other Americans and even other conservatives, were more willing to agree with stereotypes about black people and immigrants. Obama could seem like the very embodiment of right-wing populist fears: he was black, he was a former community organizer who had worked on behalf of the poor (assumed also to be black), he had a Muslim-sounding middle name and a Kenyan father, and he was also an Ivy League–educated lawyer and a Chicago politician. That combination packed a potent number of stereotypes into one man.

But the distinction between productive citizens and freeloaders that many Tea Partiers voiced has a long history in American populism, and not just the right-wing kind. And so it is not that strange that grassroots Tea Partiers (unlike, often, the politicians or elites who were speaking in their name) distrusted the government but supported Social Security and Medicare—programs they felt they had earned. Populism has always separated the "producer" from the "parasite," and that tendency has allowed anti-elite movements to be sidetracked into anger toward those at the bottom.

CORE TO THE DEVELOPMENT OF AMERICAN POPULISM WAS THE PRO-ducer ethic, or "producerism": the idea that only those who worked hard and created wealth deserved to share in it and to participate in our democracy. "Wealth belongs to him who creates it," Ignatius Donnelly proclaimed at the 1892 convention in St. Louis that birthed the People's Party. Donnelly then quoted St. Paul: "If any will not work, neither shall he eat." Producerism sees elites at the top as parasites who leech off the work of others rather than getting their hands dirty themselves. It is fundamentally a moral argument, not a deep analysis of the structures of the economy, though it often hits on vital truths that feel real to many people.[28]

Though small-p populism existed before the Populist movement of the late 1800s, the demands and goals of that movement have particular echoes in the politics of the post–financial crisis era. A coalition of farmers, wage laborers, and small business owners, the Populists, who eventually formed the People's Party to make a bid for electoral power, aimed to overthrow what they saw as a corrupt elite and sought to create institutions that would serve them. Members of groups like the National Farmers' Alliance, the Colored Farmers' Alliance, the Farmers' Mutual Benefit Association, the Knights of Labor, the Women's Alliance, and the Citizen's Alliance created a political organization that was markedly different from the major political parties of the time.

Taking a slogan from the followers of Andrew Jackson, who had railed against a specifically financial elite, the Populists decried "the money power" and "monopolists," pointing the finger at bankers like J. P. Morgan as exerting a nefarious control over society through their power over the money supply. They demanded public ownership of national banks, a "Subtreasury System" that would have provided low-cost loans to farmers, and a postal banking system that would have made local post offices into savings bank branches. They wanted public, not corporate, ownership of transportation and communication services, in part to make their own businesses easier to run, and in part because they understood the connection between concentrated economic power and concentrated political power. They called for a national progressive income tax as a challenge to growing inequality. The Populists were less progressive when it came to race; although groups that represented black farmers and laborers were part of the coalition, the movement as a whole did not fundamentally challenge segregation or a belief in white supremacy. They failed to win a presidential election, but they left behind ideas that trickle throughout American politics to this day on both the right and the left.[29]

In addition to genuine criticisms of concentrated power, American populist movements have targeted scapegoats whose actual power may be limited; they have appealed to a broad idea of "the people," but they have sometimes worked to silence or demonize certain groups. Right-wing populist language often relies on conspiracy theories about groups within the elite—from alleged communists to academics—who are said to be working to undermine American principles in order to concentrate their own power.[30]

A kind of white middle-class identity politics developed around the producerist idea that what the middle class had, it had earned, and that it needed to be protected from those above and below who aimed to take its wealth away. Taxes, not wages, became the economic issue of this politics of resentment, which was fueled by segregationist Alabama governor George Wallace and solidified by Richard Nixon and Ronald Reagan. This ideology, espoused often by those who were already in power, figured "elites" not as the "economic royalists" that Franklin Delano Roosevelt had inveighed against in the days of the Great Depression, but as the liberals in government. Richard Nixon and his vice president Spiro Agnew painted liberals as effete snobs and rallied the "silent majority" against those "who want to take their money, and give it to people who don't work."[31]

This idea resonated because middle-class reform movements that concerned themselves with poverty often did so out of a distant sense of charity rather than a real engagement with the needs of poor people. Yet in targeting liberal politicians and professors, these populists missed the corporate titans who were quietly shipping jobs overseas and keeping wages low while managing to get their own tax rates slashed to a level that redistributed wealth upward far faster than it had been shifting downward.[32]

As for Santelli, the man who kicked off the Tea Party standing in the midst of the kind of people who had just crashed the economy, one can find his precursors in market populism. Popularized in the 1990s, with capitalism ascendant in the world and socialism vanquished, market populism is the belief that markets, not mere elections, were tools of "the people," a democratic way—as well as the only way—to organize society.[33]

The rise of market populism came alongside the massive growth in the financial industry. But it was a populism that mostly left actual people out. It was expressed in magazines and books and on trading floors, and especially in the business press, where managers and day traders were lionized as the real producers and workers the parasites. If you hadn't made yourself rich in the stock market, the theory went, it was your own fault; and if you didn't like the market's priorities for your workplace or your town, you had simply been outvoted. Meanwhile, the bankers on the trading floor, Alexis Goldstein said, considered their clients to be there for the fooling: they were sources of cash, not of democratic power. When those bankers' actions crashed the markets, the "real economy" crashed, too; and when they demanded their bonuses anyway, a number of Americans realized how undemocratic Wall Street remained.

Producerism remained alive and well. Mitt Romney, during his 2012 run for the presidency, complained that "forty-seven percent of Americans pay no income tax," portraying them as nonworkers "dependent upon government." The claim that the wealthy were the real "job creators" was another form of producerism. And Santelli's placing of the blame for the crisis not on the traders flanking him, or the bank officers who had pushed low-income people into mortgages they had no dream of paying back, but on the homeowners themselves was another such rhetorical twist: it must be because those homeowners did not work hard enough.[34]

It is tempting to blame Wallace or Nixon or Reagan for this language, tinged as it is with the kind of stereotyping we expected from those figures. But populism from the beginning was shaped in the image of white working men, making it all too easy to blame those who did not or could not find jobs, whose work was the unpaid labor of raising children or caring for elders, or who had been held back by decades of racial segregation and discrimination.

For too long, it has been far too easy not just to blame the poor for their own problems, but to take a kind of nasty pleasure in their downfall, to feel ourselves virtuous when we wagged our fingers at "welfare queens" or complained about people buying homes beyond their means. If—as we have been told by a thousand pious politicians and newspaper columnists intent on finding a "social psychology" behind the era's rampant foreclosures, low wages, and unemployment, which in some neighborhoods exceeds 50 percent—it is the fault of those foreclosed upon, jobless, or struggling, then it cannot happen to us. Victim-blaming, like conspiracy theories, is an attempt to understand the world, to find an explanation for why bad things happen.[35]

But to really prevent those things from happening, to really end poverty and ensure a more equitable distribution of wealth and power, we have to accept the unpleasant fact that, indeed, these are things that could happen to all of us, and often do happen to people who have worked hard and were hit by an unexpected crisis that derailed them financially—like the 2008 downturn. The Tea Party's response was to double down on producerism, to argue that the problems would be solved by a purer form of capitalism. But for many others, the financial crisis and the resulting precipitous drop in living standards for so many people taught a different lesson: that if the actions of people far away from us can wipe out 40 percent of our wealth in such a brief period of time, perhaps we have more in common with the people we thought were below us than we had previously imagined.[36]

And in that moment, we saw the rise of a new populist language. Those who spoke it aimed to allow the people to really take power, in order to fix the crises that the people didn't cause.

THE SIGNS WERE THERE, IF WE CHOSE TO LOOK FOR THEM. OCCUPY Wall Street, the movement that would change the way we talked about the economy, was still in the future. But while the Tea Party seemed to steer people's anger away from Wall Street, the progressive groups aligned with President Obama shifted to pushing for health-care reform, and the 2010 midterm elections provided the spectacle of candidates promising to create jobs, while denying that government in fact had any ability to create jobs, the anger at the banks that had crashed the economy had not really subsided. In fact, as what many began to call the Great Recession swelled and the unemployed edged closer to the ninety-nine-week cutoff after which even extended unemployment benefits would disappear, that anger might even have been growing.

The question, for organizers and for those looking to move off the political sidelines, was how to turn that anger into something concrete, something that would have actual power.

In 2007 and 2008, the Obama campaign had galvanized a generation of young people to get involved in electoral politics. The campaign gave them unprecedented access to new digital tools as well as training in organizing from career troublemakers such as civil rights and United Farm Workers veteran Marshall Ganz. But after the election, Ganz wrote, Obama refused to use his movement; many fell into disillusionment as the administration repeatedly told them not to act, not to challenge Democrats who wavered on policy goals. "He ignored the leverage that a radical flank robustly pursuing its goals could give a reform president—as organized labor empowered FDR's New Deal or the civil rights movement empowered LBJ's Voting Rights Act," Ganz wrote in 2010. "Threatened with losing access, and confusing access with power, the coalitions for the most part went along."[37]

Some organizations kept pushing, though. National People's Action organized a successful action at the American Bankers Association convention in Chicago in October 2009. "A thousand or so folks came the first night from all across the country," George Goehl of NPA remembered. "It was like a counter-convention." They marched to Goldman Sachs' Chicago office and occupied it, then held a bigger march with support from local unions and other community groups. The "Showdown in America" campaign, which had begun at the ABA meeting in Chicago, culminated in protests at Wells Fargo and Bank of America shareholder meetings and then a march on Wall Street. These protesters were pressing for the bank reform bill winding its way through Congress to have some teeth. On April 29, 2010, thousands marched on Wall Street, linking bankers' big bonuses to federal and state budget cuts that had resulted in laid-off public employees and slashed services for already-struggling city residents. Labor unions joined NPA and other community groups in the march and the other actions, but the press coverage, particularly in contrast to the fanfare given to the Tea Party, was minimal. The overarching narrative remained that the Tea Party was the only populist game in town.

From within the nation's biggest labor unions, which would have seemed the natural groups to challenge Wall Street power, lifelong organizer Stephen Lerner also found directing attention and action at the financial crisis and its perpetrators an uphill battle. Within unions, such as the Service Employees International Union (SEIU), the necessity of confronting finance was far from a consensus opinion, and there was a reluctance to challenge the president. "There was a group of us that were obsessed that saw this as being really big. I think most folks didn't get how big it was," said Lerner, who'd begun to look at Wall Street while organizing the Justice for Janitors campaign. The shock of the crisis, it seemed, was still an influence, preventing people from seeing the whole picture.

Still, they kept pushing. "Our theory kept evolving to be 'No more single actions,'" Goehl said. "Yes, we wanted to win financial reform, but we really wanted to spark a movement." Their marches were coupled with more confrontational actions, such as entering and occupying bank headquarters and demanding to meet with bank executives. Multiday, multicity actions steamrolled forward, and, Goehl said, NPA members had a real hunger for big ideas about the structure of the economy.

Younger people were also beginning to take action, and in many cases their political beliefs had been indelibly shaped by the 2008 crisis. Mary Clinton moved from North Dakota to New York after spending 2010 working as an organizer at SEIU, first around health-care reform and then, briefly, on financial reform. But she was frustrated to find herself working to elect Democrats, rather than for deeper change. For many in her generation, mainstream Democrats were part of the problem. She'd been involved in the 2009 protests at the Pittsburgh G-20 summit of the leaders of the world's largest economies, and she credited that event with sharpening her understanding of global capitalism and inequality.

As a graduate student at the City University of New York, Clinton joined the New Yorkers Against Budget Cuts coalition and participated in the May 12, 2011, protests on Wall Street. "It was very clear that in Bloomberg's New York, it's Wall Street running the city," she said. But simply marching, as NPA was also realizing, was not enough. "I thought, being nice isn't good for negotiations around budget cuts," she said. "We need more confrontation, we need direct action."[38]

The protests in Wisconsin in the winter of 2011 in defense of public-sector union workers inspired the New York group, as did the move-ment in Spain against the austerity measures instituted in response to the economic crisis there. In both places, protesters had camped out and occupied public space—so Clinton and others decided to have their own encampment. "Bloombergville" was named after "Walker-ville" in Wisconsin, which in turn took its name from the Hoovervilles that sprang up during the Great Depression, named for the president whose inaction had made the crisis worse. In New York, Mayor Michael Bloomberg was a billionaire whose wealth came from the Bloomberg terminals that finance traders used to analyze information and make trades. There was no better symbol for the intimate relationship between Wall Street and government. "This was an opportunity where we could be confrontational, do something that was right on the doorstep of the mayor and capital," Clinton said.

Bloombergville lasted from June 14 to July 5, 2011, coinciding with city budget negotiations, and disbanded after the city budget passed. About one hundred people slept out the first night, and while the crowd never grew to the size of the one in Wisconsin, and the press coverage didn't swell as it had for the Tea Party, the protest had left an idea in the heads of its participants.

When the Canadian magazine *Adbusters* put out a call to occupy Wall Street, many Bloombergville veterans seized on the idea. Finding no meetings or planning events scheduled, Clinton and a group within New Yorkers Against Budget Cuts called for one.[39]

Many people have claimed credit for coming up with the phrase "We are the 99 percent" at one of those early assemblies to plan Occupy. What cannot be argued is that the phrase struck a chord with people who heard it. Something crystallized in that simple phrase that seemed to allow people to discuss subjects that had formerly been taboo. It expressed a solidarity that terms like "middle class" or "regular people" or "Main Street" or even "working class" did not, while pointing the finger at the oligarchs, financiers, and miscellaneous multimillionaires hoarding the wealth.

In this view, inequality—not simple concern about poverty, or unemployment, but the sense that a small group of ultra-rich were consolidating even more wealth and political power in their hands—was the problem. Occupy gave us the language for it. CEOs had gotten a 23 percent raise in 2010. Profits were up 22 percent since 2007, and the lowest share of economic growth in thirty years had gone to the wages and salaries of the employees who worked at those companies. The transfer of public wealth into private hands that had occurred over the past several decades, combined with the collapse of real incomes, the rise in debt, the disconnection of rising productivity from rising wages, all of it had contributed to the creation of a concentration of capital that economist

Thomas Piketty a few years later suggested might be incompatible with modern democratic society.[40]

Messages don't succeed because they say something new and exciting that no one has ever heard before; instead, they succeed because they explain something that people feel but have been at a loss to explain. With the discussion of inequality, the shock, the lack of an explanation for the events of the past few years, finally ended. It was, in a way, like a fog had cleared. Our problem was not simply that we were struggling, but that our struggling benefited someone else.

Communications researcher Anat Shenker-Osorio pointed out that even the 99 percent framework was not new—The Other 98% was a progressive organization that held its first action on Tax Day 2010, one of the many groups aiming to catalyze anger at the state of the economy, but it had not taken off in the same way. The difference, said Shenker-Osorio, was that unlike "the other," the phrase "We are the 99 percent" gave people a positive identity, a big inclusive group to be in.

It both echoed and fundamentally shifted classic populist rhetoric. "We are the 99 percent" was a clear evocation of the power of the people, an anti-elite rallying cry of action. Significantly, it included everyone—not just the "middle class" or the workers, but the unemployed and the homeless and the poor as well. For a country often described as hopelessly aspirational, whose fundamental myth was the "American Dream" and the idea that everyone who worked hard could achieve, it was a radical step. It caused people to identify downward, with the poorest people. It cut out the possibility of turning producers against "moochers," those who needed unemployment assistance or food stamps or public housing. There was one enemy, and it was the people who had caused the economy to crash. Which side, the slogan asked, did you want to be on?

To Mary Clinton, a key piece of Occupy's early success was that it was new, and it was not called by an established community group or labor union or organization. You didn't have to be a member of something; as Occupy organizer Nelini Stamp pointed out, all you had to agree to was that the banks had too much power. Ruth Milkman, a sociologist who studied Occupy along with her colleagues Penny Lewis and Stephanie Luce at the City University of New York, also noted the importance of painting a clear target directly on the villains of Wall Street. And yet prior actions targeting bankers, from the Working Families Party's bus tour to the Showdown in America, had not spread across the country. In the end, just as it is impossible to assign credit to an individual for the slogan, it is also impossible to explain just why it took off.

Milkman, Lewis, and Luce tracked the rise in mentions of "income inequality" in the media at the time of Occupy, watching it spike from just over 1,000 mentions in August 2011 to nearly 4,000 in October, during Occupy's peak. In a Pew Institute survey taken in December 2011, 61 percent of respondents said they thought the country's economic system "unfairly favors the wealthy," and 77 percent (and 53 percent of Republicans) agreed that "there is too much power in the hands of a few rich people and large corporations." Another survey found a 19 percentage point increase in people who thought there were "strong" or "very strong" conflicts between the rich and poor. "It's a cliché to say it, but it totally changed how you could talk about things," Lerner said. "It would be fun to think about all the money that's been spent and all the things labor and progressives have tried that didn't equal anything and then look at the money and the time and energy and compare it to Occupy."[41]

The expression of solidarity that "We are the 99 percent" offered, that we were all in this together, allowed people to move beyond the easy politics of moral superiority or purity. One did not have to be the perfect victim in order to be part of the 99 percent any more than one had to be a producer. With one slogan, it appeared that Occupy had both pointed the finger squarely at the rich and gathered the other classes together in opposition.

It was the audacity of Occupy that seemed to work, a slogan and a strategy that seemed, finally, expansive enough to tackle the crisis.

WHILE IT WAS OCCUPIED, NO ONE CALLED IT ZUCCOTTI PARK. IT WAS Liberty Plaza, the name taken from the street in New York's financial district that bordered it on one side and in homage to the occupied squares in Egypt, Spain, and Greece. The site of the original occupation had been almost accidental, a second or third choice when the police had thoroughly barricaded Wall Street. And yet the space seemed perfect, at least at first; within it, there were always many things happening simultaneously.

I first made it to Occupy Wall Street on Day 5, September 21, 2011, and met an emergency medical technician volunteering her skills. She told me, "So far we've given out lots of Band-Aids, because everyone has blisters, lots of cough drops because nobody has a voice." There was a small group screen-printing Occupy slogans on T-shirts on one of the park's stone tables, and there was a sign for a child-care center, though no children were currently there. There was a fully stocked kitchen. At any given time, there might be a march departing, whether to head down to the real Wall Street half a block away or simply to lap the park, making some noise. At each end of the park, protesters stood holding cardboard handwritten signs, including "Collective liberation," "Too big to fail?," and "NYPD: Wall Street is After Your Pension!"

No one paid much attention to the occupation for the first few days. Then the police made a few mistakes—pepper-spraying a girl in the face in front of the live-streaming cameras on several occupiers' cellphones, then, on Saturday, October 1, arresting some seven hundred people marching across the Brooklyn Bridge—and it was on.

Mary Clinton remembered that on the first day, September 17, there was yoga in the park and a folk musician playing before the march set off. Kept out of Wall Street, they turned into Zuccotti Park, held a general assembly, and stayed.

Most participants you ask about Occupy remember the organic way things happened. How the food station grew from a food committee that prepared peanut butter sandwiches the first night. How donations started to come in and committees began to decide how to spend the money. How the library grew, and people deemed themselves librarians. How the celebrities and famous leftists began to show up and speak, from Roseanne Barr to Naomi Klein to Angela Davis. How the unions began to show up, and how the protesters began to support them in return. Of course it was work, the hard work of committed organizers who spent their time sleeping in a park. But after waiting for something to happen for years, people had finally managed to make it happen.

Nelini Stamp thought it was going to be just another protest—at the time, she was an organizer with the Working Families Party, and she had been to plenty of marches. "But I saw something that was different," she said. "I saw dedicated people who had been so disenfranchised their entire lives, finally feeling like they had a voice." She wound up sleeping on a piece of cardboard in the park the first night, and staying.

Alexis Goldstein had quit her Wall Street job in 2010, disgusted by the financial crisis but unsure what she would do next. She was teaching some coding classes and considering a career developing computer and iPhone products. The video of the police pepper-spraying the girls drove her to the park, where she began to think more deeply about her time on Wall Street. When Naomi Klein gave a talk on Wall Street, a person next to Goldstein asked, "What's Glass-Steagall?" She found herself explaining the Depression-era law, repealed in 1999, that kept investment banking separate from the day-to-day banks most people use, and realized that her knowledge as a former Wall Streeter could be helpful. The next day, she held a teach-in on the finance industry.

The movement went viral, spreading across the country in weeks. According to one count, from the original occupation in New York, Occupy quickly mushroomed to over six hundred encampments around the country, with at least one in every state. Mary Clinton was excited when she found out that people in her home state of North Dakota had begun planning their occupation—the last state to start a camp. The smallest town to have one may have been Mosier, Oregon, population 430.[42]

The desire to occupy public space, to camp out and create what political analyst and writer Matt Stoller called a "church of dissent," was common to post–financial crisis protests the world over. It was a response to the privatization of public space and services of the past few decades as well as a way to get beyond the deeply isolating way that the crisis seemed to operate; as politicians brayed that all was well, it was easy to feel as though you were a unique failure. The decline of social institutions, from labor unions to political and ethnic clubs, had left people longing for connection once again. "It was kind of a shot in the arm," Alexis Goldstein said. "Our system isn't working. People are frustrated. There is corruption that we don't know how to vote out of office, because it is everywhere. We want to put a flag in the ground and stake our own new society temporarily for a very small geographic space."[43]

In holding the space, the occupiers gave outrage a location. While many people moved into the camps, many others were able to be a part of the movement simply by dropping by once in a while, attending a general assembly, eating a sandwich, joining a march, hearing a lecture, or becoming part of a "working group" addressing everything from the continued need for food and blankets to planning direct action.

Institutional public spaces were the domain of existing elites. Even Zuccotti Park, a part-public, part-private space maintained by Brookfield Properties, was not free of elite influence, though the unique rules that kept such public-private spaces open in New York were what allowed the encampment to stay. A people feeling increasingly disconnected from the way politics operated also felt left out or locked out of the public spaces designated as the locations for political debate. Instead, they carved out their own space, and in it created a society that had books and lectures, good food, committees for comfort, cleanup, security, and free medical care. It accepted everyone. It didn't require your money, though the constant flow of donations from outside, from individuals as well as supportive institutions like labor unions and community groups, allowed it to keep existing as a space where cash was unnecessary.

The space was never without tensions: between those who slept there and held the space and those who went home to beds at night, between different groups with different goals—and the ever-present standoffs with the ever-present police. When the tents began to go up in Zuccotti Park, the communal feeling of the space changed, and there was a limit to how long major cities were going to allow protest camps to exist in their midst. Yet the spaces allowed something to grow, something that felt new.

You didn't have to wait for permission to declare yourself part of Occupy. You simply did it. As Mary Clinton said, you could be part of it just by thinking it, by submitting your story to one of the blogs that turned up, like the "We Are the 99 Percent" Tumblr page. Perhaps the most compelling part of the movement, and the one that most confused outside observers, was the commitment to "horizontalism," often misdefined as leaderlessness or structurelessness.

Horizontalism at its base was a declaration that no one in the movement was more important than anyone else; its appeal seemed to answer some deep need in people who had been burned time after time by political and economic elites or by bosses who denigrated and fired them. It was fueled by the same kind of skepticism of elites that had driven the Tea Party's structure, but heightened by ideals that had come from anarchism, feminism, and the 1990s movement against rapacious trade policies. The movement had come together in response to three years of failure by elected officials to deal with the Great Recession and an increased sense that the government had responded to and bailed out the rich but left everyone else to figure out their own solutions as best they could. Doing things for yourself—not waiting for permission, as Clinton said—was key.

For the young occupiers, especially, Ruth Milkman noted, it was almost completely anathema to talk about electoral politics as making any significant change. "There's almost no circumstance under which they can imagine taking that seriously, which is not true for the older people who see the limitation of it and also see the uses of it," Milkman said. The Tea Party, in contrast, made up mostly of older people, had consciously worked to influence elections.

There was another structure that contributed to the movement's horizontalism as well: the Internet. While holding public space was key, without the Internet, and in particular, social media like Facebook and Twitter, the movement would not have spread, let alone gone real-world viral the way it did. On the Internet, horizontality is the norm, and leadership beside the point, and Occupy was shaped by this as well. Goldstein described it in computer-programming terms: "It is this idea of an API. Here is a set of tools that you can use to do a thing. And anyone can do it. You can just use my toolkit."[44]

The movement began on the Internet when people saw the *Adbusters* call, and Facebook invitations were key to making the occupation happen. Clinton remembered adding people who had RSVP'd to the *Adbusters* event and messaging them as Occupy Wall Street, asking if they were coming, if they needed a ride, what they could bring. The Occupy email address at one point was getting messages every six minutes—mostly, at the beginning, from people who had suggestions for what the movement needed to do. The challenge, Clinton said, was getting people to make their ideas happen themselves, rather than bringing suggestions for other people to enact. But at meetings, there would often be a moment when someone else would say, "I had that idea too!" "When you connect those people, then you have strength," she said.

Goldstein agreed. "At first I was like, 'Why don't they X, Y, Z?'" she said. "Then I just became involved and started doing what matched my particular skillset." That included getting "Occupy the SEC" started, and cowriting a comment letter to the Securities and Exchange Commission that helped shape financial regulation. Writ large, that was how the movement spread, as people who wanted to see an occupation in their hometown simply made it happen.

Social media served the movement well when it came to getting around the mainstream media: when at first the movement was ignored, and then misrepresented by reporters who didn't understand that there was no leader to contact, occupiers simply told their own stories. The prevalence of smartphones and new, easy live-streaming technology allowed protesters to capture actions as they were happening and share them in real time on Twitter. One study captured Occupy-related Tweets beginning October 12, 2011, and observed some 120,000 Occupy-related Tweets on a typical day that November; it found a peak of over 500,000 when the police raided Zuccotti Park on November 15.[45]

Many protest campaigns in recent years have revolved around personal storytelling, and like those campaigns, Occupy did broadcast personal tales of woe, particularly on the "We Are the 99 Percent" Tumblr page. But there was also something new in the way Occupy communicated itself to the world. It was less about the personal stories and more about writing the history of the movement as it was happening. The media was just another failed institution to the occupiers, who operated on the maxim of former punk singer Jello Biafra: "Don't hate the media; become the media."

Occupy was shaped by what British journalist Paul Mason noted were "the very values of free-market capitalism—individualism, choice, respect for human rights, the network, the flattened hierarchy." In other words, it was shaped in some ways by the very thing against which it protested.[46]

And yet for many within the movement, it was not about reforming or tinkering with capitalism: they wanted something else, something better. To Mary Clinton, talking about capitalism was like finally addressing the elephant in the room. It made it possible to discuss inequality and power, and it didn't seem to scare people off as they had been warned it might. Even Clinton's father, a Fox News fan, told her he was proud of her time with Occupy.

Where Occupy's best-known slogan, "We Are the 99 Percent," was populist, its day-to-day structure was shaped as much by anarchist practices. Decisions were made by consensus rather than by majority rule—everyone had to agree, or at least decide not to disagree publicly, for an action to be taken. Hand signals were used at the general assemblies where those decisions were made; people "twinkled" their fingers in the air pointing upward if they agreed or voted yes, pointed down for no, or pointed straight out in front if they were iffy on the subject. They crossed their arms on their chests for a "block"—something beyond a no vote, designed to halt debate.

An early innovation, created when amplified sound was banned in Zuccotti Park, became one of the movement's most memorable practices—the "people's mic," where listeners would repeat back a speaker's words, sentence by sentence, to ensure everyone could hear. The people's mic cut down on speechifying; it functioned itself as a sort of consensus process, bringing people together in what they had to say. Manissa McCleave Maharawal wrote of the experience, "There is something intense about speaking in front of hundreds of people, but . . . it is even more intense when that crowd is repeating everything you say. . . . Hearing yourself in an echo chamber means that you make sure your words mean something because they are being said back to you as you say them."[47]

The people's mic also turned into a tactic for disruption when protesters began to use it to shut down events taking place in other venues. An Occupy offshoot that worked on education issues used it to great effect early on, particularly in December 2011 at a Panel for Educational Policy meeting in New York. Occupiers called out "Mic check!" and then rose, person after person, to speak their minds about the mayor's education policy. One protester is easy to remove; many of them, each repeating the other, is much harder.

The consensus process became more and more unwieldy as the movement grew; it was hard to make decisions on little things when hundreds of people felt compelled to have a vote. Occupy struggled with making its processes work, and most of its offshoots moved away from consensus models. Yet when it did work, it was compelling to watch—hundreds of twinkling fingers in the dark, hundreds of voices chiming in unison.

Occupy's lack of a singular demand was often criticized, both in the mainstream media and by the older left. But Nelini Stamp argued that it was also what drew people in. "There are no demands, so if I don't agree with you that's okay." The occupations were spaces for generating ideas and demands, spaces for experimentation and communication. By their end they had perhaps overshadowed their reason for existing, but they demonstrated the deep desire for a new form of politics in which people felt included, not excluded.

The Zuccotti Park occupation might have had its best moment at 5:45 a.m. on Friday, October 14. Mayor Bloomberg had declared that the park would be emptied so that it could be cleaned. The occupiers, in response, had gone on a cleaning binge of their own; the people's mic had echoed, "We are now creating a society that we envision for the world. Being responsible for ourselves is at the heart of that." Emails rocketed out from supportive organizations, ranging from MoveOn to the AFL-CIO. Everyone I ran into that morning said the same thing: "I knew I had to be there."

When the unions arrived that morning, it felt like the beginning of a war. Richard Kim of *The Nation* compared the moment to the scene in *Lord of the Rings* when the elves arrive at the last battle. There were the orange shirts of the laborers, blue for United Auto Workers, red for National Nurses United. I scribbled notes and circled the park, waiting for the police to arrive, choking down a dry bagel from a food truck. In line behind me at the truck were a man in a clerical collar, another man in a keffiyeh, and a Santa Claus. The line between protester and press was gone at that moment. We all simply wondered what would happen.[48]

I saw the announcement on Twitter first, from my friend Phillip Anderson: "Looks like @MikeBloomberg just blinked. Hard. Brookfield postpones cleaning of #LibertyPlaza."[49]

Ragged-voiced, Nelini Stamp was in the center of three waves of the people's mic, reading from the message that had just been received. "They are postponing their cleaning! The reason why is they believe they can work out an arrangement with us, but also—because we have a lot of people here!"

In front of me, a burly man in a bright orange laborers' union shirt held up his phone so that his mother, a veteran of the movements of the 1960s, could hear the cheers erupting.

"This is power," he told me.

CHAPTER TWO

MIDDLE-CLASS MELTDOWN AND THE DEBT TRAP

"I TRIED FOR MANY, MANY YEARS TO BE 'MRS. ALL AMERICA.'" Nancy Daniel said, sitting in a coffee shop in a northern suburb of Atlanta, Georgia. "I married a guy in the military and divorced him. Had two kids. Tried to do everything right, or what I was being taught was right. And it didn't work that way. It just didn't." She'd greeted me with an embrace, telling me, "I'm a hugger," although we were there to talk about a sobering subject. Daniel, like millions of other Americans, had been struggling since 2009 to keep her home.

She bought her condo in 1996, right after the Atlanta Olympics, when prices dipped to a reasonable level. "This is the first home I bought with my own money, my own credit. I was so proud of it," she said. "I had a lot of friends help me move in and decorate and whatnot. We had a great time. It has been a wonderful place to live."

Things started to go downhill for Daniel in the recession that followed September 11, 2001; she lost her job at a commercial refrigeration company when construction slowed and the company downsized. She described feeling shame the first time she needed to go on unemployment, as if she couldn't support herself, but her friends reassured her that it was her money, that she had paid into the system for years. It took her over a year to find another job, a marketing and event planning position. "I thought, 'Well, great. This is wonderful.' Until they moved their whole marketing department to Houston," she said.

That was in the mid-2000s, and she was getting older. Marketing, she said, is a young person's game; it was hard to convince people to take a chance on a woman in her mid-fifties. She signed up with several temp agencies, developed an eBay business, and swapped services with people in her neighborhood, all the while remaining an active member of her condo association. She was getting by, but had to dip into her savings more and more often. Finally, in 2009, she filed for bankruptcy and reached out to Bank of America to see if she could refinance her mortgage. But in the years after the financial crisis, she was just one of millions who were struggling and reaching out individually to the big bailed-out banks for relief. "They just kind of lost me," she said. "They stopped returning my calls."

Like many others at the time, her mortgage had been handed off to a different company—in her case, Nationstar, a mortgage servicer. As home loans were packaged into investment securities, they were sliced and diced so many times that banks lost track of the underlying ownership. This practice occasionally ended up creating situations where banks foreclosed on a home when they no longer owned the loan, and for homeowners like Nancy Daniel, figuring out who actually owned their loan could be near impossible. For a while, she waited in limbo, not sure what was going on—until she started to get letters demanding she pay up or face foreclosure. In the fall of 2013, Nationstar began foreclosure proceedings. The banks that had created the crisis had been bailed out as a group, but homeowners like Daniel were left to struggle individually, the bailouts somehow failing to trickle down to the people at risk of losing their homes. Daniel was one of millions for whom what had seemed like a manageable level of debt—so-called "good debt," like mortgages or student loans—had spiraled out of control when the economy collapsed.

Daniel didn't remember how she found Occupy Our Homes Atlanta, only what it was like at the first meeting she attended. "The first thing they told me is, 'There is no shame here. This is a shame-free zone.' And I was full of shame. I was scared. I was begging."

At the meeting, Occupy Our Homes activist Shabnam Bashiri welcomed Daniel, reassuring her that there was hope, that they could help.

The first thing Daniel was asked to do was to write out her story and post it on the Occupy Our Homes website. "I went, 'You mean, tell people what is going on?!?' I was raised in a family and a culture and a society that said, 'If you can't pay your bills, then you are not a good person.'"

But she did it. And after her saga was published, she took a petition to a fall festival at which she was a vendor. "I sucked it up and I started asking people for signatures. I was so surprised at how many people had been in similar situations or knew people who had. I got my first, probably, two hundred signatures from the people at that festival. They were so generous, and caring, and there was no shame whatsoever. They really wanted to help. They understood."

Occupy Our Homes Atlanta had spun off from Occupy Atlanta in the fall of 2011 as part of an attempt to connect the occupation with what was going on in the broader city. Bashiri had been home in Atlanta on a break from touring with her band when the occupation began and had thrown herself wholeheartedly into activism. "I consider myself part of this generation of people. I was excited about Obama, then really disappointed, saw something on Facebook about this Occupy thing, and went," she told me. The park occupation was evicted after three weeks, which Bashiri thought was a good thing—"It had started to become about holding the space, and not really about what had led us to be there in the first place."

She remembered sending out a Tweet that told people facing foreclosure to call her number. "That was on a Monday and I got a call that Thursday, from a cop. This was ironic because we had just dealt with being evicted by SWAT teams," she said.

The police officer lived in DeKalb County and was facing a final eviction hearing the next morning; Bashiri and several other occupiers piled into a car to attend. Watching the judge sign the eviction order, she said, made the mortgage crisis real for her.

Without much further planning, they decided to occupy his house and attempt to prevent the foreclosure—and at first, they managed to stave off eviction and drew support from the neighbors. "It's a good cause," one of the neighbors said. "If we don't take a stand, who will?" Eventually, the family relented under threat of arrest, though they expressed no regrets about working with Occupy. Even though they hadn't succeeded, Bashiri thought they were on to something.[1]

They weren't the only ones. In Minnesota, Occupy had also turned to foreclosures. Cat Salonek, from the beginning, had been unsure of the value of holding onto an occupied space in a park—particularly with a Minnesota winter fast approaching. When homeowner Monique White came to the plaza and told her story to the general assembly, Salonek said, it was easy to get consensus to support her. Like the Atlanta occupiers, they moved into White's home without much of a plan, learning about the foreclosure process on the fly.

"Occupy Homes formed out of a few different needs locally," Salonek said. "One was for there to be really tangible wins, [and] what's more tangible than a whole house? Two, we needed some clear direction at Wall Street, the horrible things they had done to collapse our economy, so we were able to use this narrative that could be as reformist or as radical as it needed to be for the context."

In Minneapolis, unlike Atlanta, there were existing community groups and unions that had done some work around the foreclosure issue. But what was key in both locations was that a core group of organizers made Occupy Homes their job, living on whatever money could be raised and committing to spend all their time working on home defenses. They built a model for the fight that included petitioning, public protests at the banks, and letter-writing and phone-call campaigns as well as physical home blockades—a model that allowed different people different levels of engagement, from signing a petition in support of the effort to going to jail in defense of a home. In Atlanta, Bashiri and four others moved into a house that functioned as both home and headquarters for their organization. "We met every morning at 9 a.m. for a year," she laughed. "We basically worked all the time and there was really intense accountability, a level of accountability that I don't know that I'd ever want to replicate, but you couldn't get away with not doing your work because somebody would just come in your room and say, 'You're supposed to be doing this thing!'"

Along with the core group, both groups worked to bring homeowners in and to organize the neighborhoods behind homeowners facing foreclosure. Salonek noted that while protesting banks galvanized the anger people had, working to save a home galvanized their compassion. "It was this really powerful community," she said. "I remember hotdishes getting passed up through windows by the Lutheran moms who didn't want to go in the house and risk arrest but they'd make a casserole," she laughed. "Doing a barbecue and a potluck is just so Minnesotan."

Salonek would see people becoming politicized through the process of risking arrest for their neighbors: "We'd say, 'You should think about how the banks have controlled our communities to such a degree that you can't walk into this house without being worried.' It's powerful, for the act of sitting in someone's living room to be an act of resistance. Talking about the really big numbers of the bailout and really big scandals of Wall Street theft doesn't hit a person in their guts the way that seeing a mom trying to live in her house does."

People fighting a legal battle on their own against foreclosure mostly found the deck stacked against them. Bashiri discovered, though, that for many people, facing the failure of the legal system to provide anything like justice brought them to a point where they began questioning a system that had told them that if they worked hard, they would get what they deserved. "The number of people who tried and tried and tried and as a result of just sheer incompetency and evil on the part of these banks found themselves questioning capitalism as a whole. Hardcore Republicans." The immediacy of watching neighbors and friends struggling to keep their home seemed to transcend politics; it was more than symbolic that Occupy Atlanta's first home battle was for a police officer. People who dismissed the park occupations as silly whining from kids felt differently when those activists were willing to risk arrest to help them save the home they'd worked hard to buy, and they began to understand whose side the occupiers were on.

Even so, it was hard for homeowners to shake the feeling of shame that they couldn't pay their debt. Nick Espinosa was one of the core group of organizers at Occupy Homes Minnesota and had already fought a few foreclosures when he found out that his mother, Colleen McKee Espinosa, a nurse, was facing foreclosure herself. At first, she wanted nothing to do with the occupiers, despite her son's involvement, but he was able to win her over. "As I resolved to fight, I realized I had nothing to be ashamed of," McKee Espinosa said. "If anyone should be ashamed, it's the banks for tearing apart our communities after we bailed them out with our tax dollars." After several months of campaigning, Citibank agreed to cancel a sheriff's sale of McKee Espinosa's home and modify her mortgage, allowing her to keep the house.

Her whole life, Nick Espinosa said, his mother had never been political, "but by getting involved in a struggle that was about her life and her family and protecting the little that she's fought for her whole life to get, that made it real to her, that was transformative."[2]

Mildred Obi had always been an activist—she'd marched with Martin Luther King Jr. when she was sixteen. She fell behind on her house payments after having to leave her job on account of a disability, and in 2009, she was notified that she was in foreclosure. Like Nancy Daniel and too many other homeowners facing foreclosure, she had a hard time finding out who actually owned her mortgage, who was servicing it, and who else had a claim, and she tried to file legal claims against what seemed like a maze of banks. Despite her legal battle, she was evicted in 2012. "The same day that my personal belongings were put out on the street I received a notice from the Court of Appeals granting my motion for reconsideration," she said.

Obi had participated in rallies at Occupy Atlanta, but at first she resisted telling the other protesters about her own struggles. "After engaging the legal system and not being able to get any justice," she said, "you just reach out, you start hollering, you yell for everybody, anybody."

Obi moved back into her house with a group of occupiers, changed the locks, and resumed negotiating with Bank of America. At first, she said, they threatened to evict her again, then they offered to give her cash for her keys, and then finally they gave her the house back free and clear. "It's been tough, exacerbated my symptoms both physically and mentally, but without the help of Occupy, I don't think I would've had a victory," she said. "Public outcry was important; the resistance, the persistence was very important. We had people willing to risk arrest for me. I'll never forget that—that is close to my heart, a beautiful thing."

As the Occupy Homes groups grew and racked up successes, they also began to coordinate on national political campaigns, joining community groups and labor unions to press for a new director to the Federal Housing Finance Agency and to push for a new law allowing homeowners to buy back their homes after foreclosure. They drew on the drama of their battles to highlight those demands. Occupy Homes also worked on a Homeowner Bill of Rights, bringing homeowners to the Minnesota State Capitol to testify and using direct action to create pressure for the bill's passage. "I think there's a misconception that poor people or people of color don't have time for politics or don't care about politics," Nick Espinosa said. "The reality is that people are really hungry for that. Their lives are political."

In 2013, the Occupy Homes groups decided to take their fight to Washington in an action they called "Justice to Justice." They worked with community organizations to gather five hundred homeowners and family members who'd been affected by the mortgage crisis for a week of action in the nation's capital that included civil disobedience outside the Justice Department. "This woman Marie, she's from Chicago and she's seventy-eight years old and there was this line of DHS officers in full gear, at these flowerpots," Bashiri remembered. "They lift her up, she gets on the flowerpot, she pushes by them, and she sits down. And then all these other seniors, they're sitting. We're not moving!"

Bashiri was frustrated, though, by the lack of national action despite dramatic protests. The national mortgage settlements over massive fraud, she said, were too little too late, and homeowners have seen almost none of that money, which often filtered into state budgets. The grand promises turned into tiny sums. "The housing justice movement was one of the most wonderful, beautiful things," she said. "We had so many little victories, but on a grand scale, they got away with it."

In Minnesota, Occupy Homes began a campaign to occupy vacant homes, many of which had been sitting empty for years—in some cases "zombie foreclosures," homes on which banks had begun foreclosure proceedings without completing them, and where the homeowner moved on even though the house remained in limbo, with no one taking possession. "The homelessness rate in Minnesota was climbing to an all-time high, and so we pulled these two stories together and we organized people who were experiencing homelessness to move into vacant homes," Salonek said. They used a similar structure to the foreclosure battles, reaching out to the neighbors to make sure they were supportive, and reaching out to the banks to ask if they would donate the homes to a community land trust. But as they worked on that, the police began raiding the homes. The struggle to keep them simply became too much of a risk.

The organizing continued, though. "Occupy Wall Street was like a dandelion that got blown into the wind and seeds landed where they did," Salonek said. "Occupy Homes was one of those seeds that took and grew and then blew out all over the place again."

Nancy Daniel was still waiting to see what would happen with her home. Over the past two years, she had gone through a lot. Supporters in Texas had held a protest at Nationstar's headquarters for her, and she had sneaked into the Freddie Mac office in Atlanta—a building she describes as being like the Death Star from *Star Wars*—with supporters to deliver a petition to the government-sponsored entity. She had filed multiple complaints with the Consumer Financial Protection Bureau, among them one charging that Nationstar was illegally "dual tracking" her mortgage, negotiating with her at the same time as it was proceeding with foreclosure. She talked with people around the country who were in battles with the same servicer.

"Right now, we are waiting for something to happen," she said. "I am looking for other places to live, but rents are unbelievable, and with my credit history it is going to be hard. I have this vision of me living in a tent under I-75 downtown. I am supposed to be comfortably retired. Isn't that the American dream? That is not happening here."

THE STORY WE HAVE BEEN TOLD ABOUT THE FINANCIAL CRISIS IS THAT it was a brief period in time that has ended, that since the banks have gone back to business as usual, complete with gargantuan profits, things are going to be fine. But the foreclosure crisis lingered on and on, its burdens borne by individuals who felt isolated and ashamed. One estimate found that in 2012, years after the crisis was supposedly over, Americans lost $192.6 billion in wealth as a result of foreclosures—an average of $1,700 per family, although of course the crisis was not spread evenly, and some lost everything. Indeed, communities of color took the hardest hit. Though the foreclosure crisis has fallen out of the headlines, the stories of people like Nancy Daniel should remind us that its ramifications will be felt for generations: wealth that had been accumulated and handed down over decades was wiped out in a few months.[3]

It was nearly impossible to understand the size of the crisis, the sheer number of people pushed out of their homes, in part because there are simply no official statistics. "It's a total failure of public policy that government statistics are so terrible around foreclosures that we have to rely on private analysts, usually affiliated with organizations that want to soft-pedal the numbers," explained David Dayen, journalist and the author of *Chain of Title: How Three Ordinary Americans Uncovered Wall Street's Great Foreclosure Fraud.* Tracking only evictions or "completed foreclosures" results in an undercount because it leaves out people who were forced to short-sell their homes as well as the hundreds of thousands of "zombie foreclosures," which have the same effect on the family as a completed foreclosure. The most reliable number, Dayen said, is a count of 5.6 million between September 2008 and February 2015, according to private property data firm CoreLogic.[4]

In between the credit default swaps and the mortgage-backed securities, there were millions of people pushed out of their homes. The rate of foreclosures slowed after 2011, but remained well above the pre-crisis average. The housing crisis was the result of a housing bubble that vastly overinflated the price of housing, mostly because repackaging and reselling the loans as investment products had become Wall Street's favorite form of speculation. Why buy an actual property, when you can allow someone else to take on that risk and profit by selling their debt instead?

Wall Street, explained Alexis Goldstein, who worked there as the housing bubble was inflating and is now a senior policy analyst at Americans for Financial Reform, thought it had hit the gold mine on mortgage-backed securities. The thought process, she said, was that "this is a product that can never really go down in value. We have created a thing that is based on houses. That has inherent value. Even if the first person defaults on their mortgage, we can foreclose on their house and sell the house. So, therefore, money forever. We win." The ratings agencies bought in and rated the securities at the highest possible level, AAA. Goldstein noted that this meant investors were being told that mortgage-backed securities were essentially as safe as government bonds, but paid much better—giving investors every incentive to throw their money in.

Real incomes over the decades leading up to the crisis were stagnant or falling. But banks and mortgage lenders rushed to get more homeowners into more loans, driving up prices, spurring more construction, until the logical end was reached, and it became difficult to find people with credit decent enough to purchase a home. Which was where subprime mortgages came in. Subprime mortgages carried higher interest rates and were typically given to people with spotty credit histories; they had been, up until the mid-2000s, about 6 to 8 percent of total mortgages—until they exploded, reaching 25 percent of the market by 2006. Making matters worse, many of those mortgages came with adjustable rates, meaning they would start at a low rate and go up in the future, yet banks were only gauging the borrower's ability to afford the "teaser" rate.[5]

Working people's incomes failed to keep up with the cost of living, and government services began to be pared back. People began to seek out other sources of funds to make purchases, and home equity loans became more popular. People were not only borrowing to buy homes; once they had them, they were borrowing against them in order to buy other things. All of that debt was only sustainable as long as prices kept rising; if they stopped rising, let alone took a dive, the economy was in for a shock. When the subprime mortgages began to fail, the whole bubble burst—economist Dean Baker estimated the loss could be equal to about $110,000 per homeowner. The homes that people had bought as proof of their success became the method of their failure.[6]

As the crisis unfolded and people lost jobs, more and more of them became unable to pay their mortgages, and more and more homes fell into foreclosure. Foreclosed homes flooded the market, driving property values down further, yet banks largely refused to write down mortgages to the post-bubble value of the homes, and the crisis continued.

Like Rick Santelli, many commentators wanted to blame the crisis on subprime borrowers, who they claimed should have known better. Banks used sanctimonious speeches by policymakers as justification for not issuing modifications, and no blanket relief was forthcoming from Washington. But many of those borrowers were pushed into loans that they were not even aware they were taking out. Rampant, large-scale fraud occurred across the mortgage lending industry as the bubble inflated, a part of the story that is not told nearly often enough.

"This is a mountain that people think is a molehill," whistleblower Eileen Foster told me in 2012. "As far as this type of financial crime, things are far worse than I would have ever imagined." Foster became the head of Countrywide Mortgage's internal investigations department in 2007. She uncovered routinized fraud, out in the open—templates for fabricating documents, cases of Wite-Out for changing borrowers' names on paperwork, and a method of simply plugging falsified income values into the automated underwriting system until a number worked and allowed the lender to proceed with the loan. "One process was to cut a signature off one document, paste it and make a photocopy so it looks like an original signature," she said. "A part and parcel of everyday business was to do anything it took to fund a loan."[7]

It didn't matter that the loans were often being sold to people who were unlikely to ever be able to repay. "They'd set them up with those teaser rates they could afford, put in the income they needed," Foster said. "They were so confident that they could refinance, because property values were going up. Another part of fraud is rationalizing what you're doing."

Instead of being rewarded for finding massive fraud, Foster was pushed out shortly after Bank of America absorbed Countrywide. A report from the Department of Labor backed up her account, finding that Foster had been illegally fired for blowing the whistle.[8]

No one at Countrywide or Bank of America was punished for this fraud. In 2010, Angelo Mozilo, Countrywide's cofounder, agreed to a $67.5 million settlement with the Securities and Exchange Commission. It sounded like a lot of money, but Mozilo had made over $410 million since becoming head of Countrywide. The news also came out in 2012 that Countrywide had made hundreds of discount loans in order to curry favor with members of Congress and other government officials, including former Senate Banking Committee head Chris Dodd (D-CT) and Congressman Howard "Buck" McKeon (R-CA).[9]

Within the foreclosure process itself, the practice of "robosigning"—having low-level employees sign piles of foreclosure documents every day—created an assembly line of eviction. Banks foreclosed on people who weren't even behind on their payments, with almost no documentation proving they had the right to do so. In 2012, the five biggest banks agreed to a $26 billion settlement with the federal government over major foreclosure fraud; the money was supposed to go to help homeowners stay in their homes, but fewer than 85,000 people actually got mortgage modifications. It was as if, Goldstein said, the regulators said, "We have gotten halfway through this. We are just going to give up. We are just going to pick an arbitrary amount of money to give everyone. Sorry. You won't get your house back. You will just get three hundred bucks on thirty thousand."[10]

Modifying mortgages to keep people living at home and paying something would have made much more economic sense, even for the banks, and yet it didn't happen. The federal government, which one would assume, having bailed out the banks, had some leverage to make them do so, dropped the ball. Instead, it allowed banks to count actions they'd already taken toward the total amount of aid they promised to give, or to count mortgage modifications that actually increased a borrower's monthly payment as a modification nevertheless. That the best regulators could do was offer paltry settlements, for which the banks could actually take a tax write-off, is evidence of a massive failure by the US government to help its people. Some of them, like Mildred Obi, were able to get help elsewhere. But it would have been impossible to stop the crisis one home at a time. The individualized solutions pushed on homeowners were not remotely up to the job of fixing the housing market; they only reinforced the idea that the crisis was due to the mistakes of individual homeowners. As Goldstein noted, there seemed to be a fear that one undeserving homeowner would get relief, that some deadbeat would get a deal, and rather than have one person get away with something, "we are just going to screw over all homeowners."[11]

Meanwhile, the banks are ramping up again. In cities like Atlanta, Wall Street investors have bought up homes in chunks—private equity firm Blackstone Group bought 1,400 Atlanta houses in just one day in 2013—to sell financial products made from the rent payments it would collect on the homes. Most of the homes they acquired were foreclosures, most of them in the cities and neighborhoods that had been hit the hardest by the foreclosure crisis, where people were still struggling to get back on their feet.[12]

To Bashiri, it's a sign that the lack of real reform after the foreclosure crisis has emboldened the banks to find new ways to speculate. Financiers argue that buying up foreclosed homes is a good thing, that it is making prices rise. Blackstone even called its strategy "a bet on America." But the banks have been lousy landlords, sometimes jacking up rents by over 30 percent and using aggressive collection techniques on their tenants—some of whom are the former owners, renting back the home foreclosed away from them. And the shift away from homeownership to rentals is changing the shape of the housing market. It is leaving renters vulnerable to the whims of their landlords, who might decide to sell their properties as quickly as they bought them. "Whenever it makes sense for them to cash out and dump all those properties, they will," Bashiri said. "Then where do we land?"[13]

HISTORY IS FILLED WITH STORIES OF REBELLIONS OVER HOUSING. From the Paris Commune in 1871, to the organizing by leftists after the Great Depression, to 1960s Chicago, to Brooklyn in 2012 and 2013, tenant organizing and rent strikes have been a way for people to express some power over their living situation. Perhaps we shouldn't be surprised that modern homeownership in the United States was shaped by the desire of those in power to quell unrest.[14]

It might have been the rise of the automobile that finally convinced financial institutions to lend to non-rich people, but it was homeownership that really kicked off the spread of credit. Homeownership was promoted by the government as a hedge against the spread of socialism, a goal made more explicit after the beginning of the Great Depression, when the National Housing Act of 1934, and then the creation of the Federal National Mortgage Association (now known as Fannie Mae), helped incentivize lending to working-class homebuyers by providing government backing for private loans. The method assuaged bankers' fears of socialism because the lending remained in their hands.[15]

After World War II, the booming economy and GI Bill benefits for returning servicemen helped fuel the suburbanization of America. Developer William Levitt created the Levittown planned communities, which were built in an assembly-line style borrowed from the factories, where workers were enjoying higher wages than in the past and regular eight-hour workdays. And along with those wages and union contracts, the ongoing promotion of homeownership served to keep workers happy and content. "No man who owns his own house and lot can be a Communist," Levitt famously said. "He has too much to do." The July 3, 1950, cover of *Time* featured Levitt and declared, "For sale: a new way of life."[16]

That new way of life was what we began to call "middle class." While it was never a lifestyle as widely available as myth would have it—redlining of neighborhoods where black people lived ensured that they were ineligible for Federal Housing Administration (FHA) loans and couldn't make use of the GI Bill's housing provisions, legally enforceable racial covenants kept black buyers out of white neighborhoods, and even unmarried white women had trouble accessing credit—it was, for a period of time, widespread. Union representation was at its apex, peaking in the mid-1950s at 35 percent and helping to drive wages up even in non-union workplaces, and profits continued to rise and prosperity spread.

For a brief few decades, many families were able to subsist on one income. The GI Bill provided college funding for more than 8 million veterans of World War II—up until then, the number of eighteen- to twenty-four-year-olds attending college had always been under 10 percent, but the GI Bill started the upward trend, which reached an all-time high of 39.6 percent in 2008. People began to shake off the old "working-class" identifier; we were all middle class now.[17]

The student loan, separate from the GI Bill's grants, was born in 1958 from Cold War policy. In response to the Soviet Union's launch of the Sputnik satellite, the United States created the National Defense Education Act, pouring federal dollars into research universities and making low-interest loans to students who wanted to go into scientific or technological research. These first loans, as sociologist Andrew Ross wrote, "were explicitly aimed at creating a technically skilled workforce as an arm of the warfare, not the welfare, state."[18]

Federal student loans for everyone else came along in 1965 as part of the Higher Education Act, which at first was aimed at low-income students to supplement grants and scholarships, and then expanded to everyone. Those loans, too, were issued by private banks but backed up by the federal government. With the spread of higher education, the promise of upward mobility, for a brief period, seemed assured. The middle class seemed to have become so broad that it was, in fact, the only class, though the name still provided producerist reassurances to people that they deserved all they had.[19]

Having the trappings of a middle-class life became the ultimate goal for so many people, but once there, Americans were continually anxious about falling out. "Class in general is . . . referenced through a container metaphor," said communications expert Anat Shenker-Osorio. "So you're 'in the middle class,' you fall out of it, you climb into it." Once you're in that container, you have particular expectations for what you should be able to do: survive on one income, go on vacation, own a home, or send your kids to college. Over time, the middle-class identity became more and more closely associated with what could be bought than with stability. Symbols of class identity like televisions and then cellphones became cheaper—"Ironically," Shenker-Osorio noted, "through the same forces that have destroyed unions and destroyed large swaths of our manufacturing economy"—so that even as incomes began to stagnate in the

1970s, people could still tell themselves they had the little luxuries of a middle-class life. The influx of women into the workforce, women who had previously only worked in the home, helped to maintain the illusion, but now it typically took two incomes for a family to maintain middle-class status instead of one. Consumer credit arose to finance that big-screen TV. The goalposts of what it took to be middle class were moving.

Class, through the 1970s and 1980s, became detached from its moorings in one's position in the economy and became instead a form of political identity—an idea stoked by populists from George Wallace to Ronald Reagan to George W. Bush, in opposition to what was considered "identity politics." Class, Barbara Ehrenreich noted, was just another "form of cultural diversity, parallel to ethnicity or even 'lifestyle.'" The meaningless paeans to the middle spouted off by politicians and others deliberately disappeared the fact that class is a relation of power, not a lifestyle choice. And what we got in return—as the discussions about class obscured, rather than revealed, economic realities—was the largest wealth and income inequality since the Gilded Age.[20]

Politicians from all points of the political spectrum tout their concern for the middle class and their desire to save it. The theme is so popular that it has become meaningless; it tells us nothing about what the person promising it actually wants to do. More importantly, as Shenker-Osorio noted, in reality, the endless evocations of the middle worked to suppress action on measures to address the growing inequality.

In other words, notions of the middle class played into the same old producerist tropes. And those who bought into these notions didn't want to spare their hard-earned cash to help people who had been excluded from prosperity to begin with. As real conditions worsened for people who had been accustomed to thinking of themselves as comfortably middle class, the "fear of falling" kept them from solidarity with the people who had nowhere else to fall. The new solution that arose to the economic woes of the middle was the tax cut: playing off the resentment of the bottom by those who fancied themselves the middle, Ronald Reagan and his compatriots sliced away at the welfare state. Too many in the angry middle shrugged off the cuts as a just end to the "handouts" they assumed that the poor were getting. Meanwhile, they took out another credit card to stop their own slide.

The middle class, by several measures, has shrunk. Different studies using different methodologies estimated the shrinkage between 1980 and the mid- to late 2000s as between 6 and 14 percent. The US median household income was $4,500 less in 2013 than it had been in 2007, and was in fact less, in real dollars, than it was in 1989. Median household wealth, perhaps an even better indicator of one's class position, was 36 percent lower in 2013 than in 2003, and was down some 20 percent from 1984, meaning that not all of the drop could be attributed solely to the housing bubble popping.[21]

Even the middle class's image of itself is changing. Between 2000 and 2008, Gallup polls found that, on average, over 60 percent of Americans identified themselves as middle class; since 2012, closer to 50 percent identify that way, and 48 percent now identify as working or lower class. The US General Social Survey (GSS), meanwhile, found that the number identifying as middle class was closer to 44 percent; "working class" got a roughly equal response, even though the term "working class," with its tang of radicalism, was much less popular with politicians. Even politicians began to search for a new way, on the 2016 campaign trail, to talk about the majority of the country, as it became clear that the term "middle class" no longer felt accurate to large swathes of people.[22]

The middle has hollowed out, manufacturing jobs have gone overseas, and companies are better and more systematic about union-busting in the jobs that remain. As middle-income jobs for people without college degrees declined, the bachelor's degree became more necessary, a sort of middle-class boundary, even as college tuition grew more expensive, saddling students with yet more debt. In the years leading up to 2008, Americans were spending nearly one in every seven dollars of after-tax income on debt service. And all that debt served to discourage people from the risks of protest, the added weight of payment to make every month a damper on any trouble you might wish to make.[23]

"Debt has been the primary way that the system has extracted wealth from regular people. And it's not just that people have debt—the debt-driven system is how the rich have gotten richer. The level of debt is so great that wage increases won't make up for how much people owe," said organizer Stephen Lerner. But, he noted, debt can also be a place where those regular people have power. The old cliché, now being repeated by debt organizers, goes, "If you owe the bank $1,000, the bank owns you.

But if you owe the bank $1 million (or $1 trillion, in the case of outstanding student debt), you own the bank." Since the debt so broadly distributed throughout the population is being lent by an ever-shrinking and consolidating group of financial institutions, there is the growing possibility of debtors using their collective leverage to make some demands.[24]

BUYING A HOME WAS A SIGN THAT YOU'D MADE IT INTO THE MIDDLE class; it was "good debt" you could take on once you'd reached a certain level of stability and success. The other kind of "good debt" that helped sink what we used to call the middle class, though, came from education, as lenders increasingly exacted a price from young people just for daring to hope of one day getting a middle-class job.

In 1888, a young woman from Texas wrote to the Populist-affiliated paper the *Southern Mercury* under the pen name "Country Girl" to argue that education alone was important enough to make it worth going into debt. "Knowledge is Power," she wrote.[25]

Country Girl's advice is still given every day to thousands of American high school students, who are still told that education is their ticket to upward mobility. For this, those students sign loan documents for tens of thousands of dollars, loans that cannot be discharged in bankruptcy, for which their wages can be garnished if they do not pay.

While the debt load per student continues to rise, the job expectations for college graduates have not. Those who finished college during the Great Recession, researchers found, will likely have diminished earnings for the next ten to fifteen years. Young workers (under the age of twenty-five) typically have a higher unemployment rate than older workers; that rate has remained above 10 percent since the crisis, peaking at 19.2 percent in 2009.[26]

College graduates, unable to find jobs that suited their skills, moved into jobs that did not normally require a degree. One observer compared it to a game of musical chairs—when the music stops, the college grads have taken the Starbucks jobs, and the people who don't have a degree have no chairs left. A study from the Federal Reserve Bank of New York estimated this particular kind of underemployment, where recent grads worked jobs that didn't require their degrees, at 44 percent in 2012. Wages had fallen nearly 8 percent for college grads since 2000, and they were less likely to have employer-provided health insurance or a pension. There's little evidence, in other words, that if more young people went to college, they would be able to access better jobs.[27]

Ultimately, sociologist Tressie McMillan Cottom pointed out, part of the reason for the massive student debt bubble is that policymakers are prescribing education as a solution for what is fundamentally a labor-market problem. Rather than being considered a social good that people undertake to become better informed, more engaged members of society, an education is increasingly perceived as a commodity, something that you purchase to increase your value to an employer. Yet when the fastest-growing jobs out there are low-wage retail, food service, and home care jobs, what does it matter how many years of school you attend?

The cost of a college degree has increased over 3,000 percent since 1972, at the same time as there has been a massive increase in college attendance, notably from middle-income families. At least part of the price hike was due to state disinvestment from public universities, which shifted costs onto the backs of individual students, a trend that began before the Great Recession but intensified after it. The "corporatization" of universities—public and private—led to increased tuition, flashy new buildings, and inflated administrative salaries, on one hand; on the other, professors faced cuts and schools increasingly employed adjunct professors who worked part-time and were paid by the class rather than with a reliable salary.[28]

Easy access to student loans—and the ongoing idea, dating back to Country Girl, that student loans were good debt—made it easy to ignore the increasing costs. Between 1999 and 2011, during the same period that the country was dealing with the massive housing bubble, total student debt grew by something like 511 percent, twice as fast as housing debt did.[29]

On April 25, 2012, the total student loan burden carried by US students reached $1 trillion. Activists marked the day, which they called "1-T Day," with marches, rallies, and protests. It was part of a larger campaign waged by Occupy Student Debt, an extension of Occupy Wall Street, that aimed to bring attention to exploding student debt and the failure of universities and state and federal policies to address it. At the time, Occupy Student Debt organizer Pam Brown told me, "There is an overlapping relationship between the schools who have raised their tuition enormously, between the government which has lowered its spending and has subsidized this debt, and the banks who are profiting from it still."[30]

Student loans, just like housing loans before 2008, are big business. In 2006, just one bank, Citigroup, pocketed $220 million from student lending. In 2005, student lender Sallie Mae was the second most profitable company in the United States; in the first quarter of 2015 it posted profits of $47.7 million. In the early days of the Obama administration, the government switched from subsidizing privately issued loans through the Federal Family Education Loan (FFEL) program to lending directly to students. This change didn't get private lenders out of the business, but it did put the federal government in the strange position of profiting off of loans to its citizens. The Congressional Budget Office estimated in 2014 that the Department of Education would make $127 billion in profits over the next ten years from the student loan program.[31]

The average graduate with debt in 2015 owed over $35,000. That's a significant number, because the total amount the federal government lends per undergraduate through its direct loan program is $31,000, meaning that more and more students are taking out private loans in addition to their direct loans. And those private loans are issued by some of the same banks that had to pay massive settlements over their mortgage-crisis-related shenanigans. One report estimated that a household of two earners with a combined student debt burden of $53,000 faces a lifetime loss of nearly $208,000 in wealth. Andrew Ross, in his book *Creditocracy*, suggested we think of student debt as "precocious wage theft."[32]

Sallie Mae, like Fannie Mae, began its existence as a government-sponsored secondary buyer for private loans. It was created in 1972 and became fully privatized in 2004. It had moved into loan servicing and then originating, both under the FFEL program and privately. In 2014, it split into two separate companies, Sallie Mae and Navient; Navient serviced and collected on its own loans as well as those of the federal government, while Sallie Mae continued to make private loans and moved into banking and credit cards as well.[33]

In 1995, Sallie Mae issued the first Student Loan Asset Backed Securities. Robert Oxford, a graduate student at New York University researching the financialization of student debt and an organizer with Occupy Student Debt, explained that the securities work pretty much the same way mortgage-backed securities do—they're bundled, repackaged, and sold off to big banks and hedge funds that want an exciting investment product. The difference? "You can't foreclose on someone's education."[34]

Instead of foreclosure, collectors chasing education borrowers have a set of tools unequaled for any other type of debt. They can garnish Social Security payments. Borrowers cannot discharge their student loans—even private ones—through bankruptcy. There is no statute of limitations for student loan collection, and the fees only go up if you default. Essentially, rather than taking your home, student lenders can foreclose on your future. These policies have been so effective that the recovery rate on defaulted student loans is actually more than 100 percent. And debt collectors, many of them owned by the same lenders, like Navient and J. P. Morgan, have about a 30 percent profit margin—a better return on investment than when simply servicing the loan normally.[35]

All of this has contributed to the feeling that college is no longer the surefire ticket to a middle-class life that it used to be. In a 2015 survey, only half of the college graduates questioned strongly thought college was worth the price; perhaps not surprisingly, considering the economic problems graduates have faced in recent years, an even smaller portion of those who graduated between 2006 and 2015 thought that college had been worth the cost.[36]

The new protesters did not represent a fairly prosperous middle class fighting for the rights of those worse off, wrote British journalist Paul Mason; the student activists of the post–financial crisis era were fighting for themselves. He dubbed them "graduates with no future."[37]

Of course, in the age of inequality, some graduates are more futureless than others. The rate of default for black student debtors is some four times that of whites; LGBTQ students, who disproportionately have families that are unsupportive, carry a higher debt burden, as do undocumented immigrants, who are legally excluded from federal loans and thus must rely entirely on private lenders. Those whose parents can foot the entire bill, of course, carry no debt at all. Thus has student debt become yet another way that inequalities get magnified.[38]

The growth of the for-profit college sector in recent years is something of a bellwether for the direction in which higher education is going. For-profits, many of them "career colleges" that provide two- and four-year certifications that are supposed to be directly applicable to the workplace, accommodated a little more than 10 percent of total college students, but received around 25 percent of all federal loan dollars. They tended to be pricey—averaging around $35,000 for a two-year associate's degree that would cost around $8,300 at a community college—and most of their students were first-generation college attendees who were unfamiliar with the college-application process and fell victim to a high-pressure sales pitch with equally high promises of job placement. In a weak job market laden with low-wage jobs, promises of a future as a medical assistant or a paralegal or manager were especially enticing, but many of those promises turned out to be overblown. "In some ways it is subprime all over again," Alexis Goldstein said. "You take this thing that is sold to the American public as part of the dream. 'To be an American is to own a house. To be an American is to pull yourself up by your boot-straps by getting an education.' And you turn it into a product that then ruins people's lives."[39]

The debt problem attracted the attention of elected officials from President Obama on down, with proposed solutions ranging from income-based repayment plans to refinancing to full-on loan forgiveness. The debt forgiveness idea was included as an economic stimulus plan cosponsored by Representative Hansen Clarke (D-MI) and a dozen other members of Congress in 2012. But the graduates with no future were beginning to grow restless with the lack of movement from elected officials, and they decided to take matters into their own hands.[40]

IT WAS 2011 WHEN ANN BOWERS DECIDED TO GET BACK INTO THE workforce. Now fifty years old, she had been sidelined with a disability for ten years. Before that, she had worked in marketing, and she thought that by taking some classes to sharpen her skills she could make herself more appealing to future employers. Perhaps it would make up for the gap in her résumé.

One night while watching television, she saw a commercial for Everest College; the promise that she could get a degree from home appealed to her, and she called to find out more about its business marketing program. "The fact that they said they were going to help to put me into a position after graduation was very enticing," she said. After a few follow-up calls from Everest, she decided to enroll and began taking online courses from her Florida home.

Across the country, in Los Angeles, Nathan Hornes found Everest when he went looking for a back-up plan. He'd moved to LA in 2008, after high school, to pursue his dreams of being a pop star; two years later, he was still working in fast food, though he'd performed at venues large and small, starred in a web series, and even released two songs on iTunes. His mother suggested he look into going to college, so when he heard about Everest, he remembered that a cousin of his had attended an Everest school in Missouri, where he'd grown up. He and his sister Natasha decided to go check it out. Nathan recalled a lot of pressure to enroll right away. The college told him that if he didn't sign up now, he'd have to wait six months. He decided to get a business degree; Natasha enrolled in a two-year program to become a paralegal.

Everest College was a subsidiary of Corinthian Colleges, a for-profit college chain that had over one hundred campuses and over 77,000 students at the time that Bowers finished her associate's degree. But what the Horneses and Bowers did not know was that Corinthian's empire was already unraveling at the time they signed up for classes. While they were completing the degrees they thought would help them find better jobs, the federal Department of Education and multiple state attorneys general were investigating Corinthian for false and misleading job placement claims. In the summer of 2014, the DOE shut off the flow of student aid dollars that made up some 85 percent of Corinthian's revenue. Its main source of income gone, the chain announced that it would fold. The DOE stepped in and provided a bailout of sorts, releasing $35 million to keep the school afloat while it orchestrated the sale of eighty-five campuses to Educational Credit Management Corporation (ECMC), a company that had zero experience running a college, but plenty of experience chasing indebted students, as it was a debt collector for the education department.[41]

Corinthian's remaining twenty-eight campuses were shuttered in April 2015, leaving 16,000 students with no degree and a mountain of debt just weeks before many of them would have graduated. Corinthian had continued to enroll new students in the months leading up to its closure. To Bowers, the DOE had enabled Corinthian to keep making money despite its failure. Meanwhile, she said, "we're the ones facing all the consequences."[42]

The Horneses had been noticing red flags at Everest for a while. "My classes weren't in order," Natasha said. "I'd have to take a third trimester course my first trimester. Teachers got fired, we'd have empty classes. I felt like my education wasn't really an education." Her brother agreed, saying he'd had one class that had three different teachers over a twelve-week period. "I asked how I was supposed to take this final," Nathan said. "They said, 'Oh don't worry about the final, we're just going to give you an A on it anyway.' Are you kidding me?"

When Natasha finished her program, she found that the big promises of job placement were "not worth the commercial that they're on." When she did go on interviews—ones that she lined up for herself—she found that even though she'd graduated with honors, she didn't have skills employers were looking for. She wound up moving back to Missouri, where she got a job at a grocery store, because she couldn't afford to stay in Los Angeles and make payments on her $50,000 in loans.

Nathan finished his bachelor's degree in 2014 still wanting to believe that the promises he'd been made meant something. But instead, he said, he was given job listings from Monster.com and Craigslist. "If I wanted those job leads," he said, "I could do that myself."

When the news broke that the Department of Education had been investigating Corinthian for a while, Nathan Hornes decided that enough was enough. Together with some friends, he created the Everest College Avengers group on Facebook, which quickly attracted hundreds of members. "There is no way on God's green earth that the government has been investigating them for the last five years, they've allowed this company to continue to do what they do, we'll give them a slap on the wrist and everything's going to be okay," he said. "We thought, 'This is ridiculous, we're not doing this anymore, we're going to fight back.'"

Ann Bowers was still working on her online program, even serving as an "ambassador" for Everest by mentoring other online students. Then a friend of hers sent her a link to the Facebook group and broke the news to her. "I found out that they had lied to me repeatedly," she said. "My student adviser disappeared, they cut off communication with students and their advisers. When you'd call your adviser it would go to a central answering device."

The Facebook groups were also how Ann Larson and Strike Debt found the Corinthian students. Strike Debt had been founded by Occupy activists looking for ways to intervene in the debt crisis; they'd tried the Rolling Jubilee, a campaign that raised funds to buy debt on the secondary market for pennies on the dollar and then abolish it. Strike Debt had managed to make its first student debt buy, purchasing and forgiving $3.8 million in debt from 2,700 Everest College students, in the fall of 2014, and it was hoping to organize a type of action that would allow the debtors to get personally involved. The Rolling Jubilee, Larson said, "was a neat hack of the debt system, good for educating the public about how the secondary debt market worked and doing a really great thing for the few lucky people who got their debt canceled." But it was still a gift from above, a kind of charity, rather than a way to build power for and with debtors themselves. That's how they came up with the idea of the Debt Collective, a union for debtors, where people who owed the same creditor could find each other and take collective action.

The idea of a debt strike had been floating around since the early days of Occupy Wall Street, but the original plans had been simultaneously too ambitious—a website where one could sign up to pledge to stop paying once a million other people signed up—and too nebulous. The Corinthian students were a better place to start. They were unambiguously screwed by a failing institution, and yet instead of simply forgiving their loans, the Department of Education had bailed out that institution—and was still demanding that they pay back their debts. The Consumer Financial Protection Bureau (CFPB) negotiated a 40 percent write-down on Corinthian's privately issued "Genesis" loans, but since the vast majority of the debt held by students like Nathan Hornes was in federal student loans, that wouldn't do very much to reduce their debt load.

Legally, student loans can be discharged if an institution closes, but the DOE was encouraging students to transfer elsewhere and continue—even if, like Bowers, they had used up all their federal student loans on credits that often wouldn't transfer. And students were expected to continue under the new owners after their campus was sold—even if, according to the CFPB, their program of study was no longer on offer. The debt strikers filed legal "defense-to-repayment" challenges, but, as had been true of the foreclosure crisis, it was impossible to solve such a massive problem one debtor at a time.

In February 2015, the Horneses, Ann Bowers, and twelve other students went on debt strike and began a full-court press campaign, calling for all Corinthian student debt to be discharged. Their slogan was, "Can't pay, won't pay." Their numbers quickly swelled to over two hundred strikers, and the Education Department granted them a meeting. In June 2015, the DOE announced debt relief for Corinthian students, but still in an individualized manner—students were required to apply individually for loan forgiveness. The department appointed a "special master" to review their claims, but months in, only a tiny fraction of the loans had been canceled. Students continued to be harassed by debt collectors. Just as with the mortgage crisis, Alexis Goldstein, who worked with the Debt Collective, said there seemed to be a fear that one undeserving person would get benefits. "I think they are afraid that there is going to be one story that Fox News is going to get a hold of: 'This person got their debt canceled, and look at them living high on the hog.' But because of the fear of that one person, we are just going to screw everybody else."

The Debt Collective responded by creating an online "Defense to Repayment" tool to make it easier for students to file their individual claims. The Collective also continued to pressure the DOE to do better. "It has been interesting to learn that there are all of these places in the Department of Ed's authority to cancel debt," Goldstein said. "There are a bunch of different ways they can do it. It reminds me so much of the problems we have with financial reform. It is all about will, regulatory will."

Sociologist Tressie McMillan Cottom pointed out that the for-profit students' problems were also indicative of broader problems in higher education. "This is not a problem isolated to the for-profit college sector. You see it there first because these are the institutions and the populations that are the most fragile," she said. "This is the rest of higher ed in ten years. Even if you're not in trouble right now with your $100,000 in debt and your Harvard degree, you could be in an instant." She pointed to the twenty years of shifts in higher education policy, from privatization to bankruptcy law changes, and noted, "Everything that for-profits say they're doing are all things being proposed for the rest of higher ed. No faculty governance, high enrollment, centralized curriculum, diminished [study of the] humanities for applied, job-oriented credentials. It's only our hubris that says that's not us."

The Debt Collective didn't plan to stop with the for-profits, either, though they were making plans for another, broader debt strike across the entire for-profit college sector, with students from schools like ITT Tech and the University of Phoenix ready to join. On their website, other debtors could sign up to find each other and strategize; there was an active message board that included Sallie Mae and Navient borrowers as well as Corinthian strikers. "We're definitely looking to expand," said organizer Laura Hanna.

The students who chose to attend the for-profit schools, McMillan Cottom pointed out, were often very aware of how bad the labor market was, and how little remained of the social safety net. That was why they had gone into debt to get an education in the first place. Education, too, failed them, even though they had tried to do everything they could to live up to society's expectations.

Their determination kept them pushing even as the Obama administration appeared to be dragging its heels, attempting to propitiate the strikers with promises of eventual reform. Ann Bowers was appointed as student representative to a committee the DOE assembled to set standards for how and when the department would cancel loans for students who attended schools that broke the law. The committee was also looking at ways to crack down on schools that receive federal funds. Bowers hoped to use her position on the committee to press for broad reform, and meanwhile, she and the others remained on strike.

"I want big changes in the whole education system," said Bowers. "I don't think big business belongs in education. People are getting rich off of schools like Everest that are predatory, preying off people who want a better life for their family." On a more personal note, she said, "You're told you should go that way your whole life; you go and you end up in worse shape than you were in to begin with. It makes it hard to trust anyone. They destroyed our trust, they destroyed our faith in education. What do we have? Nothing but debt."

CHAPTER THREE

WALMART, WALMART, YOU CAN'T HIDE, WE CAN SEE YOUR GREEDY SIDE

T HE FIRST TIME VENANZI LUNA WENT ON STRIKE MADE HISTORY. Luna was one of about forty employees across several Southern California Walmart stores who went out on the first-ever strike at the world's largest retailer on October 4, 2012. "You didn't know what to expect," she said. "You didn't know how management was going to react, how the associates were going to react, but it was really emotional that we actually did it. We noticed that we can do this, we can do a lot of things."

Walmart was and is the nation's largest private employer, and it is known for paying low wages, but up until that point, labor unions' attempts to crack the retail giant had met with nothing but failure. Luna was part of a new organization, though, one that functioned more or less like a union but had several key differences. The Organization United for Respect at Walmart (OUR Walmart) was backed by the United Food and Commercial Workers (UFCW), and its first one-day strike kicked off a new set of tactics for labor in the face of the growing service economy.

Luna was one of OUR Walmart's first members. Her niece's stepmother recruited her to the new organization in 2010. "I said, 'I'm sold, let's do this,'" she told me. "Fear is always going to be there, but if you don't take a stand on it you're never going to know."

She found out quickly why Walmart employees were afraid to organize. "When the company ended up finding out about the organization, that I was organizing the store, they started recording me—who I talked to, how long I took my lunches—every little move I made, Walmart was on top of me," she said. She was written up twice for minor infractions, but when they tried to give her a "third strike," she had had enough. "I said, 'I'm not going to sign the paper, you just messed with the wrong person.'"

OUR Walmart helped her file a complaint with the National Labor Relations Board (NLRB). Regardless of whether workers are officially union members, organizing to improve the workplace is protected activity under federal labor law—but before this, Luna and many of her coworkers didn't know the law. Now, she did. And right after she filed the complaint, she said, human resources at Walmart wanted to talk to her, and made her write-ups go away. People at the store still called her "the union girl," but after her coworkers saw what happened to her, she was able to get more of them to join OUR Walmart and to join that first strike.

Across the country in Laurel, Maryland, Cynthia Murray became another of the earliest OUR Walmart members. She had taken a job at Walmart in 2000, and at first she found it a decent place to work. There were little benefits that made her and her colleagues feel appreciated, like getting "good job" pins when she went above and beyond, which she could trade in for a share of company stock when she got three of them. Occasional merit raises also helped. But about eight years ago, she said, things started to change. It was gradual, but she no longer felt like Walmart valued the workers.

Murray decided to do something about it the day a young coworker walked past her desk in tears. On her way by, the girl told her, "They're coming for you next." She didn't believe it at first, but the next day she was called into personnel and told that she was going to have to start doing more heavy lifting. Murray had an old injury that had caused nerve damage; her doctor had given her strict limitations on what she could lift. She offered to have her medical records sent over, but she was totally unprepared for the manager's reaction. "She leans up on the desk and spit's coming out of her mouth and she's screaming at me, 'What are you doing threatening me?'" Murray said. "At that moment, while she's screaming, I thought, 'No.' My upbringing tells me that this isn't right. This isn't the way any company should be run."

As Murray made her way back to her workstation in the fitting rooms, someone handed her a palm card from the UFCW. "I think God is good and he puts everything into motion and in action," she said. She sat down at her station and considered her options. "God said, 'Call the UFCW.' And I did."

Murray decided to be a voice for the other workers at her store who were being intimidated by management. But Walmart had already put so much effort into scaring the workers away from unions—she recalled being brought into a small room with her coworkers and lectured about the evils of unions—that she figured they needed to do something different. The new organization gave them the freedom to try unorthodox tactics and to take action without waiting to sign up every worker at every store; it also, Murray said, gave some workers the freedom to be "secret" members, planning strategy and supporting the others but not yet risking their jobs by making their membership public. They flashed a hand sign—three fingers raised, thumb and forefinger making a circle—to signal support to one another while at work.

Murray's favorite moment with OUR Walmart came shortly after the first strikes, on October 10, 2012, when a hundred OUR Walmart members from all across the country brought their demands to Walmart's Home Office in Bentonville, Arkansas. It really drove home to her the fact that everywhere across the country, Walmart workers were facing the same problems. "Walmart would say to you, 'That's just happening in your store.' But a hundred of us from across the country? What was happening to me was happening in California, Texas, you name it; wherever there was a Walmart. This was a practice that we knew was coming from Home Office," she said. "We did a survey, and the workers from across the country said the first thing that they wanted was respect."

Venanzi Luna was there that day, too. Wearing bright green OUR Walmart T-shirts, and amplifying one another's voices using the Occupy "people's mic" technique, Murray, Luna, and fellow workers confronted a suited representative of Walmart in the parking lot outside of the long, low building that houses Walmart's deeply centralized corporate operations. "We are on strike against retaliation," Luna, leading the people's mic, announced.

"We are more than happy to allow you the opportunity to speak one-on-one with some of our HR team," the Walmart representative told them. "We are not here individually, we are here as a group," the crowd replied in unison.

"I think we all thought at that defining moment, here you are with the same crutch," Murray said. "They want to see who they can break down and intimidate. That's how Walmart operates. And at that moment we were all like, 'You can't intimidate us! There's a hundred of us standing here together today, telling you that we will no longer take your intimidation. When they realized that they couldn't break us down and make us do a one-on-one, they said they didn't have enough room. We said, 'Take twenty of us.' We were willing to take twenty leaders and send them in together, but we were not going to let them intimidate any of us one on one."

Over the course of nearly four years covering the unrest at Walmart, the company repeatedly refused my requests for comment. In statements, Walmart consistently argued, "The crowds are mostly made up of paid union demonstrators and they are not representative of our 1.3 million associates across the country." One Walmart manager, who spoke anonymously to a reporter out of fear of retaliation from the tightly managed company, said that he tried to handle complaints from his workers when he had the time, but that he faced a lot of pressure from above because the company was cutting staff. "I think it's important for the associates to know that not all managers are monsters," he said, though he conceded that "there are some people that are certainly bad managers out there." He added: "There are a lot of managers–and I'm, you know, personally speaking to managers at my store and managers at other stores—that are unhappy with the direction that the company's going. It's a lot different when you're working at a store than when you're sitting behind a desk in Arkansas."[1]

Colby Harris wasn't at the protest in Bentonville; he first went on strike on Black Friday, 2012, in Lancaster, Texas. The day after Thanksgiving was the biggest retail shopping day of the year, and it became central to the OUR Walmart protests—a way for what was still a small organization to maximize the impact it had on the store's bottom line.

Like many of the other Walmart workers who got involved in the organization, Harris spoke first about others: about the inadequate scheduling and pay faced by the mothers who worked at his store and their struggles to find child care; about the sexual harassment complaints; and about the pallet jacks used for offloading the trucks full of merchandise that arrive from Walmart's massive distribution centers daily—part of the company's famed "just-in-time" distribution system—which some workers claim are often broken and can cause injury. And despite Walmart's lip service to the value of the associates (its term for employees like Harris, Murray, and Luna), he said, managers didn't treat them like equal partners in the success of the store.

There were quite a few members of OUR Walmart at Harris's store, but when it came time to walk off the job, he said, most of them were too afraid of being fired. "It was eye-opening to see how fearful people that really had issues were of Walmart," he said. "It just really showed how important it was for me to be out there, because I felt like a lot of people, not just in my store, but all the stores surrounding my store, had these issues."

Harris had always wanted to do some kind of activism—"I've always had a passion for people," he said—and so he felt like he found something important by becoming part of OUR Walmart. Even when the retaliation started in earnest, when he was "coached" (Walmart's somewhat Orwellian term for getting written up) and his family started to express fears that he would lose his job, he kept going. "I felt like we were only getting 'coached' because public perception was changing," he said. "I felt like it was a sign that things were working. They were scared of workers coming together and doing what we had the legal rights to do. So I was more motivated after being 'coached,' because I knew it wasn't right."

Harris was fired in September 2013, purportedly for "absenteeism." He and OUR Walmart, contending that it was illegal for Walmart to fire him and the other strikers, filed a complaint with the NLRB. And instead of leaving the campaign, Harris became a full-time organizer.

Outside the Walmart in Secaucus, New Jersey, on Black Friday 2013, Harris sat down in the street, a boilermaker on one side of him, a postal worker on the other, behind a banner reading "WALMART = POVERTY." Joining the rally were Occupy activists from New York and New Jersey;

fast-food workers who had also been organizing with the Fight for $15; restaurant workers; and the Rude Mechanical Orchestra marching band. Thirteen people were arrested in front of that Walmart for civil disobedience; nearly a hundred more were arrested around the country. As the police cuffed Harris's hands behind his back, he shot me a giant grin through the crowd.

"I've never felt more complete in my life," he told me later. "I'm glad that I'm here, because now I have twenty-four hours a day, and weekends if I choose to work them, to go out and organize. And not against Walmart, but for the workers. There's a difference, because this is not an 'Us Against Walmart' thing; this is 'Walmart Against Us,' and we're trying our best to protect ourselves." As for his dismissal, he shrugged, saying, "We knew that was a possibility, but we didn't care, because change had to happen. Major change only happens as a result of someone losing something. Just like in the civil rights movement and the gay rights movement. People lost their lives and were imprisoned, but all those negative things actually transitioned into positive changes."

THE IMAGE CONJURED BY THE TERM "WORKING CLASS" IN THE UNITED States has been one of mostly white men toiling in a factory, wearing hard hats and those oft-evoked blue collars. Our labor policy was shaped around those men and the assumption that workers get health insurance from their jobs, have a pension on which to retire, and make a "family wage" that allows them to support a wife, who stays home to take care of the kids and the cooking and cleaning.

And yet with each year, that picture becomes less and less reflective of reality. The working class never was all white or all male, but now, more and more, the real story of the working class is the story of people like Colby Harris and Venanzi Luna, black and Latina, working in retail, restaurants, or another form of service work. The real story is not that women and people of color have moved into positions of power, but that more men are in "casualized"—that is, in temporary, part-time, or presumably "unskilled" service jobs.

The occupations projected to add the most jobs between 2012 and 2022 are retail sales, personal care and home health care, nursing, and food service workers, including fast food. Except for nursing, those fields have a median annual income of around $20,000. That's less than half, adjusted for inflation, of the family-sustaining wage paid to unionized factory workers in their heyday.[2]

The story of outsourcing—of plant closures and "free"-trade deals and managers swaggering into the shop and announcing that the jobs were ending—has been well told elsewhere. We have also been told a story of our brave new information economy, where knowledge will prevail. But the fact remains that even as Americans go into debt for advanced degrees to get those technical jobs, they're more likely to end up in the service industry. The choice to call what we have a "knowledge economy," rather than a service economy, was just that—a choice, one that sounded more exciting than the reality of low-wage feminized service work for the majority.

Service jobs as a share of US working hours increased 30 percent between 1980 and 2005, and their prevalence has only grown since the Great Recession. One 2012 study found that although two-thirds of the jobs lost during the recession were mid-wage jobs, 58 percent of the jobs regained by the time of the study were instead low-wage, paying less than $13.84 per hour. Retail sales alone added well over 300,000 jobs in this period, at an average wage of $10.97 an hour; just behind was food prep, paying an average of just over $9 an hour. The trend had begun before the crisis, but after the crisis hit, it was impossible to pretend that something fundamental hadn't changed.[3]

There could be, and have been, plenty of decent jobs in service industries; to assume otherwise is to mistake the historical conditions that produced stable jobs and high wages in manufacturing for intrinsic characteristics of the industry. In 2014, I spoke with Rosa Ramirez, a temp worker who had been shuffled through multiple factories outside of Chicago, sometimes for just a couple of days at a time, doing work that was once done by unionized full-time workers. Her experience and that of thousands of others like her should remind us that there's nothing inherently good or bad about any type of work; safe conditions, regular hours, decent pay, and respect can do a lot to improve even the worst job.

The rise of customer service work and its attendant demand for "people skills," such as patience and communication—which are typically associated with women, and often assumed not to be skills at all—created a crisis for the old masculine producer narrative. Service labor certainly was not new, but it had long been ignored by a labor movement mostly focused on industrial work. When that industrial work began to fade, labor's lack of a foothold in the growing service sector made it harder for it to withstand increasing attacks. Labor had failed to recognize and value service work, leaving the door open for the conditions in service jobs to creep into the rest of the economy. Factories that had employed full-timers with benefits could drive wages down by employing temps like Rosa Ramirez, temps who were easily fired and were paid less than permanent employees. Even the once-strong automobile industry is now rife with lower-paid temporary workers.[4]

Women were commonly assumed not to need full-time jobs because they would have a husband who worked; women were presumed to prefer part-time or short-term gigs that would allow them to be home with the family while making a little "pin money" for themselves. Those assumptions continued to be held even in the 2000s. Women who joined the *Dukes v. Walmart* sex discrimination suit reported being told by their managers that male coworkers made more money because they had to support their families.[5]

The emotional labor that went into a day's customer service work—managing irate customers, soothing wounded egos, spending hours helping people find just the right item—was likewise not seen as skilled work. Skills were valued—or perceived at all—based on how much power the workers who had them wielded in society, not the tools they wielded on the job. The men who built the labor movement in the skilled trades and on factory floors won power for themselves, but they had their own incentives for not helping women workers build power of their own—incentives that wound up dovetailing with the interests of the boss. Leaving women and their work out of the labor movement wound up hurting the movement and working people as a whole; this is one of the reasons why organizing service workers like those at Walmart is so important.[6]

Retail workers used to be excluded from federal minimum-wage laws—John F. Kennedy made their low wages a campaign issue in 1960, though Walmart founder Sam Walton famously simply refused to pay the new wage when it first passed. Today, while retail is governed by wage and hour laws, other service workers still fight to be covered by them—and service workers who get tips, from waiters to the people who push wheelchairs in the airport, are legally mandated a minimum of only $2.13 an hour by federal law.[7]

A study by economist Catherine Ruetschlin found that a wage floor of $25,000 a year for a full-time worker in retail would affect more than 5 million retail workers and their families. More than 95 percent of those workers were over twenty, not teenagers, and more than half of them were responsible for providing at least half the family income. Such a raise would actually grow the economy and create new jobs, not kill them, as is commonly claimed. Low-paid workers spend nearly everything they make; if they had more money to spend, they would be much more likely to spend it than their bosses, who make far more than they can spend at any time.[8]

Scheduling, too, became a central issue in retail and food service work. Once, manufacturing workers fought for the eight-hour day; their battles shaped the workday and workweek that we now think of as normal, resulting in the Fair Labor Standards Act and time-and-a-half pay for overtime for waged workers. But restaurants and retail shops are open at different times—in part so that those working a nine-to-five day in other sectors of the economy have time to eat and shop—and make different demands on their employees' time.

In somewhat of a nasty coincidence, computerized scheduling systems entered the retail world around the same time as the financial crisis was wiping out jobs around the country. In an already weak job market, workers are less likely to push back on encroachments made by the boss, and so few challenged a system that rapidly worsened. Patricia Scott, a sixteen-year Walmart associate in Federal Way, Washington, had had a set schedule for ten years. This regular schedule allowed her to make plans in advance, and she was able to count on a certain amount of work each week. But when the computers came in, her hours changed. "They always tell me, 'Well, it's not us, it's the computer!'" she told me. "I'd say, 'Tell the computer to fix it!'"[9]

Walmart might have been the leader in computerized scheduling, but other firms quickly followed. The software saved managers time they would otherwise have to spend making up the schedule, but it also wrung every last dime in labor costs out of the system. It calculated staffing needs based not only on availability, but also on sales numbers, so that stores would be staffed with just enough people to get the job done throughout the peaks and valleys in sales during the workweek. Computerized scheduling systems prioritize workers who have unlimited availability, but that makes it hard for workers to get a second job. And if you have children to care for, forget it. Many of the women who populate these industries struggle to find child-care options that are flexible and affordable; one low-wage field feeds another as more workers, mostly women, do the child care, often for less than minimum wage. "Just-in-time" scheduling means workers' needs come last, their hours sliced and diced as hours and minutes are shaved off of shifts. The money adds up.[10]

The eight-hour day movement demanded fewer working hours, but post-2008, workers were often fighting to get more. Involuntary part-time employment, when workers can only find part-time jobs but would prefer full-time, spiked in the recession years (from 644,000 in 2006 to 1.5 million in 2010), and retail workers made up 18 percent of those who were involuntarily working part-time jobs. Fifty-eight percent of those making up the involuntary part-time retail workforce in 2015 were women. That means there are a whole lot of adults who would like to have a full-time, steady job with a schedule they can rely on and a paycheck that can feed their families, but who instead are making do on eight or nine dollars an hour, twenty hours a week. That doesn't add up to a living.[11]

The slack for all these low wages and insufficient hours is being picked up by all of us in the form of government programs that provide food assistance, health care, housing, tax credits, and more. A 2013 congressional study estimated that Walmart alone costs taxpayers between $3,015 and $5,815 per worker. That's money that we should understand as a subsidy to Walmart, not to the workers—it allows Walmart to save billions in wages and benefits by pushing those costs onto the rest of us. And those Walmart and McDonald's workers are taxpayers, too.[12]

Bene't Holmes, a twenty-five-year-old single mother, told me, "Recently I was forced to apply for food stamps just so my son and I don't starve. Walmart is the country's biggest beneficiary of food stamp dollars, and many of those dollars are coming from its own workers, like me." She was right—some $13.5 billion every year in Supplemental Nutrition Assistance Program (SNAP) funds are spent at Walmart. After Bill Clinton, from Walmart's home state of Arkansas, signed welfare reform into law, most welfare benefits for mothers like Holmes became short-term, yet Walmart continued to pocket welfare dollars, without a deadline.[13]

Retail and the restaurant sector both have "upscale" and "downscale" markets, and while "upscale" dining or shopping doesn't guarantee the workers are getting a bigger cut of the cash, it is certainly true that Walmart and fast-food restaurants cater to people at the lower end of the income scale. It is this argument that is used to claim that raising wages is impossible because it will drive up prices, even though profits at large chains have returned to prerecession levels and executives and shareholders continue to be compensated handsomely. But the service economy is no more required to be filled with low-wage, unstable jobs than the manufacturing sector was before it. It was shaped this way through particular historical and political circumstances.

"THE ECONOMIC VISION WE CALL NEOLIBERALISM, THATCHERISM, Reaganomics, or free-market fundamentalism could also claim the title of Wal-Martism," according to Bethany Moreton, author of *To Serve God and Wal-Mart*. The influence of the world's largest retailer is impossible to overestimate, and the influence through it of a particular set of values has helped to create the economy in which we now live. If Wall Street is half the story, the other half is Walmart.[14]

Walmart was born in Populist country, in a place steeped in the values of that movement, in its critique of an elite-dominated capitalist economic system coupled with a faith in the ordinary people to reform it. It was also, of course, the Bible Belt, where preachers were regular features of both campaigns for economic justice and paeans to big business. Sam Walton was able to evoke these traditions to win support for his discount chain even when it made him fantastically wealthy—and when he didn't share the wealth.[15]

In 1962, the first Walmart was born in a practically all-white part of northwestern Arkansas. Walton staffed his stores with Christian women, most of them in their first jobs off the farm, who didn't expect high wages but took a deep pride in giving good service. Walton learned from his employees and customers to value service work and to link it with spiritual values. Service work in a store didn't carry the same stigma as domestic service, which was still associated with black women and, particularly in the South, with slavery. Being part of Walmart was different. They were all part of the (Christian) family. The idea of Walmart as a family business may seem like a stretch now that it employs 1.5 million Americans, but many of the longtime workers I spoke to, like Cynthia Murray, still felt a connection to the family.[16]

Paying lip service to the emotional labor and people skills of the women who worked its entry-level jobs was easier than paying them higher wages, and as Walmart's earliest employees weren't accustomed to receiving wages of any kind, they were unlikely to complain. The families who shopped at Walmart had little in the way of disposable income, so they appreciated Sam Walton's rock-bottom prices and familiar atmosphere. Walmart had adapted capitalism to conservative Christianity and rendered women's work outside the home unthreatening.[17]

Its down-home image, though, concealed a massive, high-tech distribution system that allowed the company to simultaneously save money and control the conditions of production without owning a single factory. "Logistics," as these distribution systems are now called, became the heart of its business and Walton's chief innovation. Walton invested in "distribution centers," which existed not to store goods long-term but to process and ship them out as quickly as possible in Walmart's famed just-in-time system. Walmart collects enough information from bar-code scans to fill a data warehouse comparable in size to that of the National Security Agency.[18]

All that information is used to determine what Walmart will buy and who it will buy from. Most of its products come from China, where its world buying headquarters are located. Walmart sells enough of any given product to be able to demand its own price, and manufacturers bend over backward to meet its demands. The working conditions of the laborers who make the electronics, clothing, and toothpaste that line Walmart's shelves may not be directly under Bentonville's control the way the thermostats in its stores are, but downward pressure on prices has meant that manufacturers cut costs wherever they can, and "labor costs" are often the first costs to slice.[19]

Walmart actively denies responsibility for overseas labor conditions, famously refusing to sign on to a labor rights accord developed after the collapse of the Rana Plaza complex in Bangladesh, which killed more than 1,100 workers, some of whom had worked on jeans destined for Walmart's shelves. Walmart instead announced its own safety plan, which Scott Nova of the Worker Rights Consortium called "nonbinding and unenforceable." Yet the amount of data Walmart has on workers in its own stores indicates that it could, if it wanted to, do a much better job keeping an eye on the people who make its products. The company has an "Office of Global Security," set up by a former official with the CIA and FBI, and a "Threat Research and Analysis Group," which recruits from military intelligence and keeps an eye on bloggers and activists who might pose a threat. A 2015 story revealed that Walmart had hired Lockheed Martin, one of the world's largest defense contractors, to monitor activists, and coordinated with the FBI's Joint Terrorism Task Forces. Such surveillance helped the company keep abreast of any worker organizing in its stores and maintain its unblemished union-free record.[20]

Walmart's much-vaunted stock option program, too, served a purpose. It created the illusion that low-wage associates had as much riding on the continued success of the company as did the surviving Waltons, who own about half the existing Walmart stock. (They also control more wealth than the bottom 42 percent of the US population does.) But the high turnover rate for associates guarantees that most of them are unable to build up much equity, and low wages mean that even the company's matching policy—15 percent of the first $1,800 of stock purchased—doesn't get them much. Some of them even find themselves selling stock back to cover the gaps in their household budget.[21]

Walton and his wife and heirs spent a lot of money making sure that the United States—and the world—remained hospitable to Walmart's business model. Their donations through the Walton Foundation to charter schools and other organizations that aim to make public schools run more like a business are well known, as is their support for politicians who promote their particular views of trade and the market economy. They invested in business programs at Christian colleges, promoting a particular brand of "Christian free enterprise" and seeding a generation of already loyal graduates from which to choose management trainees. Students in Free Enterprise (SIFE) existed to train young activists as champions of the free market. One Walmart executive explained that the company supported SIFE because "young people today are being given an opportunity to understand really—not what capitalism is, because I cringe a little bit with the word 'capitalism,' but what free enterprise is and how it fits with the democracy that we enjoy in these United States."[22]

Walmart contributed, then, not just economically, but also politically, to the new consensus around globalization that formed after the end of the Cold War. Capitalism was ascendant, free trade the order of the day, and in the United States, both parties were loudly singing the praises of the market. These supporters were led by President Bill Clinton, the former Arkansas governor, whose wife, Hillary, had been the first woman on the Walmart board. The view has circulated in recent years that working-class people voting for conservative, pro-business politicians were doing so against their own wallets, often because they were won over on "social issues." The Walmart ideology of Christian free enterprise, though, expertly blended those social issues into a campaign to convince people that its policies were, in fact, in their economic best interests.[23]

The company's best argument for its low wages has been that they are necessary to keep its prices low so that newly strapped Americans can afford to buy microwaves, designer knockoff jeans, and DVDs. Former Walmart CEO H. Lee Scott bragged in 2005 that the company's low prices were equivalent to a raise for hardworking people, and that the company "act[ed] as a bargaining agent for these families—achieving on their behalf a power, a 'negotiating power' they would never have on their own." In other words, it was sort of like a union.[24]

Walmart's corporate populism dovetailed nicely with market populism: both caught the public's attention in the 1990s, the period after the collapse of the Soviet Union, when the idea that there was some competition for capitalism in the world began to fade. Masquerading as nonpartisan, and indeed nonpolitical, market populism turned wealthy elites like Sam Walton into heroes for the little guy and decried as elitist anyone who called for a raise in the minimum wage, advocated regulations on business practices, or stood in the way of trade deals.

In the Walmart brand of market populism, the consumer, not the producer (who might be a worker who would have a claim on the company's profits), is the everyman to be championed. Other companies embraced this framing, too, though few to the extent that Walmart did. The rise of consumer identity marked a change in populist rhetoric but still purported to promote the many, the People, against the interests of the few. When consumerism is what we have in common, the workers disappear from the picture entirely, a worthy sacrifice to the greater good.[25]

At the end of the 1990s, Walmart's populist image faced its most serious crack yet, from the same underappreciated, underpaid women workers who had built the company's massive wealth. *Dukes v. Walmart* was a landmark class-action sex discrimination lawsuit representing 1.6 million women. The suit charged Walmart with discrimination in promotions, pay, and job assignments in violation of Title VII of the Civil Rights Act of 1964. Arguing that Walmart's highly centralized command structure made it likely the discrimination was systemic and dictated from the top, the Dukes plaintiffs aimed to change the company's patriarchal culture and expressed disappointment, like many OUR Walmart members, with the shattering of the company's Christian family-friendly image. Though the retail giant had expanded far outside of its base in the Ozarks and women at work were no longer a new phenomenon, Betty Dukes and her co-plaintiffs had much in common with the "Walmart Moms" at the core of the company's image. Sam Walton's dream employees had turned against his company.[26]

The US Supreme Court dismantled the suit, ruling in 2011 that the workers did not qualify as a class; like the Walmart spokespeople, the Court majority argued that the workers should address their grievances individually. Nevertheless, the case had put cracks in the company's reputation, cracks that would only get bigger when Walmart workers joined the wave of post-2008 unrest. The workers, it seemed, weren't done trying to resolve their problems as a class.[27]

WHEN I ASKED DAN SCHLADEMAN, CODIRECTOR OF OUR WALMART, for one sentence that summed up what made its efforts different from prior attempts to organize Walmart workers, he said, "Walmart workers lead." It was a nod to the hard work of associates like Colby Harris, Cynthia Murray, Patricia Scott, and Venanzi Luna, and also an acknowledgment that earlier attempts to organize the retailer had been driven more by desperation, the understanding that wages and conditions for other workers, some of them union members, were being driven down by Walmart, and that if things didn't change there, the unions would be unable to counter the tide. As Walmart went, so went America.

Unions and worker organizations often face the charge that they are self-interested groups that only want workers' dues. A Walmart anti-union video that leaked to the Internet informed viewers that "unions are businesses, multimillion-dollar businesses that make their money by convincing people like you and me to give them a part of our pay-checks." A more accurate criticism would be that they have often failed to adapt to a changing workforce, clinging instead to a fading model de-veloped decades ago in massive factories. Today's working class is more likely to be serving burgers and fries or folding shirts and stocking soap at Walmart. "Anytime that 94 percent of private-sector workers can't ac-cess the model, it's time to start looking for something else," noted Da-vid Rolf, president of Service Employees International Union Local 775. "This is a system that has been less and less accessible to workers in the private sector every year in each of the fifty states since 1958."[28]

The UFCW, the union that backed OUR Walmart at first, had made several attempts at organizing Walmart stores. "We have the luxury of being able to learn from so many of the different approaches out there," Schlademan said. Mostly, they were able to learn from previous failures. Unless the management of a business willingly agrees to bargain with its workers, unionization is a process that requires a lengthy struggle and an election certified by the NLRB, then a usually arduous negotiating pro-cess that leads to a first contract. (This is, in part, why labor had staked its future on the Employee Free Choice Act, legislation that would have made unionization easier. Labor spent big on Barack Obama in the 2008 elections in the hope that he would prioritize this bill but did not challenge him much thereafter, and the legislation died.) Nearly 80 years after the unionization process was set down in law, companies have gotten very good at beating unions by dragging out the process, espe-cially by holding (perfectly legal) meetings where antiunion consultants give speeches, and often make threats, to a captive audience. As Venanzi Luna described, they also spy on known pro-union staffers. The NLRB process, Schlademan noted, often does not allow workers to really lead, as the path is scripted for them.

If the meetings aren't enough, Walmart has used other tactics to un-dermine the process of unionizing. In 2000, when the UFCW was at-tempting to gain a foothold through organizing one department at a time, eleven meat cutters at a Texas Walmart Supercenter actually won an NLRB election. Walmart responded by eliminating meat cutters in 180 stores, across six states. The UFCW briefly tried to organize workers at multiple Walmart stores across Las Vegas, a union-heavy town that the union figured might be a good place to launch a citywide campaign. Walmart's response, Schlademan said, "included heavy surveillance of organizers in their hotels." What did not happen was a win.[29]

The next attempt came in the Canadian province of Quebec, where labor law is generally more worker-friendly. Workers in 2005 voted to unionize at a Walmart in the city of Jonquière. This time, Walmart shuttered the entire store. In 2014, the Supreme Court of Canada ruled that the closing violated Quebec labor law and ordered that the workers be compensated, but the store never reopened.[30]

There were outside pressure campaigns that aimed both to block Walmart's expansion and to demand better wages and conditions for Walmart's workers. In the mid-2000s, the AFL-CIO, SEIU, and UFCW worked with the Association of Community Organizations for Reform Now (ACORN) in Florida to organize Walmart workers into a dues-paying, nonunion movement with some success. "We're the gumbo of all of these different strategies," Schlademan said. "We were able to really look at and see what was working, what wasn't, how the company reacted, and it really helped us as we were thinking about it."

As the organization that would become OUR Walmart was coming together, unrest was also creeping up and down Walmart's supply chain. Guestworkers from Mexico, who worked at C. J.'s Seafood in Louisiana preparing crawfish for distribution in Walmart stores, went on strike in 2012 after they were locked into their workplace, denied breaks, and threatened with beatings. "Some of us work from 2:00 in the morning 'til 5:00 or 6:00 in the evening and get no paid overtime," Marta Uvalle, one of the strike leaders, told me at the time. Brought into the country temporarily, guestworkers are particularly vulnerable to threats, since they depend on getting their jobs renewed year after year. This pressure made their 2012 strike even more remarkable. Working with the National Guestworker Alliance, these workers targeted Walmart specifically in their actions, demanding that the ultimate beneficiary of their labor require better of its suppliers. Saket Soni, director of the Guestworker Alliance, asked, "If Walmart can't guarantee safety and meet the complaints of eight workers in a small town in Louisiana, how is it going to guarantee the standards of literally hundreds of thousands of workers across the country?"[31]

The next strikes came one step up the supply chain, at distribution centers in Southern California and Elwood, Illinois. The distribution centers were also run by subcontractors, yet these workers, too, stressed that Walmart was the company that was ultimately responsible for their plight.

Elle Hoffman (not her real name) was working at the Elwood distribution center at the time. She was hired as a temp in the fall of 2012 for the holiday rush, and remembered the first time she had walked into the massive building. "I think the reason they required experience is so when you saw pallets and boxes on boxes teetering on these metal spears you weren't like 'Oh, we're going to die,'" she joked.

Near the railroad, an army base, and a prison, the warehouse was a terrifying place to work. Despite the fact that she had arrived at the job along with her boyfriend, she said, her supervisor asked her out three times before her first lunch break. The packages were covered with dust—"We called it 'China death dust,'" she said, because it left them constantly coughing—but the gloves they were given would rip and never be replaced. Without shin guards, workers would cut themselves on pallets while unloading. And all the while, the temps were pushed to get their cases-per-hour rate up in order to be considered for direct hire so they could stay on past the holidays. "You were treated like a machine," Hoffman said.

The strike began in Elwood with a petition for dust masks, gloves, and shin guards, which workers presented to management. The workers who had complained were punished, and a group of them walked out. They stayed out for three weeks before the company conceded to all their demands. Leah Fried, who had been part of the Republic Windows and Doors occupation, was one of the organizers who helped support the warehouse workers.[32]

After the strike, Hoffman remembered, "there was this shift in power. Our bosses would come to us and say, 'Do you need anything?' I said, 'Yeah, I need gloves,' and they'd go get gloves. 'Do you need anything else?' 'Yeah, I need shin guards. I heard some guy got stitches.' They started waiting on workers instead of ignoring people."

Neither the guestworkers nor the warehouse workers had been members of a union; in neither case did every worker walk off the job. Many of the workers at the warehouses were also immigrants or formerly incarcerated—people who were the most vulnerable to having their rights violated. Yet these workers managed to bring about change through their strike actions, a technique that OUR Walmart would accelerate.

Without owning a single factory, Walmart is the world's third-largest employer, after the US and Chinese armies. Add in the number of workers across the globe who work in Walmart's supply chain, and the number is staggering. One of the most important steps OUR Walmart took was to link the retail workers' struggle with that of workers from the supply chain, whether they were subcontractors in a US warehouse, packers at a crawfish plant, or garment workers at a factory in Bangladesh. When those workers get together, Schlademan said, "they all begin to see that each one of them is treated not as human, but as merely a cost of doing business for Walmart. It's always explosive to watch how they support each other, stand with each other, and link each other's struggles."

Schlademan credited Occupy with helping to lay the groundwork for the campaign to take off and helping the Walmart activists think about new tactics. "In many ways, the conversation that we can have about the Waltons really was much harder to have before Occupy," Schlademan said. "Walmart would always position itself as the 'Protector of Customers,' and whatever we wanted was going to raise prices on their customers. It became impossible for them to make that argument when Walmart has created the single richest family on earth." Similarly, Black Friday Walmart protests incorporated Black Lives Matter activists in 2014 after police shot John Crawford III, a young black man, while he shopped at the Walmart in Beavercreek, Ohio. "We're in a place now where everybody's understanding that at the foundation, what's wrong is pretty similar: the abuse of power that's happening in our country," Schlademan said.

OUR Walmart was designed from the beginning for something very different from an NLRB election campaign. It was an organization that did not rely on winning a majority at any one store in order to be effective; it was meant to spread horizontally across the country, to allow workers to take action in different ways, and to encourage them to act on their own without the supervision of an organizer. Horizontalism allowed workers to feel as though the organization was theirs; it didn't mean the movement was leaderless or existed without professional, full-time organizing staff, but that anyone who wanted to be a leader could be one. The leaders who emerged included workers who had believed in Walmart and wanted it to live up to its promises, workers who had been natural leaders in their stores, and workers who wanted to stand up for their coworkers who were afraid.

The strategy of minority unionism, of acting like a union without waiting for a majority vote, also allowed workers to act without inconveniencing their customers, making it easier for customers to side with them. It's a tactic particularly suited to a low-wage retailer that trumpets the value its low prices bring to its customers. Walmart pits customer against worker; OUR Walmart wanted to pit customer and worker against a massive, global corporation squeezing both for its bottom line.

The labor movement's biggest successes were often kicked off by a small group of workers who managed to disrupt business as usual and inspire others to join them. OUR Walmart tapped into that history at a time when unions had been shrinking for decades. Although only a few workers might strike at any given store, there was nearly always a willing crowd of supporters to accompany them in protest and to walk them back to work the next day.[33]

Walmart's expansion from its Ozarks heartland into the cities and suburbs on the coasts also helped the workers challenge its image as a Christian company. Although the Walton vision of Christian populist free enterprise might have had some traction in Arkansas, in workers like Colby Harris and Betty Dukes Walmart confronted a very different spiritual tradition. In Catholic churches connected to Latin American liberation theology, or in black churches with civil rights movement ties, Christian values connected easily to fights for economic justice. "A lot of us do have some type of faith, or specifically, some type of Christian faith," Colby Harris said. "Our issues go right along with what a lot of faith groups believe in, that people are supposed to be treated with respect. It's all interconnected. The pastor goes in and shops at Walmart, too. And so does the congregation. So we're all tied in together." Inequality, for Harris, was a moral issue.

The first Walmart strikes, in Southern California, took place far outside of Walmart's home turf, in an area with a history of labor and social justice organizing. "If you want to expand into these places," Bethany

Moreton told me, "those are currents that are going to come all the way back to Bentonville."[34]

The final key to OUR Walmart's success where previous efforts had failed was its online organizing. Jamie Way, an organizer with the campaign, told me frankly, "We're never going to match them in terms of resources, we're never going to have an organizer or a community supporter on the ground in every one of their [more than] 4,000 Walmarts." What they did instead was build a network online that connected organizers with Walmart workers, using Facebook to find new workers through targeted advertising and worker-led groups. An example was the LGBT worker group moderated by OUR Walmart member Lucas Handy, who had been motivated to join the organization because of a manager's homophobic slurs.[35]

Colby Harris, who spent a lot of time doing online work, said the Internet allowed fearful associates to get comfortable sharing their problems and move toward taking action in their stores. "It has really allowed us an opportunity to make sure that we're not missing out on anybody," he said. "Because everybody's on social media, whether it's Instagram, Facebook, Snapchat, Twitter . . . something."

Schlademan agreed that social media is critical. He acknowledged that there is still plenty of skepticism from people who think online work is merely "clicktivism," just signing an online petition that disappears into the ether. But OUR Walmart considered it "online-to-offline" work: that is, they were using social media to distribute tools to workers and supporters to help them hold their own actions in their own towns. It allowed OUR Walmart to punch far above its weight class in terms of both paid staffers and actual worker members who were willing to strike, enabled it to learn from workers who might not yet be willing to risk their jobs, and educated people who saw Walmart as the epitome of a flawed system about how to step up and support the people most affected by the company, rather than protesting in ways that harmed the workers.

Campaigns like OUR Walmart and the Fight for $15 relied on unions' willingness to spend their money on workers who were not and might not ever become dues-paying members; the $5 monthly that OUR Walmart members paid in was not enough to sustain an organizing campaign, so outside funding was needed. In 2015, change came to OUR Walmart when the new leadership at UFCW cut the budget for the Walmart campaign by more than 50 percent. Dan Schlademan and cofounder Andrea Dehlendorf were let go from the union's staff. The UFCW shifted toward an advertising-heavy strategy, rolling out big targeted ads just before Thanksgiving.[36]

OUR Walmart regrouped, reached out to funders and to the network of labor and community groups with which it had allied in the past, and relaunched in the fall of 2015, determined to continue organizing Walmart workers. Groups like National People's Action and New York Communities for Change, think tank Demos, and online organizations Color of Change and CREDO, Jobs With Justice, and the National Domestic Workers Alliance joined the partnership. "OUR Walmart has always been focused on the workers, and giving us a voice, so it's always been independent and worker-led, but we did always have a large support of funding from UFCW," Tyfani Faulkner, a Sacramento, California, OUR Walmart member, told me. "They decided that they were going to change the direction, and so this caused the workers to be more on the front lines and be more in control of our own organization. We're all stepping up and taking on the responsibility to make that happen."

OUR Walmart counted victories not in union contracts, or even in raw membership numbers, but in its ability to get a reaction from Walmart. The announcement from Walmart in April 2015 that it would raise its wage floor to $9 an hour that year and $10 an hour in 2016 was the biggest win for the campaign, but there were others—a change in the company's policy for pregnant workers, and some concessions on scheduling, for example—that came about through the work of a relatively small group of active workers. In January 2016, an NLRB administrative law judge ruled that Colby Harris and fifteen other OUR Walmart members had been illegally fired and ordered them reinstated with back pay; the company also had to post notices in thirty-one stores and hold meetings in twenty-nine stores informing workers that they have the right to strike and vowing not to discipline them for doing so. Walmart, of course, planned to appeal.[37]

There were setbacks aplenty, from the layoffs of workers to the closing of stores to the UFCW's shift back to an advertising-heavy strategy. The important lessons, for a still-struggling labor movement and for the millions of workers who didn't have a union, came from a confrontational strategy that trusted workers to lead and didn't wait to win an NLRB election in order to act like a union. "Nobody can say that these campaigns have not had a huge impact," Schlademan said. "We are demonstrating that there is a different path here to victory for workers."

IT STARTED IN THE AIRPORT.

As I waited for my flight to Charlotte, North Carolina, to be called, the one that would connect me to my flight to Bentonville to go to the Walmart shareholders meeting June 5, 2015, the gate agent announced that they would need to check carry-on bags. I got up and stood in line behind a lanky young man, who handed the gate agent his boarding pass to check his bag. "You're going to Walmart," the gate agent said, looking at the young man's ticket. I started to laugh, partly because we were both going to the same place, partly because one glance at our tickets was enough for this Philadelphia airline employee to know that most of us who were flying through the Northwest Arkansas Regional Airport were going to Walmart's home office. When I asked, he explained, "They own everything. They paid for the airport."

It started in the airport for the OUR Walmart workers, too. Tyfani Faulkner told me, "We were on a plane full of store managers. It's very interesting, the people you end up on planes with when you come here. You definitely have to be on your Ps and Qs."

Ray Scott, a department manager at the relatively new Chicago Walmart, echoed her. "Since I got on the plane I have felt nothing but hatred toward OUR Walmart," he said. "I can feel the presence of this being Walmart's turf. Right now we're behind enemy lines."

From the planes full of management to the busloads of associates from all over the world to the signs on local banks and Chick-fil-A stores welcoming Walmart shareholders, the Bentonville area was certainly Walmart's turf. It's one of the few remaining company towns, and you can feel the money suffusing it when you cross the city line. Big houses with white pillars lined one side of the street that I took to find my way to the Walmart Museum, while the other side was still weathered one-story homes. Less well-known is how beautiful the landscape is, with rolling hills, trees, and rich red dirt. I could see why the Waltons kept their empire based there.

The Walmart Museum, located on the Bentonville town square, was blocked off by a bus when I reached it. A gray-haired man with an impressive handlebar mustache greeted me and told me the shop and the ice cream parlor were closed, but I could go into the museum. This very spot was the birthplace of Walmart—it's where Sam Walton opened his first five-and-dime store.

Walmart's corporate populism was on full display inside. In a video, new CEO Doug McMillon explained that the purpose of Walmart was to help people save money and have a better life. Another video showed George H.W. Bush awarding Sam Walton the Medal of Freedom and recognizing him for sponsoring scholarships for students from Latin America. In yet another, Sam was dancing a hula on Wall Street. The museum displays included his old truck, his baseball caps, a collection of the products sold in the original Walmart, and full-page ads for Walmart's discounts. Walton's old office was preserved behind glass, complete with a hat on a chair, piles of magazines, and family photos. "Ours is a story about the kinds of traditional principles that made America great in the first place," declared a pull-quote from Walton emblazoned on one wall.

Walmart's Home Office was just a five-minute drive from the museum. I arrived just in time to hear the tail end of the famed Walmart Cheer, inspired by a trip to Korea that Sam Walton once took. "Give me a W! Give me an A! Give me an L! Give me a squiggly! (This a reference to the now-defunct dash or star in the company's name.) Give me an M! Give me an A! Give me an R! Give me a T! What does that spell? Walmart!" The people doing the cheer, presumably Walmart associates, had just streamed off one of several buses in front of the long, low building.

Patricia Scott had been part of the first OUR Walmart delegation to Bentonville in 2012. "It was different compared to what I thought," she laughed. "You always hear about Home Office, you think this big castle in the sky, and then you get there and it's just this little flat building. It's like, that's Home Office?"

Scott was there the day I arrived, too, part of a group of OUR Walmart workers standing on the sidewalk in front of the big blue Home Office sign. They held a neon green sign of their own calling for $15 an hour and full-time schedules. Dressed in matching bright green OUR Walmart T-shirts, the workers had a response to the Walmart cheer: "We don't want no squiggly," they chanted. Venanzi Luna grabbed a bullhorn and called for her colleagues to get louder. Even on Walmart's turf, they got a few supportive honks and waves from passing cars. A small phalanx of police watched them from the other side of the parking lot, apparently to ensure they remained on public property and didn't try to step on Walmart's grounds. Arkansas is one of several states in which Walmart has succeeded in obtaining a legal injunction preventing employees of OUR Walmart or the UFCW from setting foot on its property—except in order to shop.

Inside Home Office, the workers were likely being feted. Outside, the group of workers marched down the sidewalk, waving to the associates who were pouring off the buses, and ended their rally with a chant of "We'll be back!"

That year, OUR Walmart had brought a smaller group of workers to the meeting, but, Faulkner said, they had more people scheduled to speak inside than ever before. There were still enough of them to create a visible presence on the street across from the University of Arkansas on the morning of the shareholder meeting. Holding their green sign, they waved to the shareholders who sat in stop-and-go traffic on their way to the Bud Walton basketball arena on the university campus.

Music was already playing when I walked up to the arena and presented my proxy statement. (I was denied a press credential for the meeting, and so the UFCW helped to connect me with a shareholder who was willing to allow me in as a nonvoting proxy.) I sat next to Patricia Scott and one seat down from Tyfani Faulkner. Colby Harris was in the row behind me. Venanzi Luna and Cynthia Murray were down below, where the presenters of the shareholder resolutions waited their turn to speak. Other presenters were Mary Watkines, a colleague of Scott's in Federal Way, Washington, and Michael Brune, executive director of the Sierra Club, who would be speaking on behalf of OUR Walmart member Mary Pat Tifft.

At the center of the arena was a massive, triangular stage with three screens, all lit in blue. Seated section by section around the arena were Walmart associates dressed in color-coded shirts: yellow for Sam's Club, green for logistics and supply chain, blue vests for retail associates, red for e-commerce, colored hats and flags for international. On that stage, Reese Witherspoon, star of such films as *Legally Blonde, Sweet Home Alabama,* and the Johnny Cash biopic *Walk the Line,* greeted everyone with a big grin and a played-up southern accent as the host of that year's meeting. (In previous years, Tom Cruise and Hugh Jackman had graced the stage.) Musicians Bryan McKnight, Ricky Martin, Mariah Carey, and in the big finale, Rod Stewart, would all take the stage, but not before a group of Walmart employees performed their own musical number.

In that space, there wasn't a lot of official business to accomplish. Executives ran down sales numbers (perhaps notably, comparing them to numbers from twenty years ago), but H. Rob Walton, while evoking his father Sam's early challenges to his employees, cautiously refused to make any predictions for the future. The Walton family controls about 50 percent of outstanding Walmart stock, and high-paid executives a good chunk more, meaning that any challenge to family control doesn't get very far. Rob Walton, who came onstage in one of his father's trucker caps and placed it reverently on a pedestal as he spoke, was retiring from his position as chairman of the board. He introduced his successor, Greg Penner, with glowing words of praise for his time at Goldman Sachs, noting his commitment to the company. Oh, and "he was smart enough to marry my daughter."

"They call it the Walmart family," Ray Scott commented to me. "I do give them credit on that. They do make a family. We're not part of their family, but they do make a family." He had joined OUR Walmart when the managers at his store told him that in order to get a promotion, he would need to help them fire several of his coworkers. "Wasn't it you guys that were just saying that we were a family? Family doesn't do that to each other," he said.

Reinforcing that family atmosphere was what the shareholder meeting was all about, though. Clips of Sam Walton praising his associates were interspersed with inspiring stories of associates who went above and beyond and a cutesy clip of Witherspoon clumsily learning to be a Walmart retail worker. Walmart's US CEO Greg Foran came onstage in a Walmart associate vest to explain the new "investment" Walmart was making in its employees: "As a symbol of our commitment to you, we gave you a new name badge." The slogan "Our people make the difference" would be returning to associates' nametags. Other changes included a relaxed dress code, the return of Walmart Radio, and a one-degree raise in the temperature in stores—controlled, of course, by Home Office. The only announcement that evoked cheers from the OUR Walmart members sitting near me was the mention of an improved sick leave policy. The name badge comment drew a snort from Patricia Scott.

When it was time for shareholder resolutions to be presented, Cynthia Murray declared the recent pay raise at Walmart a victory for OUR Walmart; she then called for shareholders to be allowed to nominate board members. The Sierra Club's Michael Brune read Mary Pat Tifft's resolution calling for the company to cut back on greenhouse gases and demanded that associates be paid $15 an hour. Mary Watkines denounced the "double standards" in pay at Walmart, pointing out that when workers like her missed targets, their bonuses disappeared, but when Walmart itself missed targets, CEO McMillon still got a $17.5 million performance bonus. And Venanzi Luna, her voice quivering at first, told her story of being laid off suddenly when Walmart closed her store with five hours' notice.

"Our managers say our stores closed for 'plumbing problems,' but the real reason is that my store has been speaking out for change at Walmart. We were the first store to go on strike, and we have been vocal in standing up for $15 an hour and full-time, consistent schedules," she said. "Walmart executives are punishing 2,000 associates because we are trying to make our company a better place to work and shop."

She called for an independent board chair—not someone who had been "smart enough" to marry into the Walton family. Luna's speech apparently riled Jeff Gearhart, the executive presiding over the resolution portion, enough to get him to answer back; he proclaimed that the company had been generous enough to provide sixty days of pay to the workers who had been laid off due to the store closures. (That sixty days of pay was mandated by the federal Worker Adjustment and Retraining Notification Act.) Ultimately, 16 percent of the shareholders voted for the independent chair resolution, or about 32 percent of the non-Walton shareholders.[38]

When the last notes of Rod Stewart's performance faded and the lights came up, the OUR Walmart crew reunited on the floor of the arena, where Doug McMillon was glad-handing associates. Luna stepped up to him, flanked by her colleagues, and asked whether she would be rehired when the "plumbing problems" at her store were fixed. McMillon, good at projecting emotion, looked her in the eye and told her he was sorry about what happened, but he didn't make any promises.

When the group turned to find new board chair Greg Penner, he was already moving away, flanked by besuited executives. "He's running away," someone commented.

"They haven't given me a new job. And they're not going to," Luna told me. "If they say they don't retaliate against associates, well, I'm a proud OUR Walmart member, start with me. You prove to me that you're not retaliating against us."

For many low-wage workers, jobs are temporary. Walmart's turnover rate for hourly employees has been estimated at between 44 and 70 percent. Workers like Venanzi Luna and Colby Harris, when let go from one retail job, most of the time simply find another. That they instead continued to fight to improve the company that cut them loose was something that Walmart should value. They were dedicated. That they stuck around, as Tyfani Faulkner said, speaks to their integrity. Their commitment should also remind us of the realities of America in the early twenty-first century: retail jobs and other low-paying service gigs are the jobs that exist, and Walmart is an industry leader. If their only options are Walmart or someplace else that takes its guidance from Walmart, then changing Walmart is really the only choice they have.[39]

For OUR Walmart members, Walmart was a bellwether for the future of stable, decent-paying jobs, and they were willing to fight hard for it. As Cynthia Murray put it, "We realized early on that if we could change Walmart, then we could help change the country back in a better direction. And we're seeing it happen."

CHAPTER FOUR

CHALLENGING THE AUSTERITARIANS

ALEX HANNA WAS IN EGYPT WATCHING A REVOLUTION UNFOLD when she found out that the governor of her state back home was proposing to eliminate her union rights. Hanna was copresident of the Teaching Assistants Association (TAA) and a graduate student in sociology at the University of Wisconsin at Madison when Scott Walker was elected governor; she and others within the union and its parent union, the American Federation of Teachers (AFT) of Wisconsin, had been concerned that the Republican, swept into office as part of the Tea Party wave of 2010, would be bad for union workers. But they hadn't expected anything like Act 10.

The act that Walker proposed as a "budget repair" bill on Valentine's Day, February 14, 2011, mirrored what was being called "austerity" in Europe, purporting to balance the state budget with cuts to salaries and benefits for public employees as well as cuts to services. The cuts were to be expected in the still severe economic downturn, but few had predicted that the governor would eliminate or severely curtail the rights of most public employees to collectively bargain. What was really shocking was the way austerity seemed to serve a kind of disciplinary function; the moralistic language Walker used to describe the bill presented this belt-tightening not only as a response to the crisis but as a punishment, and the punishment was aimed at the victims of the crash rather than its perpetrators. Hanna and the TAA saw the bill as a naked attack on their rights in the workplace by a governor who had run promising to bring jobs back to their struggling state.

The TAA had already planned a rally for Valentine's Day, in a pre-emptive strike against likely cuts to the university, and Hanna was deluged with emails asking her to come home. She was observing the popular revolution that had begun in Egypt in the winter of 2011, part of what came to be known as the Arab Spring. But the attacks on the union and the university were serious enough that she returned just in time for the February 14 action. The TAA led a crowd of marchers up State Street from the university campus to deliver a thousand valentines protesting Act 10 to Walker at the Capitol. It was an impressive showing, but marches were common enough in Madison that few expected this one to be different. Jenni Dye, a lawyer based in Madison, was downtown eating brunch and saw the protesters. "I thought, 'Oh look, another Madison protest.'"

The next day, the Joint Finance Committee of the legislature held a hearing on Act 10. The TAA and other union protesters had planned a "people's filibuster" of the bill, lining up hundreds of people to speak against it and extending the comment period all day and all night. The repeal of collective bargaining rights, they argued, had nothing to do with "repairing" holes in the budget; freezing their wages was one thing, and even increasing the amounts they had to contribute to their pensions and health insurance could at least be vaguely connected to a need for funds, but getting rid of their right to negotiate for a raise higher than the cost of living when the economy improved was very different and had little to do with the current budget problems. People were incensed. "We had people stuffed in the overflow room of the Capitol, people in line, and the unions were agitating outside," Hanna said. As the comments stretched on into the evening, the protesters created the Defend Wisconsin Twitter account to send out updates. At the beginning of the day, Hanna said, they'd been told that testimony would continue until everyone had been heard, but sometime after midnight the legislators cut off the speakers, announcing they'd heard enough.

"We decided we were just going to stay," Hanna said. She and her colleagues sent out messages via Twitter and Facebook, calling for people to join them at the Capitol and to bring sleeping bags. The TAA members invited their students, and they camped out in the Capitol rotunda. At 5:00 a.m., Hanna looked at the person next to her and said, "I guess this is happening!"

Protesters and pundits began to compare the Wisconsin protest to Tahrir Square. The comparisons to Egypt seemed overblown to Hanna at first, but as the occupation went on, similar structures to those in Tahrir Square began to take shape, structures that were later echoed and expanded at Occupy Wall Street. Hanna had found the protests in Tahrir Square vibrant, almost carnivalesque, unlike anything she'd seen before. "It felt very safe, very communal," she said. There were people selling or giving out food, people giving speeches, people camped out. In the Wisconsin Capitol, too, were medics, food distribution, action planning, all of which seemed to arise spontaneously as people took it upon themselves to make things happen and provide services that were being slashed by the state. The space itself provided a concrete alternative to the austerity the government was pushing. Although organizations like the TAA, the AFT, and other labor unions with elected leadership were present, and helped build the occupation, inside the space things were open and horizontal. Like the occupation of Tahrir Square, the Wisconsin occupation, and later Occupy, held a space that was politically significant—the Capitol building, the "people's house," a symbol of Wisconsin's famously open and transparent governance.

For Jenni Dye, who was the daughter of a Wisconsin teacher but not a union member herself, it was the process by which Act 10 was pushed forward as much as the content of the bill itself that motivated her to join the protests. "Part of it was about standing up for the middle class, for workers, and for the everyday people in Wisconsin that are your friends and neighbors," she said. "What was happening was just not the way that we did business in Wisconsin. We didn't rush huge policy changes through. We didn't meet in the middle of the night and shut out public testimony." She felt that what was happening was profoundly undemocratic, and it roused her sense of solidarity—it was unacceptable that Walker was blaming the rough economy on her family and friends.

In cities and towns across the country, many of the people who watched the Wisconsin protests unfold had the same reaction Dye did. Union members and organizers, of course, were roused to defend their institutions, but it was the power grab, the high-handed way Walker dismissed the protests, that made people realize that something more than a march was needed. Brett Banditelli, at the time the producer for the Rick Smith Show, a Pennsylvania-based labor radio show, was following the protests via social media. He began to reach out to fund-raisers to see if he could get money to take the show to Madison to cover the protests. At first, funders thought it was simply a local story, but then Ohio's governor proposed a similar bill—one that didn't carve out firefighters and police officers, as Walker's had, but took rights from all, inspiring unlikely coalitions between cops and leftists.

When Banditelli arrived at the Wisconsin Capitol with Rick Smith, the first thing he saw was a massive sign made out of a bedsheet fluttering from a balcony high above the rotunda floor. It read "Kill the Bill!" The occupation had been going for a week by then, and the Capitol was thronged with people bundled up for Wisconsin winter, many of them in red shirts with a blue fist in the shape of the state on it. Handwritten "Kill the Bill!" signs waved in the crowd and hung next to professionally printed union signs—not just from the public-sector unions under threat, the AFT, the Service Employees International Union, and the American Federation of State, County and Municipal Employees (AFSCME), but also from the once-powerful industrial unions like the United Steelworkers. Banditelli and Smith were far from the only people who had driven all night to join the protests: labor had answered the call. A group of firefighters, who had been excluded from the cuts in Walker's bill, marched through the Capitol playing the bagpipes, led by their young, charismatic leader Mahlon Mitchell. Three levels of protesters on the rotunda joined in a sing-along of "Do You Hear the People Sing?" from the musical *Les Misérables*.

The sign Jenni Dye remembered best was one she spotted on an outdoor march one snowy day. The man holding it "looked like the ultimate Packer fan," she said. "He had this big bushy Wisconsin beard and a winter hat on and his jacket was green and his sign said, 'All the faith that I have lost in the government I have found in the people.'" For her, that was the story of the protest.

As the protests continued, Walker doubled down, announcing a budget for the next two years that the local paper said "remold[ed] Wisconsin government at every level." It slashed roughly $1 billion from public schools, laid off 1,200 people, sliced 11 percent of the University of Wisconsin's budget—and lowered corporate taxes even more, on top of $100 million in tax cuts the governor and his legislative cronies had already passed. Cutting taxes for the rich while cutting rights for workers seemed, to the protesters, to be an obvious example of what the Chicago Teachers Union (CTU) would later call "being broke on purpose"— eliminating a source of revenue in order to justify cuts that those in power already wanted to make.[1]

It was in part Wisconsin's strong labor tradition that made the protests happen—the state famously taught labor history in public schools. It was partly that open government tradition that Dye cited, rooted in Progressive-era reforms. But it was partly something else as well—as the protests grew, there was a sense that finally, working people were standing up against the blame that had been flung their way since the beginning of the financial crisis. It made people from around the country want to take part.

There was also a sense that Walker's bill was a direct attack on a particular kind of worker who was more vulnerable than others and seen as less worthy of respect. Cindy Clark, a second-generation Wisconsin teacher, pointed out that her mother had seen unionizing teachers in the state as a way to get equal pay for women. Austerity for union workers would hit everyone, from the small businesses that relied on public workers' dollars to children in the schools and patients who rely on home health aides. But most of the unions that were facing the loss of their rights were made up of care workers: these majority-woman workplaces would take the brunt of the cuts. While Clark assumed at the time that Walker had carved out the male-dominated unions because he would come for them later (an assumption proved correct in subsequent years), she felt that there was an element of scapegoating women in Act 10's measures. The public sector was also a field with a higher-than-average proportion of workers of color, many of whom had sought those public jobs because they had stronger protections against discrimination. It was at the intersection of race, gender, and class that the bill did its worst damage.

The Wisconsin uprising was the first major US protest to be covered and spread primarily by social media, and it changed the way people around the country followed the actions of movements. Although local and independent media (including my employer at the time, Laura Flanders) did arrive to cover the actions, following Twitter hashtags like #wiunion and #notmyWI remained the best way to see what was happening. Things changed rapidly, and Twitter coverage had an immediacy that traditional media could not match. Dye used Twitter from work to research and share information. When fourteen Democratic state senators left the state to prevent a vote on Act 10, she found out via Twitter and dug into the law to see which rule it was that allowed them to hold up a vote by denying a quorum. "I didn't want to wait for the media story to come out the next day, and so we were in real time scouring laws and talking about them on Twitter to figure it out," she said. From work, she could help determine where people could drop off water or deliver food—like the pizzas, famously ordered through Ian's Pizza from as far away as Egypt. Before the protests, her Twitter account had been private; afterward, she not only opened it up but vowed to respond to everyone who Tweeted at her, even to opponents of the protest.

The live-streaming technology that would be so prominent during the Occupy protests less than a year later was still in its infancy, but videographers made edited clips of the actions and posted them to YouTube for easy broadcast. Few unions had invested much in social media programs at the time, so activists simply experimented, learning from what worked, fueled by anger and the adrenaline of being part of something rather than rules and best practices. In Ohio and then Indiana, where similar bills were moving forward, similar protests sprang up and took their direction from what was happening in Wisconsin.

"I think the occupation and the engagement on social media really lowered the barrier for engagement," Dye said. During the 2010 election, she had a hard time figuring out how to get involved. After the election, her group of friends, all, like her, in their late twenties or early thirties, felt like they didn't have the time that they'd had in college to be activists, or the money to donate to campaigns. They were looking for a way to connect. "We started talking about how could we get more engaged and make change for the future, and then all of a sudden this protest exploded in our hometown," she said. With the occupation, it was easy to take part, and with Twitter, it was easy for people on the other side of the country to pass on information and to feel connected. (I "met" Dye and Banditelli via Twitter during the Wisconsin protests.) Social media, Dye said, allowed complete strangers to feel a real connection, to understand what solidarity felt like.

Despite the protests, which at their peak drew 80,000 protesters to the Capitol, Walker and the state legislature remained intent on passing the collective bargaining restrictions. Security in the Capitol began to increase, and one night after a big sit-in, the building was locked down with a small group of protesters still inside. Dye arrived the next morning for a quick check-in before heading to work and found the door locked. She and a few other people stood there, checking Twitter to see what had happened, and she Tweeted, half joking, that they should stay outside until they were allowed in. She had to leave for work, but that evening, people showed up. "So many people felt the same way that I did. This was our building. We deserved entry and we weren't going away," she said. "We slept outside. It was 13 degrees overnight. One of the nights that we were out there it was so windy that the blankets kept blowing off of us. It was three in the morning and I just gave up and started laughing because there was nothing we could do. We were stuck outside this building and the blankets wouldn't even stay on us but nobody was giving up."

On March 10, the collective bargaining portion of Act 10 was stripped out of the budget bill and pushed forward on its own. This didn't require the fourteen state senators, who were still camped out in Illinois, to be there for a vote. Hanna was on the university campus when she heard the news and sprinted for the Capitol, ducking into cafes with a megaphone and shouting "They're passing the bill!"

"At that point it seemed a little more militant," she said. "We went to the vestibule in front of the assembly chambers and were going to sit in front of the seat of power here and not allow this to happen." The police, who had been relatively restrained through much of the occupation, carted out protesters, and the bill was passed in the middle of the night. Walker signed it in a private session.

The idea of recalling Walker had been floated early in the protests. With the bill's passage, it seemed clear to Dye that he and his colleagues in the legislature were not going to listen to the demands of the public, and removing them from office was the best option. But she was also considering what she could do, herself. "Even at the early stages, I thought maybe I should run for office," she said. She was pretty happy with the legislators in her district, but after she spoke with a family friend who had been on the county board of supervisors, she realized that the supervisor for her area was a Walker supporter. She decided to jump into the race, though she'd never even worked on a campaign before. But her inexperience helped, too, as she was not wedded to the conventional wisdom as to who would vote and who was worth reaching. She spent hours each night knocking on doors and meeting people. In the spring of 2012, she won her election.

The recalls were rougher going. Walker had to be in office for at least a year before he could be recalled, so in 2011, activists focused on trying to remove some of the Republican state senators who were eligible. Walker supporters, meanwhile, targeted some of the Democratic state senators who had left the state to delay the vote. In total, six Republicans and three Democrats were up for recall in 2011; two of the Republicans, Randy Hopper and Dan Kapanke, lost their seats. Then, in the winter of 2012, the activists turned in petitions to recall Walker.

The shift to an electoral strategy was rocky. Early recall successes buoyed the idea of running against Walker, but by the time Walker could be recalled, the energy around the Capitol occupation had cooled somewhat. Still, Dye said, the effort put into the recall petitions was "phenomenal."

There were a few Democrats who wanted the spot to challenge Walker. Most of the people I spoke with—not just Dye and Hanna, but other state union leaders as well—favored Kathleen Falk, the former Dane County executive, largely because she was the candidate who went the furthest in promising to reverse Act 10. Tom Barrett, the mayor of Milwaukee, won the primary but refused to commit to undoing the law—Hanna remembered confronting Barrett at a union meeting, but the answer he gave her, she said, was mostly meaningless. Although Mahlon Mitchell, the firefighter union leader and a hero of the protests, became Barrett's running mate, the TAA ultimately chose to endorse Walker's recall but not Barrett as a candidate. Despite the fact that the massive protests at the Capitol around Act 10 had led directly to the recall, establishment Democrats seemed to think that union rights were not a winning issue.

Meanwhile, from before the beginning of the campaign, outside money from big donors like Charles and David Koch had been pouring into the state to support Walker, who was able to define the recall while the challengers were still seeking a candidate. Walker challenged the very idea of a recall, arguing that it was inappropriate to try to remove him from office over Act 10, and it worked. Hanna spent the recall day canvassing voters; by the time she reached the Capitol just fifteen minutes after the polls closed, the election had already been called for Walker. Though they had succeeded in flipping one more seat and turning the state senate away from Walker's allies, he was still governor. In Ohio, where the similar bill itself, rather than a politician, was on the ballot, voters overwhelmingly came out in an off-year election and overturned it, by a larger margin than the one by which Governor John Kasich had won office.

To Dye, many of the questions asked after the recall missed the point. It was not a question of whether electoral strategy was worthwhile or whether other forms of action were necessary, but rather a need for more of both. "We were fighting for people who are actually hurting in the moment and we should have been going at them on every level," she said. In her own life, she took up that strategy, serving on the Dane County board and giving up her legal practice to become a full-time political activist. After the election, she took a job as the executive director of NARAL Pro-Choice Wisconsin, learning the ropes of running a nonprofit—which were very different from turning up at the Capitol for a free-flowing protest—and then, after a year and a half, she became research director of the nonprofit progressive advocacy organization One Wisconsin Now. "Being here almost brings me back full circle to being in the Capitol those first days," she said. The new position allowed her to bring together the issues she was passionate about, from labor to abortion rights. "All of us, the Black Lives Matter movement, the labor movement, reproductive health, are part of this Venn diagram that has so much more overlap than we acknowledge when we're working in our silos," she said. "We have to work together."

But after the recall, it has been harder to turn out massive protests or to get people to see different issues as being connected. Some, like Hanna, were simply too burned out by nearly two years of work and the loss that came at the end. Others continued to be siloed into single issues, turning out when Walker proposed abortion restrictions but not to protest a so-called right-to-work bill that attacked the private-sector unions he had previously promised to leave alone, or to protest the right-to-work bill but not budget cuts to the University of Wisconsin system, or the voter ID law that would make it even harder to mount an electoral challenge.

Assuming that failing to recall Walker meant the whole effort had accomplished nothing would be shortsighted. Elections are easy to measure for political observers and pundits: there is a winner and a loser and there are a lot of exit polls to parse and murmur over. Counting how many Jenni Dyes were produced by the protests, and whether they counter the people who stepped back, is harder. In 2015, organizers with the Young, Gifted and Black coalition joined forces with Wisconsin Jobs Now and other groups to protest the police killings of young black Wisconsinites and the right-to-work bill together. They thronged the Capitol, the sight calling up memories of 2011. Jennifer Epps-Addison of Wisconsin Jobs Now told me, "What we need to do is make our case and build relationships between working-class white folks outstate and communities of color in Milwaukee, Madison, and Racine, to understand that we're all in this together, and that these forms of institutional classism and racism impact everyone."

In the winter of 2015, I walked through the Wisconsin Capitol with Jenni Dye. She pointed out the bench on which she'd slept, the spot outside where they'd come with sleeping bags when they were locked outside. At noon, a small group of people, mostly dressed in red, began to assemble in the rotunda. They unfurled banners over the edge of the balcony: one read "Solidarity"; the other featured a heart with the state of Wisconsin inside of it and read, "We'll be here until [the state] gets better." The Solidarity Singers gathered every day and sang protest songs—for the holidays, they had rewritten Christmas carols, singing, "O come all ye workers" to the tune of "O Come All Ye Faithful."

"I don't think that Scott Walker succeeded in dividing us and conquering us, but he did succeed in dividing us," Jenni Dye said. "We're not conquered yet. There are so many people who are still fighting harder than they were before Scott Walker was a name that they acknowledged or knew, but the divisions here are really deep."

WE DIDN'T ALWAYS HEAR WHAT WAS HAPPENING IN THE UNITED States referred to as "austerity"; in Europe, the policy had a name and often brutal enforcement, while in the United States the metaphors of "belt-tightening" and "spending within our means" were more common. But the results were the same. The Obama administration proposed an economic stimulus plan early on, but it met with resistance in Congress from budget hawks squawking about deficits; the stimulus that did get passed wound up being, according to several prominent economists, too small to succeed. When it appeared that the Democrats in power weren't doing enough to turn the economy around, the Republicans rode a Tea Party wave to victory in the 2010 midterm elections, sweeping Scott Walker, John Kasich, and Chris Christie, among others, into governor's offices. They won largely because of their promises to do what the Democrats seemingly couldn't or wouldn't do: put people back to work.[2]

What the Tea Party actually wanted, though, was not very clear. While grassroots activists opposed the bank bailouts and stimulus spending, which they saw as handouts to the undeserving, researchers and pollsters found that many Tea Partiers had no problem with public spending on programs like Social Security and Medicare, which they felt were "earned." They were not, despite the policies attached to the Tea Party brand, lining up to demand austerity cutbacks to popular programs; nor were they clamoring to dismantle labor unions once and for all, as so many Tea Party governors seemed bent on doing. Tea Partiers, for the most part, were even willing to support tax increases on the wealthy to keep Social Security functioning. Nobody campaigned on wage cuts, budget cuts, and the removal of union rights.[3]

Meanwhile, the wealthy conservatives who adopted the Tea Party name and poured money into funding events were spending lavishly on candidates. The Kochs, who supported Walker and many others, did have a particular set of policies in mind, as did many of the other rich ideologues whose money helped Republicans take the US House of Representatives and several statehouses. Austerity, to them, was less about cutting spending for its own sake, and more about cutting programs to which they were politically opposed while consolidating their own power. It often included selling off public resources and utilities to private companies and pumping public dollars, in some cases, to the very people who had created the economic crisis in the first place. A big barrier to that consolidation of power had always been the presence of labor unions, which despite shrinking clout still served as a force in the workplace and in politics for working people. The post-crisis shock moment seemed, to the powerful, to be the perfect time to wipe out unions for good.

The difference between the grassroots and the donor class became visible when plans like the overhaul of Medicare, proposed by Congressman Paul Ryan (R-WI), failed to gain traction with the broader public, even though they were considered "Tea Party" policies. Debbie Dooley, the Atlanta Tea Party activist, complained to me about Scott Walker, who "calls himself a conservative," for spending public dollars on the Milwaukee Bucks' stadium, which she considered a handout to the team's wealthy owners. Republican officials, including former house majority leader Eric Cantor (R-VA), occasionally found themselves facing an uprising from grassroots Tea Party candidates—Cantor lost a primary to a professor who proclaimed, "I will fight to end crony capitalist programs that benefit the rich and powerful."[4]

Politicians argued that the cuts that came in Wisconsin, Ohio, and other states in 2011 were necessary in order to bring about economic stability, but those cuts also revealed a host of ideological preferences. The financial crisis, not the salaries of teachers and social workers, had blown the holes in state budgets, but Walker and others blamed government spending, and particularly those public workers. They pointed fingers at bloated pensions, when in fact pension funds were missing cash thanks to the bankers who had caused the crisis: Ohio's pension fund had bought mortgage-backed securities from Lehman Brothers, where John Kasich was an investment banker from 2001 to 2008, and lost tens of millions. Kasich became governor of the state in 2011 and pushed forward his own attack on collective bargaining rights. The crisis was a great opportunity to slice away the budgets that politicians aligned with the wealthy and powerful already opposed and take aim at the protections that workers had spent decades solidifying.[5]

The term "austeritarian" was coined by Greek activists, a portmanteau used to point out that austerity policies were often imposed by authoritarian means, on populations still reeling from the shock of a collapse. In Wisconsin, the attack on collective bargaining was the epitome of austeritarianism: though Walker argued that Act 10 would save the state billions, it is hard to argue that collective bargaining itself had a price tag the same way health insurance or a pension plan did. What the law did was to change the relations of power between public employees and their employer. Walker and his allies pushed through the bill despite thousands upon thousands of people pouring into the State Capitol in protest, cutting off public comment sessions, holding meetings that were supposed to be open behind closed doors, and celebrating the result of the power struggle to their backers. It was the undemocratic process that led Jenni Dye to see the protests as a counterweight to an electoral system that had not worked.

It wasn't just Republicans. Working people felt let down by both parties—Democrats, as political scientist Thomas Ferguson noted, have delivered less and less for working people even as their needs grew greater than ever. After decades considering themselves the party of labor, Democrats had largely shifted to relying on wealthy donors, assuming that unions, a fading relic of a bygone era, would come along because they had no better options—benign neglect from the Democrats was better than the hinted-at destruction from the Republicans. Yet without a compelling alternative, Walker won handily, and continued to win, even after Act 10. Conservatives were prepared to attack unions, but liberals were not prepared to defend them.

Disconnected from workers, the Democratic Party was caught flat-footed, first by the financial crisis and then by the Tea Party. That Wisconsin Democrats' solution to the Walker recall was to run the same candidate who had just lost to Walker in 2010 should underscore the problem—there was no pipeline for candidates who seemed both competent to do the job and able to excite a long-ignored working-class base while bringing in enough money to compete. The protests helped bring people like Dye into the political process, but she was not ready to run for governor. And it takes a lot of on-the-ground organizing and enthusiasm to counter the waves of corporate cash.

The big donors, Ferguson said, have been calling the shots in both major parties for a long time—from well before the Supreme Court's *Citizens United* decision drew the attention of activists to the "money in politics" problem. What we often call money in politics is a problem of power and priorities. Unions spent millions to elect Barack Obama and other Democrats in 2008, but they got little for their efforts: labor's biggest priority, a bill known as the Employee Free Choice Act, which would have streamlined the union election process, was tabled. Their contributions were simply dwarfed by much bigger donations that came in from bankers and corporate titans. Most of that money gets spent on TV ads, many of them negative ads that drown out useful information with a heady buzz of emotional appeals and near-falsehoods in ways that can increase cynicism more than they can encourage interest in an election. All the while, voter turnout has been plummeting, to the point where the 2014 midterm House elections drew only 36 percent of eligible voters to the polls. Even the Wisconsin recall, a dramatic national story powered by grassroots energy, drew a turnout of less than 60 percent. "It seems plain," wrote Ferguson and Walter Dean Burnham, "that the American political universe is being rapidly reshaped by economic and cultural crisis into something distinctly different."[6]

Labor continues to struggle when it comes to electing candidates to office. Ballot initiatives require less faith in the promises of an individual—it was easier to vote down the antiunion bill in Ohio than to oust Walker in Wisconsin. The pipeline problem remains when it comes to electing officials who have an authentic relationship with labor and who understand working people's needs. After the failed recall, the Wisconsin Democratic Party's next unsuccessful candidate for governor was Mary Burke, an executive at Trek Bikes who had run one winning campaign for school board, not exactly a working-class firebrand. Translating the groundswell of a movement into elected power will take more time, and requires the building of institutions rather than one-off campaigns.

Austeritarianism contributes to the lack of faith in electoral politics, the feeling that politicians are answering to someone other than the voters who elect them. And so Americans have turned to protests, to occupations and dramatic direct actions, in hopes of making change that way. "People are really taking to the streets instead of just going to the ballot box, and when they're talking about the ballot box they want better choices," Jenni Dye said. "Democracy is more than a full-time job."

THE DECISION, BY WALKER AND HIS CRONIES, TO TARGET PUBLIC workers' unions had been a long time coming. For nearly as long as there have been government employees, there have been conflicts about the political position of those workers, hand-wringing about their patriotism and loyalty, and attempts to squeeze more work out of them for less pay. The history of public-sector unions is often discussed as an afterthought to the industrial unions that dominated the New Deal era, but many of the struggles they undertook over the decades are being repeated right now.

The teachers' unions of today were predated by teachers' organizations that were established in the mid-1800s, beginning with the National Education Association in 1857. But it was not until 1897, when working-class Chicago teachers created the Chicago Teachers Federation (CTF; it later became the Chicago Teachers Union, or CTU), that teachers began to exercise some power. Almost all women—the result of decades of propaganda about the proper role of working women—the teachers were paid much less than men and could not yet legally vote, and yet through actions and strategic alliances with the mostly male labor movement of the time, they challenged a school board appointed by the mayor and pressured by rich citizens to keep school budgets low. They demanded not just higher wages, but more control over their own working conditions in the schools. Without legal collective bargaining, those teachers became community organizers, collecting petition signatures in their neighborhoods and challenging the "tracking" of working-class children into vocational education. They did strategic research, discovering that for-profit utility companies were costing the city millions in unpaid taxes, in a precursor of today's battles over funding. Students protested on the side of their teachers, and male unionists supported them. From the CTF was born the American Federation of Teachers, the national union, in 1916.[7]

The ability to fire teachers was and remains a contentious issue. Tenure, or the right to due process before firing, was granted to teachers well before the right to collective bargaining, but beginning at the time of World War I, teachers who were insufficiently patriotic and unions with radical beliefs came in for special scrutiny. New York's Teachers Union, known for its "social movement unionism," was targeted after it challenged the austerity policies that came in on the heels of the Great Depression. Thousands of teachers were investigated for supposed communism, and many lost their jobs.

At the same time as the teachers were flexing their muscles, other public-sector workers were organizing. Wisconsin was the birthplace of the American Federation of State, County and Municipal Employees, which was founded in 1932 by civil service workers. Early public-sector unions expanded during World War I and the Great Depression as federal spending did, rising, according to historian William Jones of the University of Wisconsin, from the same political crises that created the Congress of Industrial Organizations (CIO) in 1935. In the 1940s, the CIO moved to organize public-sector workers at the same time as it began its "Operation Dixie" push into the South. Public workers had been excluded from the labor protections of the New Deal, including collective bargaining and Social Security, but many of the unions they formed, despite, or perhaps because of, this exclusion, had a vibrant organizing culture and a tradition of fighting for women's rights and the rights of workers of color. They managed to bring quite a few local governments to the bargaining table.[8]

Radicals in the CIO merged two unions into the United Public Workers of America in 1946 and organized custodial and laundry workers, teachers, garbage collectors, hospital workers, and the mostly black professors at a few historically black colleges and universities. The union even fought for the rights of West Indian immigrants working in the Panama Canal zone. The public sector had been more welcoming to black workers and consisted of quite a few feminized fields, meaning that even without radical political beliefs, the union would have been pressed to organize women and African Americans, but the communist organizers made a particular commitment to egalitarianism.[9]

The United Public Workers of America union was expelled from the CIO in 1950 during the purges of leftists, and Public Workers members joined other CIO unions and AFSCME. The Building Service Employees International Union (BSEIU, now known just as SEIU) absorbed the biggest Public Workers local, a militant Los Angeles union that represented janitors and garbage workers as well as hospital staff. In the 1980s, after a wave of privatization, that local would begin the "Justice for Janitors" movement, which succeeded in winning union contracts for mostly immigrant janitors through private contractors and provided a model for the organizing logic behind the Fight for $15.

Wisconsin was also the first state, in 1959, to pass a state law allowing collective bargaining for public-sector workers, a law that was imitated in states across the country and that solidified the gains that public-sector workers had made. President Kennedy issued an executive order in 1962 that allowed federal workers to unionize. AFSCME alone quintupled its membership through the 1950s, 1960s, and early 1970s, a time when the rest of the labor movement was seeing losses as the beginnings of deindustrialization crept across the country. By the 1970s, public school teaching was the most-unionized profession in the country. Strikes picked up, too: between 1950 and 1961, AFSCME recorded 200 of them, and between 1960 and 1980 there were more than 1,000 teachers' strikes.[10]

In addition, during the 1960s, public-sector unions bucked the trend in the broader labor movement to be disaffected with the era's social movements. AFSCME organizer Jerry Wurf, later the union's president, had deep connections to the civil rights movement, helping to found the New York branch of the Congress of Racial Equality (CORE). Later he brought Martin Luther King Jr. to Memphis to march with striking sanitation workers. The United Federation of Teachers (UFT), which won collective bargaining for New York City teachers in 1961, also had early civil rights connections, though it wound up in a battle with black activists over "community control" of schools that soured relations for decades. For the most part, labor's gains both in power and in diversity came through the growth in the public sector.

As the economy began to stumble in the 1970s, ending the long postwar boom, public-sector workers became targets. The fiscal crises in New York and other cities were blamed on fat municipal budgets bloated with union pension dollars, and the resentment Americans began to feel against taxes was personified in the greedy public worker, whose union-won benefits began to look like an unearned privilege— particularly when those workers were black, Latino, and women, groups that were already objects of deep resentment. The schools, sites of battles over desegregation and busing, made a particularly easy target, and battles like the one the UFT fought in Ocean Hill–Brownsville pitted the union against the community, allowing union opponents to begin a long-lasting trend of painting themselves as the ones who truly cared about children of color. The unions, which had gotten out of the habit of organizing alongside nonmembers, suffered for it.

All of this came to a head in 1981, when Ronald Reagan broke the Professional Air Traffic Controllers Organization (PATCO) strike. PATCO had endorsed the Republican president against Jimmy Carter after experiencing rough relations with the Carter administration, but found that its endorsement carried little weight. The strike was already technically illegal under a little-used 1955 provision banning strikes by government workers, and Reagan deemed it a threat to national security and ordered the strikers back to work. When they refused to comply, he fired over 11,000 of them and banned them from public service jobs for life. It was one of the most prominent examples of politicians biting the union that fed them, but more importantly, it signaled to both the private and the public sectors that it was open season on unions. "It's such overkill—they brought in the howitzers to kill an ant," one controller said.[11]

The frequency of strikes plummeted after PATCO in both sectors. Attacks on unions increased, breaking them down faster than simple deindustrialization would have done. Inequality spread—the decline in middle-class income share has tracked almost exactly with the decline in union membership. The public sector, however, hung on to more of its gains than the private sector: at the writing of this book, over 35 percent of public workers were union members, compared to under 7 percent of private-sector workers. In 2010, public employees came to represent more than half of all union members in the United States.[12]

It is no surprise, then, that the public sector came in for greater attack than ever in the wake of the financial crisis. Many who had always been ideologically opposed to unions made their move while people were still in shock from the crisis. Public workers had long been stereotyped by the broader public as privileged and, particularly in the case of teachers, unfit for their jobs. With working people everywhere pressed for money, it was all too tempting to turn to what some call "negative solidarity," which focuses on tearing down those who seem to have it better than you rather than demanding that your circumstances improve. That public-sector workers still make less than comparable workers with private employers does not seem to matter. In Wisconsin, before Act 10 took effect, public workers made 5 percent less, on average, than their private-sector counterparts. Afterward, their wages plummeted, in some cases by an additional 10 percent.[13]

Contrary to what the Scott Walkers and John Kasichs of the world have argued, the labor movement for a long time saw itself as a social movement to represent all working people, not just an organ to win raises and better health insurance for its members. In 1938, the CIO's newspaper declared, "The interests of the people are the interests of labor, and the interests of labor are the interests of the people."[14]

It wasn't just propaganda that led to unions being perceived as a narrow "special-interest" group. For decades after the New Deal was passed and the postwar compromises struck, the majority of the nation's unions did stick primarily to collective bargaining for their members. The willingness of some union leaders, from American Federation of Labor (AFL) founder Samuel Gompers to longtime AFL-CIO president George Meany, to assume that the role of the union was as partner in capitalism—to cut deals with corporations and cozy up to longtime opponents like Richard Nixon—certainly contributed to that image. An insider strategy for labor didn't always lead even to short-term gains, as PATCO discovered in 1981. It also, as Stephen Lerner, architect of the Justice for Janitors campaign, said, made unions miss the bigger picture and underestimate the challenge they faced. In 1947, the Labor Management Relations Act (or Taft-Hartley bill, as it is known) prohibited a laundry list of union tactics and legalized the passage of so-called right-to-work laws, which diminish union funding by requiring unions to represent everyone, while allowing workers to choose not to pay fees to the union. Since that time, legislative restrictions on unions have been part of a long-term strategy to eliminate unions entirely. But unions tended to think deals were still possible. Why, Lerner asked, would you make a deal with someone who wants to kill you?

In Wisconsin, people from inside and outside of the labor movement stood up for something more than just the right of nurses and teachers to negotiate their salaries. The Wisconsin uprising was the awakening of a sense, long dormant, that labor unions are still a counterweight to the power of big money in American life. "Without the ability to organize, to have some group with some organized voice to say, 'No, this is wrong,' then [decent health care and working conditions] can go away, not just for union members but for everybody," Cindy Clark said. Wisconsinites stood up for the idea of working people coming together to counterbalance the power of the billionaire class.

Union activists in Wisconsin even considered a general strike—the ultimate expression of labor as a social movement, a strike that extended across all workers in a given location. The South Central Labor Federation as well as many activists on the ground called for it, and while the general strike did not officially happen, reporter and Wisconsinite John Nichols argued that the mass protests came close, and that an actual general strike would have been possible.[15]

And in Chicago, where the teachers went on strike in 2012 and challenged the austerity budget and the conditions in public schools, the union made issues of the common good part of its bargaining process, bringing its particular leverage to bear on an institution on which the whole city relied.

Teachers come in for particularly heavy criticism when they dare to make demands about their working conditions. In part, this response dates back to an ideal, promoted by early reformers like Catharine Beecher, implying that teachers ought to be selfless because their love for the children comes above all. When teachers and other care workers strike, this same ideal is used against them and they are declared insufficiently caring. Wealthy "education reformers" and politicians argue that they, instead, are the ones who care the most about students. "Teachers have been an easy target, primarily because we're not used to fighting," said Karen Lewis, president of the Chicago Teachers Union. "We're used to saying, 'Whatever you want me to do, I'll do it because we all care about what's best for kids.' We're supposed to think that the elite, who are very wealthy and very well educated and don't send their children to public schools, care more about black and brown children they don't know?"[16]

The CTU organized like a movement—within the community—talking to parents and students and incorporating their needs and desires into a broader political strategy; when the teachers shut down business as usual in the city, those parents understood that the teachers were not just looking for higher wages and better health insurance.

A strike succeeds by stopping production, even when "production" isn't the construction of widgets but the schooling of children. It also, as writer and political strategist Matt Stoller argued, is a visible demonstration of labor's power and struggles, something largely missing since Reagan crushed PATCO. "People might *only like unions when they see strikes,* otherwise all they hear about is backroom negotiations," he wrote. "Perhaps effectively striking is actually the way to force people to ask questions about what kind of country they want to live in." If a protest is a request, a strike is a demand.[17]

The CTU strike, like the uprising in Madison before it, created space for labor to think about itself as a force to fight for a better economy for all, and to sway political opinion by making public demands coupled with action.

IT DIDN'T TAKE KENZO SHIBATA LONG, AFTER HE BECAME A TEACHER in 2003, to realize that something was wrong with the Chicago school system. School closures shuffled students around, forcing them into classes with students from rival gangs; under those tensions, violence in the Bronzeville high school where he taught had increased. When he began to research the reasons for the closings, he discovered that Arne Duncan, at the time CEO of the Chicago Public Schools (CPS), and Mayor Richard M. Daley were proponents of closing "failing" schools and replacing them with new charter or contract schools. But to Shibata, those very policies seemed to be causing the problems.

Chicago's schools had been a battleground for years. The city was an early laboratory for the "education reform" agenda of more testing and more accountability, which usually meant firing teachers when their students' test scores didn't increase and handing schools over to private companies. The city's public schools were deeply segregated—over 70 percent of the black students attended schools that were over 90 percent children of color. Education reformers argued that schools should be run more like corporations. The Chicago schools had a CEO rather than a superintendent, Shibata noted, because the job didn't have to go to an accredited educator. Instead, the head of the schools was installed by the mayor, who through "mayoral control" of the schools appointed the school board as well. Duncan, who later became President Obama's secretary of education, was one of the very public faces of "ed reform," which Shibata began to understand as a plan to put public resources under private control.[18]

Shibata tried to turn to his union as a way to take action. He began blogging about his experiences as a teacher. Then he reached out to the editor of his union's newsletter, offering to write articles, but got no response. A colleague of his, Jackson Potter, invited him to a meeting of like-minded educators at the United Electrical, Radio and Machine Workers hall, the home of the union that had led the 2008 occupation of Republic Windows and Doors. The problems in the schools, they agreed, were part of a broader agenda happening across the city, one of privatization of public goods and consolidation of wealth, and the union wasn't doing much to help. They started a book group to learn more about the issues they faced, and the first book they read together was Naomi Klein's *The Shock Doctrine*, in which she tells the story of neoliberal policies imposed by governments on peoples reeling from crisis.

That book group grew into a caucus within the union that called itself the Caucus of Rank and File Educators (CORE). At first, Shibata said, they aimed simply to push the existing CTU leadership to step up and challenge the rhetoric coming from the authorities who were blaming the teachers for the crumbling, underfunded schools. They began to organize their coworkers and to listen to their complaints, and they made connections between everyday problems—like a lack of paper or air conditioning—to the austerity budgets that were being passed. The financial crisis, Shibata said, had become an excuse for the "reformers," allowing them to speed up a process that had been underway for a while. Taking a page from Klein, in outreach to union members CORE argued that the crisis was being used "not just to bust our union but to defund our schools and essentially sabotage the system." The existing union leadership, however, which had been in power for nearly forty years almost without interruption, seemed more interested in consolidating its own power than in mobilizing its members; according to Shibata, it became apparent that making real change within the union would require taking it over.

In 2008, as it organized with parents and community activists around the next round of planned school closures, CORE ran a warm-up campaign, nominating two of its members as pension trustees. Early on, Shibata used social media as an organizing tool, mobilizing members to post messages about CORE on Facebook. CORE used the race to educate members about the importance of the teachers' pension, since teachers in Illinois are not covered by Social Security. Their candidates both won, and CORE moved into the union leadership election with confidence.[19]

CORE member Karen Lewis was chosen to run for union president. Charismatic, funny, and fierce, Lewis had been the only black woman in her Dartmouth class, and thereafter she had spent twenty-two years as a high school chemistry teacher. She was backed up by Jesse Sharkey, another early CORE member. Though the papers would focus heavily in the coming years on Lewis as a personality, it was the ground organizing that CORE had built up that led to its win in the spring of 2010, and it was a tradition the members kept up as they took over running the union.

"To shift unions from the service model to an organizing model takes not just a few people that want to do it; it takes the will of rank-and-file members to become empowered in their schools and in their union," Lewis said. CORE staff cut their own salaries in order to create an organizing department; Shibata took a position in communications and began holding social media training sessions for members. He taught them how to get the message out about their own schools and struggles and helped them feel more involved in their union.

CORE had only a short time to strengthen the CTU before Rahm Emanuel was elected mayor of Chicago. When he took office in 2011, he almost immediately took aim at the union. Jennifer Johnson, a high school teacher on the city's North Side at the time, said, "He made it very clear that the teachers union was public enemy number one. 'Chicago Students Get the Shaft' was his first headline about us." Meanwhile, a massive education reform bill was making its way through the state legislature, one that targeted the Chicago teachers in particular. It required the union to get 75 percent of the union's membership to vote yes in order to authorize a strike, a bar that the bill's supporters figured the union would never be able to cross. Like Walker's bill in Wisconsin, Senate Bill 7 was about power, but disguised as a cost-cutting measure. It was designed to strip the union of its most potent weapon.

But Emanuel and the state legislators had badly underestimated the CTU. An organized, militant union that was in constant touch with its membership was a relative rarity, even though Chicago teachers had a long tradition of such work. A union that understood its fight as political, as a challenge to the austerity agenda that was now in such vogue that the Democrats who dominated Illinois politics were all in its sway, was nearly unthinkable. In addition to its internal organizing, Johnson said, the new leadership had created a research department. That department tracked city spending, and the union began criticizing the Tax Increment Funding system by which property taxes were diverted from public schools to building projects and subsidies for private businesses. The CTU put out a report, entitled *The Schools Chicago's Children Deserve*, that called for smaller class sizes and more counselors, nurses, and social workers. It criticized the continuing segregation that routinely sent the poorest children, most of them black and Latino, to schools that were falling apart.[20]

In preparation for negotiations, the teachers held a massive rally on May 23, and a sea of educators and their allies showed up in red CTU T-shirts. "There were probably 8,000 people marching through the streets of downtown to signal to the city that our platform is for real, we care about kids, we've got the power of numbers," Johnson later said. Shibata, at the rally, heard someone shout, during Lewis's speech, "Karen for mayor!" to thunderous applause. That moment, to him, crystallized what their fight was about: it was bigger than a union contract. The same bill that had raised the bar for a strike vote had also said that teachers could only strike over their own pay and benefits; but the CTU had done its work organizing in the community and made sure that the city knew its demands. The 2012 contract bargaining process was carried out by a team of between thirty and forty teachers, classroom educators who could back up their demands with evidence. The strike vote, when it was taken, saw 90 percent of the teachers vote yes.

"The community had a better sense than normal that we weren't just striking over a pay raise, we were striking because we wanted to call attention to serious inequality in our schools," Johnson said. "It struck a chord with people. There was some of that baiting thing, we didn't care about the kids, but we had already undercut that argument by making ourselves the educational experts in our communities. Sixty-seven percent of [Chicago Public School] parents supported us in the strike. That's pretty unheard of."

The workers in the Walmart warehouses were on strike at the same time, and some of them joined the teachers on marches and on the picket lines, connecting the Walton family's support for the education reform agenda to their opposition to the power of workers on the job. Parents and students joined the teachers, too. Israel Muñoz was a senior at a high school on the Southwest Side when the strike began. "There was a lot of talk about so much inequality in the education system, so much emphasis on testing," he told me. "I really connected with a lot of these issues because I had gone to Kelly High School experiencing all that." He supported the teachers and began to organize among the students for a union of their own.

The mainstream media was squarely opposed to the strike, with even normally liberal pundits expressing concern that children were being harmed by missing classes. But Shibata and the members he'd trained used social media to get out their own story. They shared video clips from the picket line (a "strikebot" made by two robotics teachers at Lane Tech got a lot of attention) and refuted the idea that their strike meant they didn't care about the kids.[21]

The strike lasted nine days. Nine days of educators in red lining the streets of the city, in rich and poor neighborhoods, black and white and Latino neighborhoods. Journalist Micah Uetricht reported being given a free yogurt and a bus ride simply for wearing a red shirt by workers who told him, "We gotta support the teachers." Rather than outrage, Chicago reacted with solidarity—and a little bit of glee. People seemed happy to see the powerful union so publicly challenge the mayor and the idea that they ought to make do with less. The energy of Occupy and its Chicago offshoots, too, contributed to the support for the strike, as the Wall Street connections of Mayor Emanuel fueled anger at policies that heightened inequality.[22]

The contract the CTU accepted wasn't perfect, but the teachers counted it a win. Seventy-nine percent of them voted for the contract, which included provisions that guaranteed textbooks on the first day of class, held testing to the legal minimum, and held steady the amount that teachers had to spend on their health insurance. Emanuel had been defeated. But the mayor came back the next spring with an announcement that Shibata saw as "flexing his muscles": Chicago would be closing fifty-four schools.

About 90 percent of the students in those schools were black. Lewis decried the closings as a racist policy, and the teachers joined with parent and student activists to fight for the schools. Israel Muñoz and some other students formed the Chicago Student Union, holding a march to Emanuel's office during spring break to deliver a letter to him demanding that he save their schools. The school closings were much more disruptive to students' education, Lewis argued, than the nine-day strike had been. "It wasn't like these were the worst performing schools. It just seemed arbitrary and capricious."

The school closings were austeritarianism at its worst. Emanuel argued that the closings would save money and that the schools in question were not only failing academically but also in disrepair—as though, Lewis noted, the building was at fault. Despite massive protests from the parents and students involved, the appointed school board persisted in the policy. "Public pressure only works if you have leaders who are accountable to the public," Shibata said. The powerful people named to the school board, whose fancy résumés were constantly touted—Penny Pritzker, the Hyatt heiress, later became Obama's commerce secretary—were not likely to care about working-class parents' protests. "As much public support as we could have possibly had during the school closings campaign," Shibata said, "it doesn't always translate into the same kind of leverage that a large-scale strike could."[23]

Shibata had realized back before the strike that something needed to change in the balance of power in Chicago. But it took the school closings to show, as the CORE members had earlier realized about their union, that maybe the only solution to their problems was to take power themselves.

"I hate politics, actually," Lewis said in 2013. "For a long time I've felt we live in a one-party system. We just have two branches of it. The key is to use the political system to hold our elected officials accountable through mass movements." But even that, Lewis noted, was an uphill battle. In 2010, after cuts to their pensions, the teachers' unions in Illinois withheld donations to Democrats—and got Senate Bill 7. They shut down the city with a strike, and got school closures. They built power, and got only retaliation. "When you're playing on somebody else's turf, you don't have control," Lewis said. "So the key is to change the rules of the game."

Emanuel was up for reelection in 2015, and Lewis began to seriously consider running. Other candidates who might have been able to challenge the incumbent were stepping back, unwilling to go up against the well-funded mayor and his Wall Street connections. Shibata was going to organizing meetings in local churches to collect petition signatures to put Lewis on the ballot, and other organizations and unions were showing interest in a challenge. The schools weren't the only issue—there had been organizing around low wages, as Chicago had been the second city to join the Fight for $15 and had a particularly militant group of workers at its core, and long-standing fights against police brutality and prisons.

But in October, the news broke that Lewis had been diagnosed with a brain tumor, which would prevent her from running. Jesus "Chuy" Garcia, a Cook County commissioner, stepped forward and won endorsement from the CTU, and the coalition that had begun to form around Lewis shifted to support him. To Shibata, Garcia might not have been a dream candidate, but he was a local official with deep community ties in his neighborhood, the opposite of Emanuel, someone who would be accountable to the people and not to big donors.

"The big gift of Karen even thinking about running was that it changed so much of what was considered possible in many of our minds," said Amisha Patel, director of the Grassroots Collaborative and a key part of that coalition. Garcia had not been central to a popular struggle the way Lewis had, but he was able to benefit from the momentum that Lewis had kicked off. SEIU Healthcare Illinois and Indiana joined the coalition, as did the Transit Workers Union and Workers United. Community groups, too, jumped in, and together they built a new political organization, United Working Families. But other unions, including other SEIU locals, backed Emanuel. For many people, Patel said, the Garcia campaign was their "Obama moment," because they were throwing themselves into electoral work for the first time. But the core of the coalition remained the same people who had been challenging the mayor for years.

As the center of the campaign, though, Garcia did not inspire the same excitement that Lewis had. Lewis had been a public figure for years at that point. From the time of the early CORE reading groups, she had put forth not just arguments for her union, but also strong arguments against the austerity agenda in the city, and a clear vision for a more economically and racially just city. Emanuel was still unpopular, but Garcia was not well known, and Chicagoans had little idea what he stood for. That allowed the negative ads that flooded the city to define him in the voters' minds. "People realized that they weren't going to be able to sell Rahm as much as they were able to cast doubt in people's minds about Chuy," Shibata said.

In the February election, Garcia got enough of the vote to force a runoff election. It was at that moment that more activists began to jump into the fight. SEIU's state council reversed its earlier decision and endorsed Garcia. "It would have been really great to have had that from the beginning," Patel laughed. Pushing Emanuel to a runoff forced him to spend time and money on his campaign that he otherwise might have pumped into getting his allies elected to the council. This opened up space for CTU and its allies to have an impact; CTU members ran in several aldermanic races, and Sue Sadlowski Garza and Tara Stamps also forced runoffs. In April, Garza won her race.[24]

Garcia did not, in the end, defeat Emanuel. There were fair criticisms of him as a candidate, but he managed to win 44 percent of the vote. It's tempting to wonder whether Lewis could have won. Early on, she was polling higher than Emanuel, though during the course of what would undoubtedly have been a nasty election those numbers may well have changed. Her illness denied the city and the country the chance to see what a candidate who had a real base in an organized movement could have done in a major election. Lewis's prominent role had given her the name recognition and connections to consider a run. But, Shibata noted, that itself demonstrated the danger of having too much invested in one strong charismatic leader—when that leader is removed, it is hard to fill the spot.

The leadership development within and around the CTU allowed for other leaders to step up, whether they be Garza, who won her seat on the council by drawing on her strong working-class roots and her family's ties to the Steelworkers and the CTU, or Timothy Meegan, who did not win his race, but created a strong, independent organization outside of the Democratic Party in his North Side neighborhood. "They're continuing to build, they're supporting other candidates, but they're also doing a lot of organizing on the ground. That's a ward that I'm definitely going to keep my eye on," Shibata said.

The campaign against Emanuel gave many of the organizers a taste for independent politics. They were disappointed both in Chicago's storied Democratic machine politics and in the new Republican governor, multimillionaire Bruce Rauner. Rauner had ties to Emanuel and planned to bust public-sector unions. Austerity, after all, was a bipartisan game, as was market-based education reform. In the face of austerity, Patel said, it is important to put forward a positive alternative vision, to offer suggestions for where the money can be found, and to talk about what the schools should look like. In the fall of 2015, a group of parents, teachers, and advocates went on a hunger strike to reopen one shuttered school, Dyett High School; they offered a plan to create a green-technology-focused, open-enrollment school in partnership with the CTU and the Chicago Botanic Garden. They succeeded in winning a promise to reopen the school, but their own plan was rejected. They called off the strike after thirty-four days upon the realization, as strike leader Jitu Brown put it, "that they will let us die."[25]

Facing such enemies, electoral politics is likely to remain part of the fight for the CTU and United Working Families. But it has not been and will not be the only strategy—2016 brought another stalemate in contract negotiations for the CTU and another overwhelming strike vote. The union was busy connecting the conditions in the schools to the police violence that killed seventeen-year-old Laquan McDonald, and to Emanuel's participation in a cover-up of that killing. Polls showed the union had three times the support in the city that the mayor did, laying the groundwork for yet another successful strike.[26]

On April 1, 2016, the CTU managed to pull off what, if not quite a general strike, was certainly the closest thing the country had seen to one in decades. Pulling together allies in at least 8 unions, including National Nurses United and AFSCME Council 31, and 40 community organizations, and building off of momentum from the successful campaign to remove Emanuel ally Anita Alvarez from the Cook County State Attorney office, the one-day strike saw 15,000 people turn out for a downtown rally that effectively stopped business as usual. Fast food and retail workers with the Fight for $15, child care and health care workers, and members of BYP 100 and other groups from the movement for black lives also joined the actions. Sarah Chambers, CTU member and teacher at Maria Saucedo Scholastic Academy, called it a "historic strike" and described picketing at the schools, direct actions around the city, and an end to the "broke on purpose" mentality starving the city's people of public services.[27]

"This is one of the first strikes in a very long time where we're pushing for progressive revenue. It's not just about a specific contract; we're actually fighting as a group for economic demands and we're getting close," Chambers said. "I'm hoping that what we do in Chicago with this massive strike will spread around the country, because the same types of social service cuts and austerity agendas are spreading throughout the whole country, and frankly, the world."

CHAPTER FIVE

RACE TO THE BOTTOM

A T THE EARLY TEA PARTY RALLIES, AMID THE SIGNS CALLING to "Take Our Country Back" and the American flags, there was another noticeable pattern: signs that remarked upon the race of the new president.

Some called for his birth certificate, or played on the fact that Barack Obama's father was Kenyan. One woman giggled as she read off her two-sided sign. "What's the difference between the Cleveland Zoo and the White House?" the front asked. "The zoo has an African lion and the White House has a lyin' African." Others were blunt: "Don't Blame Me, I Voted For the American." There were pictures of Obama as a witch-doctor, a reference to the health-care reform bill in the works in Washington. Outright racist slurs were rare, but the implication that the nation's first black president was somehow un-American, an outsider, or otherwise incomprehensible to the people who rallied in anger at town halls or outside the nation's capital was fairly common. Black members of Congress, including civil rights icon John Lewis (D-GA), former chairman of the Student Nonviolent Coordinating Committee (SNCC), and James Clyburn (D-SC), were greeted with racial slurs at a protest against the health-care bill; Emanuel Cleaver II (D-MO) was spat upon.[1]

Obama's election would probably have inflamed avowed racists at the best of times. But he came into office during a massive economic crisis, one that had thrown millions out of work, obliterated retirement savings, and caused a wave of foreclosures that was accelerating and that would continue long after recovery had supposedly come. The combination was destabilizing even to many who would never have admitted to a belief in white supremacy. As people scrambled to protect what they had and cast about for someone to blame, suspicions flared. Anyone else's gain felt like it might come at one's own expense. All of that tension made it harder for people to see what they had in common and to imagine working together to make things better.

J. D. Meadows joined the Council of Conservative Citizens (CCC), which hosted a Tea Party protest in his hometown of Ripley, Mississippi. The group's economic message hit home for him; factory closings in his town had put his aunt and uncle out of work, and meanwhile, he had watched the government bail out the banks and the bankers get richer. "Most people around here, whether they're Democrat or Republican, liberal or conservative, are fed up with the government in some way or form," he said. Asked about the CCC's position on race, Meadows said, "The media plays races off against each other when the races should be united for liberty." Pressed further on the subject, he said that he would leave a rally where there were overt racist themes promoted.[2]

But the CCC's organizer in the area, Brian Pace, was convinced that he could bring members like Meadows around to white supremacist beliefs. Pace, who sold Confederate flag memorabilia as a sideline, explained that he began conversations by talking about the economy and slowly "educated" people on race.[3]

Tea Partiers were conscious of the fact that the racist signs gave them a bad name, and many of them worked hard to counter that reputation, posting guidelines on their websites on how to deal with racist outbursts, inviting black conservative speakers to address their gatherings, and reiterating, in interviews, that they had no problem with immigrants or black people. But even when they decried the kind of overt racism that has become déclassé in recent years, surveys found Tea Partiers more likely to agree with statements like, "If blacks would only try harder, they could be just as well off as whites," and, "The Obama administration favors blacks over whites." People who agreed with statements like these might never utter a racist epithet, but their belief that there were no structures of racism remaining in the United States fueled resentment—a resentment that was inflamed in times of crisis.[4]

Those periodic flare-ups obscured the fact that the people who had been hit hardest by the financial crisis were black and Latino, and that far from getting a handout from the new black president, black people had seen nearly half their wealth wiped out, compared to just under 30 percent for US families overall. Tensions had been heightened during a polarizing election, and the crash piled on yet more pressure, inspiring some people to point fingers and others to offer solidarity.[5]

By seeming contrast with the Tea Party, other activists taking to the streets after the financial crisis and the election made fighting racism part of their strategy. When Occupy Wall Street erupted in New York City in 2011, for example, among the signs that dotted the park were proclamations that "I Am Troy Davis." Davis was executed in September 2011 for a crime he maintained he did not commit; an international movement sprang up around his case, but it was not enough to save him. "Race is everything in this case," Representative Lewis had said in 2008, noting that Davis, a black man, had been convicted of killing a white police officer. After Davis's execution, one occupier bore a sign that read, "Troy Davis would still be alive if he had been rich and white." Across the country, when Occupy Oakland took over Frank Ogawa Plaza outside of Oakland's city hall, the occupiers renamed it "Oscar Grant Plaza." Grant, another young black man, was prostrate on the ground when he was shot in the back by a white Bay Area Rapid Transit officer in 2009.[6]

Among the young protesters, the term "intersectionality," coined by legal scholar Kimberlé Crenshaw in 1989, was often used to describe the way people face multiple axes of oppression at once—for instance, a black woman does not face racism or sexism separately, but rather as intertwined, overlapping experiences. Sociologist Ruth Milkman, who studied Occupy, noted, "This generation uses the word intersectionality as if it were a household label."[7]

Earnest attempts at color blindness within Occupy didn't always go smoothly, though. Often they revealed a disconnect between the activists in the parks and the people they desperately wanted to reach. There were valid criticisms of the way the slogan "We are the 99 percent" could elide real differences. Manissa McCleave Maharawal was unsure about Occupy at first, having heard that it was mostly white people. She went anyway, and felt a connection to the movement, but when she stopped by the occupation one night with some friends, on the way home from a South Asians for Justice meeting, they saw a problem unfolding. The movement was about to agree on its "Declaration," which contained a line about "being one race, the human race, formerly divided by race, class," that put them off. If it made them uncomfortable, they worried it would warn other people of color away entirely.

"Blocking" the Declaration was hard, although the movement's consensus process theoretically gave anyone the right to do so. A "block" was supposed to be taken very seriously—it was supposed to be something you were willing to leave the movement over. Maharawal wrote later, "There in that circle, on that street-corner we did a crash course on racism, white privilege, structural racism, oppression. We did a course on history and the Declaration of Independence and colonialism and slavery. It was hard. It was real. It hurt. But people listened. We had to fight for it. I'm going to say that again: we had to fight for it. But it felt worth it."[8]

At Occupy Atlanta, another "block" made news when Representative Lewis stopped by and asked to speak. The assembly debated the proposal, as they did everything—loudly and in public—and decided to ask the congressman to address the assembly later, at the time scheduled for public speakers. Lewis couldn't stay, and he appeared unruffled by the decision, telling reporters that the process represented "grassroots democracy at its best." But someone caught the event on video, and it shot around the Internet. The movement's horizontal ideals—that no one, not even a member of Congress, was more important than any other—seemed to clash with the respect due to a hero of a past movement, particularly to a black hero of the civil rights movement. The image of white protesters rejecting the black congressman was hard to shake.[9]

But frequent clashes with police were beginning to show some occupiers what it was like to exist under the gaze of armed officers day and night, and began to create connections that went beyond lip service to communities of color. For white protesters, being surveilled by police was a new experience; for a black Latina like Nelini Stamp, it was a fact of life, a problem that she had grown up with. The deaths of black men like Amadou Diallo and Sean Bell at the hands of police had shaped her work as an organizer and her practices of activism and civil disobedience.

In New York's outer reaches, community organizers were building a movement to challenge the New York Police Department's "stop-and-frisk" tactics—a policy that encouraged officers to stop people who appeared "suspicious" and pat them down, ostensibly for guns, more often for drugs—and the occupiers began to take notice. White protesters began to venture to marches in Harlem and the Bronx and the far reaches of Brooklyn's East New York. Experienced organizers, Stamp noted, deployed the white activists, who would be treated with more deference by police than the black and Latino residents of those heavily policed neighborhoods, to make audacious demands, using their privilege as a shield.

On February 2, 2012, an NYPD officer burst into the Bronx apartment where eighteen-year-old Ramarley Graham lived with his grandmother. Graham was shot in the bathroom; his grandmother was thrown to the ground as he died in front of her. The police said they were pursuing Graham, who was unarmed, for possession of marijuana, and activists took to the streets, demanding charges against the officers. They made the connection between the pursuit of Graham and stop-and-frisk; ostensibly used to try to find weapons, the tactic most often resulted in minor pot arrests. That year, 85 percent of the people frisked by police had been black or Latino. Graham's death activated networks that had been strengthened by Occupy, but protests remained local. And then on February 26, seventeen-year-old Trayvon Martin was shot in Sanford, Florida.[10]

Martin's killer, George Zimmerman, was a neighborhood watch member, not a police officer, who had tailed the black teenager on his way home from a convenience store. At first, Zimmerman was not arrested for the crime. Authorities cited Florida's Stand Your Ground law, which allows individuals who have used force against others to claim self-defense when they are in a public place and have a legitimate fear for their life. But to those already in motion around the abuses of the police, Martin's death was on a continuum with Graham's, another black teenager killed because society considered children like him a threat. "This is not just a state violence problem, it's our country's problem," Stamp said.

The undercurrent of racism that had long simmered in the United States seemed to be bursting into the open, stoked by economic strife, the discomfort of some with a black president, and a new culture of protest. For people around the country, Martin's death became a flashpoint;

the claim that wearing a hooded sweatshirt had somehow made him seem suspicious angered many, including Daniel Maree, who called for a "Million Hoodie March" in New York on March 21. Maree founded the Million Hoodies network, which helped push an online petition calling for Zimmerman's arrest to over 2 million signatures. Celebrities like basketball superstar LeBron James, musicians Frank Ocean and Ludacris, and even members of Congress made speeches, took photos, and turned up to protests in hoodies, challenging the oft-trotted-out line that black men and boys would be safe if they'd stop dressing like thugs.[11]

Ciara Taylor was a student at Florida A&M University in Tallahassee when she heard about Martin's death. His story was a turning point for her because it put the lie to pretty fables about respectability and upward mobility. "Trayvon still had two very loving parents who would nurture him, he lived in a suburban community, and he was killed in his neighborhood by this guy who calls himself a neighborhood watchman," she said. "In this country they tell you if you work hard you can live in these communities that are supposed to be safe and everyone is equal and free." Like Martin, Taylor had grown up black in the suburbs, and she'd believed that story; although she had still experienced some level of racism, she had mostly bought into the myth of progress. That belief was now shattered, the possibility of individually escaping the tendrils of racism exposed as false.

Taylor had participated in some activism in high school—she protested the controversial presidential election in Florida in 2000, when the US Supreme Court had stepped in to resolve disputes over the vote count and put George W. Bush into the White House. Taylor remembered "thinking how much it sucks I'm basically yelling at my neighbors," while decisions were being made behind closed doors that neither side could influence. In college, she organized in favor of a living wage for campus workers and in opposition to the budget cuts that discontinued her major the year before she was due to graduate. She didn't remember how she found herself on that particular phone call to organize a response to Martin's shooting, only that she was skeptical that anything would bring justice.

Organizers Gabriel Pendas, Ahmad Abuznaid, and Phillip Agnew (who has since changed his name to umi selah) knew each other from college activism around the death of yet another young black man, Martin Lee Anderson, in 2006. Pendas had just returned from an event

celebrating the anniversary of the 1965 march from Selma to Montgomery, and suggested a march from Daytona to Sanford. Taylor remained
skeptical, but she was angry enough to try anything. They scheduled the
march for April 6.

Nelini Stamp got a call from a friend who worked with the progressive
"netroots" organization MoveOn; the friend was looking for someone
with experience in direct action to help the march organizers plan the
event. Stamp accepted the offer of a plane ticket and flew down to join
the march, even though she had only the barest connection to the Florida group. Martin's death, she said, made her wonder about the value of
the economic justice organizing she had been doing. "What's it worth,
if we can still be killed because we're walking around who we are?" she
asked. When she arrived, she saw that the group was smaller than the organizers had expected, with just forty people. Nevertheless, they set out.

Taylor, envisioning the photos of civil rights leaders in suits marching
arm in arm, had worn dress pants to the march. She laughed at herself
later, remembering the heat. But even in that heat, people pulled their
cars over on the side of the road to join the march for a while, calling
home for a ride later on. Taylor also recalled racist slurs shouted from
passing cars, and a gas station owner who wouldn't let them in to buy
supplies or use the restroom. They spent nights in African Methodist
Episcopal (AME) churches with a civil rights history, and members of
the Student Nonviolent Coordinating Committee came to meet with
them. They sang civil rights songs, and Stamp rewrote a song she had
written for Occupy Homes into a marching song for Trayvon.

Most of the marchers were not members of any organization; they
were students or alumni of Florida schools who had done some activism
in the past but had regular jobs. Ahmad Abuznaid had just taken the bar
exam; umi selah was a pharmaceutical salesman. But as they marched,
they began to feel that they couldn't go back to the life they'd had before. "We all said, this can't be it, this weekend can't be it," Stamp said.

As the marchers got closer to Sanford, rumors began to fly. They heard
that the Ku Klux Klan and other white supremacist groups planned to be
in town as well. When they reached the church where they were staying
that night, Taylor was asked to address the crowd of local residents and
elected officials that had gathered. "I had the elected officials and law
enforcement stand up and people started automatically applauding,"

she said. "I said 'These people are the people who could've had George Zimmerman arrested from day one and they haven't.'" The atmosphere in the room changed after that. Taylor challenged those in power to pick a side rather than issuing platitudes about how tragic it all was.

That night at the church, the group stayed up most of the night finalizing plans for a sit-in at the Sanford police station. The legal and financial support they were expecting evaporated; some of the organizations and celebrity backers the group had heard from earlier were now deciding against having their names associated with such an action.

Although only a small portion of the group, including Taylor, was still willing to risk arrest, the whole group marched to the police station from the church, singing as they went. "We went to the doors, knelt and just sort of prayed," Taylor said. "We didn't know what was going to happen."

Instead of getting arrested, the group was asked to come in to meet with local elected officials and police. State attorney Angela Corey, who had been appointed as special prosecutor in the case in March, was on the phone. And after an hour or so, Taylor said, they were told Zimmerman would be arrested. There would be an investigation into the Stand Your Ground law. The direct action, coupled with the intensifying national protest and 2 million petition signatures, had finally brought the local officials around.

It felt like a tremendous victory to them. But to some members of the Sanford community, it wasn't so simple. Many felt disempowered by an outside group coming in to take action. The group that would become the Dream Defenders realized, Taylor said, that in the future they wanted to help give people the skills they would need to fight their own battles.

Zimmerman was arrested on April 11 and charged with second-degree murder. Nelini Stamp went back to New York to pack her bags. "I'm moving to Florida for a while," she told me at the time. "I think what's happening there could be the new SNCC."

It was not that Trayvon Martin was more deserving of these protests than any other young black man dead at the hands of a guardian of order, self-appointed or official. Indeed, as Ciara Taylor said, the protests were for everyone—they were for thousands of lost futures as much as they were for Trayvon's. The networks were in place that allowed these protests to take off: the infrastructure of the Internet, which allowed more people than ever to plan and communicate with one another quickly, and the networks of trust formed through earlier protests, which then brought in new people and their own social networks. And it was not that George Zimmerman shot a teenage boy in a hoodie because of the lousy economy or a black president, but that the tensions were stretched to the breaking point already, with people's anger, fueled by repeated social breakdowns, driving them to take sides.

"The economic downturn and the election of the first African American president present unique drivers for right-wing radicalization and recruitment," warned a 2009 US Department of Homeland Security report. Among the examples it cited was the shooting of three police officers in Pittsburgh by a man influenced by racist ideology. Border militias expanded, fueled by fear and anger at immigrants from Latin America, who were perceived as taking American jobs. In May 2009, white supremacists Shawna Forde, Jason Eugene Bush, and Albert Gaxiola killed nine-year-old Brisenia Flores and her father in a robbery that Forde had planned; she intended to use the stolen money to fund her Minutemen American Defense group. Brisenia's mother was shot during the raid and heard her daughter plead for her life; the invaders had pretended to be law enforcement when they knocked on the door.[12]

It's impossible to trace specific acts of violence to any particular inflamed rhetoric, but there is no doubt that heated debate after 2008 had violent undertones. On March 23, 2010, Sarah Palin Tweeted "Don't retreat, instead—RELOAD!" with a map of "targeted" election districts in the crosshairs of a gun. That rhetoric exploded on the 2016 campaign trail, where Donald Trump's calls for deporting undocumented immigrants and registering Muslims for surveillance led to rallies where black protesters and reporters were punched and dragged out by security. Trump declared at one campaign stop, "I could stand in the middle of Fifth Avenue and shoot somebody, and I wouldn't lose any voters, OK?" Actual violence seemed to be lurking around every corner, from a stepped-up rate of mass shootings (including one on January 8, 2011, that nearly killed Congresswoman Gabrielle Giffords [D-AZ], who had been on Palin's map and whose opponent in 2010 had held an event to "Get on Target for Victory in November" by shooting a fully automatic M16) to the deaths of Trayvon Martin, Jordan Davis (a black seventeen-year-old shot at a gas station in Jacksonville, Florida, by a man who wanted him to turn his music down, November 23, 2012), and Renisha McBride (a black nineteen-year-old shot while knocking on a stranger's door for help in a Detroit suburb on November 2, 2013). Inflamed rhetoric ran high, while actual security—the economic kind that allows one to pay the bills—was in short supply; for those who already saw their gun as the thin line of defense between themselves and government tyranny or encroaching hordes of immigrants, the grip on the trigger might be even tighter.[13]

In times of economic crisis, producerist beliefs often take on a nastier tone than usual as more people begin blaming the "moochers" off the state for the broader condition of the economy. Such scapegoating can easily adopt racist language, and after the election of President Obama, it did: many believed "Obamacare," for example, to be a handout from the black president to black and brown people; others considered the stimulus package to be a handout to the undeserving, a measure that left the (white) middle class to fend for itself. In that space, existing white supremacist groups won new converts.

Groups like the Council of Conservative Citizens, a descendant of the white Citizens' Councils founded in the civil rights era to battle desegregation, had a resurgence, fueled in part by the Tea Party movement. Gordon Baum, the leader of the CCC until his death in 2015, claimed that the organization saw its most dramatic growth after Obama's election. "Our nose is being rubbed into the fact that Obama's black and we better all recognize the fact that he's a black man and he's our president," Baum complained.[14]

The Citizens' Councils were created in Mississippi just after the 1954 US Supreme Court *Brown v. Board of Education* decision desegregated the schools. They were made up of self-proclaimed "concerned and patriotic citizens" fighting "communism and mongrelization." Scholar Charles Payne described them as "pursuing the agenda of the Klan with the demeanor of the Rotary Club." When Baum went to build his new organization, the CCC, it was the mailing list of the Citizens' Councils that he used—he'd been their Midwest field organizer.[15]

The distaste for talking about racism in the United States allowed groups like this to operate under the radar, and they were able to recruit people who might otherwise have avoided them had they been more up-front about their beliefs. That "demeanor of the Rotary Club" gave them a veneer of respectability that was important. Scholar of right-wing populism Chip Berlet argued that people like J. D. Meadows might have joined another organization if there had been one available that found a way to talk to people like him about their economic troubles. And on the other side, when liberal organizations and pundits acquiesce to the idea of a "color-blind" nation and time, they allow everyone to act as if racism is a thing of the past, to pretend that the structures of slavery and Jim Crow have left no marks on our current economy, and to detach phrases like "states' rights" from their deep connection to secession and George Wallace in the schoolhouse door, keeping black students out of the University of Alabama.[16]

We forget the violence that was used to maintain structures of racism, that race as we now understand it was created by violent acts. Most people, if prodded, will mouth the truism that "race is a social construction," often in service of the idea that race is over if we want it to be, that anyone who brings up the persistence of racism is in fact the one perpetuating it. If American society is unequal, we want to believe it is because some people simply aren't working hard enough. Never mind the ferocious irony contained in believing that the descendants of people brought here as slaves to labor for decades under the constant bite of the lash have not worked enough. We did not see the violence that created and maintained slavery, and color-blind ideology allows us to pretend not to see the violence that continues to maintain inequality.

When we say "race is a social construction," what we mean is that there is no biological distinction, no scientific reason, to think that people with brown skin are different from people with white skin. But what "social construction" also means is that European settlers in this country needed a justification for dispossessing the people who were already here of their land and their very lives, and needed another justification for why certain people were slaves and others were not. Racism, as scholars Barbara Fields and Karen Fields wrote, created our idea of race, not the other way around. It was created in order to build the structures that produced wealth for those settlers, the wealth that has been handed down through generations in this country.[17]

Racism—and racist violence—maintains race even today. W. E. B. Du Bois concluded in 1923 that what made a person black was that he "must ride 'Jim Crow' in Georgia." The boundaries might be more porous to-day; we cannot say in the same way that a black person is one who is pushed into a subprime loan when she qualifies for a prime one, or that a black person is one who can be killed by police with impunity, though both of those things are much more likely to happen to black people than they are to white people. But Du Bois's description reminds us of the force required. It would have been impossible for Trayvon Martin to argue with George Zimmerman that he did not identify as black, that he was post-racial, when the gun was aimed at his head. There might have been no law that prevented Martin and his father from living in a mostly white suburb, but that didn't stop Zimmerman from feeling justified in using force to try to eject him from it.[18]

"Everyone has skin color, but not everyone's skin color counts as race, let alone as evidence of criminal conduct," the Fieldses wrote. "The missing step between someone's physical appearance and an invidious outcome is the practice of a double standard: in a word, racism." The belief in "race" as a fixed category disappears this racism, leaving even the most well-meaning people writing sentences such as "her real crime was to be black" when discussing the pointless arrest of a young woman. Blackness is not a crime, and we know that, but somehow to write "the real problem was that the police officer was steeped in the beliefs of American racism" is too much.[19]

Without an understanding of power and who wields it, some argue that the existence of black churches is equivalent to the establishment of Jim Crow laws. Yet on June 17, 2015, the Reverend Clementa Pinck-ney and eleven of his congregants at Emanuel AME Church in Charles-ton, South Carolina, demonstrated the difference when they welcomed a young white man to their Bible study meeting. The young man sat with them for an hour before pulling out a gun and shooting nine of them dead. Dylann Roof decorated his car and clothing with the flags of white supremacist regimes: Rhodesia, South Africa, the American Confederacy. He'd been turned on to white supremacy, a manifesto traced to him explained, when he found the website of the Council of Conservative Citizens while trawling the Web after the death of Trayvon Martin.[20]

Politicians scrambled in the days after Roof's manifesto was discov-ered to give back political donations they'd received from the president of the CCC. The Confederate flag, which still waved in front of the South Carolina Capitol, had been a battleground in the state for decades, since it was raised in the days after the *Brown* decision. Protesters thronged outside of the Capitol, demanding the flag's removal, in the summer of 2015. A South Carolinian who showed up to defend the flag, John Anthony Miller, said his grandfathers had fought under it. "I had no use for the flag being on top of the Capitol. It did not belong there. That was put up there for spite," he acknowledged, but he argued that he was hurt that people wanted the flag removed from the grounds. "Last time I checked these grounds are a museum," he said. "This is a war memorial for my grandparents. That's a memorial for those who died for what they believed in . . . states' rights, having stuff crammed down their throats by the federal government."[21]

Miller decried Dylann Roof's violent acts, and decried racism, but he wanted to maintain the flag and went and spoke with the other side; online, behind anonymous comments, others declared support for the flag in more vicious terms. "Here we see a moderately-sized clique of primitive savages, and a few White Leftist bottom-feeders, launching a tribal raid on a group of Southerners attempting to defend their heritage from cultural genocide," one blog wrote of a group of counter-protesters at a Confederate flag rally. Brian Pace wrote a letter to his local paper arguing that Mississippi should keep the Confederate battle flag on its state flag and identifying himself as the president of something called the European American Front. The pro-flag rallies spread, spiked by the removal of the flag from the South Carolina Capitol. The first removal was carried out in civil disobedience on June 27, 2015, by North Carolina organizer Bree Newsome, who scaled the flagpole and brought down the flag, risking a jail sentence alongside her ally James Ian Tyson. The second time, on July 10, was by the vote of the South Carolina state legislature. Debate about Confederate flags and memorials continued to rage, reaching well beyond the South—students protested Yale's Calhoun College, named for a famous alumnus and relentless battler for the spread of slavery, John C. Calhoun, and were waved off as unserious by commentators on both sides of the aisle. It is easy to decry racism in the wake of a brutal, blatant attack; it is harder to shake the way such beliefs wind their way into mainstream politics and into our culture's most venerated institutions.[22]

VIOLENCE WAS EMBEDDED IN THE UNITED STATES' POLITICAL AND economic systems from the very beginning. It took violence to take the land, violence to move African people here and hold them as slaves, and violence to make them work and to force them to innovate, and get more productive each year. That violence is embedded in the Constitution if you know where to look for it: in the language counting slaves as three-fifths of a person, for example, and in the amendment linking imprisonment to slavery at the moment of its abolition ("Neither slavery nor involuntary servitude, except as a punishment for crime whereof the party shall have been duly convicted . . . ").

The way we talk about the effects of racism today can make it seem as though it is a hate that simply happened rather than an ideology developed to justify keeping millions of people (around 20 percent of the population in 1800) in forced labor. That labor produced the main raw commodity of the industrial revolution. Slavery created massive wealth for many people—not just the direct enslavers of other people, but factory and mill owners, retail salespeople, speculators, and perhaps most importantly, financiers. And when it ended, though the slaves were free, the rest of that wealth was not distributed back to the people who had created it. The legacy of inequality remains.[23]

It was in the interests of the wealthiest planters to encourage as many white people as possible to own slaves; it ensured that even if they had little else, they had the feeling of belonging to the white upper class. And many others, including in places like London and New York, where slavery was abolished fairly early on, sunk their money into bonds made by securitizing slaves—humans who were still working on plantations, but who were mortgaged to raise capital by their owners in a process that historian Edward E. Baptist likened to the home mortgage–backed financial products that created the financial crisis of 2008. Companies like Lehman Brothers, which collapsed in 2008 and kick-started that crisis, got their start providing capital to slaveholders. Slavery was not a system outside of modern capitalism; it helped to build it.[24]

It took violence to end slavery, too, the massive bloodshed of the Civil War, in which more than 600,000 people died. It took federal troops stationed across the South after the war's end to allow black people some semblance of actual freedom. Underlying the rationale for expanding and perpetuating slavery had also been the fear of slaves' retribution, a fear concretized by the Haitian Revolution, where black people rose up and drove out their enslavers. It was that fear—as well as by then deeply inculcated racist beliefs that reiterated, despite the end of slavery, that black people were not whites' equals, that they were capable only of hard labor or brute violence—that led to the organization of groups like the Ku Klux Klan, which aimed to maintain white supremacy through violence.

While many of the laws that were set up under the Jim Crow regime explicitly to prevent black people from exercising political rights, such as poll taxes and literacy requirements, also disenfranchised poor white people, the group violence of lynching allowed those white people a way to feel like citizens who were invested in protecting the security of their communities, according to historian Robin D. G. Kelley. Lynching not only served to terrorize black people out of making demands—for higher wages, for voting rights, for reparations, for a share of the wealth they'd created—but also helped create a unifying "white" identity, one that expanded to take on the European immigrant groups who came to the country in waves before and after the Civil War. That white identity served as what Du Bois called a "public and psychological wage," a supplement to the meager wages that the so-called "white working class" was paid. Even the word "boss," borrowed from the Dutch, was used so that white workers could differentiate themselves from slaves—slaves had "masters," while free white workers had a boss.[25]

In order to push for economic advancement and political rights, former slaves and their descendants had to challenge a justice system that was mostly based on mob rule. "Black Codes" criminalized the tiniest of infractions, including vagrancy, absence from work, insulting white people, and perhaps notably, the possession of guns (and have their echoes in today's "broken windows" policing).[26]

Discrimination was written into the New Deal's labor laws: farmworkers and domestic workers—mostly black men and black women, respectively, at the time, and work that had been done, until emancipation, by slaves—were left out of the protections of the Fair Labor Standards Act (FLSA, 1938) and the National Labor Relations Act (NLRA, 1935), making them ineligible for the protections of a union and for minimum wage and overtime pay. These exclusions and others were not explicitly racist, as their implicit racism would spill over to affect non-black workers in these fields, but the exclusions disproportion-ately affected people of color, and they would last well beyond the civil rights era, and are still having an effect today.[27]

With labor unions given official sanction by the NLRA in 1935, the labor movement grew exponentially, but even outside of the South it was lukewarm about organizing black wage workers. Communist organizers argued that excluding black people from unions would drag down wages and conditions for all by undercutting the contracts that unions won, but others simply refused to admit black workers. Even famously pro-gressive leaders, like those in United Auto Workers Local 600 at the Ford River Rouge plant outside of Detroit, faced impromptu wildcat strikes in the 1940s by white workers when black employees were transferred into all-white units. Operation Dixie, the major attempt of the Congress of Industrial Organizations to organize the nonunion workplaces of the South, foundered in the early 1950s on its inability to break down the resistance of white people to interracial unionism and its unwillingness to challenge the racist violence that black workers still faced. As a result, the South remained mostly unorganized. Pretending racism didn't exist, it turned out, was a poor strategy for bringing black and white workers together. Antiunion right-to-work laws were pushed through in most southern states, promoted with explicitly racist language by people like Vance Muse and his "Christian American Association." Muse argued, "From now on, white women and white men will be forced into organi-zations with black African apes whom they will have to call 'brother' or lose their jobs."[28]

In the face of all this oppression, the decision of what we now know as the civil rights movement to embrace nonviolence as a strategy can seem even more amazing, but it also makes a particular kind of sense. Surrounded by white people with guns and a criminal legal system that mostly served to lock them up or kill them after sham trials (all-white ju-ries, of course, were common, as denying black people the right to even register to vote kept them off jury rolls as well), black people could have little hope of winning an armed conflict. Yet as Charles E. Cobb Jr., jour-nalist, professor, and former Student Nonviolent Coordinating Commit-tee activist, wrote in his book *This Nonviolent Stuff'll Get You Killed*, armed self-defense was also a part of the struggle. And it began not among the Black Panthers or with Malcolm X, but among tenant farmers and grandmothers in the rural South, where a gun wouldn't win you equality but might stave off the lynch mob. As one farmer explained to nonviolent organizers, "I wasn't being non-nonviolent; I was just protecting my family." Others tartly noted that nonviolent strategies were being taught all over black communities, while no one had volunteered to teach nonviolence to the Klan.[29]

The rights won by the civil rights movement guaranteed some measure of protection for black people's political rights, access to the ballot, and some measure of justice through fewer all-white juries. The schools were legally desegregated; George Wallace had to step out of that schoolhouse door and let the black students through. But Wallace and others managed to ride a wave of white resentment of desegregation and a newly rocky economy to new prominence. The Confederate flag was raised again over the South Carolina capitol in 1962 in defiance of desegregation, a symbol of the backlash to the black freedom struggle. Martin Luther King Jr. was killed in Memphis, where he'd gone to join sanitation workers whose strike slogan, "I am a man," was echoed in 2013 by fast food strikers in New York.[30]

Desegregation and affirmative action hit just as the economy skidded downward. White workers didn't want to hear that they'd had the benefits of the affirmative action of whiteness for decades when they were hunting for a job. As historian Jefferson Cowie wrote, "diversity arrived to American industry just as industry was leaving America," and the answers from politicians often made things worse. The truck drivers who moved freight at the nation's ports had been a strong, unionized, mostly white male workforce, but rather than pushing the unions to accept women and workers of color while maintaining a standard of living, elected officials chose to deregulate the industry, allowing bosses to classify the drivers as "independent contractors" who were responsible for maintaining their own trucks. The quality of the work and the take-home pay plummeted just as black workers and women were allowed in—and that story was repeated around the country.[31]

There was a brief attempt at fixing this problem in the late 1970s, as Senator Hubert Humphrey (D-MN) and Congressman Augustus Hawkins (D-CA) pushed forward a bill that would, in its original incarnation, have created an extensive apparatus for ensuring full employment. The bill was to provide the universal right to a job, and to do so it would have required the US government to do something like economic planning, an idea that turned out to be a bridge too far for members of Congress steeped in anticommunism. The bill was mostly defanged, and the version that was passed in 1978 had little effect.[32]

And so scarcity continued to inflame racist feelings as the economy began to take the shape with which we are now familiar. Incomes for those at the top continued to grow, and everyone else was forced to make do with less. While some tried to organize across race lines—Jobs or Income Now and the Young Patriots in Chicago worked alongside the Black Panthers on issues like police brutality as well as economic justice—too many others were susceptible to the charms of Ronald Reagan. Reagan put a smiling face on cuts to the welfare payments that supported so many, white as well as black, through economic rough patches. And too many were won over by the strategies of Republican campaigner Lee Atwater, who explained in 1981, referring to the infamous "southern strategy": "You start out in 1954 by saying, 'Nigger, nigger, nigger.' By 1968 you can't say 'nigger'—that hurts you. Backfires. So you say stuff like forced busing, states' rights and all that stuff. You're getting so abstract now you're talking about cutting taxes, and all these things you're talking about are totally economic things and a by-product of them is blacks get hurt worse than whites. And subconsciously maybe that is part of it."[33]

IT WAS THE VIOLENCE OF SLAVERY, THE VIOLENCE OF A WHITE SU-premacist regime enforced with burning crosses, lynch ropes and bullets, and a racist legal regime on top of it, that left black families with dramatically less wealth than white ones, right up to the present. As Robin D. G. Kelley said, these ideologies structured capitalism in the United States, and those effects are still with us today. The lowest that the black-white wealth gap ever got was in 1995, when the ratio between the median white and black households in terms of wealth was seven to one. Then the 2008 financial crisis wiped out about half of black wealth.[34]

Most of that wealth was in homes. For decades, policies and predatory sellers combined to ensure that when black families did manage to buy homes, they still wound up with less equity, less appreciation, and less of a financial safety net stored away in those homes. The Federal Housing

Administration was created by the same New Deal administration that left black farmworkers and domestic workers out of labor protections, and like the labor laws, it wrote black people out of the gains that families would make from its backing of private mortgages. Its decision to insure a mortgage would lower interest rates and down-payment sizes, but that decision would be based on the home's location on a map, which rated neighborhoods A through D—A was the best, D was where mostly black people lived. Those areas were colored red; thus the term "redlining."

It wasn't that you couldn't buy a home without FHA insurance. It just opened you up to a host of predatory schemes. Speculators bought up cheap properties in black neighborhoods and sold them "on contract" to black buyers, a process by which the seller held on to the title, and if the buyer missed a single payment, forfeited everything they had put into "their" home. The home that they had hoped would allow them to build wealth instead took all they had.[35]

In those redlined neighborhoods, public services were lax and private businesses unlikely to invest. Public schools, which draw their funding from property tax revenue, were underfunded. Redlining was officially outlawed by the Fair Housing Act of 1968, and activists pushed for the 1977 Community Reinvestment Act (CRA), which required federally in-sured banks to lend in the low-income neighborhoods where they took deposits, to make up for some of the damages done by decades of rac-ist policy. But all the CRA did was ensure that qualified borrowers were not shut out of mortgages because of their neighborhood. It could not replace the generations of wealth that the black working class had been denied.[36]

By 2005, the median black household had a net worth of $12,124; for white families it was $134,992. Home equity was the lion's share of that wealth, some 59 percent for black families. The disparity in homeowner-ship between black and white families was 25 percent in 2007. And then the housing bubble burst, exposing what journalist Kai Wright called "the myth of the black middle class." People who had just begun to have the trappings of a middle-class living, who had bought a home, were making payments, and had a decent job, but nothing put away in case of emergency, were wiped out when the layoffs began. When their home values plunged, what little they had was gone, and if their jobs disap-peared, they had no way to keep making payments.[37]

The social safety net that many people might have relied on in rough times had been gutted; "welfare reform" (what President Bill Clinton glowingly called "end[ing] welfare as we know it") had arrived, following a campaign loaded with racist stereotypes, alongside the deregulation of the financial industry that allowed for the growth of the speculative bubble, which was inflated by financial products made out of mortgages. People of color, regardless of income, were steered into subprime loans, often in the same neighborhoods that had been previously redlined. Wells Fargo paid out more than $175 million to settle allegations that it had pushed black and Latino borrowers into subprime mortgages when white people with similar credit and incomes were given normal "prime" loans.[38]

Perhaps the worst part of the subprime scam was that large numbers of those loans were refinances of existing mortgages, and many of those probably unnecessary. "A lot of our older African-Americans were house rich but cash poor. So lenders came up with these scams to siphon the wealth away," Center for Responsible Lending researcher Nikitra Bailey told Kai Wright. Around the country, 57.5 percent of refinance loans to low-income African Americans were subprime, as were 54.3 percent to moderate-income black borrowers. These predatory loans stripped what wealth existed in these communities, so recently hard-won, and put it back into the pockets of wealthy lenders. By 2009, the median black family had just $5,677 in wealth; the white median was still over $100,000. Black homeownership was down to 44 percent.[39]

This raiding of black wealth would have been bad enough without a crash, if homeowners were simply paying too much interest, struggling to keep up with variable-rate mortgages. But when the crisis hit, black unemployment went through the roof—and at the best of times, it has always been higher than the rate for white workers. Back in 2007, when the unemployment rate for white workers was 3.9 percent, it was 8.2 percent for black people. By 2009, black unemployment was near 15 percent; in the spring of 2011, two years into the supposed recovery, it was still higher, over 16 percent. Even black workers with college degrees were twice as likely to be unemployed as white workers with college degrees. Wages, too, were already lower for black workers. By 2015, the actual number of black children in poverty, 4.2 million, was higher than the number of white children in poverty, 4.1 million, despite the fact that there are more than three times as many white children in the United States.[40]

The history of redlining and white flight from the cities turned neighborhoods into disaster zones, and those neighborhoods were where the double whammy of job loss and foreclosure hit the hardest. In Baltimore's Sandtown-Winchester and Harlem Park neighborhoods, the unemployment rate in 2011 was one in five, almost twice that of the whole city, and about a third of the residents lived below the poverty line. Almost a quarter of the neighborhood's buildings were vacant, and the ones that were occupied were health hazards—the neighborhood had three times more lead paint violations than the rest of Baltimore. Freddie Gray grew up in Sandtown-Winchester and suffered lead paint poisoning as a child; at age twenty-five, he was killed in the back of a police van. In neighborhoods like Gray's, interactions with the police for low-level infractions are all too common, the only solution the state seems to have for rampant poverty. In "those neighborhoods," black and brown people get arrested for violations like "obstructing pedestrian traffic," and the excuse given is that "those neighborhoods" are where the crime is.[41]

It's not enough that people like Gray were blamed for their own deaths, for being in the wrong place at the wrong time with brown skin. The people in "those neighborhoods" were also blamed for causing the entire financial crisis, a shift of blame that would have been laughable if it hadn't been nearly pulled off by a whole chorus of sanctimonious columnists and congressmen intoning pieties about "moral hazard" and people signing up for mortgages they couldn't afford. "Political correctness," they said, was to blame for the collapse, because lower-income people simply couldn't be trusted to own homes.[42]

The Community Reinvestment Act was the target of their ire, although, as many pointed out, the biggest subprime lenders were private-sector companies that were not subjected to the rules of the CRA. It is also worth noting that the idea of the "ownership society," of getting every person to own a home as a way of involving them personally in American capitalism, was as dear to the hearts of Republicans like George W. Bush as it was to Democrats like Jimmy Carter, who signed the CRA into law. But what those arguments really meant was that the people who finally got mortgages after the government stepped in had been unworthy of that effort, that in fact they had deserved all along to be shut out of the process, that racism had had nothing to do with it. Such an argument not only washed clean the hands of banks like

Wells Fargo but absolved all of the architects of redlining as well as the lenders who managed to profit from it.[43]

Shifting the blame served to make those who escaped relatively unscathed from the recession feel better about their good choices, and to feel less inclined to share what they had to make the victims of the crisis whole. And since the implicit message behind so much of the victim-blaming was that trying to help black people only made things worse for everyone, it was okay to simply write them off instead.[44]

In this context, with what little wealth black communities had been able to amass crumbling away, and demagogues blaming them for their own suffering, the death of Trayvon Martin took on a meaning that was larger than life. It spurred people around the country into action. And in the context of protests around the country against inequality, activists began to connect the violence they faced with the economic crisis that had been ongoing, even permanent, among black people.

CHARLENE CARRUTHERS REMEMBERED RIGHT WHERE SHE HAD BEEN when the verdict in George Zimmerman's trial for shooting Trayvon Martin came down. At the time, she was still director of digital engagement at National People's Action. Cathy Cohen, founder of the Black Youth Project, had called a convening to discuss what black youth organizing could look like, a gathering of one hundred young black activists from around the country, in the summer of 2013. And on July 13, 2013, the Zimmerman verdict was announced while they were together: not guilty.

Out of that moment of collective trauma, they formed the BYP 100. Carruthers began devoting herself full-time to building an organization that would create a new vision of justice, one that didn't depend on the courts, and that would bring a black feminist and queer lens to its work for racial and economic justice. "I wholeheartedly believe that if we were not together in that particular moment, this organization wouldn't exist," Carruthers said.

Ciara Taylor was in Jacksonville when the news broke. She watched on social media as hundreds of people Tweeted their grief. Calls to action came from students at her alma mater, and hundreds rallied at the Florida Capitol. She was political director for the Dream Defenders, who were at the time scattered across the state, organizing in different regions around the school-to-prison pipeline and racial profiling, issues they had seen at work in the story of Trayvon Martin.

In the intervening year, they had registered voters alongside Vote-Mob and the League of Women Voters. They had also committed civil disobedience outside the Boca Raton, Florida, presidential debate, demanding that the candidates speak on immigration and privately owned detention centers, police brutality, education, living wages, and criminalization of drugs—issues that had been largely missing from the campaign season. Taylor found the voting work frustrating. Many people, she said, were simply turned off by the entire process, feeling disempowered. "Nobody wants to vote," Nelini Stamp agreed. "People are saying no, you're not representing me, the electoral system in this country has been broken for a while. It was born broken."

But although people didn't want to vote, and turnout remained low, more and more people seemed willing to come out for big protests. In New York, before she'd moved to Florida, Stamp helped organize a massive silent march—a tactic first used by the NAACP in 1917 to protest lynchings in East St. Louis—against stop-and-frisk tactics. It brought together labor unions like 1199 SEIU, the NAACP, the American Civil Liberties Union (ACLU), elected officials, community activists, and occupiers, who flooded Fifth Avenue in opposition to the policy. To Stamp, the fact that the mainstream organizations were willing to take part in an unpermitted march down a street where protests were usually not allowed represented a step forward.[45]

Alicia Garza had been an activist since she was twelve, at first around sex education and reproductive justice, and then in college around issues of race and class. In 2013 she took a job with the National Domestic Workers Alliance, organizing a group of mostly women workers who were still held back by the connections of their work with slavery and their racist exclusion from the New Deal. At previous moments in her lifetime, activism had surged around police violence, and in particular, around the killings of Amadou Diallo and Sean Bell and the beating of Rodney King. Garza, along with Patrisse Cullors and Opal Tometi, also longtime organizers, wanted to create something that would look different from the activism of generations past, where black organizing was often led by charismatic men of the church. After the Zimmerman verdict, they formed Black Lives Matter, initially as a set of online platforms meant to connect people to offline actions.

Around the nation, social-media-amplified anger and grief fueled protests. The Dream Defenders decided to do something more dramatic than a rally or a march. At a rally in Jacksonville—for Trayvon Martin and Jordan Davis, who had died in that city—they announced that they would be heading to the Capitol. "We couldn't really give people much more information than that. Partly because of security, partly because we didn't really know what we were going to do," Taylor laughed.

The Dream Defenders planned to demand a meeting with Governor Rick Scott to discuss the Stand Your Ground law, the school-to-prison pipeline, and racial profiling. Inside the Capitol, a receptionist told them the governor was unavailable, but they refused to leave. "When night came, there was a decision, do we leave or do we stay? We said we'll stay," Taylor said. "We didn't have food, water, things to sleep on. Next thing you know people who were with us, older people from our community, were just like, 'I'm going to buy you food and I'm going to buy you all water.' This woman came with sleeping bags. We understood the love that we had for our community, but I don't think we really understood the love our community had for the work that we were doing."

There was technically no law, at that point, that said they couldn't stay. On the third day, Taylor had to leave to go back to Jacksonville for a meeting, and that was the night that Governor Scott arrived. He showed the protesters his boots, which were adorned with the Confederate flag alongside the US flag, and told them there was nothing he could do. He suggested they organize a prayer vigil.[46]

Some of them may have prayed. But rather than leaving the decision to God or the governor, the Dream Defenders found a law that allowed citizens to petition lawmakers for a special session. They began organizing a letter-writing campaign to call for such a session and for lawmakers to pass "Trayvon's Law," which would amend the Stand Your Ground law, eliminate zero-tolerance policies, and end racial profiling. They also met with the Florida Department of Law Enforcement. During that time, they maintained a presence in the Capitol rotunda and in the hallway outside Scott's office, using the space as a training ground, giving workshops and building support. The actor Harry Belafonte joined them for a rally.

The Capitol guards, Taylor said, would try to drive them out, leaving the lights on at night, turning on loud music suddenly while they tried to sleep, or preventing people from bringing in supplies. Republican lawmakers refused to vote for the Dream Defenders' special session, instead passing a law against people staying in the Capitol in the future—nicknamed the "Dream Defender law." But the Dream Defenders called a "People's Session," inviting members of the community to vote on the policies that the legislators refused to vote on, and left with their heads high—on their terms, not Rick Scott's.

To Stamp, it had been a question of when, not if, a movement would go viral in the same way Occupy had. She knew the energy around stop-and-frisk and Trayvon would at some point turn into something more concrete. While not everyone surrounding the new racial justice movement was willing or able to risk arrest, the Dream Defenders' Capitol occupation was a symbol of a new militancy, a willingness to move beyond the boundaries of electoral politics. Activists held public spaces that for them held symbolic meaning while allowing them to disrupt business as usual—what John Lewis, when I spoke with him in the summer of 2013 as the Dream Defenders were still in the Capitol, called "finding a way to get in the way. Finding a way to get in trouble, good trouble, necessary trouble."

To Alicia Garza, what was new in that moment was "a real emphasis on leaderfull events, that have multiple leaders and that also aren't reliant on the charismatic leader to lead the masses to victory." The groups that emerged in the wake of Trayvon Martin's death often did have directors, founders, people with titles and official positions, but they still encouraged others to step up and organize actions and to expand their networks. They used social media not just to inform people about their actions but to share tactics and strategies, so that the work the Dream Defenders did in Florida or that the BYP 100 did in Chicago could be replicated elsewhere.

In 2013, Malaya Davis was recovering from the presidential elections. A student at Wright State University in Dayton, Ohio, she'd grown up in Cleveland very aware of her own race and class position. She had begun organizing with other black students, became president of the NAACP on campus, and then discovered the Ohio Student Association (OSA). The organization, which was born out of the successful fight against Ohio governor John Kasich's antiunion bill and the local Occupy movement, used language that seemed to fill a gap she had been missing in her own work. "Many oppressed people, we're told that power is something that we don't want to have, because we see it as something that is manipulative and something that is top-down—power *over*," she said. "I never had a real, intentional conversation about power *with* other people, and how power *with* folks and power *with* resources can build the type of things that we want."

OSA members had worked with the Dream Defenders and other student organizers to put on the National Student Power Convergence in the summer of 2012 in Columbus, Ohio. Kirin Kanakkanatt, project director at that convergence, joined the Florida Capitol occupation. She was part of a loose network of activists working on racial and economic justice that was coalescing. In the summer of 2013, just two weeks after the Dream Defenders left the Florida Capitol, many of them planned to attend the 50th Anniversary March on Washington and to be part of the actions around that event. The young organizers held a march on the American Legislative Exchange Council (ALEC), the conservative bill mill that had pushed Stand Your Ground model bills in several states, in conjunction with the anniversary commemoration, and umi selah of the Dream Defenders was scheduled to speak at the official march.

But at the last minute, selah and Sophia Campos from United We Dream were cut from the program—denied even the two minutes each had been allotted. To Davis, the omission was ridiculous. "We are talking about the fiftieth anniversary of the March on Washington and the entire time we were just commemorating the fifty years, as if there was no possibility that the next fifty years could even happen." The Dream Defenders released selah's speech online and encouraged young people to record their own two minutes. The clips of young black and brown people speaking about their work—their value to a movement that is happening now, that didn't end fifty years ago—resonated across the Internet and embodied a tension that would continue between the young activists (and quite a few movement elders who supported their work) and those who had gotten used to positions of power and a performative way of acting that had long ceased to produce results.

In the wake of the march, Nelini Stamp said, young activists decided to celebrate the fiftieth anniversary of Freedom Summer not with "pomp and circumstance," but with action. Members of BYP 100, of Dream Defenders, of OSA, United We Dream, and others came together to plan a network for actions. Freedom Side was born out of that meeting, a coalition of groups and individual activists of color who were committed to the fight for racial justice. "Together," their statement read, "we defiantly claim that our lives matter."

Kanakkanatt, who had just taken a job as field coordinator at LGBT organization GetEQUAL, helped craft their first statement, and she had conversations with some members of the group who had done little work with queer and transgender people. The important thing, she said, was that everyone came to Freedom Side with a spirit of openness and learning, an understanding that "we're fighting for these different political agendas, but actually what we're fighting for is for each of us to love each other fiercely." Malaya Davis agreed: "Solidarity is a verb."

Stamp left her job at the Working Families Party once again to be the coordinator for Freedom Side full-time, and they put together four anchor actions, in Mississippi, Florida, Ohio, and Texas. "The idea was for all of us to show up to each other's fights," she said, to model what "deep solidarity" might look like. They convened throughout the year, and many of them traveled to different states to support each other. Freedom Side allowed groups to coordinate, but also left them space to do different types of work, according to Charlene Carruthers. "It makes movement work more intersectional. And more open for many people to enter in different ways."

Direct action and disruption remained central to the movement. "We call it 'Stopping business as usual,'" Alicia Garza said. "It forces people to say 'Where do I stand? I don't get to be wishy-washy about this. I can't continue on with my life until I decide which side I am on.'" It is a declaration that the current system is intolerable and must be changed, and a demonstration of a different kind of power, a power that comes from a group of people acting together, challenging traditional figures of authority.

In July 2014, a Freedom Side group went to Nashville, Tennessee, to hold an action at the National Governors Association meeting, to challenge those governors about the criminalization of young people of color. That was the first time Malaya Davis had ever been arrested. "It shifted reality for me and for a lot of us in this work at that point," Davis said. They had not planned on being arrested, and so the larger network had to jump into action to react, to raise funds. "There was a graphic made within thirty minutes of us being detained. It was awesome. We were able to bring resources together and get five folks out of jail within six hours," she said.

Only a few days after Davis and the others got out of jail, on July 17, the news came that Eric Garner had been killed by a New York City police officer. Two weeks after that, on August 5, John Crawford III was shot by police in a Beavercreek, Ohio, Walmart, and just four days later, August 9, Michael Brown was shot and left for four hours in the street in Ferguson, Missouri. The response of young people in Ferguson was explosive, but it helped that there were networks in place of people who could help support them.

Davis and OSA began organizing actions to demand that police turn over the surveillance tapes from the Walmart store to Crawford's family. The videos, like the video of Eric Garner in New York, became central to the struggle, but also something of a double-edged sword. Videos existed of Garner's death, and of Crawford's death, but the officers in both cases were not indicted; meanwhile, the repeated exposure to videos of black people dying was both traumatic and desensitizing. Davis said, "If we allowed ourselves to react emotionally and physically and all these ways that a human being should react to these horrific instances, we would drive ourselves crazy."

The videos did serve, though, to remind people that racism was not just a southern problem, not just a Florida or Mississippi story. Historically, Davis pointed out, Ohio was the "safe state," a free state. "Folks who escaped slavery and migrated from the South, once you got to Ohio you were safe," she said. But every state in the nation was touched by slavery's reach and retains a history of racism. "Ohio has never been a safe space for people of color and for black people," Davis said. "Racism is something that we know transcends a geographic area of the country."

With the existing networks in place, it was easy for organizers to put out guidelines and templates for action, to host conference calls, and to create an initial list of demands. Those demands ranged from the specific—arrest or fire police officers who kill—to the broad-ranging, even revolutionary—end capitalism and white supremacy. To Nelini Stamp, having the smaller, more winnable demands was necessary to keep people moving forward, and backing up those demands with action created space for the bigger ones, what Robin D. G. Kelley called "transformative demands." Transformative demands attend to a specific crisis but then are ratcheted up to question the logic of the system itself—the system, in this case, of white supremacy. BYP 100, in the spring of 2016, released an "Agenda to Build Black Futures" that was an excellent example of such demands. The agenda included a demand to pass the Employment Non-Discrimination Act and for investigation by the Consumer Financial Protection Bureau of predatory mortgage lending; it also included reparations for slavery, mass incarceration, and redlining. It included a guaranteed living income regardless of employment. "I think we need to be very clear about what it is that we want. We want freedom, but what does that really mean?" Malaya Davis said. "If we can get to the point where we are naming and can explain the things that we want, then we can better figure out how we are going to get there."[47]

Challenging that system means ending the violence, whether it comes from the state in the form of police officers or from racist vigilantes like Dylann Roof. But it also means fighting for economic justice, as BYP 100 did with its Black Work Matters campaign and its Agenda to Build Black Futures. "When we think about economic justice, the Fight for $15, any workers' rights struggle," Carruthers said, "it is essential that racial justice and also gender justice is central to the analysis and also how folks attack their organizing." Nelini Stamp underscored the necessity of understanding white supremacy, capitalism, and patriarchy as intertwined systems that could also stand alone. The movement for black lives stressed the "white supremacy" part, but it was also acutely aware of how these systems intersect, and how black women like Rekia Boyd, shot in 2012 in Chicago by an off-duty police officer who was deemed "beyond reckless" by a judge, and black transgender women, like Islan Nettles, beaten to death in 2013 in Harlem while she was out walking with friends, were caught at the intersections.[48]

The networks that had begun after Trayvon Martin's death expanded to become something different altogether. From its beginnings as an online platform, Alicia Garza said, Black Lives Matter became an organizing network of local chapters—there were twenty-six of them as of 2015—"with a really radical analysis and a commitment to praxis in a way that I feel like I haven't seen in a really long time. Every single one of those chapters is moving a campaign on the ground that has clear demands and a clear target, analysis of how to build power."

The Dream Defenders, too, reorganized, going from a chapter model mostly based on college campuses to a more community-focused approach. Ciara Taylor's title became "director of political consciousness." She learned from traveling, studying movements in countries from Brazil to Palestine, and began to push for a way to talk about politics that went beyond the binary of Democrats and Republicans. "We're really trying to figure out how to develop our own organizing model for change," she said. "We're trying to make sure that we are eradicating any semblance of oppression from our means, and bringing people to a true place of understanding these issues and thereby being able to move forward, in collective strategy, where we're not having a few people dictate the direction of the movement."

After scaling the flagpole and taking down the Confederate flag in South Carolina, Bree Newsome put out a statement stating her lineage as an activist, beginning in North Carolina with Moral Mondays. She had joined the Dream Defenders in Florida and marched with the Ohio Students Association in the streets. She recalled her ancestors, sold in the slave market in Charleston. "This action required collective courage just as this movement requires collective courage," she said, thanking the group of people who planned and supported the action. It was a striking display of the values of the movement that trained her.[49]

It was necessary, Taylor said, to keep breaking down barriers that prevent more Bree Newsomes from taking action and stepping up to lead, barriers that include internalized sexism and racism as well as external pressures. Taylor said: "Until we address those barriers, until we address the unconscious behaviors, we're not going to be able to win, because you can't fight for justice and freedom and liberation if you don't believe you deserve it in the first place."

CHAPTER SIX

A MORAL MOVEMENT

B ARBARA SMALLEY-MCMAHAN REMEMBERED EXACTLY WHEN she had had enough. It was 2013, and the new state legislature in North Carolina had rolled out a series of bills that slashed funding to schools, health care, and unemployment insurance for thousands who were still jobless from the financial crisis, while starkly restricting access to the vote. The state legislature held a public forum that spring to allow legislators to hear from their constituents, and Smalley-McMahan resolved to go.

An ordained American Baptist minister who had spent thirty years as a pastoral counselor, Smalley-McMahan had been part of some protests in her youth, and more recently, she had volunteered for Barack Obama's presidential campaign. But mostly she preferred one-on-one settings. At the forum, though, as she watched over a hundred people get up and speak, she noticed that the legislators seemed more interested in their smartphones than in their constituents. "They would clearly text something and look across the way and laugh at each other and it really made me angry," she said in her soft southern accent. To see the disrespect they openly displayed—"I was undone," she said. Instead of speaking about public schools as she'd planned, she stood up and said, "When I was a kid, I used to have a nightmare that I was lying in the road in front of my house and one Mack truck after another was running over me and all I could do was dodge the wheels.'"

At that, she said, they put down their phones. She continued, "You rolled into town like a fleet of Mack trucks, loaded down with laws that you've intended to pass here, and those laws are intended to mow the people down. When I was a kid all I could do was dodge the wheels. But I'm not a kid anymore and neither is anybody else speaking before you today. We are adults and we are out in front of those Mack trucks and we're telling you to stop."

Shortly after that, another pastor, the Reverend William J. Barber II, called together a meeting of people who wanted to do more to challenge the legislators' agenda. The meeting was held at Pullen Memorial Baptist Church, where Smalley-McMahan was a member and where, back in 2002, the Reverend Nancy Petty became the first lesbian pastor to lead a Baptist church in the South. (The American Baptists have long been more progressive on gender and sexuality than the Southern Baptists.) That meeting led to another, a church service in the city of Durham. Smalley-McMahan didn't know when she arrived that the service was going to lead into a training for those willing to engage in civil disobedience. But when she found out, she thought, "Why not?"[1]

Rev. Barber had become president of the North Carolina NAACP in 2005, when Democrats still controlled the North Carolina legislature. To him, the advocacy groups in the state fighting for labor rights, for LGBT rights, for public schools, and for environmental and racial justice seemed disjointed. "We didn't need a new organization, but we needed to understand the intersectionality of all of our issues and make sure that we developed a way of working together that put antiracism, anti-poverty and pro-labor at the center of our work," he said. In 2006, he and some other leaders pulled together a meeting of fourteen organizations working on various issues, and from that meeting, they created a fourteen-point agenda.

They decided to hold annual "People's Assemblies" around that agenda in front of the state legislature's General Assembly, as well as local assemblies, and to come together to have a collective "People's Lobby Day," where people would be able to lobby for all of their issues at once. Inspired by the examples of Reconstruction, after the end of slavery, when Populists and Republicans came together in North Carolina, as well as the civil rights era, they aimed to build a fusion movement, a movement that brought people together in an understanding that their issues were connected, that they would only gain power by working together. After a few thousand people showed up to their first People's Assembly on a Saturday in February 2007, they marched to the General Assembly and, like Martin Luther with the theses that kicked off the Protestant Reformation in 1517, hung their agenda on the door. "In my speech that day," Rev. Barber said, "I said a new ethic was now being infused into the political veins of North Carolina. It was not about Democrat or Republican. It was about our deepest moral, our deepest constitutional values." Moral values had been the language of social conservatism for a long time, but to Rev. Barber, it was time to take that language back. He wanted to give people space to define moral values, whether it was through their faith or outside of faith.

That coalition had a few early wins, including the passage of a same-day voter registration bill that made it easier for people to access the ballot. Rev. Barber believed it helped drive up turnout in the presidential election of 2008; but democracy, not electing Democrats, was the goal.

In 2010, Republicans took back the state legislature with majorities in both houses, and they were able to redraw the legislative districts into what Rev. Barber called "the worst form of gerrymandering we've seen since the nineteenth century." The redistricting took back the small-d democratic gains the coalition had made. According to a *Washington Post* analysis, three of the ten most gerrymandered districts in the country were now in North Carolina. They packed the state's likely Democratic voters (including large swaths of the black population) into long, sprawling, odd-shaped districts that made no geographic sense. In 2012, Pat McCrory, the former mayor of Charlotte, who was viewed as a moderate Republican, won the governor's office. And with that, the Mack trucks of Barbara Smalley-McMahan's nightmares rolled in, slashing education funding, cutting unemployment benefits, and forcing through voting restrictions. That was when the burgeoning coalition decided it was time for a more disruptive strategy.[2]

Jacob Lerner and Ivanna Gonzalez first heard that the NAACP was planning civil disobedience at a meeting of Student Action with Workers (SAW), a campus student-labor alliance at the University of North Carolina at Chapel Hill, when they were both just weeks away from graduating. Laurel Ashton, a friend of theirs who worked with the NAACP, came to the meeting and told the gathered students that there would be a protest at the General Assembly that would involve civil disobedience. For both of them, that meeting was a turning point, but for different reasons. For Lerner, who had grown up in an activist family—both his parents and his brother are labor organizers—it had always been a question of when, not if, he would get arrested standing for something he believed in. North Carolina, though, was a place where he'd built his own community, away from the world he'd been raised in. The moment felt right.

For Gonzalez, the equation was different. She was nervous for the next couple of weeks after that meeting, trying to come to a decision about whether to participate. Born in Venezuela but raised in Miami, she had found her way to labor activism after a study abroad program in London that happened to coincide with a massive public-sector worker strike. That led her to SAW and to a whole new set of skills as an organizer. Yet even through major campus protests, she had avoided getting arrested. She worried about losing the job she had lined up after graduation, and a future with a criminal record, especially as an immigrant. The decision looming in front of her took on new significance. "This was the culmination of my undergraduate years," she laughed. "Not my finals, not my classes, but whether or not I was going to participate in this act of civil disobedience."

The first Moral Monday protest was just a few days later, April 29, 2013. Seventeen people, including Rev. Barber, were arrested blocking the doors to the General Assembly. The following week, the group doubled in size, and Barbara Smalley-McMahan was arrested for the first time in her life. Gonzalez still hadn't decided what she would do, and still worried about how she would explain an arrest to her family. But when she and Lerner arrived at the training meeting, and Rev. Barber began to speak, she said, "It felt like I had no other option. There was just so much going on that despite everything I felt like I had at play, I was still significantly more privileged and in a position to do this than a whole lot of other people."

The Moral Monday coalition had lawyers giving "know-your-rights" training to ensure that the participants were prepared. And then Gonzalez and Lerner were approached by an NAACP staffer, who asked if one of them would speak to the press to represent the young people present. Both Lerner and Gonzalez remember another woman leaning over and asking, "Ivanna, are you going to let a white man be the face of the movement?"

The speech she gave, Gonzalez remembers, was one that she wrote in three minutes on a napkin. Outside of the General Assembly, some six hundred supporters gathered for a rally, and then, two by two, those willing to be arrested walked inside, singing protest songs. Inside the building, Rev. Barber spoke, and then Gonzalez. She said: "I am here as a student to stand by the liberal arts education that made me who I am today. As a woman, I am here to declare that this body is mine. As an immigrant, I am here to remind everybody that at some point our families were from somewhere else. And as a human being, I am here because I know that the attacks on my gay friends, on the people that I love in immigrant detention centers, on the housekeepers on UNC's campus are all interconnected."[3]

Fifty-seven people were arrested that week, their hands zip-tied behind them. As they were loaded onto police buses, the crowd outside cheered their support for the protesters. Those who had been arrested were taken to the Wake County Detention Center, where they were booked on charges of trespassing and failure to disperse. Gonzalez remembered being pleased that the process seemed to be going quickly, but just before she was to find out what her bond was, she heard someone say, "Wait! Is that Ivanna? ICE needs to talk to her."[4]

She'd been warned by a friend, also an immigrant, that Immigration and Customs Enforcement might turn up. The friend had been arrested previously, and she had packed her passport to prove that she was a US citizen. When the officer asked Gonzalez, "Ma'am, are you here legally or illegally?" she replied, "I am an American citizen." She gave him her Social Security number and told him where to find her passport. Laughing wryly, she remembered the relief he expressed. "Glad this is a relief for *you*," she said.

But even after he retrieved her passport from her bag, he still took her fingerprints a second time. "That actually allowed me to have a more meaningful conversation with my parents," she said. "I had a cousin who was in immigrant detention at the time. He had been in for almost six or seven months, flipped like a Ping Pong ball in different jails all over

Florida. It was helpful to say this was what happened. I don't have an accent, I look like a white girl, and I have an American passport, and this is what happened to me when I was in there. This is partially why I did it."

For Gonzalez and many other Moral Monday arrestees, the experience itself was a chance to demonstrate the way that different issues intersected in their lives. Being a woman, a student, an immigrant, and a worker were all parts of her life, identities that couldn't be pulled apart. Those issues of racism and sexism, of economic and social rights, had to be addressed all at once, not out of an urge to be politically correct, or even simply to broaden the size of the coalition, but because they affect people at their intersections. Gonzalez could not separate the attacks on her bodily autonomy through the legislature's attempt to deny access to abortions from the attacks on her right to move freely as an immigrant. She could not separate the attacks on the programs at her university from the low wages paid to the workers at that same university.

When the arrestees were freed, they were greeted by supporters who came bearing home-cooked food and good cheer, the kind of "jail support" that can be as important as legal training. Eventually, Lerner said, the police streamlined the arrest process to speed Moral Monday arrestees through, because their numbers just kept increasing: in week five, 151 were arrested. By the end of the summer, there had been nearly 1,000 arrests, and the national media was paying attention to what was happening in North Carolina, in the oft-written-off South. The arrestees were black and white, clergy and professors, young activists like Lerner and Gonzalez as well as older people recently drawn into action, like Smalley-McMahan. The well-planned actions, the repetitive, almost ritualistic nature of the events, and the constant presence of the charismatic Rev. Barber helped to create an atmosphere where people felt comfortable facing arrest. The crowds did skew older and whiter, Lerner noted, and that probably influenced the way they were treated by the police—for young people of color, those like Gonzalez, the experience of challenging police is a very different and usually more violent one.

"What civil disobedience does is dramatize the seriousness, the shamefulness, and the urgency of the moral and economic failure," Rev. Barber said. "When we get arrested, we do it to arrest the consciousness of the state and to guarantee that what they are doing will not be done in the dark." For him and other people of faith who were involved in the protests, it was important to see their call for justice as a moral one, not simply a technocratic call for better policy or a partisan demand. They put their bodies on the line for what they believed was right and just. Moral Mondays drew the largest crowds that had ever come to a US state capital to take part in civil disobedience, said Rev. Barber, and they culminated in the largest march the South had seen since the famous 1965 Selma march for voting rights. The numbers seem all the more impressive when you consider that North Carolina cities are not particularly dense, that some people drove for hours to join a protest in Raleigh, and that unlike some northern states that have labor unions and community groups that regularly turn out members for marches, North Carolina had little in the way of infrastructure for protest.

"When I was in seminary we used to talk about the priestly and prophetic functions of ministry," Smalley-McMahan explained. "I always saw myself in the priestly function, sitting with people who felt disempowered. I felt very comfortable behind my closed door with my clients helping them find their own center and sense of self, and I thought that's where I would stay. But the number of laws those guys rolled out in 2013 pushed me over the edge. So then that gets into the prophetic, when you stand up to the powers that be and say no, what you're doing is abusive and it's not going to continue."

After the civil rights movement, Rev. Barber argued, advocates for a more equitable economic system, for an end to racism and sexism, gave up talking about morality, and those who opposed gay rights and abortion rights took up the framework. But to him, ending poverty, creating a green economy, ensuring that children can go to good public schools, protecting the right to vote, providing health care, and dismantling the system of mass incarceration are moral issues. "Personal matters are between you, your priest, your pastor, your imam," he said. "The issues in the public square that people of faith ought to be dealing with have to do with the common good."

Women's groups and LGBT organizations, as well as individual women and queer and transgender people, had been part of the Moral Mondays actions from early on, many of them inspired by Amendment 1, the ban on same-sex marriage passed in 2012 by North Carolina voters. In July, the legislature introduced the Faith, Family and Freedom Protection Act, which coupled restrictions on abortion providers with a ban on considering Islamic Sharia law in family courts. Moral Mondays were well-established by then, said Tara Romano, president of the board of North Carolina Women United (NCWU), a coalition of women's groups; there had even been a Women's Moral Monday to focus on the way the economy did not work for women. There was a bit of concern among some in the Moral Movement that centering on abortion would cause division, Romano said, but women made up such a large part of the coalition that it was impossible to ignore their role. Planned Parenthood took the lead in bringing people out, and on July 8, 2013, the Moral Movement put the issue of access to abortion front and center. Protesters in pink and purple T-shirts, with slogans like "Married Christian Man for Choice," singing "We Shall Not Be Moved" under the banner of "morals," presented a vastly different image from the one normally cast by those claiming to support "moral values."

To Romano, it was important for faith leaders like Rev. Barber to challenge the idea that the only people who placed moral values at the center of their politics were those who opposed gay rights and abortion. While marriage equality, she noted, could be a way of assimilating queer relationships into mainstream culture, and thus into a commonly understood "moral" paradigm, many people have a hard time considering access to abortion a moral value. And yet the need for abortion, and the right of those who might get pregnant to control their own bodies, do not happen in a vacuum—abortion, too, is an intersectional issue. It comes down, Romano said, to a question of, "Who really counts in North Carolina? They use the issues of voting rights and keeping you economically insecure and controlling reproductive rights as a way of making sure that you are never going to be one of those people that counts."

While many of the Moral Monday arrestees did community service to fulfill their sentences, often with organizations that had been part of the Moral Monday coalition to begin with (Gonzalez laughed that the state legislature, in its rush to crack down on the protesters, wound up strengthening its own opposition), Rev. Barber and other leaders within the Moral Movement took their movement on the road, "going after the consciousness of the state." In particular, Rev. Barber wanted to challenge the "southern strategy" of dividing white from black people around economic issues. The movement picked a few local struggles to join, in particular the battle over the closure of the Vidant Pungo Hospital in Belhaven. Rev. Barber was also invited to Mitchell County, a nearly entirely white county, mostly Republican, and known, he said, for being home to some paramilitary groups. At first, he wanted to refuse, but he eventually went and spoke to two hundred people, laying out his moral argument for health care and education. "Now we have seven branches of the NAACP in Western North Carolina that are all led by primarily white people, like it was in the early days of the NAACP," Rev. Barber said. "The liberal versus conservative, Democrat versus Republican, is too puny for where we are right now."[5]

The movement held a Mountain Moral Monday in Asheville, and even a Moral Monday in Yadkinville, a town of 2,800 people just west of Winston-Salem. Wooten Gough, an organizer with LGBTQ group GetEQUAL and cofounder of the immigrant rights group El Cambio in rural North Carolina, helped pull together the rural Moral Monday action, where about seventy-five people turned up. Members of El Cambio, undocumented workers from the area, and faith leaders from the NAACP all spoke.

Gough and others from Yadkin County took a bus back to Raleigh to join the massive Moral March to be held on February 8, 2014. In previous years, the march had been known as the Historic Thousands on Jones Street, but that year the turnout was higher than it had ever been. "That was, at least in my lifetime, the biggest statewide push for some kind of collectiveness," Gough said. "People in our area were taking an action who I have never seen taking action before."

William Barber III had planned to take a path for his life that was different from his father's—in college, he studied energy engineering. But growing up around Rev. Barber, he absorbed more than he'd thought, and when the General Assembly had proposed a voter ID bill that would ban students from voting where they attended school, he became involved with his college chapter of the NAACP. It was important to him not only to learn from movement elders, but also to forge his own path; when the March on Washington anniversary event excluded the voices of young organizers, he connected with Freedom Side, and he went on to help bring members of the network to the Moral March that February.

Kirin Kanakkanatt of Freedom Side and GetEQUAL was one of those who came down from New York for the march. It could have been like the March on Washington, she said, another parade with little connection to the present. There was a little of that in terms of who was speaking—Ivanna Gonzalez noted that she spoke as part of a relatively small "youth contingent." But what Kanakkanatt remembered the most was how queer-friendly it felt; how Planned Parenthood handed out pink beanies for the cold, which dotted the crowd; how rainbow flags flew everywhere. "That march felt better than any single Pride I've ever been to," she said.

THE REPUBLICAN WAVES OF ELECTION WINS, BEGINNING IN 2010, continuing to a lesser extent in 2012, and then increasing again in 2014, can mostly be chalked up to a floundering economy and a sense that the Democrats hadn't fixed things. The coalition that became the Moral Movement had begun when Democrats ran North Carolina, before the financial crisis exploded and exacerbated the struggles many people already faced. The conservative sweep in North Carolina was much like the one in Wisconsin: it was fueled by a promise of jobs, jobs, jobs—after he became governor in 2012, Pat McCrory even promised Rev. Barber and the coalition partners that he would focus on jobs.[6]

In North Carolina, there were no unions to scapegoat; despite decades of rule by the party that supposedly was friendly with organized labor, public school teachers and other public-sector workers in North Carolina still lacked the right to collective bargaining. By 2013, the employment rate had begun to creep upward from its crisis level, but recovery was still far too slow and for too few people. And then the new legislature came into office. Despite poverty rates of nearly 30 percent in parts of the state, and over 40 percent of black children living in poverty, the new legislature rolled back the Earned Income Tax Credit for 900,000 people, refused federal money to expand Medicaid, cut off unemployment benefits for 165,000 people, cut funding for prekindergarten, gave the wealthy a tax cut, and shifted nearly $1 billion from public schools to voucher programs to send students to private school. The outrageousness of the cuts spurred many people of faith who took the demands to care for the poor in their religions seriously to consider their moral obligations to act.[7]

The legislature topped all of that off with House Bill 589, which Rev. Barber called "the worst voter suppression bill we have seen since the days of Jim Crow." After the Supreme Court's decision in *Shelby*

County v. Holder ruled part of the 1965 Voting Rights Act unconstitutional—the section that required certain states and counties, including forty in North Carolina, to get clearance from the Justice Department before changing their election laws—the North Carolina legislators proved why the act had been necessary. They ended same-day registration, early voting, Sunday voting, the right of teenagers to preregister to vote, and out-of-precinct voting, and required state-issued photo IDs in order to vote. The Voting Rights Act was passed in order to protect the rights of black Americans to vote; the voter ID bills that sprang up around the country after the election of Obama were widely assumed to be designed to make it harder for black voters. There was certainly no economic rationale for making it harder to vote; the voter ID bills were about consolidating power. In a country with already-shrinking voter turnout levels, they were designed to put more barriers in the way of access to the ballot. All of this heightened the need for civil disobedience. Telling activists to "just go vote," when the legislature has made it much more difficult to do so, and your district lines are drawn to produce a party-line result, is insulting.

On top of the economic changes and voter rights changes, which already disproportionately hit people of color, queer and transgender people, and women, the new legislature took specific aim at abortion rights and, later, LGBT rights. When Governor McCrory, who continued to attempt to position himself as a moderate, threatened to veto the bill restricting abortion and banning Sharia law, the abortion restrictions were then snuck into a motorcycle safety bill (dubbed the "Motorcycle Vagina" bill). Opponents of the bill tried to connect its provisions with the denial of Medicaid to low-income people or the lack of sex education in schools, but were ruled off-topic by Thom Tillis, the state Speaker of the House, who went on to the US Senate in 2014. The simultaneous attacks on so many rights and freedoms at once, paired with budget cuts, helped cement the connections that the Moral Movement was trying to make.[8]

North Carolina wasn't the only place where so-called "social issues" came to the fore while the economy was still struggling. Ohio's John Kasich allowed an executive order banning discrimination in state employment based on sexuality or gender identity to expire; he later reinstated the ban on sexuality, but left out gender identity. In Wisconsin, Scott

Walker's 2011 budget slashed funding for contraceptives and reproductive health care; he later signed a bill that banned abortion after twenty weeks. In Congress, where the Tea Party wave of 2010 swept Republicans to power in the House of Representatives, two antiabortion bills were pushed through with the support of some Democrats. The No Taxpayer Funding for Abortion Act would have restricted funding to those who were victims of "forcible" rape, meaning that those who were drugged and raped, or who failed to physically resist hard enough, would no longer qualify for the rape and incest exception to the Hyde Amendment, which already prevented taxpayer funding for abortion. The Protect Life Act would have redefined "conscience" clauses for medical providers to allow them to let pregnant persons die if saving them would harm the fetus. Between 2010 and 2015, states enacted 215 different abortion restrictions. Moreover, in the first half of 2015 alone, more than 100 anti-LGBT bills had been filed in state legislatures around the country.[9]

The view among many for a while had been that such "social issues" were a distraction from the real issues and were being used to convince working-class people to vote against their own self-interest; the most prominent example of this argument was Thomas Frank's book *What's the Matter with Kansas?* But the push for anti-gay, antiabortion bills in the wake of a devastating financial crisis, with unemployment in many places in double digits, felt more like Naomi Klein's *The Shock Doctrine* in action, a way to pass restrictive bills that would hit already marginalized people while they were still reeling from the collapse of the economy. These bills, as Tara Romano argued, were a way of perpetuating inequalities, of defining who would and would not "count." The "culture war" was not just a wedge. It was a way of securing economic and political power.[10]

The push for abortion restrictions and opposition to gay rights was particularly notable because the biggest conservative movement at the time, the Tea Party, was ambivalent about such issues. While many Christian conservatives did become Tea Party activists, there were also plenty of what Theda Skocpol and Vanessa Williamson deemed "secular minded libertarians, who stress individual choice on cultural matters and want the Tea Party as a whole to give absolute priority to fiscal issues." There was often tension between Christian Tea Partiers and other Tea Party members around the government's role on so-called moral standards—one Tea Party leader even split her group into two, one

Christian and one secular. In a national poll in 2012, only 14 percent of Tea Party supporters had said that "social issues" were more important than economic ones.[11]

The separation of political issues into "social" and "economic" in any case is a false dichotomy, and the idea that one's economic self-interest has nothing to do with whether one can control one's own pregnancies or maintain a job without discrimination is simply wrong. "Social" issues serve to create and perpetuate inequality, erecting barriers to full participation in society for certain groups. They shape our idea of who is a full citizen, and they also shape the very real material conditions of people's lives. Those who would maintain hierarchies with themselves at the top are as interested in what political scientist Corey Robin called "the private life of power" as they are in hoarding riches; they pass bills to restrict the rights of women, workers, people of color, and queer and transgender people in order to maintain their own position.[12]

Angel Chandler, who at the time was an organizer with GetEQUAL and an abortion clinic escort in Asheville, North Carolina, reached out to me in 2011 after I wrote a series of articles profiling the Democrats in Congress who supported anti-choice and anti-gay legislation. Chandler's own congressman, Heath Shuler (D-NC), was one of them. "If you're fighting on one issue you're usually on the front lines about all of it," Chandler said. Democrats like Shuler, as I wrote in that series, were usually conservative on a host of issues, that is, conservative as Corey Robin explained it—patriarchal, militaristic, and opposed to the kind of government spending that helps poor people. And all of this gets painted as a commitment to "moral values." Shuler again is instructive: while he was in Congress, he lived in the C Street home of "The Family," a secretive elite religious organization founded in 1935 that opposed the New Deal and has ties to repressive governments around the world. Shuler was recruited to run for Congress as part of Democrats' outreach to people of faith.[13]

To Rev. Barber, that's where they went wrong—in assuming that people of faith are more like Shuler than like, say, himself. "Two thousand scriptures in the New Testament, the Old Testament, have to do with how you treat the poor, how you treat the stranger, how you treat women, how you treat children," he said. "Now, at best, there may be five or ten scriptures in the whole text that deal with homosexuality. None that deal with abortion. And the ones that deal with homosexuality do not negate that the ultimate call of scripture is to love your neighbor." Yet politicians and the media alike only call people of faith to talk about issues of sexuality; they assume that those are the "moral" values.

The Moral Movement was designed to challenge that ideology head-on. For Barbara Smalley-McMahan, it was time to remind people that "Jesus was about standing up, being radical, about empowering the people that were marginalized and taken advantage of by the Roman government. Exploited." The perpetuating of hierarchies of power, the construction of certain people and certain groups as "less than," she said, "needs to be dismantled."

IT HAS ONLY BEEN RELATIVELY RECENTLY THAT ABORTION AND GAY rights were assumed to be the major concerns of people of faith. For much of US history, when politicians took a stand based in their faith, it was likely to be a prophetic call for justice, for liberty, and for redistribution of wealth to the poor. The abolitionists, in challenging the institution of slavery, drew on a deeply moral language: it was an outrage to enslave and abuse another human. John Brown, the white abolitionist who was hanged for his 1859 raid on Harpers Ferry in an attempt to start a slave revolt, was driven by his faith, as was Nat Turner, a popular religious leader among his fellow slaves who in 1831 felt that God had called him to rebel and lead them to freedom. William Jennings Bryan, the early twentieth-century orator nominated for president by Democrats and Populists, used Christian imagery to deride what he saw as an obsession with profits over people: "Man, the handiwork of God, comes first; money, the handiwork of man, is of inferior importance."[14]

The famed "Scopes Monkey Trial" pitted Bryan against another Populist-identified attorney, Clarence Darrow, in a 1925 legal case over teaching the theory of evolution in the public schools in Tennessee. The trial helped drive a wedge between Christians and secularists, beginning a trend among urban secularists, often liberal, of mocking believers for their beliefs. It did not put an end, however, to calls for economic justice based in moral language. Eugene Debs, the labor leader and five-time Socialist Party presidential candidate, was known for his preacherly style and his ability to hold audiences rapt for hours as he appealed to their sense of justice on behalf of the working class.[15]

For nearly as long as economic reformers have appealed to moral values, there have been moral panics that revolved around controlling sexuality and what was considered "vice." Reformers like Anthony Comstock, of the New York Society for the Suppression of Vice, tried to stamp out prostitution and ban access to birth control (or even its mention). There was also a healthy dose of moralizing about the behavior of the poor among the Progressive-era reformers, arguments that were updated in the twentieth century into the "culture of poverty."

Anticommunists used moralistic language against the Communist Party's labor and voting-rights organizing among black workers, accusing the party of intending to nationalize white women and associating it with promiscuity, free love, and homosexuality. Queer people and communists both were seen as corrupting America's moral fiber, destroying families, and plotting to undermine the country.[16]

The civil rights movement, particularly the pieces of it that remain in the forefront of Americans' memories and in history classes, may be the most prominent justice movement in US history to rely heavily on biblical language and moral appeals. Rev. Martin Luther King Jr. and the other members of the Southern Christian Leadership Conference (SCLC) drew on skills they learned in the pulpit to captivate crowds, even while drawing upon the strategic talents of Bayard Rustin, who was openly gay and a former communist. J. Edgar Hoover at the Federal Bureau of Investigation tried to undermine King precisely by attacking him on moral grounds, threatening to out his extramarital affairs.

The kind of moral values that many Americans had assumed were universal did not hold up to the demands of the new social movements that sprang up in the 1960s. While the 1950s had been a time of conformity, with a record number of people marrying young and having children, the 1960s upended that ideal. The identity-based movements—Black Power, feminism, gay rights, Chicano rights, and more—challenged that image of America and reminded us that it had never been good for everyone, that there had always been people pushed to the margins. And what those movements wanted was not to assimilate, but to fundamentally change structures of power.[17]

The Black Panthers combined innovative social programs and organizing for black self-determination with militant confrontation. Though painted by law enforcement as a threat to white America, the Panthers in Chicago worked in coalition with other groups, including the all-white Young Patriots, who had taken to heart SNCC organizer Stokely Carmichael's admonition to organize white people against racism as well as the systems that kept them, too, in poverty.[18]

The gay rights movement exploded onto the public consciousness with the Stonewall uprising in 1969. Manhattan's Stonewall Inn was a gathering place for queer and transgender people, some of them in the sex trade, and was also a frequent target of police. On one particular night when the police raided, the regulars at Stonewall decided they had had enough and chose to resist. Marsha P. Johnson, a black transgender woman, famously threw the first brick. Rather than fleeing the scene, the queer community rallied around the inn, embracing a newly confrontational stance. They discarded the sense of shame with which they had been expected to live.

Although the new liberation movements were often made up of individuals like Johnson who were at the intersection of race and gender identities, such identities were usually conceived of as separate. The feminism of the period coined the motto "The personal is political" to point out that problems often assumed to be individual were in fact broadly shared. But even within the women's movement, not all women faced the same issues. Women of color, queer women, and working-class women worked to define a feminism that reflected their lives, not just the lives of the well-off white women anointed as leaders, as much by the press as the movement itself. Within the black liberation struggle, too, black women developed feminist and womanist politics, but the common public perception was that these identities were distinct and that the movements didn't overlap.[19]

The "white working class" of the time developed its own form of identity politics, one pandered to by politicians like George Wallace and Richard Nixon, who positioned themselves against demanding movements that they termed "special interests." Although, as sociologist Penny Lewis explained, white workers were not monolithically opposed to the 1960s movements, the perception that they were, shaped by events like the 1970 "hard hat riots" on Wall Street, affected the politics of the age. At the same time as the new liberation movements were rising, the economy was stumbling. Women and people of color were moving into previously white-male-dominated jobs at the same time as those jobs were disappearing. The conservative labor movement of the time wasn't prepared to deal with this new reality or to share its power. Nor was it able to reconceptualize power altogether in the way that these radical movements urged.[20]

The legislation won during the 1960s seemed to codify the difference between the identity-based movements and earlier struggles. Labor rights, though they originally excluded many women workers and workers of color, were collective rights, rights to organize and bargain as a group; they operated on the principle that improving conditions for all was more important than individual striving. By contrast, the non-discrimination provisions of the Civil Rights Act protected individuals' rights to a job or a promotion, with the emphasis on the ability to sue after discrimination rather than to proactively come together and have a voice on the job.[21]

The movements of the later 1960s and the 1970s mostly put aside moral appeals for sharp political analysis and demands. Moral calls seemed too much like asking the oppressor politely to take his foot off one's neck. The anti–Vietnam War movement had built moral calls into its framework, incorporating the Catholic Left, but despite huge mass mobilizations, the war dragged on. And the moral-values language was being adopted by a new group of activists, this time on the Right, who were growing in power.

It was the Supreme Court's 1973 *Roe v. Wade* decision striking down state abortion laws, and ruling it unconstitutional to ban abortion, that kicked off what came to be known as the "religious right." Before that, said Adele Stan, a reporter who has spent over thirty years covering the Christian conservative movement, Catholics and evangelicals were "like oil and water except for patriarchy." Abortion was not a hot topic for evangelicals at that time. Some liberal Protestant clergy had even taken part in the movement to liberalize abortion law, helping to refer people for abortions, and several Protestant denominations issued resolutions supporting women's moral right to have an abortion.[22]

In the aftermath of the decision, activists Richard Viguerie, known for his innovation of direct-mail techniques; Paul Weyrich, founder of the Heritage Foundation and the American Legislative Exchange Council; and Howard Phillips, founder of the US Taxpayers Party, realized that anger around *Roe* and changing social mores could be leveraged to create electoral victories. They relied on the feeling that the "traditional" family, with the male breadwinner at work and the woman at home raising children, was falling apart, although they mostly ignored the economic realities that were helping make that change. Desegregation had also contributed to the feeling of white Christians that their values were under attack; in the South, religious schools were a way to avoid sending children to integrated schools.

Viguerie, Weyrich, and Phillips recruited televangelist Jerry Falwell to become the public, Protestant face of the Moral Majority, founded in 1979. Falwell credited legalized abortion and gay rights with his decision to get involved in politics. The organization, Adele Stan noted, was set up to play a long game, to reshape politics, and particularly the Republican Party, in its image over the course of decades. Women like Phyllis Schlafly, who was Catholic, and Anita Bryant, a Protestant and a former beauty queen, took leadership roles in the fight against the Equal Rights Amendment and laws that would have banned discrimination against gays and lesbians, respectively. These women adapted the language and practices of the feminist movement to explicitly antifeminist goals: Schlafly extolled the "right" of women to stay at home and to be cared for by their men, a language that hit home for many working-class women whose journey into the workplace was likely to be low-wage, low-status drudgery.[23]

Ronald Reagan seamlessly blended the new religious conservatism with the antiunion, pro-business politics he'd learned during his time at General Electric. He struck a populist pose, updating Nixon's "Silent Majority" by railing against "special interests." He depicted anyone who opposed his proposed budget and tax cuts as part of a kind of elite akin to the robber barons and bankers of an earlier age, rather than people who had been shut out of the political mainstream in the United States for most of its existence. Reagan and his backers repackaged the language of solidarity and interdependence—traditional values of the labor movement—to describe the patriarchal nuclear family. Not only had the religious right laid sole claim to Christian values; it was staking its claim to the secular values of its usual opponents as well.[24]

After the folding of the Moral Majority in the late 1980s, the values language was picked up by the Family Research Council, which branded its yearly conference the "Values Voter Summit," solidifying the idea that "values voters" were those who were opposed to abortion, gay rights, and equal pay for women, and in favor of low taxes, school vouchers, and, by the George W. Bush era, war in the Middle East. After the 2004 election, which swept Bush to a second term amid a wave of state ballot initiatives banning same-sex marriage, exit pollsters trumpeted their findings: 22 percent of Americans had said "moral values" were the reason they chose a candidate, and of those voters, 80 percent had chosen Bush. Evangelicals had not increased their turnout in that election as a whole, and presumably some of them had considered the economy, terrorism, or the war in Iraq as pressing issues, too. But the polls—and the pundits' obsession with them—sealed the narrative.[25]

THE NUCLEAR FAMILY THAT HAS BEEN THE FOCUS OF SO MUCH HAND-wringing and moralizing in recent years was not a product of human nature but rather of a particular period in US capitalism. The family wage, designed to allow a male breadwinner to support a wife and children, was bargained for by the labor movement and accepted, though uneasily, by business leaders during the New Deal period. It allowed many working-class women, as well as their wealthier sisters, to stay home with their children; as discussed earlier, it built the middle class. The family wage—that is, material conditions—shaped our ideas of the male and female role in the workplace and in the home, in public and in private.[26]

It also shaped the "moral values" of the period. Men took pride in their work and in their ability to provide for their families; women took pride in their children and in their caring skills that held the family together. The family wage helped to normalize certain ideas about women's work and its value and about gender roles. If women were to be supported by their husbands, they didn't need to make a living wage, and could be paid less when they were in the workplace—and despite the popular mythology, some women were always in the paid workforce. If women should be at home, social systems for child care were unnecessary, and in fact were examples of the state usurping the private rights of families.

Those moral values were constructed in reaction to the position that working people were pushed into. Black men and women, who did not enjoy the same economic position during the New Deal order, also had different relationships to the nuclear family. While the upper classes did not have to invest their sense of self-worth in their labor in the same way, working people found ways to take pride in what the world had given them.[27]

It is interesting, then, that the same politicians and activists who profess to want to maintain the nuclear family have done the most to help dismantle it by reducing wages for most people, making it necessary, whether women like it or not, for them to work.

Marxist feminist activists in the 1970s, under the banner of "Wages for Housework," argued that the work women did in the home in fact did have economic value, and that it was deserving of a wage. Their demands were mostly dismissed as unworkable, but the commitment of conservative women to their role in the home as the Christian right grew in power is related to their argument. These women might not have been demanding wages for housework, but they did demand a kind of acknowledgment for the reproductive labor done in the home, even if it was mainly lip service.

Into that context the *Roe v. Wade* decision hurtled. To antiabortion women in particular in the 1970s, the Supreme Court seemed to have devalued not only the fetus, but also the labor of the women who bore and raised children. The decision was not, sociologist Kristin Luker argued, simply about pregnancy; it was about the social role of women. Not just childbirth, but the entire spectrum of work that women did, the caring labor of tending to the feelings and needs of the family, seemed to be on the verge of disappearing. Men were not about to pick it up—indeed, antiabortion women often argued that abortion allowed men to skirt responsibility. While many working-class women embraced abortion as a way to plan their families and save themselves money and stress, family planning alone was not enough to solve their economic issues. Particularly for women whose entry into the workforce likely meant more supervision, less control over their time, and less symbolic value for a fairly meager wage, often in a service job, staying in the home didn't seem like a bad choice.[28]

"Family values," framed as concern for reproductive labor and support for the traditional, patriarchal nuclear family, became a political obsession as the economy was transitioning away from industrial, family-wage union jobs to a service economy in which more and more women worked away from home. Those service jobs relied on the same "people skills" that women were already expected to possess. The Christian emphasis on service, adopted by corporations like Walmart, allowed bosses to pay the same lip service to women in the workplace as they had to women in the home, in both cases in place of a wage.[29]

Homosexuality, too, was perceived as an affront to the traditional roles of men and women. It fit into the particular set of "family and moral values" concerns put forth by the newly organized religious right. The overall moral decline that so angered religious leaders like Jerry Falwell included any sex outside of marriage, but gays and lesbians came in for particular loathing because they seemed to upend traditional roles. Pointing the finger at them allowed straight male leaders to detach themselves from any responsibility for the moral decline they so lividly condemned. Although the later gay rights movement came to focus much of its energy on marriage rights, asserting the similarity of queer couples to straight ones, the early gay rights activists reveled in the challenge the movement presented to the existing family structure.[30]

The movements of the late 1960s, particularly the feminist and LGBT rights movements, had stepped away from the kind of charismatic leadership model that was so recognizable in the civil rights movement and earlier eras. In part, because these movements were posing a direct challenge to the structures of patriarchy, they had little choice. Queer groups like ACT UP, formed in response to the 1980s AIDS crisis in an effort to break through the barriers that homophobia had erected around dealing with the disease, were organized horizontally, with affinity groups and caucuses. They used facilitators to structure meetings and encouraged groups to take independent action. Feminist groups, which often sprang up as a result of "consciousness-raising," eschewed formal leadership, but struggled with what activist Jo Freeman called the "tyranny of structurelessness," as formally nonhierarchical groups in practice found themselves with people who exerted control without having been selected as leaders—often along lines of race and class.[31]

The post-2008 movements drew from these models, mostly putting aside hierarchies for more open-ended structures. In this, Moral Mondays was an outlier, a movement that clearly had a charismatic leader in Rev. Barber, who in speech and style harkened back to the civil rights movement. Adele Stan noted that even when the left turned its back on religion, and even in some cases began to mock the faithful, the civil rights movement and the liberation tradition of the black church was always excepted. Hence Rev. Barber was able to draw in even nonbelievers to a movement that used moral language and a preacherly style. It is not entirely surprising that a movement using the language of moral values had something of a patriarch.

"People trust him and are inspired by him and there's a power to having that trusted person," Jacob Lerner said, noting that the almost reverent style of Moral Mondays in a way felt like going to church. The media, too, has an easier time covering a movement with a clear leader to interview; having an obvious person to call contributed to the large amount of mostly positive coverage that the Moral Movement received. There was less of a need to rely on social media storytelling when the movement was more legible to the media.

And yet there is power in allowing more people to step up and take leadership roles or to act independently. People tend to stay involved with a movement, Lerner said, when they feel crucial to its success rather than just like one more person showing up. Although some people felt incredibly energized by Moral Mondays, others, like Angel Chandler, did not see themselves in it. Long-term, a movement's ability to survive relies on many people stepping forward, and those people need to feel that they have space to speak and are empowered to act. Moral Mondays remained strong and powerful for the first summer, and continued to hold events that drew large crowds, but as with any disruptive action, what at first is a shock to the status quo becomes normalized, and those in power adjust to it. There is a constant need for new tactics to keep a movement growing, and the more people feel that the movement belongs to them, the more they will believe that they can try something new.

Even during the civil rights era, when Dr. King commanded headlines and phone calls from the White House, there were many others who did hard work with much less acknowledgment, from the domestic workers who walked and carpooled to make the Montgomery bus boycott a success to the distributed organizers of SNCC in counties across the South who painstakingly registered black people to vote. That labor, too, is gendered, with women doing the less-visible labor of care and organization, from powering the phone trees and stuffing the envelopes for the antiabortion movement to maintaining the phone and email lists of the Tea Party to creating safe spaces for protesters and organizing jail support teams in Raleigh and Ferguson. That work is wrongly assumed to be less important, less a demonstration of "leadership." As Bethany Moreton and Pamela Voeckel have argued, movements themselves are a form of reproductive labor.[32]

By including from the start issues of reproductive justice, sexuality, and gender identity alongside the more traditionally male issues of political rights and the workplace, Moral Mondays were able to bring in many women and queer and transgender people, who in turn did the important work of organizing, door-knocking, running meetings, and providing support for arrestees. Their work shaped the movement. As Wooten Gough noted, intersectional organizing requires more than just bringing in different people in a sort of laundry list of struggles; it means putting people who face multiple attacks at once front and center. These issues, as much as any others, shape what class means in America today.

Today our values have been shaped by the workplace and the world around us just as much as the values of the people living in the New Deal era were shaped by the world in which they were living at that time. And they are very different worlds. Our twenty-first-century world has been shaped by birth control and access to abortion; the service economy and the notorious "two-income trap," in which two working adults became necessary to maintain the living standards that used to require just one; the Internet and social media; and the mainstreaming of queer and transgender people. Even Rev. Barber, who at first glance could appear to be an old-fashioned leader, spoke the language of intersectionality and argued for the need for distributed movements across the country. "Helicopter leadership doesn't work in this environment and it never really has," he said.

THE SUCCESS OF MOVEMENTS IS OFTEN JUDGED, FAIRLY OR UNFAIRLY, by their ability to get candidates elected. In North Carolina, where the right to vote has been such a central part of the struggle from the beginning, that criterion was of special interest. If the movement fought to maintain and to expand access to the ballot, surely it must believe that voting is the way to create change. But battling simply to maintain access to the ballot is a different struggle from putting together a strategy to win elections.

At her sentencing, Barbara Smalley-McMahan announced that she would be doing her community service with Democracy North Carolina to register voters and get out the vote. She organized a group of twenty-one people who would meet at PieBird, a restaurant in her Raleigh neighborhood, for breakfast, and then go out to register voters. She wound down her counseling practice, devoting herself instead to the voting work, to putting together workshops that would help educate people around systemic racism, to making public change.

The fiftieth anniversary of Freedom Summer, the massive civil rights–era voter registration drive in Mississippi, was the summer of 2014, and William Barber III and his colleagues in the youth section of the NAACP decided to use it as an opportunity to push the Moral Movement further. "We began to ask ourselves, what could we do to really honor that legacy as well as engage in the moment that we were in?" he said. They decided to make the summer into their own Moral Freedom Summer. They would place organizers in forty-nine counties across the state for twelve weeks to build relationships, train people in the issues, and register voters. "We had black, we had white, we had poor, we had middle class, we had LGBTQ, we had straight, we had a representation of the movement," he said.

Despite all that work, the 2014 elections saw Republican Thom Tillis, the Speaker of the North Carolina House often targeted by the Moral Movement, narrowly defeat incumbent Democratic US senator Kay Hagan. Democrats won a few seats away from Republicans in the statehouse, but the conservative supermajority remained in place. Around the country, the story was the same—from Wisconsin to Florida, politicians continued to win despite pitting themselves, in some cases, directly against popular movements in their states.[33]

In North Carolina, part of the story was the heavily gerrymandered districts—even conservative Democrat Heath Shuler dropped out of his race for reelection to his seat in the US Congress in 2012 because his district was redrawn in a way that would be less favorable to him. The NAACP, along with the ACLU and the League of Women Voters, continued to fight legal battles against the voter ID law, and in the winter of 2016, federal judges threw out two congressional districts, ruling that they had been drawn specifically to consolidate black voters. The judges ordered them redrawn before another election was held in the state; lawmakers appealed to the Supreme Court, which declined to stay the order, forcing the state to reschedule its congressional primaries.[34]

But the other part of the story was that many people, inspired by social movements and direct action, were less thrilled when they were told to go vote. The NAACP does not endorse candidates, and while a few Moral Monday arrestees went on to run for local office, the non-partisan movement's momentum was hard to translate into the very partisan field of electoral politics. Angel Chandler echoed a sentiment I heard around the country—that electoral politics is the problem, not the solution. "It's the two-party system, that is where we get screwed every single day," she said. "Even if one side, you feel, doesn't do as much harm, if you're just buying into that system, to me that's the biggest part of the problem."

Rev. Barber, too, though he continued to fight for voting rights, saw the role of the movement as less about elections than about shifting consciousness. "You have to change the context in which elected people operate. That is what makes them do something," he said. "We don't just decide what we are going to do based on one election. We are long-term in our focus. Persistent in our actions. Consistent in our principles." Democracy was about more than just voting.

Being persistent in their actions was made a little bit harder by changes enacted at the legislative building in response to the protests. Massive protests in the Halifax Mall behind the General Assembly building were barred, and the legislators' schedules shifted so that the protests began to move from Mondays to Wednesdays. The actions slowed from once a week, but continued, Tara Romano said, to draw big crowds and make plenty of noise. In the fall of 2014—just before the election—the Wake County district attorney dropped charges against hundreds of protesters following two judges' rulings that the arrests had violated their rights to assemble and speak. But that didn't stop the legislature from trying to shut down protests.[35]

The existence of Moral Monday also served as a draw for other organizing in North Carolina. To Jacob Lerner, it seemed unlikely that labor unions would have put money into the least-unionized state in the country until Moral Mondays proved that there was energy around economic justice; after the protests began, the Service Employees International Union began a local Raise Up for $15 low-wage worker campaign. The movement for black lives also intersected with Moral Mondays, focusing on the cases of Jonathan Ferrell, a black man shot by a police officer in Charlotte in 2013, and Elisha Walker, a black transgender woman found murdered in 2015. Bree Newsome, who scaled the flagpole and took down the Confederate flag outside of the South Carolina Capitol, was also a Moral Monday arrestee.

The North Carolina legislature, after the shootings in Charleston, passed a law protecting Confederate monuments. Once the flag became such a flashpoint, Smalley-McMahan found conversations with her more conservative friends, which had seemed productive, cut off. Previously, they had found common ground in some areas, including money in politics, funding for public schools, a raise in the minimum wage, and even reproductive rights. "Even if there may still be some agreement, we can't talk about it because the big thing up front is the flag and the statues and raising up people who basically promoted white supremacy," she said. "They think it's heritage. It's not heritage, it's white supremacy."

Despite the cries for local control and states' rights coming from Confederate flag supporters and the General Assembly, Ivanna Gonzalez said, legislators in fact worked to cut off local control. The bill protecting Confederate monuments required the General Assembly to vote on removing such a monument, superseding local government authority. And the General Assembly moved to redistrict the Greensboro City Council in a move that packed black voters into fewer districts. Still, Gonzalez said, there remained plenty of energy on the local level in cities around the state—and Wooten Gough stressed that rural organizing, too, was making strides in building an intersectional movement.[36]

Perhaps the biggest success that Moral Mondays can claim is that it has been replicated—not just in southern states like Georgia and South Carolina, but also in northern states usually considered much more liberal. In the spring of 2015, I joined protesters in the "War Room" of

New York's Capitol in Albany. Beneath paintings of muscular colonists battling Native Americans, a circle of protesters held signs proclaiming, "Faith Stands Up to Pharaoh" and "Black Lives Matter." They were black and white, young and old, Christians, Jews, Buddhists, and atheists. Like Moral Mondays in North Carolina, their events had a theme; this one was "The New Jim Crow Has Got to Go." Activists read letters from prisoners detailing the conditions in solitary confinement, quoted the Bible, and handed around a list of demands, ranging from "freedom from mass incarceration," to "full employment and living wages for all," to "the right for all people to self-identify and express their gender with freedom from violence, poverty and discrimination." There were also specific policy asks and bill names.

The range of demands, from the mundane and even wonky to the transformative, was a feature of this and other movements, a way for organizers to build momentum, small victory by small victory, even as they kept their eyes on major social change. "The ethic that guides the movement is that part of what your obligation is as a person who is fighting against prisons is to also be concerned about the material conditions of people who are in prison now," said Angelica Clarke, executive director of the Albany Social Justice Center and an organizer of the day's action. And then, too, she noted, is "that bigger-picture value demand of a world beyond prison, a world that sees justice not as punishment but as a rehabilitative opportunity or as restoration."

Emily McNeill of the Labor Religion Coalition of New York State had found the moral-values framework compelling as a person of faith. But, as she explained, whether they were religious or not, people were "hungry for a way to express something deeper than just, this is a good policy or this is a bad policy." In New York, with a Democrat in the governor's mansion, McNeill said, the moral language was powerful because both Democrats and Republicans were serving the interests of the wealthy. It also helped different groups who often didn't see their interests as overlapping to come to understand their struggles as connected: that ending prisons would require living-wage jobs, that prisons were built in counties that had lost their manufacturing or agricultural bases as an alternative to real economic development, that prisons contributed to inequality, and, as Clarke noted, that New York was the most unequal state in the country.

Civil disobedience was not yet central to Moral Mondays in New York, but in Illinois, said Toby Chow, chair of the People's Lobby and a Lutheran pastor-in-training, civil disobedience was essential to feeling as though Moral Mondays Illinois was making an impact. Their first action that involved arrests was outside of the Chicago Board of Trade, where Rick Santelli made his famous rant. They brought a big puppet of Governor Bruce Rauner with hellfire surrounding him and, inspired by the Bible story of Jesus turning the moneychangers out of the Temple, also set up a table with riches on it and flipped it over. From there, a group of protesters blocked the street in front of the Board of Trade, bearing signs reading "Rauner Repent," and "What Would Jesus Cut?"

"I think there's a few aspects to civil disobedience," Chow said. "One is if you're willing to risk an arrest, you're going to be able to more effectively shut something down. That's crucial, because part of what we want to do by staging these direct actions is to generalize the crisis. The politicians and these rich people who are funding them, they're imposing this crisis on a vast majority of people, but as far as they're concerned there is no crisis, it's not part of their life."

Chow continued, "It's a form of self-assertion that really transforms the people who go through with it. Once you cross that line and say no, I'm not going to leave when the police tell me to leave, and if they have to carry me away then they're going to carry me away, it expands your sense of freedom about what you're willing to do and what you're capable of doing. It has a really liberating effect on people."

Barbara Smalley-McMahan, as part of a delegation from the Baptist Peace Fellowship, attended the massive Moral Monday action in St. Louis on August 10, 2015, that marked the first anniversary of Michael Brown's death at the hands of Ferguson police officer Darren Wilson. "We were there to learn," she said, "and the leaders in the movement there that we were most in contact with were all young and very radical, very disrespectful." She meant that in a good way. As she explained, "there was a whole theology of disrespect that was really new and really good to hear about while I was up there." She heard it from the likes of Cornel West and Rev. Osagyefo Sekou, who has called it "the liberation theology of Ferguson." West and Rev. Sekou, the latter in his clerical collar with his dreadlocks pulled back, climbed over the barricades that Monday with more than fifty others and were arrested at the Thomas Eagleton Federal Courthouse. "In the early days of August a poor queer black and female Jesus took up a cross and faced tanks and tear gas," Rev. Sekou said. "A cry from the wilderness could be heard: Fuck the police!"[37]

Smalley-McMahan, already changed by the Moral Mondays in her home state, came home changed again. She joined a protest days later but found it too rigid, too strict, too concerned with the right way to hold a sign. "That way," she told me, "doesn't work." She began to consider how what she learned in Ferguson could be applied at home.

Rev. Barber called it all the birthing stages of a third Reconstruction, a transformative moment when all the strands of different movements began to reconnect into a fusion movement, from the Fight for $15 to Black Lives Matter to the new environmental justice movement to Occupy. "I think that we, all of these movements, are social defibrillators," he said. "Our job is to shock this nation's heart again."

In the fall of 2014, Rev. David Forbes addressed the North Carolina NAACP convention, and Smalley-McMahan, sitting in the audience, was struck by what he said. "He talked about King David when the Philistines were the powers that be. David wanted to go after them with the army, and God said to wait until you hear the rustling in the top of the mulberry trees; it will sound like people marching, and when you hear that sound of people marching, the fullness of time has come, and it will be time for you to go out," she said. "We hear the feet, the feet are marching, the leaves are rustling in the top of the mulberry trees, the fullness of time has come, and that's when change happens. I believe we are in a new time in history and something radical is coming. I don't know what it means in terms of our capitalistic system. I think something about that's going to change."

CHAPTER SEVEN

RED SCARES AND
RADICAL IMAGINATION

Kshama Sawant took the microphone at her victory party on November 17, 2013, and called one of the Seattle region's biggest employers an economic terrorist. "If Boeing executives insist on relocating the factories out of Washington," she told a cheering crowd at the headquarters of Service Employees International Union Local 775, "the only response we can have to reject this blackmail is to tell the CEOs if you want to go, you can go. The machines are here, the workers are here, let us take this entire productive activity into democratic public ownership and retool the machines to produce mass transit."[1]

Yes, Kshama Sawant is *that* kind of socialist. And her speech, just after her election to the Seattle City Council, got a standing ovation. Local 775 had endorsed her opponent, incumbent Richard Conlin, but by the time the final vote count showed Sawant had won, the union was lending her its hall. She paused, grinning, to let her supporters clap. "We need to fight on behalf of the Boeing workers, we need to fight on behalf of Metro workers, we need to fight for $15 an hour, but that is not going to be enough," she said. "We are fighting against the system of capitalism itself, and look how spectacularly it has failed in meeting even the most basic needs of human survival."

A year and a half later, I sat in Sawant's office in City Hall, listening to her recall the Boeing workers' rally that had taken place the next night. The state legislature had just voted to give Boeing a package of tax breaks worth $8.7 billion, at the time the largest subsidy ever given to a single company in US history, and at the same time Boeing was demanding that its union workers give up their pensions—or else the company would move production to nonunion South Carolina, where Governor Nikki Haley had bragged about wearing high heels to kick the unions.[2] Haley, like Sawant, is of Indian descent, but there the similarities most definitely end. After riding the 2010 Tea Party wave into office, Haley had flaunted her hatred of worker organizations; Sawant, by contrast, argued that both Republicans and Democrats had abandoned working people. And Sawant's election to the City Council seemed to be evidence that Americans, increasingly, were ready for answers outside of the previously accepted political consensus.[3]

Sawant came to socialism in 2009, after hearing a member of the group Socialist Alternative speak at a postelection event. "When he spoke it was everything that I was thinking about; it was an analysis of why we need to fight against capitalism and why we need an organization like Socialist Alternative, and for me it was like boom, it makes sense," she said. Growing up in India, she had been "obsessed" with the problems of poverty and hunger. "It got more and more obvious as I got older that this was something systemic—it was not inevitable—meaning you could change the system and have a different kind of outcome."

Until she encountered Socialist Alternative, she hadn't found a political organization that made sense to her. Single-issue campaigns or nonprofits held little appeal. She moved to the United States at age twenty-two and worked as a computer programmer, but her questions about poverty and inequality led her back to school, where she earned a PhD in economics. She moved to Seattle and began teaching at Seattle Central Community College. That's where she was when the Occupy movement broke out in Seattle in the fall of 2011. "I can hardly remember a day that I didn't go—I would finish teaching my classes and then walk downtown to the occupation," she said. When the city government wanted the encampment moved out of the public park it had taken over, Sawant helped negotiate space for the occupiers on the campus of Seattle Central.

When Occupy faded, Socialist Alternative began to consider new ways to get involved in politics. The 2012 election was looming, and the pressure was on for movement activists to get in line behind the Democratic Party. But what if they could demonstrate a different kind of political campaign, one that took issues seriously but was uncompromising about its anticapitalist politics and deliberately outside of the two major parties? Socialist Alternative, Sawant explained, is an activist organization, not a political party—it calls for an independent workers' party—and so it took a serious debate for the Seattle group to decide that it wanted to run an electoral campaign. Sawant was even more surprised when her colleagues nominated her to be their candidate. "I was quite stunned," she laughed. "Nobody can even say my name in this country. How are we going to make any impact with my name on the ballot sheet?"

David Goldstein was a writer for the Seattle alternative weekly newspaper *The Stranger* when Sawant ran her first campaign, which was for the state legislature. "We're used to having what we call 'clown socialists' come in," he told me, "who are there just to be angry and dour-faced and spout a little Marxist rhetoric about how corrupt the whole system is, and then that's all they do—they don't really run races."

But Sawant, seeking *The Stranger*'s endorsement in her race against state representative Jamie Pedersen, seemed different. She had specific plans and could discuss the ins and outs of the budget. *The Stranger* staff felt that they had to endorse Pedersen, who had been a champion of the marriage equality measure on the ballot that year. But Goldstein suggested endorsing Sawant in another race, against the Speaker of the House, Frank Chopp, as a write-in candidate. They did, and she made it through the first round of both primaries. For the November election, Sawant chose the race against Chopp and went to court to make sure the ballot identified her as coming from Socialist Alternative. She lost the election to Chopp, but she still managed to win 29 percent of the vote with "Socialist" next to her name.

The City Council elections came up the following year and, buoyed by its success against a powerful statewide figure, Seattle Socialist Alternative decided to challenge Councilmember Richard Conlin. Meanwhile, halfway across the country in Minneapolis, another Socialist Alternative member with ties to Occupy, Ty Moore from Occupy Homes Minnesota, was running his own City Council race. "Ty at that moment, ironically, was our winnable campaign," Sawant recalled. "This campaign was a long shot because this was a citywide campaign; that was a ward-based campaign and we were such underdogs at that time."

"Running a viable campaign as a socialist isn't just a matter of audacity, clever tactics, and the right program (though those are all crucial)," Moore said. "You need to have built up some kind of base in advance." He won endorsement from SEIU's Minnesota state council, immigrants groups, and worker centers, and ultimately lost by just 229 votes.[4]

Another campaign was heating up at the same time as the Seattle City Council race. For years, workers at Seattle-Tacoma International Airport, in the nearby suburb of SeaTac, had been trying to organize, backed by several local unions. Alex Hoopes, a twenty-five-year veteran of the airline industry, was one of those workers. He had seen his job fall from a unionized, stable position with a living wage to a gig that started at $8.72 per hour. He worked as a baggage handler and ramp agent for AirServ, a contractor that provided staff to clean the planes, load them, and provide security. He had reached out to SEIU Local 6 about organizing, but the union was having little luck getting the airlines to come to the table and negotiate with the workers. Instead, the union and its allies moved to raise wages for the many low-wage workers at the airport and its surrounding hotels, restaurants, and other businesses by putting the wage issue before the voters. Hoopes collected petition signatures to put a $15 an hour measure on the SeaTac city ballot that fall. It was the first time that voters anywhere in the United States would consider a wage that high; only a few months before, striking fast-food workers calling for "$15 and a union" had begun the drumbeat on the streets of New York.

It wasn't long ago that calling for a $15 an hour minimum wage would have gotten you branded a dangerous communist and laughed out of the political debate. But in 2013, members of Socialist Alternative thought it was their key to mainstream success. "We felt that the $15 demand was really going to fix itself on the consciousness of a large base of the working class nationally, not just in Seattle," Sawant said.

Heather Weiner, a longtime labor movement strategist, was working on the SeaTac campaign at the time, and remembered the first time

Sawant and Socialist Alternative arrived at a hearing on the $15 an hour measure. The SeaTac City Council had the option to adopt the measure rather than sending it to the ballot, and airport workers and local residents were lined up to speak. "Kshama and her crew showed up in their red shirts from Seattle and start giving socialist rhetoric," Weiner said. "I remember I thought, 'What are you doing?' But the crowd *loved* her, and I thought, 'All right, I don't need to control this, I just need to sit back and relax and watch what happens here.'" The socialists, she said, were making her campaign look like the moderates in the room.

Back in Seattle, few people thought Sawant had a chance. Despite her vocal support for $15 an hour, most of organized labor endorsed the incumbent, Conlin. Some, though, recognized that there was an opening for someone who was prepared to challenge what Robert Cruickshank, a former aide to Mayor Mike McGinn, called the "very comfortable liberalism in Seattle." Cruickshank explained, "Voters in Seattle were ready for political change in City Hall, and I think Kshama captured that in the right way. They wanted something more progressive."

The Fight for $15 campaign in Seattle timed its fast-food strikes and actions to line up with key points in the mayoral race in order to put pressure on the candidates. Early on, Sawant was the only one who supported it. Mike O'Brien, at the time one of the most progressive members of the City Council, shrugged off $15 an hour as a fringe demand at first. The speed with which opinions changed on the issue, he said, was incredible. "It was just a matter of months before I said, of course I'll support this, and then it was a few more months when I said, there's no way this doesn't pass." The growing movement for $15 tapped into something that was out there, he said. "Successful movements don't go tell people what they need, they tell them what they already know."

The country in general, and Seattle in particular, were ripe for this message. The financial crisis, Cruickshank said, had made people start to think about capitalism, creating a newly fertile ground for big ideas and washing away the remnants of the red-baiting that had so defined debate for so long. In Seattle, where tech money from companies like Amazon was flowing and rents spiking, the city was perhaps even more primed for Sawant and for $15. David Rolf, executive director of SEIU Local 775, which backed Working Washington, the group organizing fast-food workers in the area, thought that people had been ready for a left-populist economic message for decades. "It's just that, until very recently, there has been a silent agreement between the two major political parties and their consultants and handlers and pollsters that that's not something they're willing to offer."

It didn't hurt that Socialist Alternative ran what turned out to be a very effective grassroots campaign. "We had about four hundred volunteers toward the end of the campaign," Sawant said. "As many of the people we ran into told us, they couldn't walk a few blocks without seeing one of us. It was incredible." They held a "hundred-rallies" campaign in the last few days counting down to the election, studying a map of the city to decide which street corners to hit at what times. But most people in the city's political class assumed the City Council races were all safe. "Had anybody polled that race in late September, early October, and the Establishment realized she was in striking distance," David Goldstein said, "they would've put an extra $150,000 into that race and she wouldn't have won."

Sawant's ultimate margin of victory was over 3,000 votes; because the City Council was elected citywide at the time, that meant that over 93,000 people in Seattle voted for a socialist. The SeaTac ballot measure won, too, by 77 votes out of 6,003. It became clear that what had been a wild, utopian demand for a livable wage was something that voters were willing to endorse, both in the person of Sawant and explicitly, in the SeaTac ballot campaign.

To Sawant, the victory showed that her message, and its appeal to the working class of a wealthy city, had resonance. "People don't need some kind of detailed graduate-level economics lesson; they understand that the market is not working for them. The market is making them homeless. The market is making them cityless. And they're fed up, and they're angry." Angry enough, it seemed, to take a leap of faith and support a candidate whose ideas had only recently been presumed to be unthinkable.

ON TWITTER, IF YOU MENTION THE WORD "SOCIALISM," YOU GET A preprogrammed reply from an icon of long-dead senator Joseph McCarthy, the man who was so famous for his red-baiting that his name became synonymous with the entire ideology. The "RedScareBot" adds a bit of nonsense commentary, like "Leninist soda" or "Hot to Trotsky," to each reply, a parody of the anticommunism that once pervaded every aspect of American life that underscores the ridiculousness of red-baiting in 2015. As red-baiting itself has lost its power, it can be easy to forget that it destroyed lives—some of them not that long ago.

In the fall of 2008, as the financial industry was shuddering from the collapse of Lehman Brothers, and when Hank Paulson was trying to push a $700 billion no-strings-attached handout to banks through Congress, the most pressing concern on the campaign trail was whether Barack Obama was secretly a socialist. On October 3, George W. Bush signed the Troubled Asset Relief Program into law. On October 12, Barack Obama had a campaign conversation with a man who became identified as Joe the Plumber, a man who became, in the media, a symbol of Obama's supposed disconnect from white working-class voters. The future president explained his tax plan and commented that "when you spread the wealth around," it's a positive thing. Sarah Palin jumped on the phrasing. "Friends," she told a crowd in New Mexico, "now is no time to experiment with socialism."[5]

But Palin's attacks on Obama's commitment to an economic system that was spectacularly failing didn't gain much traction with people who had just watched their retirement savings or their future jobs go up in smoke. Even as the red-baiting hit another level, thanks to Fox News's Glenn Beck and his jeremiads against "socialized medicine," and even as Tea Partiers turned up to protest at town hall meetings held by members of Congress, it seemed that the reaction to red-baiting from younger Americans was to turn a favorable eye on socialism. A spring 2009 poll found that 20 percent of Americans of all ages thought socialism would be preferable to capitalism, and 33 percent of people under age thirty thought so. Just 37 percent of people under age thirty stuck it out for capitalism, with the rest undecided. Maybe, contra Palin, it was time for some new ideas.[6]

Those polls didn't save Van Jones's job. In the spring of 2009, Jones, an African American activist with a background in a socialist organization, had been appointed to the White House Council on Environmental Quality as special adviser for green jobs, enterprise, and innovation. He was dubbed Obama's "green jobs czar." But Glenn Beck's red-baiting drove Jones out of the administration. There were power and profits at the heart of the fight over Jones—as reporter Adele Stan and Tea Partier Debbie Dooley noted, the Koch brothers and others who backed the campaign against Jones made a lot of their money from the kind of dirty energy that Jones was brought on to fight.[7]

The attacks on the Association of Community Organizations for Reform Now, which began in earnest during the 2008 elections, also centered on political power. The group was a membership-based community organization, mostly of working-class people of color, and had for decades organized around raising the minimum wage and fighting for affordable housing. It had challenged subprime lending and other bad banking practices, and most notoriously, had registered people to vote. It was those voter-registration efforts in communities of color that led to the election-season attacks on the group, with which Obama had worked in the 1990s. John McCain, in the third presidential debate, harped on the theory that ACORN was perpetrating massive voter fraud. The "fraud" was some registration forms filled out falsely, some of them very obviously so—Mickey Mouse isn't going to turn up to vote—by workers hired by ACORN to be part of a voter registration drive. ACORN had turned over the fraudulent forms, and no one voted using them.[8]

The election over, the attacks on ACORN continued. Glenn Beck continued to accuse the group of being part of a leftist conspiracy to impose socialism, alongside the "union thugs" at SEIU, and even of using "Alinsky-ite intimidation tactics" to pressure banks into making subprime loans. (Saul Alinsky was a groundbreaking community organizer from the 1930s through the early 1970s who published a 1972 book, entitled *Rules for Radicals*, that described his disruptive methods.) That Beck's arguments were barely coherent mattered little. The end came for ACORN after a video created by activist James O'Keefe purported to show ACORN staffers helping a "pimp" evade taxes on his prostitution ring. Congress voted to cut off grant funding to the group in September 2009; ACORN declared bankruptcy in November 2010, its state affiliates having dissolved and in some cases reformed. Investigations found that the video had been heavily doctored, but none of ACORN's allies—certainly not the president—were willing to stand up for the group.[9]

At the same time, though, something else was happening. Economist Richard D. Wolff remembered getting calls from Tea Party groups asking him to come and lecture. "I would say to them, 'You know I'm a Marxist, right?'" he told me. "'We don't care,' they'd say. 'You're saying that what happened is unfair, that the little guy got screwed, [and] we want to hear you.'" When he was first hired at the University of Massachusetts, Wolff said, he had asked the university for a letter acknowledging that he would teach Marxian economics, in case some legislator came after him for being a socialist. But each year after the financial crisis, he got more calls asking him to come speak, and by 2011, he was no longer getting calls just to critique capitalism. People were looking, he said, for something more, for what comes next.

Bhaskar Sunkara was in college at George Washington University when the financial crisis hit, and he decided to start a leftist magazine. He had been the editor of the blog for the Young Democratic Socialists, but *Jacobin*, the print magazine he launched in 2010, was designed from the start to attract a bigger audience. It succeeded beyond anyone's expectations, buoyed not only by the rise of the Occupy movement but also by mainstream support for its unapologetically socialist ideas. It didn't hurt that the magazine (for which I have written) was sleek and glossy (it was designed by Rhode Island School of Design graduate Remeike Forbes), and looked about as far from the newspapers still printed by socialist organizations as it could. It even got support from conservatives: *National Review* writer Reihan Salam praised its "vital left-of-left-of-center" perspective in the *New York Times,* and *Times* conservative columnist Ross Douthat, in a piece entitled "How to Read in 2013," suggested *Jacobin* as one of many outlets worth reading for those who wanted to be "a well-informed and responsible American citizen."[10]

Despite the Obama administration's overreactions, it was beginning to seem as though red-baiting had lost its power. "There's been such a massive shift in the times," Kshama Sawant told me. "Often people would ask me, especially when we were running the campaign, 'Aren't you worried about the S word?' And certainly there is truth to that because of the Cold War–era propaganda and everything. But the recession and the collapse of the American dream among young people, who are going to have worse-off standards of living than their parents for the first time in American history, for them it's not so much about the S word. It's the C word. Capitalism is the dirty word."

THE DECLINING EFFECTIVENESS OF "THE S WORD" AS A WEAPON FOR silencing progressive voices in recent years is significant because for so many decades it was a defining obsession of American politics. For a nation committed to its revolutionary beginnings, the United States has had a deeply fraught relationship with its radicals. It has arrested them, deported them, hounded them out of jobs, and hanged them. In the 1800s and early 1900s, the enemy was "anarchists" and radical unionists. In 1886, a bomb was thrown into a crowd during a rally for striking workers and the eight-hour workday at Chicago's Haymarket square. The perpetrators were never identified, but that didn't stop the city from hanging four leftist rabble-rousers, August Spies, Albert Parsons, George Engel, and Adolph Fischer, for the crime. In the absence of evidence that any of them had lobbed the bomb, the court mainly relied on their political writings. Parsons was the editor of the English-language paper *The Alarm,* which announced itself as "A Socialistic Weekly"; Spies was the editor of the *Arbeiter-Zeitung* (German for "Worker's Newspaper").

Many in the left of the labor movement were immigrants—German, Jewish, Italian, and others. Antiradical "witch hunts," then and now, have contained a xenophobic streak identifying rebellious politics with foreignness. The demands for Barack Obama's birth certificate are part of a long history of such fearmongering. Crackdowns on labor organizers also had the effect of mitigating the demands of labor leaders; after the Haymarket bombing, the persecution of radicals caused American Federation of Labor leaders, such as Samuel Gompers, to argue for putting labor on a "business basis." Talk of class struggle was off the table.[11]

Fears of the communist threat grew after the 1917 Russian Revolution. The US government passed the 1917 Espionage Act and then amended it with the 1918 Sedition Act, ostensibly to protect American soldiers during World War I. The laws made it a crime to "interfere with the war effort" by criticizing it, the draft, or the US government. Labor leader and Socialist Party presidential candidate Eugene V. Debs was jailed under the Espionage Act. He had already run for president four times, beginning in 1900, and ran another presidential campaign from prison in 1920, receiving 919,799 votes, 3.4 percent of the total, the most ever for a Socialist.

Anarchist feminist agitator Emma Goldman was deported under the 1918 Alien Act, which was specifically set up for the deportation of foreign-born radicals, and the 1919 and 1920 "Palmer Raids," named for Attorney General A. Mitchell Palmer, rounded up thousands of suspected "aliens" on little evidence. The prisoners were held under horrific conditions that included beatings, little or no food, and no communication with the outside; eventually, public anger forced the release of most of them. J. Edgar Hoover, future FBI head, organized the raids. Local ordinances also played a role in the Red Scare, banning "radical" literature, which sometimes included publications like *The New Republic* and *The Nation*.[12]

The Special Committee on Un-American Activities was first created in 1934 to investigate pro-Nazi sentiment in the United States. Its second incarnation, however, launched in 1938 and dedicated more robustly to chasing communists, was the one that stuck. Alongside it came a wave of antiunion legislation, including the 1947 Taft-Hartley Act, which among its many limits on the power of organized labor required labor leaders to file affidavits declaring that they were not members of the Communist Party or any similar organization.

Who benefited from the Red Scare? Then as now, it has been big money—finance and major corporations trying to banish any vestige of demands for a more equal share from their workers. Red-baiting was a tactic in the war on workers, and it had a lot of success. Taft-Hartley kicked off a purge within the labor movement of the radicals who were the main proponents both of militant, democratic unionism and of organizing for racial and gender equality. The National Labor Relations Board would turn over the names of anyone insufficiently vehement in their denial of communism to the Justice Department to be investigated for perjury; their tax returns were scrutinized by the Internal Revenue Service, and if they were born outside the United States, the Immigration and Naturalization Service looked for ways to deport them.[13]

The Congress of Industrial Organizations expelled eleven communist-aligned unions representing around 1 million workers. "Red Harry" Bridges, of the International Longshoremen's and Warehousemen's Union (ILWU), condemned the purge of the biggest communist-led union, the United Electrical, Radio and Machine Workers, saying, "I don't find a single charge that says that the UE has not done a good job for its members. Not a single economic charge is leveled. So now we have reached the point where a trade union is expelled because it disagrees with the CIO on political matters."[14]

Bridges, who was born in Australia, successfully avoided deportation in part because no one could ever find proof, despite years of surveillance, that he'd actually been a member of the Communist Party. His West Coast longshore workers' union remained in the CIO, while the UE survived, much diminished, on the outside, long enough to help the Republic Windows and Doors workers take over their factory in 2008, and to support striking warehouse workers in Elwood, Illinois, in 2012. The influence of Bridges and the ILWU continues to be felt in Washington State—Robert Cruickshank suggested that the survival of the ILWU's radicalism "helped preserve that left-wing political activism through the 50s and into the 60s" in Seattle.

The foreign communist threat of the Soviet Union and the internal threat of leftist unions, David Rolf of SEIU noted, made the owners of businesses more likely to figure out who to bargain with and how to construct deals that left the free-market system intact. So while the Chamber of Commerce was publishing anticommunist materials and implying that the New Deal was a Red plot in 1946, General Motors negotiated the famed "Treaty of Detroit" with the United Auto Workers. UAW head Walter Reuther had earlier denounced the anticommunist witch hunts, but by 1952 he was assisting the House Un-American Activities Committee (HUAC) to investigate remaining leftists within UAW's massive Local 600. He wasn't the only labor leader to do so. HUAC would often schedule hearings on a union to coincide with an NLRB election, particularly if the election was to choose between a communist-affiliated union and a noncommunist one.[15]

Red-baiting and race-baiting often went hand in hand. Eugene "Bull" Connor, the Birmingham public safety commissioner infamous for setting dogs on civil rights marchers, less famously wrote laws that banned communist organizing. Red organizers were often the ones who insisted on organizing black and white workers together, arguing that one could not fight the power of the boss without also fighting racism. Such "social equality" was frightening to many white workers at the time, and that fear helped lead the collapse of the CIO's "Operation Dixie" campaign to organize the South.[16]

Outside of the labor movement, the Red Scare most famously went after Hollywood. Attacking movie stars was great publicity for HUAC, allowing it to raise its profile and intimidate many more people than it would ever be able to haul in for a hearing. The hearings were a spectacle, designed to punish those who had committed no crime, to turn friend against friend, to divide. Going after Hollywood was also a way to attack ideas. The idea that Reds would brainwash the masses into a revolution by means of musical comedy or noirish drama seems ridiculous now, but it was common at the time. That fear itself, however, was a kind of admission that there might be something appealing about socialism to the American people.

The Hollywood blacklist was only the most visible front of the Cold War at home. There were many means of cracking down on radicals, from HUAC and the NLRB to the Internal Security Act of 1950, which authorized concentration camps for interning communists; there were private agencies that specialized in blacklisting, as well as security programs within some companies to root out communists among employees. The FBI would also pass information about suspected Reds to the employers of those who had come under suspicion and leak the information to the press. Suspected radicals were evicted from their homes, denied passports, and occasionally denied unemployment or Social Security payments.[17]

Senator Joseph McCarthy (R-WI), the most public face of the Red hunts, was a skilled populist orator who aimed the Senate Permanent Subcommittee on Investigations squarely at suspected communists within the federal government itself. McCarthy managed to flip the class politics of communism, making his campaign against those who wanted workers to rule into a battle against "the bright young men who are born with silver spoons in their mouth." For years, people were afraid to challenge him, both for fear he would turn on them and because he appeared to have broad popular support.[18]

The Red Scare was about narrowing the scope of what was politically acceptable, and it did its job admirably. Although the most famous Red-hunters might have been Republicans, Democrats, including Hubert Humphrey, joined in the fun. Liberals fought bitterly over whether the best thing to do was to support the Red Scare's targets, and open themselves up to accusations of being part of the "Un-American" conspiracy, or to attempt to clear themselves—to present their clean hands to the country and free their preferred political programs of any socialist taint.

After the 1950s, the most intense part of the Red Scare was over. The Supreme Court ruled that many of its weapons violated the Constitution, including the anticommunist portion of Taft-Hartley. Yet long-time labor organizer Stephen Lerner remembered being required, as late as the 1970s, to sign his own undated resignation letter that would allow a union to fire him if he was discovered to be a Red. McCarthy was disgraced, dying in 1957 after having been censured by Congress. But Hoover was still in charge at the FBI, and Bull Connor in Birmingham, and the anticommunist tactics rolled over into fighting the civil rights movement. The FBI infiltrated and harassed a number of civil rights and "New Left" groups, from Martin Luther King Jr.'s Southern Christian Leadership Conference to the Black Panthers to Students for a Democratic Society, through COINTELPRO (for Counter Intelligence Program), which began as a red-hunting program. In the final years of the Cold War, under Ronald Reagan, there was an attempt to ramp the red-baiting back up, with the Senate Subcommittee on Security and Terrorism attacking organizations such as the National Lawyers Guild and the investigative magazine *Mother Jones*. As journalist JoAnn Wypijewski remembered, liberals once again joined in the posturing. It was still a fight, she wrote, "to preserve space for the insurrectionary thought."[19]

The legacy of the purges left us with the myth of classless America, a distrustful place where everyone was out for herself, where solidarity had been largely forgotten, and where big, radical ideas were suspect. Talk of inequality, of any deep-rooted problems within the US economy, was simply taboo. We cannot understand why it took so long to notice the inequality that was creeping up on us without understanding the intense campaign, enveloping both the public and private sectors, that was undertaken to beat the idea out of us.

BY 2012, IN THE WAKE OF WISCONSIN AND OCCUPY, SPACE HAD ONCE again been carved out to talk about inequality without the fears that had hovered around such talk throughout the Cold War and post–Cold

War years. Many groups were looking for a way to use the rekindled radical imagination to create concrete changes. New York Communities for Change (NYCC), the group that arose from the ashes of ACORN in New York, had been organizing workers at local grocery stores and car washes across the city. These workers, mostly immigrants, were often the victims of wage theft, and labored under the fear of deportation, yet they had been able to win several victories and even a few union contracts through a partnership with the Retail, Wholesale and Department Store Union (RWDSU) and the community organization Make the Road New York. Rather than going store by store, the campaigns attacked the business model of the whole sector head-on, noting that the problems were often endemic to an entire industry. If one car wash raised its prices to raise wages, that might just run it out of business and destroy any gains made for its employees.

The energy of Occupy had added vigor to these and other labor campaigns in the city; Occupy's labor working group had created a collective called 99 Pickets, which would turn out to support workers both on picket lines and through direct action across the city. Once again, there was a vision of a labor movement that could make big demands. In this environment, the partnership between NYCC and SEIU was born that would result in the Fight for $15.

The idea of organizing fast-food workers had been bouncing around SEIU and within NYCC for a while, backed by Jon Kest, NYCC's leader since the ACORN days, who died shortly after the first strikers walked out on November 29, 2012. The day before the strike, I spoke to Jesska Harris and Saavedra Jantuah, who both made less than $8 per hour. "The managers are telling us that we don't have power. In reality we do have power; they're trying to suppress our power," Jantuah told me. "They want to keep us down so they can be up and I think that's not fair."

Like the car wash and grocery store campaigns, what was then called Fast Food Forward targeted an entire sector: workers from McDonald's, Burger King, KFC, Domino's Pizza, and Taco Bell joined in. Like the Walmart strikes earlier that fall, the first actions taken by the new campaign were one-day strikes, supported by raucous rallies with community members, clergy, and elected officials. Dancing on Brooklyn's Fulton Mall outside of Burger King, fuchsia-haired Pamela Flood told a crowd that she wanted to make enough money to take her two sons on vacation, like her bosses did.

From the beginning, the movement called for $15 an hour and a union. At first, it seemed like an impossible demand, even in expensive New York City. But it was a big enough demand to be exciting, to make workers like Flood think about what they could do if they were paid a living wage. It was enough of a demand to dream about.

The next city to go on strike was Chicago, where community group Action Now also partnered with SEIU and took workers out on a one-day strike in April 2013. The movement there built on momentum from the 2012 teachers' strike and embraced that city's radical history, traveling to Forest Home Cemetery to visit the memorial to the men who had been executed for the Haymarket bombing, and learning about the Latina background of Lucy Gonzalez Parsons, the widow of Albert Parsons and a lifelong radical organizer. Striker Trish Kahle wrote of her decision to organize when her college degree didn't get her a "good" job and her Whole Foods job didn't pay the bills. "In my store, when I faced disciplinary action for violating the attendance policy we had been organizing against, I demanded union representation in my disciplinary meeting and my co-workers prepared to take action if they decided to try and fire me. Management backed off. The disciplinary meeting never even took place."[20]

In Missouri, the third state to go out, the campaign named itself Show Me $15, taken from the state's nickname, the Show Me State. There, leaders like Rasheen Aldridge would hone skills that would be deployed a year later in the protests over the shooting of Michael Brown by Ferguson police. In different cities, SEIU partnered with different organizations, but the pattern remained: organizing fast-food workers across the sector, and bringing them out on a single strike day that culminated in a massive rally that drew support from the community, from existing labor organizations, and from sympathetic elected officials.

The movement seemed as much about changing politics, the minimum-wage law in particular, as it was about organizing workplace by workplace. Since most fast-food chains operate on a franchise model, the immediate boss in most workplaces is operating on a thin profit margin, kicking back a required payment to the corporation at the top, and wringing profits out of the workers by keeping them at minimum wage or just above. By targeting the sector, and particularly the biggest names in it (McDonald's, Burger King), the campaign was saying that the extremely profitable brand-name corporations and their exceedingly wealthy executives were in fact responsible for the conditions in their franchises. The National Labor Relations Board backed that claim up, ruling that the fast-food giants could indeed be considered "joint employers" of the workers making burgers and fries on the front lines.[21]

One hot week in the middle of the grueling summer of 2013, the air conditioning at two fast-food restaurants in Chicago and New York went down. Workers at those stores walked off the job and refused to return until the air was fixed. Regardless of whether the NLRB recognized them as such, the workers were beginning to act like a union.

Crystal Thompson, who worked at a Seattle Domino's Pizza, attended the first Fight for $15 conference in Detroit and met other workers there. She kept in touch with them, sharing strategy and support, but was still too nervous to go out on the first strike in Seattle. The organizers continued to include her in the planning, she said, remembering how they would use the term "go bowling" as a code for going on strike. The first strikes in Seattle were dramatic, and they drew more workers in. "My directive was to create chaos," said Sejal Parikh, director of Working Washington, the organization that backed the Seattle Fight for $15. Workers struck, shut down their stores, and demanded the city's attention. What was at that point a national campaign still differed greatly from city to city, and in the Seattle area, where the effort to gain a $15 wage was already in motion, the city fizzed with energy.

There was national momentum around $15, a number that was high but not so high that it seemed impossible, and the fact that Sawant was bringing it to the campaign trail helped make it the center of debate. In turn, because of the strikers' demands, Seattleites began to see Sawant not as the bogeyman of Glenn Beck's fears, but as a candidate who might have something to offer. "The fact of a well-resourced, very media-intense campaign happening within our media market at the SeaTac airport, at the same time that we had the launch of the fast-food fight for $15 in Seattle, at the same time that we had the municipal elections, created a compression zone around $15 and around wages and work and inequality," said David Rolf.

As election day drew nearer, tiny SeaTac, with just 12,000 registered voters, drew more and more attention. The BBC even arrived on election day to do a live feed, despite the fact that Washington State votes by mail. "It was a once-in-a-lifetime campaign. It seemed as if the general public outside of SeaTac understood the issue, understood about the economic inequality," Heather Weiner said. "If the people can do it in a small suburb like SeaTac, they can do it anywhere."

The results on Election Day were close enough that neither the $15 campaigners nor Sawant knew they'd won that night. Rolf met Sawant properly for the first time days after the election, as they both waited for a final count. They both realized, he said, that at least one of the two had to have a victory in order to be able to win $15 in the city of Seattle; eventually, they both did.

Martina Phelps, the daughter of a welfare rights activist, had joined the Fight for $15 in Seattle just before the election. The first action she took part in was a march from SeaTac to Seattle, an eight-mile hike in the November cold. Marchers carried lit-up signs to symbolize $15 moving from the suburb to the city. "I can't even explain how that was," Phelps laughed. "The walk was horrible, but I spoke at the end. That was my first time ever speaking in front of a crowd like that."

It was the efforts of people like Phelps and Crystal Thompson and Malcolm Cooper-Suggs that changed the story in Seattle. Without workers in motion, the process would have been entirely different. "Voters have changed their opinions on whether they support higher minimum wages," said Sejal Parikh, "and this was done not through traditional knocking on doors or phone-banking; this was done through workers rising up and gaining the attention of people in their communities."

The workers' pressure eventually brought around the mayoral candidates, too, beginning with the eventual winner, Ed Murray, who used the issue to differentiate himself from the incumbent. After the campaign, Phelps, Thompson, and Cooper-Suggs made trips to City Hall to meet with council members and share their stories; they also kept up the strikes and actions, enough to convince business owners to come to the table and hammer out a compromise bill that would gradually get to $15 over seven years. Through the process, Sawant and Socialist Alternative continued to threaten to take $15 to the ballot in Seattle if the City Council didn't act. On the day of the final vote, Sawant offered amendments that would speed up the process of getting to $15, which were rejected by the other council members. The audience jeered and booed each rejection, and many assumed Sawant would vote against the bill. But the final vote was 9–0 in favor of $15. "It was an incredible victory," David Goldstein said. "It was also important that it was passed by ordinance. Because it showed that this wasn't some fringe thing that a bunch of angry voters did. 9–0. This is a mainstream idea. You can get to $15."

Sawant stressed that the narrative should not be that the political establishment—"a few people at the top"—sat down and worked out the details. "If this fairy tale is what people are fed then two things happen. One, it eliminates the reality under capitalism, which is that there is a fundamental conflict between the interests of big business and the interests of the working class. The other part is, it's such a disempowering message. So you have to wait for some mythical do-gooder at the top who's going to do something for you?" The message, instead, that she wants to stress is that this was an "organized collective struggle" by people who may all disagree on politics, but who agree that income inequality as it exists "is absolutely unacceptable."

When you talk to the workers who made the $15 wage a reality in Seattle, you can hear the power that they feel. Being part of the campaign changed Crystal Thompson's life. She didn't vote before she got involved in the Fight for $15; now she can rattle off policy priorities like a seasoned wonk, from mental-health services to the exact number of homeless sleeping on Seattle's streets. "Now I'm actually a part of something bigger—it's pretty empowering," she said. "To have my kid watch me and say, 'My mom helped do this,' he's proud of me. It's pretty cool."

TO DAVID GOLDSTEIN, SEATTLE'S LEADERSHIP ON THE MINIMUM-WAGE issue, and the push for economic justice more broadly, are part of an obligation Seattle has to the rest of the country. The tech wealth that suffuses the city comes from companies like Amazon, which might be a high-wage employer within the city—it didn't oppose the $15 minimum wage—but around the country mostly creates low-wage warehouse jobs similar to those at Walmart distribution centers. "We're like Rome," Goldstein said. "We have this moral obligation, because we're benefiting tremendously."

After the vote for $15, Seattle workers found themselves answering questions from others around the country. It was hard, Martina Phelps said, for some of the workers in New York and Chicago, who had been in motion for months before Seattle's first strike, "for us to just pop up and get it within a year—no one really knows what they're doing wrong." Malcolm Cooper-Suggs noted that the political situation was different in Seattle than elsewhere—in New York City, for example, where the city was unable to raise its own minimum wage without state approval. Political pressure had to build across the state, finally escalating to a point where Governor Andrew Cuomo, who had formerly opposed raising the wage, empaneled a wage board in 2015 that formally approved a $15 an hour wage for the fast-food industry by 2021.

In Seattle, a socialist candidate taking up the demand helped move it to reality; in New York, the circling corruption investigations of major politicians in the legislature helped to bring Cuomo to the table. Looking for friends, the unpopular governor took up the demand of the still-growing movement, which had added child care, home care, and other low-wage workers to its ranks, and bragged about New York's "leadership"—though San Francisco had already followed Seattle to $15 through a ballot initiative by the time Cuomo changed his mind, and Los Angeles became the largest city to vote for $15 an hour in July 2015.

In most places, the measures implemented did not immediately raise the wage, but phased it in over a period of years. Phelps and Cooper-Suggs were wary, too, of attempts to cut their hours alongside the raise, and talked of the need to stay active in their stores. "We have power; these stores don't run themselves, we make these stores run," Cooper-Suggs said. "I tell people to organize within their stores—stay strong; if you guys have a common issue, raise the issue, stand strong together on that issue, that's how you get things done."

The second part of the "$15 and a union" demand was harder to come by, Sejal Parikh noted. Winning a legislative fight was a big deal, but immediately after the wins in SeaTac and Seattle, there were attacks on the measures, including attempts to block or repeal them. Those attempts were partially successful in SeaTac, where a court at first excluded workers at the airport itself from the benefits of the raise. (In August 2015, the state supreme court ruled that airport employees would indeed get their wage hike.) "Without a sustainable organization, how do workers join together and fight back, and make sure that they defend their wins, and do more proactive policy stuff within the city, county, state?" she asked.[22]

Cooper-Suggs and Phelps were lukewarm on the idea of a union, but they did want such an organization, and they valued the power they had built with their coworkers in their workplaces. In the aftermath of the win in Seattle, Working Washington spun off into an independent organization and began to consider what a workers' organization for the twenty-first-century workplace might look like. The questions they were dealing with, Parikh said, were how to be findable by workers, to those who use social media comfortably as well as those who don't have Internet access; how to help workers develop their demands and connect to one another; and how to be flexible enough to adapt and to be able to create new strategies as quickly as their well-funded opponents could. "We need to be quick and nimble and experimental and militant because those are the things that work," she said.

Relying on elected officials for victory, even friendly ones, only goes so far, and particularly for the labor movement, playing an inside game has been a strategy that has gotten it burned many times before. Without some actual power in the shop and in the street, campaign trail promises can often fizzle into nothing. But the combination of disruptive movements and political candidates willing to stake out a seemingly radical position has often been how change is made.

The anger that I heard over and over while reporting this book—directed at both political parties—would seem to provide an opening for more outsider candidates to ride movement energy into office. The Working Families Party, for years mostly dependent on "fusion" voting laws in states like New York that allow multiple parties to endorse the same candidate, elected its first state legislators as Working Families Party–only candidates in 2015. The first WFP-only elected official, Letitia James, became a member of the New York City Council in 2003, and in 2014 she became public advocate, the city's second-highest elected office.

The Working Families Party came close to sending a challenger, Zephyr Teachout, against Andrew Cuomo in the New York governor's race in 2014; the party's decision to endorse Cuomo earned it a good bit of criticism. Teachout challenged Cuomo in the Democratic primary, and in the general election, longtime socialist activist and teacher Brian Jones joined perennial Green Party candidate Howie Hawkins's campaign and drew a record number of votes. "Promoting a genuine independent third party may have the paradoxical effect of getting more out of the major parties and genuinely shifting the debate," Jones said. "The bottom line is that it's becoming clearer to people that it's getting hard to imagine a way that capitalism can actually solve our problems." It was the year after that challenge that Cuomo decided to take executive action on the $15 wage.

To Cruickshank, Sawant was a "canary in the coal mine" for something new, a different kind of political party or coalition outside the mainstream and defiantly disconnected from the patronage of the billionaires who pump so much cash into the electoral system.

A $15 an hour minimum wage is hardly socialism, of course. It's a decent increase in the floor for workers, but still barely enough to live on in major cities like San Francisco, New York, and Seattle. That it took a socialist to be the first to make it a campaign platform was a sign of how far away from workers' demands the political debate in the United States had moved. But it became the central demand in a time of renewed protest and attention to income inequality. Different politicians have been able to have more or less success with a worker-focused agenda, but, as David Rolf noted, "what unites them is the fact that it was in an atmosphere of real, legitimate anger about the looting of our country and leaders actually being willing to talk about it."

How much the debate had changed—and how much fear there still was that it was possible to be too radical—was visible in the 2016 presidential race, when longtime independent Vermont senator Bernie Sanders, a proud democratic socialist, entered the Democratic primary calling for a "political revolution." On his first day as a declared candidate, Sanders brought in $1.5 million; he continued to smash fundraising records, raking in $8 million from small donations the day after he defeated former secretary of state Hillary Clinton in the New Hampshire primary. Supporters of Sanders flooded the Internet with calls to "#FeelTheBern" and organized marches in their cities and towns; in New York City, former Occupy organizers held a phone-banking session in Zuccotti Park. Sanders was especially popular with young voters; by mid-March 2016, more voters under the age of thirty had chosen Sanders than both Clinton and Republican front-runner Donald Trump combined.[23]

When Brett Banditelli helped kick off People for Bernie, he said, "We wanted to inspire people not to support Bernie Sanders, but to use his platform as a way to support themselves. It had less to do with electoral politics and more to do with community organizing." The effort kicked off months before the official Sanders campaign launch, building grassroots groups around the country that would last beyond a Sanders campaign. "Would winning an election be nice? Sure. But what's more important is winning our issues and creating a new world from the bottom up," said Banditelli, who had been involved in the Wisconsin protests and Occupy. "There's a real sense of it being about us. That's the most beautiful thing. The movement can run without me. The movement can run without you. But the movement can't run without us."

Especially exciting, he noted, was the involvement of very young people—in some cases, too young even to vote in the 2016 election. There was so much talk about so-called millennials, he noted, but the actual change might come about because of the generation coming after them. "They can't remember the financial crisis, but they can see the effects. They realize capitalism has failed and see socialism as *the* answer. That's going to be the long-term lasting effects," he said.

Sanders' declaration that he would run in the Democratic primary had disappointed some who had wanted a truly outsider campaign from the well-known, well-liked senator. Kshama Sawant was one of those. "We have to think about any of these campaigns not as an end in itself but what it could do to serve to show the way forward," she said. "Victory in 2016 would be for somebody of the stature, name recognition and the confidence that people have in Sanders, somebody on those credentials running an absolutely bold independent working-class challenge to the big business candidates, and serving as an electrifying pole of attraction to especially the young people on the left, and using that campaign as a launch pad for building a party for the working class."

Still, Sawant saw the value in Sanders's campaign even as a candidate within the Democratic Party, and she appreciated the issues that he brought into the race. He spoke of breaking up the Wall Street banks, universal health care under the banner "Medicare for all," worker cooperatives, and a $15 minimum wage in a campaign season otherwise dominated by corporate-friendly candidates. But many major labor unions, despite Sanders's position on the $15 wage, continued to endorse Hillary Clinton—even SEIU, which had spent so much time, energy, and money to make $15 the center of the debate, went with the candidate who insisted that $12 an hour was a reasonable wage. For much of labor, perhaps, the ghost of the Red Scare was still too close, and it was too hard to believe that a self-proclaimed socialist could win.[24]

In the first Democratic debate, Sanders was asked if he was a capitalist. "Do I consider myself part of the casino capitalist process by which so few have so much and so many have so little? By which Wall Street greed and recklessness wrecked this economy? No, I don't," he said, to resounding cheers. Clinton jumped in with a defense of capitalism: "I don't think we should confuse what we have to do every so often in America, which is save capitalism from itself." Even in defense of the system, it seemed, one had to admit that capitalism unchecked would self-destruct.[25]

From New Hampshire to Washington, as Sanders's poll numbers brought him neck and neck with Clinton, it seemed that plenty of people were tired of saving capitalism from itself. In Seattle, Sawant was popular enough not only to get elected in 2013, but to get reelected in 2015, this time with the support of the unions that had opposed her before. She had won over quite a few of the city's Democrats despite her adamant opposition to the two major parties. "There are a lot of Seattle Democrats who chafe under the neoliberal moderate Democratic Party in the state and in this country and really want something to the left, and they see her as what they would love to have," Robert Cruickshank said. They might not all have been ready to discard the party and join Socialist Alternative, but they supported Sawant: the two Democratic Party groups whose districts overlap with her council district chose to not endorse a candidate for the 2015 election, a tacit endorsement of Sawant, who could not receive their direct endorsement because she's not a party member.

The most common criticism of her was that she was divisive and polarizing, that she was ineffective because she only wanted to stake out a far-left position. While she had been willing to take a stand and fail in order to make a point, she was often much more effective than her critics would admit. David Rolf noted that "the issues she picks to organize around and to raise rarely get settled 100 percent the way she would have crafted the policy, but always to the left of where they would have ended up without that kind of voice."

"We've accomplished a lot as a city since she's been on the council in just over a year," agreed council member O'Brien when I spoke with him. "To pretend that somehow we can still do that and just play nice, that's what we've been doing for decades. There's something about her keeping us unsettled that forces us to do a better job."

Denechia Powell, a former organizer with Occupy Our Homes Atlanta who moved to Seattle after Sawant's election and worked with the Tenants Union of Washington State, said that having Sawant in power opened up more political possibilities; it was a reversal of the Red Scare's ability to limit political possibilities for so many years. "For so long it was like capitalism is the way, it is the light, the only way of living, and so seeing that someone in a city like Seattle can win as a socialist is big," said Powell. "I remember being in Atlanta following her campaign and just being like 'YES!' It changes narratives. It allows us to imagine more, imagine a world that is actually just and equitable and with a solidarity economy."

Sawant credited Occupy with kicking off the change that Fight for $15 consolidated and that people like her have been able to ride to electoral success. "Anytime you look at historical periods in the past, you cannot see the value of movements by looking at them in an isolated fashion," she said. "They're a continuum." Sanders supporters, too, pointed to the wave of movements behind them, crediting them with propelling the unlikely candidate to victory in state after state. At the time this book went to press, Sanders had won 22 states, representing a total of nearly 12 million voters, and had raised $230 million.[26]

For decades, it had been the right that successfully took fringe ideas and moved them into the mainstream of American politics. The Tea Party has been correctly credited with pushing Republicans into office who were more conservative, and more willing to stand on principle, than the mainstream party. That now ideas are moving from the left, from workers' movements and Occupy protesters, into the public sphere, becoming policy in major cities and propelling an insurgent presidential campaign, is a sign of a shift, a sign that all of the years of the Red Scare couldn't, in fact, completely kill the radical idea that a fair distribution of wealth is possible. Seattle's organized business lobby, Goldstein noted, didn't even fund a ballot initiative opposing the $15 an hour wage in Seattle. "They would've lost."

CHAPTER EIGHT

THE MILITARIZATION
OF EVERYTHING

T HE VIDEO DOESN'T SHOW YOU WHERE THE PROTEST BEGAN, OR
give any indication as to what it was about. It begins with a
close-up shot of slim-armed white girls in tank tops, surrounded
by blue-shirted police. The title of the video tells you that they are NYPD.
The girls are pinned behind orange webbing being held up by the line
of officers, who are pushing the girls back onto the sidewalk just south
of an overpriced sushi restaurant.

One version of the video has been slowed down to draw the viewer's
attention to an arm in the white shirt of a high-ranking officer, reaching
out from the top, right-hand side of the frame, bearing a spray canister.
And then you see a girl crying. The protesters, still penned in by police
officers turning their faces away from the pepper spray, crumple to the
ground, wailing. The original clip has been viewed over 1.6 million times
since it was first uploaded on September 24, 2011.[1]

The officer was identified as Deputy Inspector Anthony Bologna, a
twenty-nine-year veteran of the force. For pepper-spraying unarmed,
penned-in protesters in the face, he was docked ten vacation days and
reassigned to Staten Island. District attorneys refused to press charges.
But his actions helped the protest known as Occupy Wall Street go viral.

The clip spread like lightning via social media, and people who had mostly ignored the encampment in New York's financial district up to that point reacted viscerally. The police mishandling of the protests managed to draw even more attention and people to Occupy. According to sociologist Ruth Milkman, "they made a series of errors that blew it up in a big way."

Possibly an even bigger mistake was the NYPD's decision to arrest seven hundred protesters after allowing them to walk into traffic lanes on the Brooklyn Bridge. My colleague Kristen Gwynne was covering the march and Tweeting until the protest was halted by a line of police. "People started screaming 'Fall back!' The police kept pushing, and suddenly we were crushed, slammed up against each other and corralled on both sides by police. It was so tight my feet were barely touching the ground," she reported. "A girl shouted, 'It's the police doing this! No one is pushing back!' Other people yelled to them, 'Stop it! Why are you doing this?'" She noted, "In the time it took them to arrest hundreds of us, we could have crossed the bridge four times."[2]

The viral spread of these incidents demonstrated the importance of social media, and particularly the new live-streaming technology, which allowed anyone with a smartphone to become her own broadcast media outlet. Americans who had thrilled to video broadcasts from Egypt's revolution were now producing their own. The police, Milkman said, "had no clue what they had blundered into."

Violent conflicts with the police were common at Occupy encampments. In Oakland, California, where police in riot gear cracked down quickly on protesters, reporter Susie Cagle described repeated experiences of being teargassed and threatened by a wall of riot-masked officers brandishing clubs, faceless black-clad versions of Star Wars Stormtroopers. The protesters were evicted on October 25 from the plaza they had renamed after Oscar Grant, a young black man killed by Bay Area Rapid Transit Police on New Year's Day 2009. They regrouped and called for the city's workers to join them in a general strike November 2.[3]

Cagle was due to write an article for me on the strike day, but the next morning I woke to the news that she'd been arrested overnight. I called the police department and was shuffled around repeatedly as I tried to find out where she was being held. My repeated insistence that she was a working journalist had little effect—a potent reminder that the First

Amendment rights of journalists, too, are limited, particularly in the police crackdown zone.

So-called "less lethal" rounds were fired at the Oakland protesters; occupier Scott Campbell filmed the rubber bullet that hit him as he panned his camera down a line of riot police standing quietly along the edge of the plaza—quietly, until the pop and flash of the shot and Campbell's scream as he fell. Cagle was arrested after sprinting from a tear-gas canister; her video showed legal observers in lime-green hats with their hands raised, standing between her and what looked like a war zone, complete with clouds of gas and the bright flashes of "flashbang" grenades. Once in jail, she reported being forced to take a pregnancy test, groped, and commanded to shake her breasts in front of a line of male inmates. All for a misdemeanor charge of "failure to leave scene of riot."[4]

Cagle's story was not the worst to come out of Occupy Oakland. That honor likely belongs to twenty-four-year-old Marine Corps veteran Scott Olsen, who was hit in the head October 25 by a police officer firing a beanbag bullet, made of birdshot wrapped in cloth, out of a shotgun. As Olsen lay on the ground, Oakland police threw a flashbang grenade toward the protesters who rushed to aid him. "You can't safely fire beanbags into a crowd after you deploy those flashbangs," Olsen said later. "You can't hit the target, because people are going to be running."[5]

The two-tour Iraq veteran had joined the Marines in 2006 as a staunch supporter of the war. His first tour of duty, he said, gave him "perspective, empathy for people's struggles around the world, against occupiers, against imperialism." He joined Iraq Veterans Against the War (IVAW) upon his return, then took part in the Capitol occupation in Madison, Wisconsin, in 2011. After he moved to San Francisco for a job at a software company, Olsen accompanied IVAW colleagues to Occupy San Francisco and Occupy Oakland. "I think people are getting able to see the way the system works, and I think people see the connecting dots of exploitation around the world that's enabled by the military and keeps our American interests flying," he said.[6]

Two years after he was shot, Olsen joined protesters in Oakland at Urban Shield, a Department of Homeland Security–funded convention, where the companies that make weapons and surveillance equipment display their wares to police departments. "We're seeing continued training in scenarios that paint the public as an enemy," Olsen said. "The police forces right in this building are buying the same weapons that they used to shoot me."[7]

Olsen won a $4.5 million settlement from the City of Oakland in 2014, much of which went to cover medical bills. "Whatever the amount is, it's certainly not enough to make up for a part of my brain that is dead and will forever be dead," he said.[8]

In Los Angeles, when the police came to evict one of the last remaining occupations, they wore hazardous materials suits, the type used to protect against biological contaminants, chemical spills, or radiation. "When those white-suited hazmat people came running from a corner of the police station we weren't aware of, it was apocalyptic," the Reverend Peter Laarman, part of Occupy LA's Interfaith Sanctuary Support Network, told me. "An audible gasp went up from people who were observing." Protesters who were arrested said they were swabbed for DNA, a practice that Michael Ratner, president of the Center for Constitutional Rights, told me was probably illegal. "It paints the protesters as a dangerous infection in America that has to be cut out," Ratner explained. The city of Los Angeles later settled with protesters for $2.45 million for what an attorney for the occupiers called "unconstitutional" arrests.[9]

Brutal crackdowns like these were designed to contain and deter protesters, and they were widespread and coordinated. Documents released to media outlet Truthout and to the Partnership for Civil Justice Fund revealed widespread monitoring of the Occupy protests by the FBI and the US Department of Homeland Security; Joint Terrorism Task Forces in multiple cities were involved at various times. FBI officials shared information with private businesses that might be targets of the movement's actions, including the New York Stock Exchange. Naval Criminal Investigative Services (NCIS) was also involved in monitoring actions at the ports in Oakland.[10]

A report issued by the Global Justice Clinic at New York University's School of Law and the Walter Leitner International Human Rights Clinic at Fordham Law School documented extensive police abuses at Occupy in New York that added up to "a complex mapping of protest suppression." Violent actions included "hard kicks to the face, overhead baton swings, [and] intentionally applying very hard force to the broken clavicle of a handcuffed and compliant individual." The white plastic flex-cuffs used by officers at protests, which function like zip-ties, clicking tighter but impossible to loosen, caused injuries. Police repeatedly denied medical care to protesters. Legal observers faced assault and arrest, and video surveillance of protesters was constant.[11]

"For protesters who previously had little interaction with police, these abusive practices have radically altered worldviews about the role of police in protecting citizens," the report noted. "For others who had long experienced official discrimination and abuse, especially those from minority and economically disadvantaged communities, protest experiences have simply reinforced existing negative perceptions." The concerns about overly aggressive, militarized policing, the report continued, came alongside a backdrop of "disproportionate and well-documented abusive policing practices in poor and minority communities outside of the protest context."[12]

What was new at Occupy, in other words, was not routinized police abuses and violation of the civil rights of Americans. That had been happening for a long time, something that the occupiers in Oakland acknowledged with their decision to name their encampment after Oscar Grant. What was new was that it was happening on a large scale, to white people, in front of cameras and legal observers. White activists might have been terrified and outraged at their first experiences being brutalized by the police. Some of them did tire of the abuse and give up; others probably stayed home altogether. But when militarized cops rolled into a neighborhood that had been saturated in dehumanizing treatment from the cops on a daily basis, the residents didn't simply get angry. They rose up.

Sometime in the summer of 2014, Diamond Latchison remembered, her father asked her if she thought her generation (she's twenty-one, a much-maligned "millennial") would rise up in protest if something happened. He had his doubts, and to be honest, so did she. But that all changed later that summer. On August 9, 2014, Latchison was at work at a local movie theater and checked Twitter on her break. "I saw a picture of a boy lying down on the ground. I thought, 'That's evil, why would you take that picture and put it on social media?'" She quickly realized that it must be nearby, as it was all over her timeline, and then saw the word "Ferguson." She thought, "Ferguson like right down the street, like ten minutes away from me Ferguson?" She kept checking her Twitter feed throughout her shift. "He was still there, on the ground."

Michael Brown Jr. was eighteen years old when he was shot by police officer Darren Wilson outside his apartment in Ferguson, a suburb of St. Louis. As his body lay in the street, residents of the Canfield Green Apartments began to gather along the police tape that roped off the street. He lay there for four and a half hours as the grief and anger built among his neighbors. Brown's mother, Lesley McSpadden, identified her son from a cellphone video.[13]

When Latchison got home, she wanted to go to Ferguson and see what was happening for herself, but her parents stopped her. She tried then to find a TV news broadcast, but there was nothing. "My only news was Twitter," she said. Even when local news began to cover it, the news she was getting from Twitter was better.

Rasheen Aldridge worked at a car rental outlet by the airport, northwest of both St. Louis and Ferguson. He, too, was at work on August 9 and saw a mention on Facebook of a young man who had been killed at the Canfield Apartments. "Honestly, I didn't think too much of it, sadly, because it just was another young man in St. Louis being gunned down, nothing's going to happen," he said. "But once I went on Twitter, I saw the details and the response of community people reporting instead of the news reporting on it, you got a different idea of what was actually going on."

Aldridge began to notice police cars flying down the highway, back toward the city and Ferguson. He called a colleague of his from the Show Me $15 organizing campaign, who worked at a McDonald's off of West Florissant, the main street that the protesters had gathered on, and she filled him in on details. They decided to go down there the next day to put the organizing and mobilizing skills they had from the labor campaign to work.

At Canfield Green, they spoke with people who had been there the previous day. "It was very emotional, to see people out there still crying, telling the story of what happened," Aldridge said. "And then after we had visited the memorial, we went down to West Florissant, where a lot of people were gathering, and started slowly protesting, walking up and down the street. The skills went out the window and the emotion took over real quick."

Seeing the approach of the police in armored vehicles, aiming weapons from the tops of trucks, shook him. Residents, he said, were just trying to grieve, to process their emotions. "The reaction was just way, way uncalled for."

Latchison, too, joined the protests, but at first kept just missing the worst of the police overreaction, including the tear gas and the rubber bullets. She would leave Ferguson and check Twitter when she got home to find out that her friends were fleeing tear gas. School was canceled as the protests intensified. In addition to the 94 percent white Ferguson police force, the St. Louis County Police and the Missouri Highway Patrol joined the fray. The governor of Missouri declared a state of emergency on August 16 and instituted a curfew, but the curfew was different in different towns. Aldridge recalled announcing through a bullhorn that the curfew for Ferguson was approaching, but that in municipalities just minutes away on either side of them, the curfew had already been in place for an hour or two. "No one knew what was going to happen in those early days. It came 11:00, they didn't do anything, we didn't do anything, 11:10, 11:20, then 11:30, that's when they came with the trucks and the tear gas, they just started shooting it at us."[14]

The National Guard was called in on the 18th, though the curfew was lifted. Documents revealed by CNN after a Freedom of Information Act request found that the National Guard used language such as "enemy forces" and "adversaries" to describe the protesters and grouped them along with the Ku Klux Klan as enemies; meanwhile, the Ferguson mayor fretted that the National Guard didn't show up soon enough to "save all of our businesses." Saving Michael Brown, apparently, was less of a priority.[15]

The images of the tanks shocked the nation. Technically, they're Mine-Resistant Ambush Protected vehicles, or MRAPs, but "tanks" is what both reporters and protesters called them. Tef Poe, a local rapper who was on the scene early on, said, "I saw some people I've been knowing all of my life—for 15 years or better—standing there by armored trucks with M-16s pointed at their chests. They don't have guns. They have their hands up. I feel like the police force is mocking us. I feel like, you know, we're assembling in peace and they're mocking the fact that we can't fight back with weaponry. I've seen pictures where they aim guns at people and another officer stands to the side with their hands in the air, mocking the chant that we've been chanting. The 'Hands up, don't shoot,' chant."[16]

The chant came from reports by witnesses that Brown was shot with his hands in the air. "Hands up, don't shoot," would have been a powerful message for protesters facing normal police, armed with pistols and Tasers. Surrounded by MRAPs, breathing tear gas, it became something else entirely.

Weapons used on the unarmed protesters in Ferguson included flashbang grenades, rubber bullets, pepper balls (which were banned in Boston after a woman was killed by one in 2004), wooden pellets (developed by the British for control in Hong Kong and Northern Ireland in the 1960s), beanbags (like the one that had given Scott Olsen permanent brain damage), and the LRAD "sound cannon" (which can produce "pain-inducing 'deterrent' tones" and cause "permanent hearing loss"). Journalists Robin Jacks and Joanne Stocker tracked the munitions from Ferguson and traced most of them to two "less-lethal contractors," Combined Systems, Inc., and Defense Technology, a division of the Safariland Group. They also uncovered the use of two tear-gas canisters that most likely date back to the Cold War.[17]

Latchison was arrested for the first time on September 28, zip-cuffed and left in a police van by herself. She has delicate hands that she gestures with when she talks; telling this story, she demonstrated how they cuffed her, and how the cuffs got tighter and tighter. That first time, she was held for five hours; her second arrest kept her in for fifteen hours, alongside people who reported being denied asthma and heart medication. Bail, too, began to be hiked for protesters, sometimes ranging to thousands of dollars for people who were simply standing on a sidewalk when arrested, as videos attested.[18]

"Even in August, a lot of the police weren't wearing badges, a lot of them weren't wearing nametags, [and] media didn't question it," said Kennard Williams, another participant in the protests. "The people who are supposed to be a part of this 'protect and serve' system have their faces covered. Why do you need concealment?" he asked. "The 1033 program," he said, referring to the US government's program to transfer military equipment to local law enforcement agencies, " . . . training isn't required for the stuff that they give them. Police officers think that they are military in an occupied country. Because people who've proven irresponsibility without the use of weapons, it's probably a good idea to give them weapons, right?"

Afghanistan veteran Paul Szoldra wrote of the scene: "In Afghanistan, we patrolled in big, armored trucks. We wore uniforms that conveyed the message, 'We are a military force, and we are in control right now.' Many Afghans saw us as occupiers. And now we see some of our police officers in this same way. . . . If there's one thing I learned in Afghanistan, it's this: You can't win a person's heart and mind when you are pointing a rifle at his or her chest."[19]

The message being sent to protesters in Ferguson was that they were the enemy, that they were not people worthy of the protection the police were supposed to provide. The protesters saw the divide between themselves and the people who were considered worthy, and they faced down a fully armed military force in order to challenge it.

THE COMPARISON TO AFGHANISTAN WASN'T A COINCIDENCE. THE AT-tacks of September 11, 2001, ushered in a new era of war in the United States, one that had no borders or boundaries. Like the Cold War, the War on Terror is a battle conceived of by its initiators as a global conflict over ideas: a clash of ideologies. "We're moving into the era of the Cold War on Terror," journalist Jeremy Scahill, author of *Dirty Wars: The World Is a Battlefield*, told me. For our supposed allies in the Cold War, the key to unlocking funds and weaponry was to oppose Soviet communism; once the War on Terror began, the code shifted from anticommunist to antiterrorist language. Just like during the Cold War, battles abroad justified a ramp-up in domestic policing.[20]

"Instead of the Communist Menace lurking in every corner, now it's the Terrorist Menace lurking in every corner," Scahill said. Terrorism gave Americans an identity to defend; Glenn Beck's Tea Party–linked project, we should remember, was called the "9/12" project in an attempt to recall a moment of supposed national unity. It also offered the possibility of traitors within to be fought. "We're militarizing our response to any perceived problem," Scahill said. "It's a War on Drugs—so there's a militarized solution to it. We have a War on Crime—so we're para-militarizing law enforcement in the US."[21]

The ramped-up militarization at home seemed to inspire militarized antigovernment sentiment, too. After Obama's election, the rise of the Tea Party brought along with it escalated rhetoric about arming in the face of a tyrannical state, from open-carry protests to the comment from Texas gubernatorial candidate Debra Medina, at a pro-Texas-secession rally, that "the tree of freedom is occasionally watered with the blood of tyrants and patriots." Sharron Angle, who challenged Democratic Senate leader Harry Reid in 2010, liked to refer to "Second Amendment remedies" and hint that she might be packing heat during interviews.[22]

The Obama years also saw a revival of the kind of armed militias that had arisen in the 1990s. Perhaps the most dramatic example took place in the winter of 2016, when armed militia members occupied an Oregon wildlife refuge in protest over the long prison sentences given to ranchers who had burned brush on federal lands. Dwight and Steve Hammond were charged under the Clinton-era Federal Antiterrorism and Effective Death Penalty Act and given mandatory minimum sentences of five years, whereupon Ammon and Ryan Bundy, already famous within the militia movement for a similar standoff at their father's ranch in 2014, led a protest that they insisted was peaceful. Nevertheless, their nearly month-long occupation ended in arrests and the death of one of the occupiers at the hands of police. They drew support from several militant and "patriot" groups, including the Oath Keepers.

The Oath Keepers were a group of largely current and former military personnel and police officers who had vowed to protect the Constitution of the United States—even from "unconstitutional" orders that might be issued by higher-ups. Sam Andrews, who grew up in St. Louis County and spent thirty years working in private security and weapons training, had found the Oath Keepers a couple of years before the uprising in Ferguson. He was dismayed by the "gradual erosion of our rights" that he saw under both Bush and Obama, citing the PATRIOT Act, the National Security Agency surveillance programs, and Hillary Clinton's private email server as examples of "both parties of this country violating our rights, acting like an elite ruling class that can functionally ignore laws at the expense of people."[23]

When the protests began in Ferguson, Andrews was disturbed by the police response, both the use of militarized weapons on a civilian population and the failure of the police to protect local businesses. He criticized the governor's use of the National Guard to protect "his rich friends' assets in Clayton" rather than the people and small businesses in Ferguson.

Along with a group of friends, military veterans, police, and Oath Keepers, Andrews went out to do what the police were not. He wound up working security for some reporters, and he began to hear the same refrain over and over, both from protesters and from black reporters: that if they carried a gun openly, as Andrews and his friends were that day, they'd be shot dead by police. To Andrews, this was a clear violation of their rights in an open carry state, and he reached out to the leadership of the Oath Keepers about planning an open carry march with black residents of the county. He was disappointed in the response, which he blamed on the fact that many on the Oath Keepers' board were police. Their reluctance to hold a march with black protesters, he said, led him to leave the organization.

What was happening in Ferguson should have been the worst fears of people like the Oath Keepers—a militarized state bearing down on its own people with the weapons of war. Andrews chalked the split up to racism. Justin King, a reporter who has spent a lot of time around the Oath Keepers, considered Ferguson the first major test for the organization, and it cracked along a fault line between police and military. "Most people in the military will tell you flat out, 'I didn't fight in Iraq to come home and have MRAPs rolling down my street,'" he said. "They're very against police militarization. Meanwhile cops are on the other side. I think the split was inevitable." He knew of three different Oath Keepers groups that left the organization.

It was Andrews's training that made him angry at police violence, especially the killings of Tamir Rice and John Crawford III in Ohio. In those cases, he said, the police officers violated clear safety guidelines, instead operating by the maxim, "Comply or die." He held his open carry march in November 2015, but entrenched fears, he said, still kept many black supporters at home. About a dozen people joined him, most of them, though not all, white.[24]

The Oath Keepers were not wrong to note the increase in militarization at home; indeed, the average local police department has enough firepower to make an attempt to out-armed-force the government a laughable proposition. The US government is, quite simply, better armed than any other force in the world, and an increasing number of those high-tech weapons are being placed in the hands of police departments—not just in major cities like New York that might be obvious targets for terror-ism, but in suburbs and small towns. The founding of the Department of Homeland Security provided both funding and an excuse to beef up as towns launched new SWAT teams and acquired MRAPs, guns, armor, aircraft, and other tools of war. Between 2001 and 2011, Homeland Security had given out over $34 billion in "anti-terror grants" to towns across America, including Fargo, North Dakota (pop. 105,925), and Fon du Lac, Wisconsin (pop. 43,021). The grants expanded under the 2009 post–financial crisis stimulus program.[25]

Some of the military equipment seen on the streets of Ferguson dated back further. "The drug war certainly laid the foundation for all sorts of mechanisms through which law enforcement works with the Feds to ob-tain both power and money," said Kade Crockford of the Massachusetts ACLU. "We saw that those foundations were massively expanded upon in the years after 9/11 and through the present." The 1033 program Kennard Williams spoke of came from a post–Cold War 1990s National Defense Authorization Act, which aimed to move weapons from areas where they were supposedly no longer needed (the military) to places where they were needed (American cities, where crime and drugs had replaced communism as the fears du jour). Section 1208 of that act allowed the military to transfer weapons and gear to law enforcement agencies that were "suitable for use by such agencies in counter-drug activities." Whether armored vehicles were actually suitable was not, apparently, up for debate. In 1996, Section 1208 became 1033, and it continued to send Humvees and grenade launchers to small towns. The companies that make these military weapons thrilled to this new market for their goods and began to target their products specifically at domes-tic police agencies at conferences like Urban Shield, where Scott Olsen joined the protests.[26]

In fact, Ferguson and Occupy were not the first time these weapons had been used against protesters at home. The protests at the G-20 eco-nomic summit in 2009 were Mary Clinton's first encounter with heavily militarized police. "That was the first time that the LRAD sound cannon was used on US soil," she said. "I would see our civil rights and our rights to protest and assemble totally violated in a way that didn't make sense.

It's actually the militarization of police and the state apparatus of protecting capitalism."

That apparatus, Crockford said, has been very visible in the so-called fusion centers, where private and public security converge. "There is a fusion center in New York called the Lower Manhattan Security Initiative, which is staffed by security operatives who work for the major financial firms that were the targets of the Occupy protests," she said. "You literally have members of law enforcement paid by the public sitting next to security officials who are employees of the largest financial firms in the country monitoring protests outside directed at those financial firms." Crockford is correct about this: the Department of Homeland Security even describes the fusion centers on its public website, and its description is consistent with Crockford's. There are over seventy federally funded fusion centers around the country.[27]

Inside the United States, particularly after 9/11—and then again after the Paris attacks in November 2015—immigrants bore the brunt of Americans' suspicions and fears. This is not new—immigrants had been targets of the anticommunist witch hunts. But in the post–9/11 age, fears of terrorism merged with a fear much closer to home for many people—the fear of losing one's job to a migrant worker who would do it for less. The militarization of the US-Mexico border (notably, not the border with Canada), and the increase in power granted to Immigration and Customs Enforcement (ICE), reflected these fears. A huge chunk of Homeland Security's budget goes to "border enforcement," which features Predator drones that, according to one report, cost more than $12,000 an hour to operate. The Immigration and Naturalization Service (INS) has its own SWAT teams, which crash into homes and businesses and round up undocumented immigrants, many of whom are then sent to private detention centers owned by corporations that spend hundreds of thousands of dollars lobbying for "enforcement-first" immigration policy. Surveillance of Muslim immigrants and Muslim Americans ramped up significantly after 9/11 and was carried out by many different agencies, from the NYPD's Intelligence Division to the FBI to the Transportation Security Administration (TSA), which was created in 2001 and then moved to the Department of Homeland Security in 2003.[28]

But policies directed at people who are designated as "other" to American society, from recent immigrants to communists to African

Americans, almost always wind up hitting the broader population. In 2015, the news broke that Chicago's police were operating a facility that lawyers compared to a CIA "black site," where arrestees were reportedly held incommunicado, kept out of official booking data, and subject to abuses that mirrored those in "War on Terror" interrogation sites. Brian Jacob Church, who was in Chicago to protest the 2012 NATO summit, was held there for twelve hours. He told reporter Spencer Ackerman of *The Guardian,* "I had essentially figured, 'All right, well, they disappeared us and so we're probably never going to see the light of day again.'" He was found not guilty, eventually, of terrorism charges.[29]

The War on Terror rhetoric is not so different from the Cold War rhetoric—the enemy is everywhere and could be anyone, and we must watch you for your own good. And that rhetoric has been used to justify massive surveillance of pretty much everyone. When former National Security Agency (NSA) contractor Edward Snowden leaked a massive trove of documents detailing the NSA's program of data collection, many Americans were shocked to realize just how big the surveillance dragnet had become. Cellphone companies were passing on customer data to the NSA; Internet companies allowed the NSA access to communications data from their servers; software allowed the NSA to search, with no prior authorization, databases containing chats, emails, and browsing histories of millions of people. And that was only the beginning.[30]

"Surveillance is secret. It is not like a tank," the ACLU's Crockford said. "A tank comes out into the street and there are heavily armed military-clad guys standing in the gun turret pointing a weapon at a crowd of unarmed protestors. That is quite an image." Surveillance programs, such as electronic monitoring, don't provide such dramatic visuals when exposed. Alongside the MRAPs, Sam Andrews, the Oath Keeper who had split off from the organization, heard reports of stingrays—devices that allow law enforcement to eavesdrop on cellphone calls and track people by their phone signals—and other electronic surveillance devices on the ground in Ferguson. Crockford noted that license-plate readers had also been used to track protesters. "It is really difficult to identify that kind of surveillance, because it is really only effective for law enforcement if they can keep the existence of those operations secret from the public."[31]

State agencies' response to questions about such devices is usually a version of, "If you're not doing anything wrong, you don't have anything to fear," or, "We need this for national security." National security, it should be clear by now, is a mostly meaningless term; this argument is the equivalent of telling protesters "because I say so."

As political scientist Corey Robin wrote, the idea of "balancing" freedom and security requires one to assume "that security is a transparent concept, unsullied by ideology and self-interest." It is nothing of the sort if you are a protester on the street in Ferguson, blinking through tear gas at the armed police pointing guns at you in the name of security. We mostly don't balance freedom and security as concepts within our own lives—instead, some people get freedom and security, and others get neither. "What a fuller analysis of the metaphor reveals," Robin wrote, "is that the items being balanced on the scale are not freedom and security but power and powerlessness."[32]

THE HISTORY OF POLICING IN THE UNITED STATES IS A HISTORY OF inequality; certain groups, defined by race, ethnicity, or political views, must be controlled, while others quite literally get away with murder.

The very first SWAT raid in the United States came in December 1969 in Los Angeles, when the tactical squad attempted to raid the headquarters of the Black Panthers using, among other weapons, a grenade launcher. Inspired by the Watts riots and strikes by farmworkers organizing with what would become the United Farm Workers, LAPD chief Daryl Gates had created the team, which he had wanted to call "Special Weapons Attack Team." The name was vetoed, so it became "Special Weapons and Tactics"—SWAT. The members were supposed to be trained in crowd control, sniping, riot response, and those special weapons. None of that training stopped their first raid from being a disaster from start to finish.[33]

Angela Davis, who was outside the headquarters when the raid occurred, described it in her autobiography. Awakened in the middle of the night by a phone call informing her that police "had tried to break into the office," she rushed to the scene to find a standoff between the armed Panthers within and the SWAT team without. The street surrounding the office, she wrote, was cordoned off for blocks. Armed figures in black jumpsuits were "creeping snakelike along the ground or hiding behind telephone poles and cars parked along the avenue," firing weapons. "A helicopter hovered overhead. A bomb had just been dropped on the roof of the Panther office," she wrote. "They were like robots. The assault was too efficient to have been spontaneous."[34]

That first raid on the Panthers failed in its immediate objectives, but it succeeded in spreading the idea that police departments might be justified in using military-style tactics against radical political activists at home—particularly black activists.[35]

Police forces go back farther than that, but not nearly as far as most of us might think. The first official police department was established in Boston in 1838; before that, cities relied on night watch systems made up of volunteers. The NYPD was founded in 1845. Early police forces started off unarmed, careful to avoid appearing too much like an army; officers came from the wards they policed and were part of the political machine. They were nominated by ward leaders and appointed by the mayor, which gave them an incentive to remain popular in the neighborhoods they policed. Some of them even ran soup kitchens.[36]

Elsewhere, police were less interested in winning people over and more overtly interested in controlling particular sets of people. The police in St. Louis began as a force to protect settlers from Native Americans. In the South, white slaveholders feared slave revolts, and so, many decades before northern cities were hiring police departments, the South had institutionalized, uniformed, armed patrols with broad powers to arrest slaves and search their residences.[37]

For those departments, the idea that the people being policed were a dangerous alien population was there from the beginning. This notion is still at the root of the problems with the modern police force. Meanwhile, the job of policing has actually grown much safer—among the jobs more dangerous than being a police officer are driving a truck or a taxicab, roofing, and trash collecting. The inequality at the heart of the policing issue is perhaps most obvious when you consider that we have reliable statistics for how many officers are killed on the job, and yet no federal agency reliably collects numbers on how many people are killed by police. The first official attempt by the Bureau of Justice Statistics to calculate such a number, carried out following the protests in Ferguson and around the country, wound up with 928 per year, on average, over a period of eight years—or about one person every nine and a half hours. *The Guardian* tracked killings in 2015 and came up with 1,139.[38]

From the Haymarket hangings in 1886, to the surveillance of labor organizers and other troublemakers during much of the twentieth century, to the infamous beatings outside of the Chicago Democratic National Convention in 1968, to Ferguson, the full brute force of the police and of the judicial system has often been turned on those who have challenged the distribution of wealth and power in society. "Red Squads" and "Un-American details" intervened in meetings armed with tear gas and machine guns; police sometimes released people into the hands of vigilante lynch mobs to be killed or horsewhipped. Such police complicity with mob violence extended well into the civil rights movement.[39]

Under J. Edgar Hoover, FBI surveillance of suspected communists evolved into COINTELPRO actively infiltrating and undermining the efforts of civil rights and New Left groups. Hoover had a special hatred for the Black Panthers, a group he called "the greatest single threat to the internal security of the country." Notably, it was not their guns, but the Panthers' free breakfast program that Hoover considered the greatest threat. An FBI informant supplied the map used by the Chicago police in the raid that killed twenty-one-year-old Fred Hampton, leader of the Chicago Black Panther Party. More than eighty shots were fired, all but one from the police. Hampton's pregnant fiancée reported hearing two bullets pumped into his head at point-blank range, and the police saying, "He's good and dead now."[40]

In the 1990s, with the Cold War threat gone, the target of "counterterrorism" legislation and militarized policing was, for a time, the right. In Ruby Ridge, Idaho, and then Waco, Texas, federal agencies participated in disastrous shootouts with separatist groups that fueled fears among the militia movement that the federal government was, in fact, coming after them. The six-week siege of the Branch Davidian compound in Waco ended with tear gas, grenade launchers, a massive fire, and seventy-six dead Branch Davidians, including twenty-six children.[41]

In Seattle in 1999, the protests at the World Trade Organization summit were remembered for their success in disrupting the event, but perhaps they should be remembered more for what they taught police about handling large urban marches and rallies. "The real story behind the WTO is that the police created a riot," said David Goldstein, who was there at the time. "My daughter was in preschool. There were families there that were marching that day, and their three-year-olds got teargassed. Just totally indiscriminate." The city wound up settling lawsuits with protesters, including one for $1 million in 2007.[42]

Nothing has shaped modern American policing more, though, than the War on Drugs. That war was first launched in the 1950s to combat "Red" as well as black threats. Richard Nixon inflated it, bringing together all the fears of the 1960s and 1970s into one big policy package designed to appease the "Silent Majority": the drug war targeted hippies and radicals alongside black people and sold it all as a crackdown on violent crime. The drug war turned the right to security from violence into an excuse to pump money into federal law enforcement and saw both major political parties decide that fighting nonviolent drug users with weaponry and harsh prison sentences was the way to go.[43]

In New York, Governor Nelson Rockefeller, who, theoretically, was a liberal Republican, proposed mandatory minimum sentences for drug possession, sending people to prison for fifteen years for posession of more than an ounce of marijuana. Mandatory minimums quickly spread, and most of the people who went to jail were black or Latino. Under Ronald Reagan, with drugs designated as a national security threat, the military and local police were pairing up more and more often, using military spy planes to search for marijuana crops, and sharing in the spoils through new asset forfeiture policies—local cops would get a cut of whatever was confiscated from crime suspects. The drug war could pay for itself—meaning new toys for new SWAT teams to use in going after more drug users. And liberals like Joe Biden drafted bills that made most of these powers possible.[44]

While hyper-militarized policing provided dramatic visuals, the criminal justice theories of the time also gave us a much less spectacular policy that ruined the lives of countless individuals, forcing mostly black and Latino low-income people into daily conflicts with the police. This philosophy was "broken windows," or so-called quality-of-life policing. Broken windows made its debut in an *Atlantic Monthly* article in 1982, in which criminologist George L. Kelling and political scientist James Q. Wilson theorized that cracking down on petty crimes and small disturbances in predominantly black inner-city neighborhoods would prevent larger crimes. Despite no proof that this strategy worked, it remains popular to this day, defended even by officials who claim to be police reformers.

As journalist Raven Rakia wrote, broken-windows theory relies on an imperfect analogy between a broken window and a person, an assumption that the equivalent to fixing a broken window is writing a ticket for riding a bicycle on the sidewalk or selling loose cigarettes. Broken windows, and its stepchild, stop and frisk, are impossible to separate from the racist outcomes they produce. The policies harken back to the "Black Codes" passed after the end of slavery, which criminalized vagrancy, absence from work, and other minor offenses, pushing the newly freed back into forced labor in prison. An ACLU study found that between 2002 and 2011, close to 90 percent of the people stopped in New York were black or Latino, and about 88 percent of the time, the person stopped had done nothing illegal. In total, that was more than 3.8 million stops of people who didn't even have a joint in their pocket. The new mayor, Bill de Blasio, vowed to end stop and frisk when he took office in 2014, but over his first seven months in office, the police made more misdemeanor arrests than they had the previous year. The disparity remained stark: 86 percent of those arrests were of people of color.[45]

Those misdemeanor arrests can often escalate. Some 55,000 arrests were made over the past decade in New York for which the top charge was resisting arrest, meaning that the original "crime" was a low-level offense. Shortly before Michael Brown was killed in Ferguson, a Staten Island man, Eric Garner, was stopped by a police officer, ostensibly for selling loose cigarettes. Garner refused to submit, complaining of constant harassment. "It ends today!" he said. The officer, Daniel Pantaleo, placed Garner in a chokehold. The disturbing video captured by a bystander features Garner repeatedly wheezing, "I can't breathe." They were his last words.[46]

This kind of policing divides society into the protected and those whom they need protection from—into those who are policed and those who are not. Those effects snowball. As Rakia noted, "The person selling items on the street without a permit may not be able to get traditional employment because they have a record—and is the same person targeted by police in the name of 'maintaining order.'"[47]

When New Yorkers protested after the death of Eric Garner, when Ferguson rose up after the death of Michael Brown, such overwhelming force was deployed in order to protect against "violence" from protesters, "violence" that was almost entirely conceived of as—literally—broken windows and other vandalism. "When things move beyond just routine poverty policing, and black people start demanding a better life for themselves and their communities," Crockford said, that's when we see the full force of the domestic military police state. It is hard not to reach the conclusion that American society values windows more than it does black lives.

As sociologists and organizers Mariame Kaba and Tamara K. Nopper wrote, "for blacks, the 'war on terror' hasn't 'come home.' It's always been here."[48]

INEQUALITY HAS LONG BEEN A RECIPE FOR INSECURITY; MAINTAINING order in a deeply unequal country has necessitated heavy-handed policing. "Guard labor" in the United States—police officers, private security guards, prison and court officials, and weapons manufacturers, among others—has risen hand in hand with rising inequality. A justice system that cracks down hard on the Michael Browns of this world while letting their killers off is only going to solidify the beliefs of many Americans that the system is there to control them, not protect them.[49]

Part of the outrage that led to the protests and to the destruction of buildings came from day-to-day humiliations at the hands of the police. It also came from the knowledge that for municipalities like Ferguson, the constant harassment had a financial motive. Standing in front of a burned QuikTrip, Ferguson resident DeAndre Smith told reporters, "This is how they eat here, this is how they receive money, businesses, the taxes, police stopping people, giving them tickets, taking them to court, locking them up. That's how they make money in St. Louis. Traffic. Everything is all about money in St. Louis." Stopping the flow of income, he said, might serve to make those in power take notice.[50]

The Department of Justice report on policing and court practices in the area released in March 2015 backed up at least one of Smith's points: "Ferguson's law enforcement practices are shaped by the City's focus on revenue rather than by public safety needs," it read. "Further, Ferguson's police and municipal court practices both reflect and exacerbate existing racial bias, including racial stereotypes." Court fees and fines pile up quickly for people ticketed for minor violations like illegal parking—one woman, who had been experiencing homelessness, did not pay a $151 fine, which multiplied to over $1,000 and six days in jail. Ferguson is 67 percent black, but 93 percent of its arrests were of black people between 2012 and 2014.[51]

Racial disparities in arrests are a nationwide problem, but the convoluted municipal court system is somewhat unique to St. Louis County, which has a population of around 1 million people divided into ninety municipalities. While poor black residents find themselves locked up, the wealthy and well-connected—like the teenage daughter of a wealthy oilman who helped an attorney get into a posh golf club, who saw her charge on illegal possession of alcohol mysteriously disappear—get off easy. Some attorneys served as a judge for one town and prosecutor in others, while at the same time working cases as a private practice defense attorney. The municipal court gigs were typically part-time—and lawyers sometimes advertised their muni court positions when soliciting for clients. Ronald Brockmeyer, named in the Department of Justice report, was paid $600 per session as judge in Ferguson and Breckenridge Hills, and, until he stepped down, was also prosecutor in Florissant, Vinita Park, and Dellwood. "If you look at some of these people and their connections and everything, the numbers indicate that some of them are perpetuating racism," protester Kennard Williams said.[52]

The combination of the denial of rights by a judicial system gone berserk, on the one hand, and the extraction of money from already-poor people, on the other, created a system for exacerbating inequality. And it was built on top of a long-existing system of inequality: segregation.

St. Louis remains the sixth-most-segregated city in the United States; its metropolitan area, among the fifty "with the largest black populations," is the ninth most segregated. "There's a big division, it's called the Delmar Divide," protester Rasheen Aldridge explained. "North of Delmar is where a majority of African Americans live, even in North County, where the incident happened in Ferguson. There's a lack of opportunities on the north side, there's not the same jobs. If you drive up on Delmar and look to one side and the other you'll see it." Job segregation had deep roots; until the 1940s, when labor activists protested, even government-job offices were split into "white" and "colored," which meant that different applicants were funneled to different jobs (and black workers were screened for sexually transmitted infections). White flight sent the suburban residents of St. Louis County over the Missouri River into

St. Charles County when black people arrived in formerly white suburbs like Ferguson. Redlining and restrictive covenants all played a part in St. Louis, as did urban renewal policies that flattened historically black neighborhoods to build industry—or simply to put up monuments. Only about half the black St. Louisans displaced by urban renewal were offered any relocation assistance at all, let alone new homes. The subprime crisis hit the area hard as well; at the time of Michael Brown's death, half of the homes in Ferguson were underwater on mortgages. After the protests, former Oath Keeper Sam Andrews said, many small businesses in Ferguson could no longer get insurance, forcing them to sell out and leave. The spaces became cheap, making them ripe for developers. "Greed is driving all of this," Andrews said.[53]

White residents of the area, when pressed, can point to plenty of incidents that helped create the racial boundaries that now exist. The Reverend David Gerth, director of Metropolitan Congregations United (MCU) in St. Louis, watched his community connect the dots. Some of the members of MCU, he told me, remembered urban renewal, while others pointed to the Jefferson Bank protests in 1963 as a turning point. The protesters in that case were demonstrating against a bank that made much of its money in the black community, but hired almost no one from it.[54]

While some white residents joined in the Ferguson protests in 2014, others proclaimed support for officer Darren Wilson and the other police. Kennard Williams compared the reaction of some to the protests to "a brand of McCarthyism." Instead of fearmongering about communists, he said, emails and pro-police Facebook pages referred to the protesters as "terrorists."

The nakedness of the police brutality the protesters faced, to Williams, revealed the force that lurked behind everyday injustices. For people in St. Louis's black neighborhoods and suburbs, there was almost no social safety net—the positive side of government power; instead, their interactions with the state were almost all coercive. Meanwhile, the wealthy, even those who committed the massive fraud that led to the financial crisis, rarely faced criminal penalties.

Many people who have been exposed to the criminal legal system, according to political scientist Vesla Weaver, "don't believe the state will respond to their needs. Such people do not think they have an equal chance to succeed and see themselves having little influence over political decisions that affect them." When looking at the numbers in Ferguson, where so many were ground under the heel of the state, it is a wonder that anyone stood up to protest at all.[55]

And yet they did—some inspired by prior movements, others because they had simply had enough—and many of them found the movement more fulfilling than anything else they had ever done. "I've never liked nine to five but really being in this, being so conscious of everything, now I can see the reason why I don't like it," protester Diamond Latchison told me. "You work these ten-, twelve-hour shifts only to get the bare minimum, you barely have enough to pay rent still. Once summer hits, I may have to quit my job again and be like 'All right! Protest full-time!'"

ON MARCH 14, 2015, I SAT ON A FOLDING CHAIR IN THE GYMNASIUM at Greater St. Mark's Family Church, just a short drive from the memorial to Michael Brown in the street where he had died. I was there with a few dozen people, a mixed black and white crowd, for the People's Movement Assembly. The assembly had been called by the Organization for Black Struggle (OBS), a thirty-five-year-old group based in the area that has had new life (and funding) breathed into it by the movement. We went over the hand signals to use to show agreement or disagreement; unlike at Occupy Wall Street, there was no "block," and the meeting would not demand that people come to consensus. Instead, the large group made a list of topics that would be discussed in order to create action plans. It was yet another step in taking the movement from simply protesting and clashing with police to building the structures that would allow for the kinds of major changes the people in that room wanted to see.

The topics written on the sheets of paper on the wall in front of us ranged from ending the drug war to raising wages; from fighting restrictions on the right to vote to creating alternatives to the police. Abortion access was raised as an issue, as was access to healthy food. The group divided the issues into several overarching topics, and participants broke out into several different rooms to come up with plans.

I followed the group that tackled policing and the courts. In that room, participants introduced themselves and where they came from;

some were union members and organizers, while others were longtime anti-prison activists. One was a member of Socialist Alternative. Kennard Williams was in the room, wearing a bright green Ferguson October T-shirt. At one point, he spoke up to politely remind people of the rules of discussion and to let others who hadn't been heard yet take a turn speaking. At the end of the day, the groups came back together to share what they had come up with. I stepped outside with Montague Simmons, the director of OBS, to talk.

The movement assembly model, he explained, had been inspired by the work of organizers in Jackson, Mississippi, who eventually put one of their own, Chokwe Lumumba, in the mayor's office. "This is a moment where we've had more people get engaged, in and around activism, period, let alone the issue of state violence or policing, than we've seen in a very, very long time," he said. "We've had a lot of folks get activated who don't know exactly where their place is." The assemblies, he said, were designed to build a movement that had intersections, that could work on a variety of issues at once and link victories in one struggle to others that remain.

Over the five days I was in the area, there were rallies outside of the Ferguson Police Department and a silent march downtown; there was "Black Brunch," where protesters from the group Millennial Activists United disrupted brunch in a mostly white, affluent part of town to ask people to consider the violence visited upon black communities with their tax dollars; and there was "Monday Mourning," where protesters awakened Ferguson mayor James Knowles III early, holding fake tombstones bearing the names of people killed by the police, and delivered a letter asking him to resign.

Everyone I met just called it "the movement." There was only one, and everyone knew what it was. It was a movement for justice for Mike Brown and a class-conscious economic justice movement and a movement to dismantle structures of inequality wherever they existed.

There were plenty of experienced leaders and community organizers involved, but they deferred to the protesters much of the time—to the young people who provided moral leadership. There were specific, narrow demands and broad calls to awareness and action. There were new organizations and an "Action Council," a structure that allowed groups to plan separately and then come together to support each other and to share the burdens. There were skills being shared and learned. There was incredibly positive energy, and a lot of trauma from repeated clashes with police.

Rev. Gerth struggled with finding his role in the movement, at first, but toward the end of September, he committed to going out to the protests. One September night, the row of clergy—many of them, like him, white—knelt in the street to pray. "All the protesters just flowed in and knelt there, and it completely disarmed the police," said Rev. Gerth. "It was an amazing thing. There was this one guy at the front, who was still banging his nightstick in his hand; he was ready to crack heads. And now we were sitting there praying—'I can't hit them when they're kneeling down praying!'"

Eighteen-year-old Vonderrit Myers was killed about a week later. "He lived in my neighborhood, and he was killed by an off-duty police officer who was paid for by my neighbors," Rev. Gerth said. "The rich street in my neighborhood pays for off-duty security. We were there within forty-five minutes from when he was killed. I was with a group of clergy that prayed on the spot where he died, not long after his body was moved out."

The next night, tensions were at their peak. Riot police occupied the intersection of Grand and Arsenal. "It was the first time that I had really been that close in front of the riot police. That's walking distance from my house," said Rev. Gerth. "I was standing next to the St. Louis Bread Company with the armored car behind me. The police department that I paid for had occupied the street where I get my Communion bread." In those moments, the white clergy experienced the state violence from which their privilege normally protected them. Creating that kind of discomfort, Diamond Latchison said, was an express goal of the protests. In a strange way it is the police violence that can be the most deeply radicalizing; it can build the movement as much as it can eventually kill it.

Most of the media coverage zoomed in on the protests outside of the Ferguson Police Department, particularly at flashpoints like the nonindictment or the shootings of two police officers. Even the best coverage was tinged with riot porn, such as photos of burning buildings. Less featured were the creative actions aimed at challenging people in power to respond.

Kennard Williams recalled the takeover of St. Louis City Hall that the protesters staged for Moral Monday in October, just after the shooting of Vonderrit Myers. The original plan had been for a relatively small group to drop a banner inside. Instead, more than sixty people showed up, and they simply flowed in and took over. "I had a megaphone with me and I was calling to meet with the mayor," Williams said. He was going to present the protesters' list of demands, which included the removal of the city police from the 1033 program, independent investigations of officer-related shootings, and a civilian review board. But he was met by an aide to the mayor, who, he said, asked him if they were hungry and wanted pizza. "I looked at him and I asked, 'Does it look like we came here for pizza?'"

The mayor's chief of staff then came to meet with him and promised to open communications with the protesters within forty-eight hours. By 9:00 the next morning, the mayor's office reached out to them, and shortly thereafter, Mayor Francis G. Slay came out in favor of body cameras on police.

"If there is any hope for American democracy, it is in the streets of Chicago and Baltimore and Ferguson," said Kade Crockford of the ACLU. Because police crackdowns remain a large factor discouraging people from joining the actions, challenging the police is in some sense necessary for any future protests to stick; thus, the Ferguson movement became, in a way, the protest that made all other protests possible. But it took a lot of work to make those protests possible. Since the beginning of the protests, Kennard Williams had gone through legal observer training, street medic training, and nonviolent civil disobedience training. Those skills allowed him to play many different roles at different actions, from being prepared when the chemical weapons came out to keeping track of people who got snatched up to organizing actions like the one at City Hall.

The Ferguson protesters eventually won a court order preventing police from using tear gas without making a declaration of an illegal assembly and giving the protesters enough time to disperse—this came after the night when it was announced that Darren Wilson, the police officer who shot Brown, would not be indicted for the killing. On that night, Williams was at MoKaBe's coffee shop, a neighborhood business that had become a hub for protesters and a safe space during protests. Police fired tear gas that night right onto MoKaBe's patio. "People tried to go out through the back door, and they fired into the back alley at the exits of the building," Williams said. "I treated two kids like nine, ten [years old] for tear-gas exposure and flushed their eyes and everything."[56]

Flexibility as well as symbolism were key to the actions in Ferguson. Diamond Latchison cited the work of artist-activist Elizabeth Vega, whose creative actions could evoke a deep emotional response. The "die-in," often timed to evoke the hours that Michael Brown's body lay in the street, became symbolically important, too, both as a gesture of mourning and as a way of holding space reminiscent of labor's sit-down strikes. St. Louis workers with Show Me $15 held a die-in at a convenience store as part of a nationwide day of action in December; Carlos Robinson, a participant in that action, told me that they were "trying to show people the significance between injustice in our workplaces and injustice in our communities."

When Show Me $15 first took off, OBS director Montague Simmons said, there was some resistance within the city to the strikes. But after Michael Brown's death, it became easier for people to understand struggle and disruption as a tactic. Fast-food workers elsewhere, such as Malcolm Cooper-Suggs in Seattle, also connected their struggle to the Ferguson movement. "Working minimum wage, you see that when you don't have money you do other things," said Cooper-Suggs. "If you don't have a legal job you do illegal things for the money, you do illegal things, you go to jail, after you go to jail you're branded as a felon for life, it's harder to get a job, you're doing even more illegal activities. . . . It's a cycle that people get stuck in, and we've got to do something to break it, because if we don't we're in trouble."

"Every facet of the movement is interconnected. You have the Fight for $15—keeping people in a low-wage position is a locus of control, that's a method to control people," Kennard Williams said. "Using those same systems to deny people health care—that's used to control people; if you have an oppressive racist police force—that's obviously used to control people and keep the status quo. With the Occupy movement, power consolidated to just a small series of corporations that control other corporations—all of it is methods of control."

After August, many of the people involved in the movement formed their own affinity groups or organizations. One of the more visible groups,

Millennial Activists United, created popular T-shirts and hoodies paying homage to black liberation leader Assata Shakur. Latchison was a member of the Freedom Fighters, a group that began working together early on in the protests. "I think in the beginning it just started so people could remain close with people they came out there with," she said. "And then it started to become, maybe we can make something out of this; since we're all fighting for the same thing, why not make an organization?"

The different groups sometimes overlapped and often worked together to pull off big, dramatic actions. In addition to being part of Show Me $15, Rasheen Aldridge was also director of Young Activists United and remained close to other organizations in the city, including Missouri Jobs with Justice. Williams, too, worked with different groups; to him, it was a good thing that different people took on different targets, and that the movement was nonhierarchical and not structured around charismatic leaders. "What a lot of us talk about with this movement is it's not just one face, because a person can get killed," he said. "You can get rid of a person, you can take a lot of steam away. We're a community of people. And that's a very powerful advantage to have." For the young black men and women of this movement, the fear of being killed or otherwise targeted was real, not only because they were deeply aware of the history of leaders like Fred Hampton, Medgar Evers, and Assata Shakur, but because of the realities they faced (and still face) every day.

A variety of formal and informal Internet networks served to connect the protesters. "Twitter has been like the mecca," Latchison said. Action alerts went out on Twitter as well as on a text-message service that anyone could opt into. FergusonAction.com listed actions around the country, and two participants, DeRay Mckesson and Johnetta Elzie, started an e-newsletter and website (wearethemovement.org). The in-person Action Council meetings allowed organizers to plan together with people they trusted.

It was also important, with all of the pressures protesters faced, for people to take some time to take care of themselves, to balance the rest of their lives with their ongoing commitment to the movement, and the different groups allowed for that. Still, it was hard, Latchison said, to step back, even if others were there to step into the gaps. People gave up jobs to dedicate themselves to the movement. "People have become dead-end broke. They had money before, but they've used their savings—all that's gone," she added.

All this meant that dealing with trauma became a significant issue for many of the protesters. "To get teargassed is so far out of our realm of experience, to feel the burn, to deal with the grenades, to deal with cops in full tac gear rushing on you," Montague Simmons said. "I can't put into words what it's going to take to really process it. I know it's not going to be immediate." People stepped up to offer therapy and healing work, to create safe spaces as well as jail support networks and bail funds. Groups held self-care nights, where they spent time together to relax and be friends.

"PTSD is not a joke," Latchison said. As we sat in MoKaBe's, I watched her flinch when an ambulance passed outside, its siren on. Having been teargassed at the coffee shop, she said, she now felt more anxious being there, even though it was a second home for the protesters—she was greeted with hugs from four or five people as we sat and talked. "Some people don't sleep. I know I don't," she said. All the stress heightened tensions between protesters—"When you're like a family, of course there's going to be tension," as Latchison put it. But at the end of the day, they all knew they were "still fighting for each other."

Particularly important for Latchison was the support she felt from other women and other queer women in the movement. "I know that black lives matter, but what makes a black life? There's more factors than just the color of your skin. Do you have mental health issues? Are you going through the foster care system? If you are queer, if you are Christian or Muslim, what makes a black life valuable?" she said. "We fight for all of that. These women have been sexually abused, have been harassed, have been raped and killed by police; that's stuff that we go through, too, and for some reason we don't get that same discussion."

Within the movement, she said, they created a space specifically for women called Black Girl Magic, a periodic get-together for women to talk about their specific struggles within the movement. As a queer person of color, Latchison said, it was deeply important to her to see other queer people in leadership roles. "I came out, but not to everybody, until all this," she said. "Finally, I have a space where I can talk about my queerness and also my blackness as well. I don't have to keep being black and being queer and being a woman in three different spaces. I can put them all together."

The media depiction of the protests, OBS director Simmons said, "misses the fact that we're not just on the streets. We are actually having discussions about policy." He and others have testified in the state Capitol and in St. Louis City Hall on bills calling for civilian oversight of police. The movement counted the resignation of Ferguson police chief Thomas Jackson in March 2015 as a victory. Rasheen Aldridge pointed to the 2015 Ferguson City Council elections as another success: turnout was higher than in other recent elections, and three of the four candidates supported by the movement were elected. The Don't Shoot Coalition, a collection of progressive groups that formed to push for legislation in the wake of the protests, was tracking more than one hundred bills in the state legislature aimed at reforming policing practices and the legal system, though only one of them passed in 2015.[57]

President Obama announced, in May 2015, that he would modify the 1033 program in order to stop "tanks and other tracked armored vehicles, weaponized aircraft and vehicles, firearms and ammunition measuring .50-caliber and larger, grenade launchers and bayonets" from going to local police agencies. For many, it sounded like too little, too late, but they nonetheless saw it as a start to challenging the militarization of police. The response by conservatives like Representative Jeff Duncan (R-SC)—who posted on his Facebook page that he regretted having voted for a defense authorization bill that contributed to militarizing the police—was possibly more noteworthy, though Congress failed to take action.[58]

Rasheen Aldridge himself played an inside-outside role in the movement. In late 2014, he became a member of the Ferguson commission that Governor Jay Nixon created to look into the conditions behind the unrest. Although several members of the commission participated in the protests, Aldridge was the youngest, and he was seen as a representative of the movement. Just twenty-one, he gave the impression of being older; soft-spoken, he smiled slowly and chose his words carefully. The decision to join the commission, he said, was not an easy one for him. His first reaction to the news was skepticism. "The governor, instead of coming down to Ferguson, talking to the residents, he just put together a commission and the thing is people are tired of talks, that's why the young people aren't going anywhere."

But Aldridge sought out advice from mentors he trusted and then applied for the post. He had to go through a bit of background-checking, but eventually was told he had made it onto the commission. For the swearing-in ceremony, he arrived in a T-shirt reading "Demilitarize the Police." He then had to miss the first meeting because he was part of a delegation to meet with President Obama, alongside his fellow commissioner Brittany Packnett and members of Millennial Activists United, the Ohio Students Association, the Dream Defenders, and Make the Road New York. At subsequent meetings, the commission discussed the police, the municipal court system, and other local issues. They eventually, Aldridge said, managed to build some trust with the community, but he still pressed for more.

While on the commission, Aldridge continued to take part in actions, including an occupation at the police department. But he also began to consider how his actions would look—on both sides. "It's kinda hard to walk that line because it's like, am I selling out?"

Ultimately, though, the commission was just one of many ways to create change, and all of them overlapped. What originally was a movement in response to the death of one young man expanded not only to include other young black people killed by the police, but also low-wage work and shuttered schools and the economic depression in black communities. When the financial crisis hit, Aldridge noted, even people with college degrees weren't sheltered. But even as the nation was supposedly struggling, fast-food restaurants were popping up, creating more low-wage jobs selling cheap products. "Police brutality is the root of it, but we're trying to spread out and get to some of these other factors because those are also kicking our asses, too," Diamond Latchison said. "We can't just fight for one thing. You've got to take the system as a whole, not just part of it."

That systemic change, Kennard Williams said, would not come simply through voting. Taking direct action, remaining in the streets, challenging institutions that are oppressive, had to be part of the strategy for change. "I think that's one of the greatest lies that people in power have been able to pull off," he said, "fooling people that they legitimately cannot change things."

People who ask what the movement has accomplished, Latchison said, don't understand what they're saying. "Liberation is not quick, freedom is not quick, there's levels to this." Aldridge compared the Ferguson movement to the Montgomery bus boycott, which lasted 381 days—and was only part of the broader civil rights movement, just a part of the bigger freedom struggle.

The day after the OBS assembly, I drove to St. Louis University and joined a meeting under the aegis of "Sacred Conversations on Race (and Action)." Put together by Metropolitan Congregations United, the event was part consciousness-raising and part action planning. I had been invited by Rev. Gerth, and after the opening address and prayer ("God has asked us to get in this fight"), I followed him to the breakout group he facilitated.

The room was mostly older—a sign, perhaps, of the demographics of church membership—and mostly white. In the breakout groups, I watched Rev. Gerth ask a group of white men to articulate the ways it had benefited them to be white. "Michael Brown was stopped for walking in the street," said one man. "In my neighborhood, people walk and run in the street all the time." An older man said that he was able to buy a house when a black man would have been redlined out of it. Another couldn't explain it exactly, but said simply, "I'm probably here today because I want to understand."

Some of them bristled at the term "privilege," while others had been learning the language of social justice movements. A man in a Vietnam veteran hat explained the term "micro-aggression," and Rev. Gerth navigated the group through its own micro-aggression when a white woman began to explain to a black man that something he'd perceived as racism might not have been. More obvious examples of racism—everyone gasped when a younger black man related a tale of his college professor calling him "boy"—were easy for the group to understand, but they grappled with tougher questions of their own personal complicity in the system of white supremacy and of what could be done about it.

"My sense was that most of the people there were looking for a way to have some impact," Rev. Gerth told me afterward. "We also have found that if you're not taking some real risk, people leave and go, 'That was too nice. We need something that is harder than that.'" Part of the plan was to move people from the emotional reactions they were having to the events in Ferguson to an understanding of the power they had to make change and the actions they could take.

At the end of the event, rather than asking for a conclusion, Rev. Gerth and the other facilitators simply asked people to identify the tension that they would hold onto going forward. It helped people immensely, Rev. Gerth said, to allow them to realize, "I don't have to have an answer. I just have to be honest about where the tensions really are. And I have to take responsibility for paying attention to them and doing something in response to them."

"One of the things we said early on is that you can't go back to normal. There's got to be a new normal, because the old normal was diseased," Rev. Gerth said. In that space at St. Louis University, in the Organization for Black Struggle's People's Movement Assembly, in the streets of Ferguson, the protests were attempting to create a new normal. It is early yet—Montague Simmons said, "It's not 1964, it's 1954"—but that was the plan, even if, as one participant in the Sacred Conversations said, some of them will not be around to see it.

In the Christian church, said Rev. Gerth, he learned the concept of *kairos* time—God's time, a special or opportune moment when the world might change. "It doesn't work on the clock," he said. "A lot of us have felt like there's something *kairos* about this."

CHAPTER NINE

CHANGE IS GONNA COME

W INTER WAS COMING IN NEW YORK WHEN WE GOT THE NEWS about Hurricane Sandy. The storm, as it moved north, had been caught up in an unusual weather pattern; in the words of one Weather Channel hurricane expert, it was becoming "a monstrous hybrid vortex. A combination of a hurricane and a nor'easter." Somewhere along the line, it was dubbed "Superstorm Sandy." We didn't know how bad it would be, only that we'd never seen anything like it.[1]

It was the end of October 2012, just after the first anniversary of Occupy Wall Street, and later than usual for hurricanes, but climate scientists had warned that warmer waters and a higher sea level had put New York City and its environs at risk of record storm surges. I stocked up on nonperishable goods; a friend of mine who lived out in Coney Island came to stay with me at my Crown Heights apartment, well away from the flood zone. That night, we sat and watched TV and checked Twitter for updates. That was where we saw the video of the water rushing into the subways.[2]

That was also where I saw the first hints of something else happening. People I followed from the Occupy days were starting to talk to each other about what they could do to help. They had come together in response to the financial crisis; now they were preparing to deal with a very different crisis.

Julieta Salgado, an organizer with the Occupy-related Free University, said it began with a group text: "Let's get on our bikes and go see what we can do." Someone suggested heading to the Red Hook Initiative, a community center in the waterfront Brooklyn neighborhood of Red Hook. Salgado and Emma Francis walked from their Bedford-Stuyvesant home. From there, they decided to knock on doors and collect donations.

In Carroll Gardens, a wealthy neighborhood nearby but outside of the flood zone, the group went door to door, asking for anything people could give—blankets, candles, food. "No one turned us down," Salgado said. The next day, when she returned to the Red Hook Initiative, she saw people who'd given her supplies the night before: they had come to help.

People in the gentrified parts of Brooklyn were happy to donate, but nonetheless, Salgado said, it was already obvious that the storm had not hit everyone equally. Red Hook was a long walk from the nearest subway, and although it had become desirable real estate for reasonably well-off, artsy types, it was also the site of high-rise public housing. Without power, and with stores in their neighborhoods closed, it was the people who were already poor who were left struggling up and down stairs in search of help. A few days later, I joined up with two friends and walked from Crown Heights to Red Hook. I'd already heard reports that the Red Cross was conspicuously absent in the storm-ravaged areas, and that community groups and Occupy activists had stepped in to fill the vacant space. The hashtag #OccupySandy had spread across Twitter; the old networks were moving.

At the Red Hook Initiative, we found a well-oiled volunteer machine distributing food, diapers, clothing, blankets, and other needed items to lines of people. It was days after the hurricane had hit, and people told us that they still had no power. Familiar faces from Occupy eventually directed us to another Occupy Sandy hub further south, because there were so many volunteers in Red Hook that they didn't know what to do with us. In Sunset Park, at St. Jacobi Church, the division of labor that had created the Kitchen and Comfort and Medic stations in Zuccotti Park was at work once again as occupiers cooked hot meals and packed donations into bags to be loaded into cars headed for Coney Island or the Rockaway Peninsula.

"It's amazing how organized we are," said Michael Premo, one of the Occupy organizers in Sunset Park. Added Salgado, "The joke is on

[Mayor] Bloomberg. The people you spent $60 million trying to destroy, we're the first people on the ground."

The next day, I joined organizer Desean Burrus from New York Communities for Change as he canvassed in the Rockaways to see what people needed. "You from FEMA?" people asked us over and over again, referring to the Federal Emergency Management Agency, which had yet to be spotted. We saw one Red Cross truck, but quite a few police cars. "All I see is cops, and they're still harassing us," said Kenyatta Hutchinson, who stood by the floodline on his neighbor's house, which was above his head. The police didn't respond to requests for help, he said, but he was afraid to take his things out of his house, worried he'd be accused of looting. The people in this working-class, mostly black neighborhood were used to being left behind and overpoliced, but after the storm had wiped out their homes, the presence of security before aid was heaping insult on very real injury.

"This whole system is built around punishment and prevention of abuse instead of providing service," said Judy Sheridan-Gonzalez, an emergency-room nurse and at the time vice president of the New York State Nurses Association (NYSNA). After spending a few days volunteering in the Rockaways, she had quickly realized that Occupy Sandy was "the organization that was willing to do whatever was needed." She had tried to work with the Red Cross, with FEMA, or the New York Department of Health, but there was so much bureaucracy that nothing was getting done. "There was no public health infrastructure preparation at all," she said.

It was a story I heard over and over again, even though the big organizations were raking in the donations. The Red Cross eventually raised over $300 million, but its spokespeople argued that disclosing how that money was spent was a "trade secret." Doctors Without Borders workers were there, running their first US relief operation in forty years; they benefited enormously from activists and organizers connecting them to local groups. Nastaran Mohit, a petite labor organizer with a commanding presence, was one of the Occupy veterans who headed to the Rockaways. Her father had been a doctor and her mother a psychiatric nurse, so when she arrived at the Rockaways hub, health care was on her mind. She connected Doctors Without Borders to the Rockaway Youth Task Force, who took the doctors into the high-rise public housing buildings that were still without power. There, they were able to offer help to any-one with health issues.[3]

Mohit put out a call for medical and mental health professionals and was overwhelmed by the response. Doctors Without Borders couldn't manage all the volunteers, so Mohit began to search for a medical clinic that might be able to serve as a hub for medical aid. There was almost nothing open. She wound up at You Are Never Alone (YANA), a new community space, and with the help of YANA's founder, Sal Lopizzo, created a clinic. "Every day I was hoping that some amazing doctor was going to walk in and say, 'I've done this before, I'll take this over,' or FEMA would come in," she said. "Then we found out FEMA was refer-ring people at their tents to YANA medical clinic for medical attention, and we had St. John's [Episcopal] Hospital referring people to YANA medical clinic for medical care, and I'm like, 'I'm a labor organizer! This isn't supposed to be happening!'"

Mohit found herself juggling patient files, trying to get prescriptions filled, and passing patients from volunteer to volunteer. "I would say every single day, 'If this is not the strongest case for a universal health-care system I don't know what is,'" she said. "You already have a strained system and now we're in a disaster and these basic prescriptions that you could get in any other country, you cannot access in the richest city in the richest country in the world."

When she wasn't providing direct care, Sheridan-Gonzalez was busy coordinating with other activist groups, both to provide aid and to pres-sure the city to do better. "It was very unclear to us what the hell people were doing," she said. "What we found, aside from the fact that resi-dents were totally devastated—we also found that most of them weren't getting good health care anyway. With flashlights and a stethoscope we provided more information and care to people than they had probably ever gotten."

Pat Kane, also a NYSNA officer, had spent the hurricane at work at Staten Island University Hospital. Once she was able to leave the hospi-tal, she and some of her NYSNA colleagues took the union's RV down to Miller Field on Staten Island, where FEMA and the Red Cross were by then set up. "Every day," she told me, "we'd talk to the FEMA ambu-lances that were being deployed to Staten Island. Their orders were to stand by at Miller Field, and every day we would more or less convince those ambulance drivers to take us out into the community. We found everything from people that were still stuck on the second floor of their homes to families living in cars to ten people living in one room with no food and no water." Eventually, the mayor's office gave them official permission, she said, for what they were already doing.

The mayor attended a rosy opening ceremony for the New York Stock Exchange just two days after the storm. Although the financial district had also flooded and lost power, big banks like Goldman Sachs had independent generators powering their buildings and remained open, beacons of light in the dark. The signal was clear—the important parts of the city were functioning, the financial capital was back in action, despite the rescue efforts still underway, led mostly by volunteers, in the outer boroughs. "There's this disconnect between how [the wealthy] live and how regular people live," Mohit said. Residents, she explained, "know what's happening to them, they know that people of color and immigrant communities always come last, poor folks always come last, and the same applies for disaster response."

The city's push to move away from the acute response to the recovery, closing down Miller Field and other aid hubs, only exacerbated frustrations. The Occupy organizers had already been motivated to battle inequality, and the NYSNA nurses were used to seeing the results of poverty and the disparities in health-care access. But what they were seeing after Sandy was on another level: "It's scary when you're in the middle of the disaster, you see what the conditions are, and then you see FEMA saying return to normal, we're pulling out, all services have been restored," Kane said. "Where?" The people on Staten Island, she said, were hearing the stories about the money that had been raised by the big agencies and wondered why it wasn't going to them.

The nurses pulled together a rally on the steps of City Hall when their demands for increased state and federal investment in disaster relief and care were not met, and they managed to get some response from the administration. But the whole situation exposed deeper political problems. Sheridan-Gonzalez likened it to being at a pool, and seeing a drowning person. If the lifeguard isn't jumping in, you're going to jump in and save them; but eventually, if the lifeguard continues to ignore drowning people, what do you do? She felt torn between wanting to do the hands-on volunteer work—which, in a way, made it easy for the city to wash its hands of the job—and wanting to do the political organizing to demand that the city, state, and federal government do their jobs. For much of the time, the political demands came second to the volunteer work, and the mayor continued to pretend everything was fine.

"I think we should applaud ourselves at Occupy Sandy that we've done such a great job, but this is not our job," Mohit said. When some Occupy organizers began using the Twitter hashtag #WeGotThis, she and others jumped to say, no, we don't and we shouldn't. The ongoing attempts to privatize what's left of the social safety net rely on the argument that the private sector can do better than the government. When government services are sliced back, as they often were in the name of austerity after the financial crisis pressed state budgets, they fail when they are needed, which provides another excuse to cut them further. But as inevitably happens after a disaster, the private donations eventually dry up (Occupy Sandy raised and spent or disbursed over $1 million, most of which came in the month after the storm), and the volunteers have to return to their day jobs. Without a state response, people are left stranded with nothing. The second-costliest hurricane in US history, Sandy had wiped out 305,000 units of housing—homes or apartments—in New York state alone. Over a year after the storm, more than 30,000 people remained displaced. The *New York Times* calculated in 2013 that less than half the people who applied for government aid after the storm received it, meaning that many people were left on their own to rebuild, a hard enough task when you have resources, but an impossible one for families surviving paycheck to paycheck. Without long-term funding and support, the occupiers could not substitute for a functional federal disaster response, though they managed, with a tiny fraction of the Red Cross's budget, to do better immediate relief than the major nongovernmental organizations (NGOs).[4]

The hurricane and the movement around it changed New York politics. Mayoral candidate Bill de Blasio, a centrist Democrat with ties to the Clintons, picked up the demands of Occupy, the low-wage workers' movement, and the movement against stop-and-frisk to make inequality central to his campaign, outflanking Bloomberg's chosen successor. He also took aim at Bloomberg's response to the disaster and joined the NYSNA nurses in protesting hospital closures in the Rockaways and near Red Hook. After he won the 2013 election, however, those fights faded to the background. The hospitals closed anyway, and the rebuilding plan still allowed for gentrification of formerly working-class neighborhoods. Most occupiers avoided electoral politics, but community groups—and eventually NYSNA—had endorsed de Blasio and then were caught between wanting to keep an ally and wanting to hold him to his campaign promises.

Mohit was frustrated by the struggles of the movement to agitate for change with a new, supposedly friendlier administration. Organizations were overstretched, trying to meet the next crisis, and deal with the next closing hospital, the next foreclosure, the next budget cut. "We're all struggling to serve our communities, and on top of that what time are we carving out to actually address these massive structural issues?" she said. "If we don't learn lessons from these disasters, they're going to continue to happen. As climate change blazes on forward, the disasters are going to be far greater and more catastrophic, and we still will not have a structure in place that actually meets the needs of these people."

Occupy organizers believed in mutual aid rather than charity—in acting in solidarity with the community members, making decisions collaboratively, getting help as they gave it. "There was certainly a struggle within Occupy Sandy about the differences between charity and organizing social justice work," said Occupy organizer Andy Smith. "Where are our resources most useful: in really deep community organizing, or to be doled out one by one?" Despite these intentions, it was hard to demand that people who were traumatized participate in anything they didn't feel inclined to participate in. In the end, Smith conceded, "Occupy Sandy did a whole bunch of charity. Which is fine."

Existing community groups and occupiers with organizing backgrounds, though, were able to do some work moving from aid to action. New York Communities for Change, Make the Road New York, and Voices of Community Activists and Leaders of New York (VOCAL-NY) developed deeper bases. They began to bring climate change into their political analysis. "Now is the time to marry climate and economic justice," said Jeremy Saunders, lead organizer at VOCAL-NY. "Poor people across the world unfortunately have become aware that this is life and death for them." Though it is difficult to say to what degree climate change causes any one storm, what is not in dispute is that as the oceans warm and temperatures change, there will be more "natural" disasters.

"This is the time for poor and working people and the organizations and unions that represent them to say, we want to rebuild, but we want to rebuild in a way that starts to address the long-term implications of what's driving these storms," Saunders said.

Yotam Marom had been considering how to move forward after Occupy Wall Street when Sandy hit and wiped out his own New Jersey apartment. When he was able to leave, he began to do political trainings to help volunteers understand the communities they would be walking into and to give the people in the hardest-hit communities some answers for why the system was failing them. Occupy Wall Street had been in the center of the richest part of New York City, but Sandy brought the organizers to the communities that had already experienced the worst of capitalism's crises—unemployment, foreclosure, homelessness, incarceration, and untreated illness. Political organizing in that space took on a different tenor.

"An organized community is a resilient community," Andy Smith said. "An organized community responds to disasters of all types. Organizing is where folks in the community learn how to take actionable steps against climate change, which is an incredibly complex undertaking." In the Rockaways, that organizing became Rockaway Wildfire, a group that turned its attention to challenging the gentrification of storm-damaged neighborhoods, where developers were swooping in to build luxury condos on storm-destroyed beachfront property. And Marom began to work on building a broader movement infrastructure.

To Nastaran Mohit, Sandy felt like an inflection point, a moment that could open the door to big changes. "I think for so many of us who are trying to build a more just world, when we say another world is possible, there were so many glimmers in this relief process that gave us a glimpse into what this world could look like. What if we did have a community clinic, what if we did have a system of mutual aid where we're taking care of one another, not based on profit?"

The disaster helped the NYSNA nurses see their union as a force for social change beyond the bargaining table, Judy Sheridan-Gonzalez said. It allowed them to link workplace struggles like the cutback on training and disaster preparedness on the job—anything, she said, that was considered "nonproductive time," that doesn't make money—to the failure of the health-care system and the political system to save lives and serve people after the storm. They made the connection between the pressure to work more and harder for lower wages and the limited amount of time people had to volunteer, and they watched as owners of small businesses began to reopen, struggling to sell products in a devastated community. "You have to start taking a look at the bigger picture, because how do you make sense of that? How do you deal with that contradiction of a little mom-and-pop business that survived by selling food in their little deli, and then a block away there's a soup kitchen providing food?" Sheridan-Gonzalez said. "This disaster has really forced people to come face to face with looking at this contradiction. It created so many questions in people's minds about how things should be. Most people don't think about the kind of society they want to have."

I BEGAN THIS BOOK WITH THE 2008 FINANCIAL CRISIS, BUT IN TRUTH, there was more than one cataclysm that kicked off the years of unrest that we have seen recently. I could also have begun in 2005, when Hurricane Katrina breached New Orleans's levees and permanently altered one of the world's most remarkable cities. Katrina, like Sandy, was a "natural" disaster made many times worse by the failure of human systems, and it opened the eyes of many to the harshest realities of racial and economic inequality. The people who were displaced and homeless, the thousands who were trapped without food or water in the Superdome, or waiting for help on the roofs of houses, were mostly black, and mostly poor. Many who evacuated still have not returned to their city.

New Orleans post-Katrina was where Naomi Klein formulated her famous theory of disaster capitalism. It was where we first learned of private security firm Blackwater, which had guards patrolling the streets. It was where the public schools were shuttered and replaced with privately run charters, and where 7,000 teachers—the majority of them black women—were fired. Housing projects that were structurally sound were bulldozed to make way for new developments of mixed-income housing, their former residents pushed out of the center of a city where many don't own cars (one of the reasons the storm was so deadly in the first place). Elections were held just three months after Katrina, with 80 percent of the city's residents still displaced. The areas hit worst by the storm, the Lower Ninth Ward in particular, were the city's poorest, their residents almost all black. When I was an undergraduate in New Orleans in 1998, I heard the rumor that the city had rigged the levees to fail, in case of a storm, in the commercially unimportant parts of the city, the poor black neighborhoods, to save the French Quarter. Untrue, of course, but shaded with the truth of the way the disaster relief and recovery would go.[5]

Those neighborhoods were also where former Black Panther Malik Rahim and a small group of volunteers from the community created the Common Ground Collective. Inspired by the mutual aid programs— free breakfast, free clothing—of the Black Panthers, of which Rahim had been a member, Common Ground was built on an ethic of "solidarity, not charity," the same ethic that inspired many Sandy organizers. The state failure in New Orleans was obvious to observers from around the world, and Common Ground was certainly unable to fill in all the gaps— Rahim would be the first to note that the city was still suffering more than ten years later. But their little collective survived even attempts to infiltrate the organization by the FBI, which was concerned about its political activities. As they had with the Black Panthers, officials considered political organizing alongside direct aid a threat.[6]

Disasters can sweep away the myths under which we live to display the kindness and solidarity that people are willing to show to complete strangers. They can also reveal the truth of who is seen to matter and who is not, in all its ugliness. The fossil-fuel industry, in particular, has a long history of disasters that have showcased the horrors of extraction to the people who don't live them every day. The people most affected by the hazards of coal, gas, and oil production are usually those already left behind or broken by the daily crises of an unequal political and economic system.[7]

New Orleans and the Gulf Coast had been hit hard enough for a lifetime by Katrina, and then, in 2010, the BP Deepwater Horizon offshore drilling rig in the Gulf of Mexico exploded, killing eleven rig workers and sending oil billowing into the water. Oil workers who had tried to organize for safer conditions had been fired. An underwater camera provided obscene fascination as people around the country watched over 4 million barrels of oil pumping into the Gulf. It took eighty-seven days for BP to cap the well.[8]

Just a few weeks prior, a methane explosion had killed twenty-nine miners in West Virginia at Massey Energy's Upper Big Branch coal mine, in the worst coal-mining disaster since 1970. A supervisor had demanded that a methane monitor be disabled because it kept going off. Two of the miners who confirmed the disabling of the monitor refused to give their names, in fear for their jobs. When coal or oil is the only game in town, as it certainly is in swaths of West Virginia and along the Gulf Coast, you might blow the whistle, but you still need to work, even if your boss is deliberately putting you in danger. Even if the company that employs you is one of those responsible for what's known as "Cancer Alley," where over 130 petrochemical plants and six oil refineries line the waterfront in Louisiana, and for the climate change that makes Katrina-like storms more likely.[9]

When protests against fossil fuels arise, companies raise the specter of job loss to keep workers in line. When there is new drilling to be done, or there are new pipelines to be built, the possibility of jobs is dangled like a carrot in front of already-impoverished communities. The risk of a disaster may seem worth taking to avert the quieter disaster of poverty, since a society that so often fails to provide aid, even after the most spectacular disasters, has also already cut its supports for everyday troubles to the bone. That the mine owners and oil CEOs pocketing millions each year—Massey's Don Blankenship made $17.8 million in 2009—remain sheltered from the ill effects of their dirty business does not change the fact that workers need to work in order to eat.[10]

Trish Kahle, an environmental and labor historian and member of the Fight for $15 campaign in Chicago, saw some hope in the 2015 strike of oil refinery workers—the first major oil strike since 1980—for a climate movement based on solidarity between extraction workers and the extractive industry's victims. The United Steelworkers union reached out to environmental organizations like the Sierra Club for support in the strike, highlighting the role that the refinery workers played in preventing disasters and keeping their communities safe. Safety, in the extractive industries, Kahle noted, is inherently an environmental concern—the workers on the front lines are also the ones whose children play within sight of the refinery, who breathe its air and will be vulnerable to a spill or explosion. The agreement reached to end the strike included attention to the workers' demands around safety and staffing along with a modest wage increase. One strike leader later joined a protest against a new oil pipeline, speaking to the protesters about her workplace issues and the damage caused by a nearby oil spill.

As many realized after the 2015 strike, the workers on the supply chain hold a lot of power over the industries, but they need to be willing to press the leverage that strikes provide them. After all, strikes that actually halt production are harder to shrug off than simple protests. They challenge the mindset that says we should all be out for our own short-term gain at the risk of hurting others, and point to another structure for society itself that is built on the kind of caring work that has been undervalued or ignored by capitalism. And it helps people realize that the oil company that is found to be grossly negligent when it comes to their safety also considers occasional spills the cost of doing business, all the while lobbying against legislation that would slow the progress of climate change. It is not surprising that nurses were central to the Sandy response, or that National Nurses United has become a leader in the labor movement on the issue of climate change. With more disasters on the way, a society based on caring for people, rather than ensuring continued profits, may be our best hope for the future.

MAKING THIS SOCIETY A REALITY, THOUGH, WILL REQUIRE A BREAK from a long history of capitalism's abuse of the environment—and of the workers whose exploitation has gone hand in hand with the pillaging of the earth.

Modern capitalism was born out of and then fueled by slave labor and then by coal, coal, more coal, and oil. Indeed, the sweat and strain of enslaved people served as substitute for fossil fuels in the American South, part of the reason that the South industrialized so much later than the North. Black people, wrenched from their birthplaces to labor at the end of a whip, were a reliable power source for hundreds of years before slavery was eliminated—and in England, when it was eliminated, reparations were paid not to former slaves but to the people who had owned them. That money was pumped back into the coal-fired plants that made the industrial revolution possible. Meanwhile, the removal of Native American people from the land—through forced migration or just plain killings—allowed settlers full access to a wealth of natural resources, including the coal and oil underneath the Native lands.[11]

Slavery in the United States ended with the Civil War, but the people who worked in coal-powered factories or dug the coal out of the ground continued to face the brunt of the abuses of the industries. Coal miners formed some of the most militant early unions; it is no coincidence, Trish Kahle noted, that many of the labor songs we remember today came from the coalfields, where workplace struggles were often a matter of life or death. What is today called "extractivism"—the mindset that sees workers' bodies and the environment simply as resources to be plundered to exhaustion—was in full force in those days, the era of unregulated capitalism.

The Progressive era saw the growth of some concern over the fate of the environment alongside concern for workers, though the high-minded ideals of white middle-class reformers presaged an environmental movement that would largely ignore the demands for structural change that working people were making. Theodore Roosevelt created the US Forest Service and preserved national forests and parks through the 1906 American Antiquities Act—but mostly to keep some pristine lands for the enjoyment of people like him. Similarly, the Sierra Club had its roots, in the words of historian Adam Rome, in "well-to-do San Franciscans who liked to go out hiking." In the cities, meanwhile, reformers challenged the factories that were belching smoke into the air, demanding some restrictions on what corporate polluters could emit. The second President Roosevelt built on this legacy with the Civilian Conservation Corps, a works program during the Depression that linked the need for jobs to the desire to preserve natural resources, something echoed in today's calls for "green jobs."[12]

What we think of today as the environmental movement developed in the 1960s and 1970s with a renewed interest in cleaning up pollution and saving endangered animals. Historian Erik Loomis has linked this renewed interest to the fact that inequality was lower in the 1960s than it had been in earlier decades. Thanks to the labor movement, he said, more Americans than ever had free time and the disposable income to enjoy wild spaces. By 1970, the year the Environmental Protection Agency (EPA) was created to administer federal environmental regulations, Loomis wrote, 69 percent of Americans expressed some concern about air pollution. Today, we remember that conservative Richard Nixon signed a raft of environmental legislation, but much less about the pressure that was on him to do so. Organizations like Greenpeace, founded in the 1970s, connected environmental conservation to the fight to end nuclear weapons, calling for a more peaceful, greener future. The 1970s also saw the first warnings about global warming as well as the first real oil crises, when oil-exporting countries turned off the spigot and left the United States questioning its reliance on fossil fuels. President Jimmy Carter put solar panels on the White House in 1979; Ronald Reagan, under the influence of the growing "drill, baby, drill" ideology, scrapped them in 1986, along with federal funding for wind and other renewable energy sources.[13]

At the same time, the labor movement, particularly in the extractive industries, was undergoing upheaval. Rank-and-file movements in the United Mine Workers and the United Steelworkers challenged leadership that they saw as too eager to collaborate with the bosses. They also began to question whether the jobs for which they were supposed to be grateful were worth the degradation they entailed. Kahle noted that these struggles arose at the same time as the modern energy conglomerate—massive corporations with interests in coal, oil, even nuclear power. These firms consolidated different kinds of energy work under one corporate name and one boss. "It suddenly made the inter-industrial connections between uranium workers, coal workers, oil workers that simply hadn't existed before," she said.

The Oil, Chemical, and Atomic Workers International Union (OCAW) went on strike in 1973, demanding better safety and health protections, and stressed the connection between their working environment and the broader environment. The reform group Miners for Democracy demanded that mine companies repair the lands they destroyed, an investment they saw as potentially producing more and better jobs than mining itself, and briefly won power in United Mine Workers of America (UMWA) in 1972 following a bitter struggle that saw its leader, Jock Yablonski, and his wife and daughter murdered. Edward Sadlowski of the reform caucus Steelworkers Fight Back argued, "With technology, the ultimate goal of organized labor is for no man to have to go down into the bowels of the earth and dig coal. No man will have to be subjected to the blast furnace."[14]

There was potential, then, for a real worker-led movement that challenged the energy industries, but we already know what happened next: deindustrialization, as companies simply packed up and left the United States, its demanding workers, and its new environmental protections behind to start over again in less-developed countries without so many pesky laws. With fewer jobs to go around, it was harder than ever for workers to refuse labor in dirty industries.

That outsourcing to poorer countries mirrored a trend that had long existed within the United States: the location of extraction, factories, and pollution in the poorest parts of the country, where people of color were most likely to breathe the air and drink the water. The environmental justice movement was a grassroots response to what scholar Robert D. Bullard dubbed "environmental racism," the intentional location of hazardous manufacturing, chemical production, or energy extraction in locations where people of color make up most of the population. Those locations, often called "sacrifice zones," are considered expendable, to be destroyed for the benefit of people who live far away and never see the destruction that makes their lifestyle possible. Faced with a mainstream environmental movement that was mostly white and centered on lobbying, environmental justice activists moved to make those sacrifice zones visible to all, and force companies to clean up their messes. In 1994, President Bill Clinton issued an executive order making environmental justice a priority under federal law, but the sacrifice zones persist, from Louisiana's Cancer Alley to the South Bronx.[15]

As climate change became the major focus of the environmental movement, the tensions between the so-called Big Green groups and more militant grassroots activists came to the surface. In 1990, on the day after Earth Day, activists disrupted the New York and Pacific stock exchanges, challenging the logic of working hand in hand with the biggest polluters and their funders to try to solve environmental crises. But the green movement mostly retained an image as a hobby for the wealthy, more concerned with saving polar bears than with the people who faced intertwined economic and environmental crises.

THE WORLD BEGAN TO SERIOUSLY CONSIDER THE NEED FOR ACTION on climate, and to negotiate toward a major climate treaty, at the same time that the Berlin Wall was coming down and the world was hailing the triumph of capitalism. There was, we were hearing, no alternative. And so even as dignitaries met to discuss the sobering realities of a warming planet, container ships were chugging across the oceans on global trade routes, spewing carbon into the air as they brought cheap consumer goods from Asian factories to Walmart's shelves. Capitalism was ascendant, and any solutions to the climate crisis that might be considered had to suit its imperatives for growing profit.[16]

We were told to switch to greener lightbulbs, taught to calculate our individual carbon footprint. The world could be saved, we heard, if we just modified our behavior a little bit. That the biggest polluters kept right on polluting was just something we were supposed to ignore in our virtuous attempts to buy the right thing. Carbon trading, a plan to allow countries or companies to buy credits that allowed them to pollute more from those that were not polluting up to their level, was supposed to use the magic of the market to incentivize a green transition. Carbon markets were established, in theory, in the 1997 Kyoto Protocol, but they have failed to produce measurable results. And yet even a basic carbon tax was too close to communism; markets were the way and the truth.[17]

We might have realized that expecting financial markets to regulate anything was a fool's errand when the financial markets imploded in 2008, the super-smart market whizzes we were supposed to trust with the planet having failed to see that they'd built a house of cards that was bound to collapse. In the wake of that crisis, while some argued for a "green New Deal"—pumping money into creating a new, sustainable infrastructure and putting the unemployed to work to create a just transition—others insisted that the only thing that mattered was the economy, that the best way forward was to "drill, baby, drill": in particular, to drill for natural gas through the new process of hydraulic fracturing, or "fracking," underground shale rock to loose the gas within. When the share prices of energy companies plummeted, losing almost 80 percent of their market value, they began to look desperately for a sure thing, and the Marcellus Shale, beneath Pennsylvania, New York, West Virginia, and Ohio, where companies had already been leasing mineral rights, seemed to be it.[18]

The new unconventional or "extreme" energy extraction boom was underway. Fracking quadrupled between 2010 and 2014, turning the United States into the world's largest producer of natural gas—the fuel once touted even by several "big green" groups as a potential bridge from carbon-based energy to renewables. Meanwhile, oil drilling, including from offshore rigs like the Deepwater Horizon, was also on the rise. The process of building the Keystone XL Pipeline, designed to carry oil from Canada's tar sands across the United States to Texas, began. Politicians who had once expressed concern about global warming now openly denied it and cheered any and all drilling and pipelines, in terms nearly as breathless as Sarah Palin's "drill, baby, drill" rhetoric on the campaign trail.[19]

There was always an undercurrent of recognition that we could not buy our way out of climate change—that no amount of gas-company-sponsored Earth Days or energy-efficient lightbulbs or hybrid cars could make up for the damage done on an industrial level. But for many activists, it was the 2009 climate summit in Copenhagen, and its failure to produce anything close to meaningful change, where they realized, as Naomi Klein wrote, "that no one was coming to save us." The elites, both the elected officials and the supposed movement leaders, had failed, and something new was needed.[20]

It wasn't just that the leaders we had counted on to solve the problem, to sit down around a table like adults and make a deal, had decided to fiddle while the world burned. No, the big energy companies, along with some of the biggest consumers of all that coal, oil, and gas, had put a lot of money—something on the order of $900 million a year, according to one study—into ensuring that no real dent would be made in their profits. When you consider that the value of the fossil-fuel reserves not yet extracted could be as high as $20 trillion, the spending begins to make sense. Debbie Dooley, president of the Green Tea Coalition of Tea Party activists for renewable energy, pointed out that wealthy Tea Party backers like the Koch brothers have fortunes largely drawn from fossil fuels, and they've poured money into fighting solar—particularly, she said, in so-called "red" states. Americans for Prosperity and the Heartland Institute, among other groups associated with the Tea Party, she said, "are looking out for the financial interest of their donors."[21]

There are, of course, capitalists who don't deny that climate change is a problem and indeed are looking forward to profiting from greener energy, electric cars, solar panels, and the like, or even touting schemes for "geoengineering" a functional climate. But in general, even as they fund environmental organizations, billionaires like the Walton family or Michael Bloomberg or the bankers at J. P. Morgan continue to invest in fossil fuels and to draw their money from polluting industries. The same elites that crashed the financial system, that cracked down on protesters, that created a low-wage economy, are not likely to create a livable planet for all of us. Instead, it's more likely that they will count on their wealth to insulate them from the brunt of climate change, just as it did when Sandy hit New York.[22]

After the financial crisis, George Goehl, director of National People's Action, had felt unprepared, as though groups like his should have done a better job of putting forward big ideas for changing the economic system and breaking up the concentrated power within the financial industry. As the realities of climate change created openings to challenge the power of the energy industry, NPA was aiming to do things differently. It was planning actions around the Obama administration's Clean Power Plan, which requires each state to come up with a plan to cut carbon emissions. The climate crisis, in other words, provided an opening for the group to use the knowledge—and the new membership base—it had gained since 2008 to try to really change the distribution of power.

It had been too easy for the victims of the 2008 crisis to feel like their problems were deeply individual, deeply private, as if they were their own fault. Everyone feels like a failure when they've lost their job. The challenge that activists faced was getting people to understand that it was the actions at the top levels of business and government that had caused the Great Recession. Climate change can have an almost opposite effect—it can be easy to forget about, until a superstorm comes through your city, sending water pouring into subway tunnels and up through the floors, and there is no one to help you when your power is out.

But after Sandy, the connections between the manmade economic crisis and the manmade climate crisis seemed more obvious—especially when some of the same names and structures kept popping up to profit off the wreckage the storm had left. Mayor Bloomberg appointed a Goldman Sachs executive to the team overseeing the recovery. A report from the Occupy offshoot Strike Debt found that people who had lost their homes or belongings were being pushed into "aid" that, like much student aid, in fact required them to take on more debt. Many of them were already suffering from lost home equity after the financial crisis, which had left their homes underwater financially long after the flood-waters receded.[23]

Many of those affected by climate change, however, argue that it is not they but the polluters who are in debt. The theory of climate or ecological debt is that the wealthy countries that created the problem owe some sort of payment for the destruction that their burning of fossil fuels has wreaked on the less-developed nations, who, after all, share the same atmosphere, often face even greater risks from rising sea levels, and are already feeling the force of storms, floods, and droughts. Climate debt has been a non-starter at the major climate talks, however, for the wealthy nations prefer to consider any payments to poorer countries as aid, as charity given out of the goodness of their hearts, rather than a debt owed or a form of reparations for past crimes. Like the activists after Sandy and Katrina, the victims of climate change call for solidarity, not charity.[24]

Such debt can also be considered within US borders, with the residents of sacrifice zones in Appalachia's coal country or New York's South Bronx the creditors and the fossil-fuel companies on the hook for payments. Such a debt, some have argued, could be paid by instituting a carbon tax, the results of which could be paid out as a basic income, something like a broader form of Alaska's oil dividend, the annual payment drawn from taxes on the state's oil industry that is given to every resident of Alaska—or what some commentators have jokingly called Sarah Palin's socialism.[25]

Naomi Klein has laid out the argument that fighting climate change will require moving beyond capitalism: that the economic system itself is responsible for the looming disaster we face and will not be able to solve it. After the release of *This Changes Everything: Capitalism vs. the Climate*, she told me, few journalists questioned her conclusions, but almost all of her interlocutors questioned whether such a thing was possible. Literary critic and Marxist theorist Fredric Jameson famously said it was easier to imagine the end of the world than to imagine the end of capitalism. Climate change and the increased frequency of environmental disasters force us to grapple with the possibility of the end of the world as we know it, and invite us to see what else, then, we can imagine. Climate change requires us to think about the future and consider what we want it to look like, because the possibility of maintaining the status quo—the insistence that there is no alternative to continuing on the way we have been—is simply no longer possible. It is, in this way, the ultimate intersectional issue, the one that makes us really consider what and who we value and how we want to live. And around the country, activists are using it to bring disparate groups of people together.

When Kirin Kanakkanatt first became a climate activist, she often found herself one of the only people of color in a room—sometimes, in a very large room. She was nineteen, it was the middle of the 2008 presidential election, and she was in college in Athens, Ohio, unsure of what she was doing, when she was invited to a Sierra Club meeting. From there, she threw herself into the movement. But she still felt that something was missing. "It never had a class analysis," she said. "The reason why black and brown people, poor people in Appalachia need to lead this is that they understand power." To tell people who are suffering daily that they need to save the planet misses the fact, she noted, that for many of them, if saving the planet doesn't include changing their lives, "a lot of us don't even want to live on the planet even if we could save it."

The People's Climate March on Sunday, September 21, 2014, was designed with that lesson in mind. A massive march through New York City, with the frontline communities marching in the lead—First Nations people from Canada who had been battling the tar sands, community groups from Sandy-ravaged neighborhoods, delegations from around the world—it was supposed to send a signal that the people of the world were tired of waiting for elite leaders to act. The march was backed by Bill McKibben's 350.org and a host of other organizations, with buy-in from labor unions, and estimates put the number of participants at well over 100,000.

But to get that many people at a march, noted Colin Kinniburgh, an organizer with System Change Not Climate Change and an editor at *Dissent* magazine, the organizers diffused the message. Many of the signs at the march were aimed at specific polluters, calling for bans on fracking or drilling, but the march overall did not make specific demands. There were thousands in town for the march, though, and organizers took advantage of that to bring a deeper analysis of the situation to the fore as well as to take more radical action. System Change Not Climate Change organized a convergence, a day of panels and workshops. They featured Kshama Sawant, Jill Stein of the Green Party, and others digging into the politics of climate justice.

Then, Monday morning, a crowd of people poured into Battery Park, most of them dressed in blue, for "Flood Wall Street," an action planned to disrupt the financial district and put out the message, as one massive banner read, that "Capitalism = Climate Chaos." Many of the organizers were former occupiers—some of whom had also been paid organizers on the official People's Climate March—and were willing to face arrest to demonstrate the need for serious action on climate change. In Battery Park, they went through a brief direct-action training and scribbled the National Lawyers Guild phone number on body parts. Then they took the streets.

"There was this incredible energy as we poured out into the streets, because everyone thought we were immediately going to be battling with the cops," Kinniburgh said. But instead, the police let them take the street and penned them in at the intersection around the Wall Street Bull. "It very quickly turned into this carnival," Kinniburgh said. There was singing, dancing, and an impromptu speak-out as the day stretched on. A group of protesters, including student organizer Biola Jeje, climbed onto a double-decker tourist bus and rode it around, waving a blue flag. A giant inflatable "carbon bubble" that had been prepared by demonstrators for the climate march was passed across the crowd; it was eventually popped by police. "We didn't know how to escalate because we'd already done the thing that we thought was going to get us arrested!" Kinniburgh laughed. At the end of the day, though, he was part of a group of over one hundred people who took arrest rather than leave the streets.

For the members of People United for Sustainable Housing (PUSH) Buffalo, the People's Climate March was an opportunity to take their place in the climate movement. "In our view, climate injustice is a function of a power structure that is intersectional, and racism, classism, and economic exploitation are the other side of the coin of resource extraction," said Aaron Bartley, PUSH's cofounder and head. PUSH Buffalo, which is affiliated with National People's Action, began its work on housing access, but to think about housing in a city like Buffalo, with its bitter winters, is to think about energy. "When we started here on the west side of Buffalo, a good half of the homes were paying more in utilities for six months of the year than they were in rent," Bartley said. The energy utility, National Fuel, had fracking interests, and its CEO was the highest-paid person in the western half of New York. When PUSH began to scrutinize the energy bills of its members, it found extra charges for "conservation," but could not find out where that money was going.

Lonnie Barlow was an organizer on the campaign that PUSH built around National Fuel. "It was a learning experience for us," he said. "We learned a lot about the makings of what an energy campaign looks like, and we evolved to energy democracy stuff that we're working on now." They zeroed in on National Fuel, holding protests outside its office that culminated in a campout in July 2012. They brought tents, signs, even had a small kitchen, all set up on public land right on the edge of National Fuel's property. Eventually the company and the state conceded, and millions of dollars from those "conservation" fees were put into weatherization programs for low-income residents. Through the energy campaigns, they created PUSH Green, a community energy-efficiency initiative that is pushing, among other things, for access to solar power for working-class communities.

The argument for energy democracy that Bartley and Barlow made to me—that people should be able to control their own power sources, rather than being forced to support massive corporations with overpaid executives—was strikingly similar to the one that Debbie Dooley of the Green Tea Coalition had laid out. "The average person cannot go out and construct a power plant, but they could put solar panels on their rooftop," Dooley said. She had become involved in energy advocacy after finding out that her state, Georgia, had passed legislation allowing Georgia Power to bill rate-payers in advance for new nuclear reactors. When she did further research, she learned that nuclear and fossil fuels still received massive subsidies from the federal and state governments, and that meanwhile, the cost of solar panels had fallen dramatically. She butted heads with Americans for Prosperity and other fossil-fuel-funded

Tea Party groups, who supported laws that made solar power more difficult for the average person to access, and she reached out to environmental and pro-solar groups to join the fight. She had even spoken on panels with former vice president Al Gore. "I care about the environment. I believe that we should be good stewards of the environment God gave us," she said. "I have a grandson and I want him to have a clean world and clean air and energy freedom and energy choice."

Both Dooley and National People's Action affiliates want an energy system that is decentralized, one that reverses the concentration in the industry that pools too much power and money in too few hands. It's not enough, said George Goehl of NPA, just to reduce carbon emissions, or even to move some jobs and funds to communities of color and low-income communities, if "at the end of the day [we] still transition from ten dirty energy CEOs to ten clean energy CEOs and not address the underlying structures of who has power and control."

Without some form of democracy in the energy system, the benefits and side effects will continue to be unequally distributed. In October 2015, I took a ride through one neighborhood that continues to feel the ill effects of fossil fuels. My tour guide to the South Bronx was Mychal Johnson of South Bronx Unite, a group that has been fighting the location of diesel-truck-heavy businesses, power plants, and waste disposal in the neighborhood for several years.

Environmental racism, to Johnson, meant that "people of color breathe different types of air and have different types of health outcomes due to the living environment around them." In the South Bronx, he noted, one in four children has asthma, and asthma hospitalization rates are eight times the national average. Their life expectancy is nearly ten years lower than people just across the river on the Upper East Side. They have almost no green space, besides the community gardens that Johnson and his neighbors have fought to cultivate, but they do have four power plants—of the ten sited across the state under Governor George Pataki years ago, Johnson noted, nearly half were in the South Bronx. Without some power over where the power plants go, the poor and people of color will continue to live in sacrifice zones.[26]

"We're only fighting for the right to breathe," Johnson said. "The first effect of carbon emission is your ability to breathe." Black and Latino New Yorkers, he said, understand the connections between the injustices they face, the slow violence of pollution, and the quick violence of the policeman's bullet—or his arm. Eric Garner, killed in 2014 when a New York City police officer put him in a chokehold, had grown up near the Superfund site of Gowanus Canal, and suffered from asthma. Johnson and his neighbors tweaked the Twitter hashtag that sprang up through the protests at Garner's death, adopting #WeCantBreathe as a slogan.

Areas like the South Bronx become sacrifice zones because the people there are considered expendable. But as the extreme energy boom heated up, the gas was where it was, and the gas companies went to it, regardless of who lived there. To them, everywhere is a potential sacrifice zone.

When the gas company first showed up to Eileen Hamlin's home in New York's southern tier, wanting to lease her land for fracking, she thought, "Isn't this wonderful? I will be able to make back the money that we lost in the crash." She and her husband were retired, and they had twenty-six acres of suddenly desirable land. But Hamlin, an activist with Citizen Action and an early member of the Working Families Party, lived within sight of heavily fracked parts of Pennsylvania, and she could see flaring wells across the river from her home. Even if it would bring in needed money, she began to wonder if fracking her land was worth the payoff.

Isaac Silberman-Gorn was studying environmental science at the State University of New York in Binghamton when Governor Andrew Cuomo proposed fracking in the southern tier. "I realized pretty early on that this was going to be the environmental site that was going to define what the movement looks like for years to come," he said. "I knew I had to get involved." Citizen Action brought in speakers, scientists, and doctors and talked to people from the fracked parts of Pennsylvania; they heard about proprietary chemical blends—the contents of which gas companies refused to disclose—about cracked cement well linings leaking gas into the water supply, and about earthquakes and health complaints. Eileen Hamlin's neighbors were still ready to sign leases, but she became involved in the movement to fight fracking. "There is just no free stuff. There is a price to be paid for it," she said. "We suffer the health consequences, so that a few people can have a few jobs for a short period of time. We need to find a better way than fracking to provide people with jobs."

Hamlin joined New Yorkers Against Fracking, which aimed for a total fracking ban in the state. "We zeroed in on Governor Cuomo and followed him around the state," Silberman-Gorn said. "Every single public event that he was at, we had people tailing him." At the same time, they put together a template for a municipal ban on fracking, one that would be passed in Binghamton and eventually in more than two hundred municipalities across New York State. It was supported by residents across the political spectrum, who began to branch out into other forms of activism. "In every single one of those towns you had groups of people organizing, going to these board meetings, winning elections on a municipal level on this issue specifically and passing legislation," Silberman-Gorn said. "I am still inspired by watching people who got into activism because of fracking, upper-middle-class white people who are standing with Black Lives Matter activists. That kind of cross-fertilization, realizing it is all part of the same struggle."

It wasn't always easy, Hamlin added. "These people around here are so poor that they see it as something that will make them rich," she said. But the example of Pennsylvania across the border provided more than dramatic visuals—there were hard numbers, and the money just wasn't panning out like the gas companies had promised. The global energy market, too, had changed, making fracking less profitable and making the potential for short-term gains from a compromise seem riskier. The damage, Pennsylvania's example showed, was real, and the possible benefits were dependent on the same fickle markets and corporate titans who had already crashed the economy just a few years earlier.

There was the labor question, too. Fracking jobs have been hard, dirty, and temporary, and so while some unions have endorsed fracking, the Working Families Party and other labor-affiliated groups were willing to come out and oppose it. Finally, in December 2014, Governor Cuomo announced that New York would not allow fracking.

Illinois People's Action (IPA), a faith- and community-based economic justice group affiliated with National People's Action, also waded into the fracking fight. When its Bloomington-Normal chapter put together a meeting to gauge interest on the issue, Dawn Dannenbring, an IPA organizer, was surprised when two hundred people turned up. IPA decided to demand a ban, not the compromise regulation that ultimately passed. From there, IPA members put pressure on the Illinois Department of Natural Resources, writing comments on what was wrong with the bill and how it would not protect the residents of the state. By the end of the comment period, they "had generated 36,000 comments," Dannenbring said. "By law the department was required to respond to every single comment that it got, so our goal wasn't just to get things addressed, we wanted to bog the process down." They managed to do so for four hundred days, creating an effective moratorium.

They also embraced disruption. IPA members occupied the offices of the Illinois Coal Association and the Illinois Gas Association. In 2014, when the McLean County Board heard an oil company's request to drill test wells, IPA and its allies packed the hearing room night after night. On the last night of testimony, Dannenbring said, members came with pictures of their children and grandchildren. As the board members spoke about their votes, one thanked the protesters who had testified against the drilling, and two others cited their grandchildren as reasons to vote no. The vote was 15–3 against drilling.[27]

Environmentalists have been decried for decades as elite "NIMBYs," short for "not in my backyard," people who are happy if a polluter is located somewhere else, out of sight. But what the anti-fracking movement and its connection to the broader climate justice movement has shown is that people who get motivated to act because of something in their backyards can put forth demands that are bigger and more holistic—because there is no safe location for fossil-fuel extraction if global warming is to be held below catastrophic levels. It is people like Mychal Johnson and South Bronx Unite who show that fighting fossil fuels isn't just about a faraway future, but about the air they breathe right now. Today's climate movement is about people taking action in their backyards, metaphorically or literally, actions that add up to an impact on the entire planet. And the influence of groups like IPA, which have brought direct-action tactics from their other organizing to the climate, is pulling normally staid green groups toward more militancy.

Before Mike O'Brien was elected to the Seattle City Council, he was a Sierra Club volunteer. It was as an activist that he got involved in the fight against Shell Oil's Arctic drilling endeavor. In January 2015, he learned that the Port of Seattle planned to lease a terminal to Shell as its home port. From there, Shell would send ships to probe Arctic waters for oil. At first, he told me, green groups simply said, "We object." But press conferences weren't going to be enough, and local activists wanted to do more. The "Shell No!" campaign came together, he said, almost organically, to the point that he couldn't even remember details. The idea of blocking the port in kayaks, he said, had begun almost as a joke, a reaction to the cynicism of those on the other side, which was "like, what are you going to do about it?"

The "kayaktivists" began to train on the water, though, and started to plan actions designed to physically block the ship's departure as well as events that people who didn't want to risk arrest could join. O'Brien was torn as to whether he should join the main action. Could he lose his job? What did it mean for a City Council member to take direct action? He'd never been arrested before and had never done anything like what he was considering. But in a conversation with a Greenpeace organizer, he said, he began to think about the position that he was in, and he decided that he could take these risks for others who couldn't.

Sierra Club executive director Michael Brune was arrested outside the White House protesting TransCanada's Keystone XL Pipeline. (I had first encountered Brune at the Walmart shareholders' meeting, when he had read a statement in favor of a resolution calling on Walmart to reduce its emissions, which in turn had been introduced by OUR Walmart member Mary Pat Tifft.) It was time, Brune wrote of the club's decision to officially take part in civil disobedience over climate issues, to change the rules, to take a few risks. O'Brien agreed and decided to join the Port of Seattle blockade.[28]

Being on the water, O'Brien said, was a powerful experience, even if the ship eventually got past them. On the morning of September 28, when he read the news that Shell was abandoning its Arctic drilling efforts because of "costs," he was even more thrilled. And then the Obama administration followed it up by canceling more lease sales for drilling rights, and weeks later, rejecting the Keystone XL Pipeline. "Maybe once in a lifetime you're involved with something like this, where everything comes together in a way—the energy is there, the timing is right, everything happens better than you expected, and it works," he said. "But that one time is built on so many other attempts." It was all the earlier attempts, the ones that felt like failures, that built energy to a point where they could win.[29]

CONCLUSION

OUR FUTURE IS NOT YOURS
TO LEVERAGE

A S I SIT DOWN TO DRAFT THE CONCLUSION TO THIS BOOK IN
November 2015, the Fight for $15 is on what is reported to be
its largest strike yet, with actions in what the spokespeople at
Service Employees International Union say is five hundred cities. On
Twitter, I am watching people I've met through my reporting joining
together in solidarity. Rasheen Aldridge is on the picket line in St. Louis
holding a Black Lives Matter sign, as activists proclaim, "Our struggles
are connected, we must love and support each other!" In North Carolina, protesters join hands and hold up signs that connect the Fight
for $15 to the movement for black lives and to the immigration reform
movement. In Minneapolis, strikers and Black Lives Matter activists
flood into City Hall, demanding $15 an hour, paid sick days, and fair
scheduling.

The day before, young people from Million Hoodies, 350.org, and
United We Dream came together in Washington, DC, under the banner
of "Our Generation, Our Choice," blocking traffic outside of the White
House and demanding attention from Congress to their movements.
The organizers of the march wrote, of their reasons for acting, "Too
often, both parties put the demands of big money over the hopes of

real people. Despite the campaign rhetoric and the noise of the 24-hour news cycle, most Americans will tell you that they think our political system is broken." They noted, "Now our movements are starting to come together to begin to speak with one voice."[1]

In Columbia, Missouri, Diamond Latchison has joined black students at the University of Missouri as their protests against racist actions at their university succeed, through a strike by the football team, in forcing out its president, Tim Wolfe. On 110 college campuses around the country, a Million Students March has kicked off, calling for free college, the forgiveness of existing student debt, and better-paying jobs on campus. On different campuses, students are also calling for justice for adjunct professors, who are paid by the class rather than a full-time salary, and tying their march to the demands of the Missouri students. And then there are the Walmart workers, who are beginning a fifteen-day "Fast for $15" in the run-up to their now annual Black Friday protests. Tyfani Faulkner plans to take her fast to Alice Walton's Manhattan doorstep and to Hillary Clinton's campaign office.[2]

All of this is happening almost exactly a year before the 2016 presidential election, which has already been shaken up by the "troublemakers"—those who "get in trouble, good trouble, necessary trouble," as Representative John Lewis (D-GA) put it, inspiring the title for this book. Bernie Sanders's very viability as a presidential candidate is largely due to successive movements making his issues mainstream and making "socialism" a less scary word. Although he stumbled at first when he was interrupted by Black Lives Matter protesters, including Ciara Taylor, at a Netroots Nation presidential forum, he has since incorporated the movement's demands into his platform. He has introduced a bill that would eliminate private prisons—an issue on which the Dream Defenders have spent a lot of time since their founding. Hillary Clinton, once a cheerleader of "tough-on-crime" policies and a Walmart board member, has called for reversing the tide of mass incarceration and pursuing a $12 national minimum wage; according to an SEIU spokesperson, she reached out to *them* about speaking to the Fight for $15 national conference.

The troublemakers on all these fronts are making their influence felt in every aspect of American politics. The very first question at the Republican primary debate that took place on November 10 acknowledged the fast-food workers outside of the Wisconsin theater where the candidates stood, and asked them if they supported a $15 minimum wage.

When even billionaire Donald Trump, riding a wave of fervor for his "outsider" candidacy and delivering speeches peppered with racist, anti-immigrant rhetoric, must answer to minimum-wage workers, something is shifting. Trump still held the power in that equation—he rejected the workers' demands for a raise—but the voices clamoring outside would not be silent, and as the campaign progresses, more and more protesters are beginning to disrupt Trump's events. In Chicago in March 2016, students at the University of Illinois at Chicago, organizers with Black Lives Matter, Assata's Daughters, and other movements for black lives groups, union members, most of them black or Latino, planned a protest that led Trump to cancel his rally. The movements have resisted lining up behind one candidate or another, instead choosing the outsider strategy of making so much noise that their demands are impossible to ignore.[3]

But during an election season in which pricey political ads blaring negativity dominate the airwaves, it's not enough to try to make more noise than the presidential candidates and the cable news pundits. The activists who recognize that American democracy has failed them are trying to change the conversation altogether. They are disrupting business as usual to make it clear that we are facing critical, even existential issues, and that capitalism is no longer the future.

In this book, we have followed the growth of a new movement, one that began with opposition to the banks but then ignited the sparks of a different labor movement and made uncompromising demands for racial justice. We have seen the potential for new radical ideas in mainstream circles, and understood that change is not going to come through violence, but through the growth and spread of ideas from movement to movement, person to person, among those who are willing to take risks in an effort to make those ideas come true. It is easy to think that all of the movements in this book are just oppositional, but many of them are putting forward transformational ideas that are beginning to point the way toward a new economy and a more equal country.

In the public spaces that became home to the various occupations, in the homes held against the sheriffs, in the People's Assembly in Ferguson, in the You Are Never Alone medical clinic after Superstorm Sandy, we saw a movement that was simultaneously against and for: that named an enemy, a corrupt political system run by and for the "one percent," and also demonstrated in a very real way what it wanted. The spaces themselves became the first demand—but it wasn't just about occupying a space for the sake of it. Instead, these occupied spaces offered opportunities to try out a better future. The movements sought to address people's immediate needs, but in the cracks left by the failure of the financial system and electoral politics, they began to consider bigger goals, to envision what real democracy might look like.

Historian Michael Kazin argued that the tragedy of the 1960s New Left was that it "discredited the old order without laying the political foundation for a new one." If that is true, then it is more important than ever that today's movements have a vision for the society that they want to see. George Goehl of National People's Action suggested that the failure of activism in the early days after the financial crisis was that there were few people publicly putting forth an idea of what an alternative to "banks-got-bailed-out-we-got-sold-out" might look like. There were exceptions—the workers at Republic Windows and Doors, on their victory tour, began to think about running the factory themselves, and now, years later, they are the owners of New Era Windows, a worker cooperative in which they are all the bosses. In early 2016, they finally got a settlement that would bring them the back pay they've been waiting on for seven years.[4]

New Era Windows is just one business, employing just seventeen people, but it is an instructive example of the power shift that the trouble-makers are imagining. Rather than asking benevolent leaders for a gift, they are envisioning a world in which power—political and economic power, but also the relatively private power of the workplace—is democratically distributed. To really address inequality requires nothing less.

In response, there is already backlash. Elected officials continue to hack away at budgets, and pundits wag their fingers about impolite protesters, but there will also be attempts to silence the movements with small gifts: Hillary Clinton's proposed $12 an hour minimum wage, perhaps, or Walmart's even smaller raise for its full-time workers; Obama's decision to cut back the handouts of military gear to police departments, or cities requiring police to wear body cameras. At best, Democrats promise a return to the New Deal social order, where incomes were relatively equal, and where détente in the form of the forty-hour workweek reigned. Why aren't you satisfied? the pundits will ask. But as the Occupy Sandy activists knew, charity maintains power relations as they are; a world based on solidarity demands that something change, and yes, it will mean that those at the top must give something up.

National People's Action is planning for big changes. Over the fall and winter of 2012, around 5,000 members of its affiliate organizations contributed to the process of creating a "long-term agenda." They took a page from the long-term agenda of businessmen who opposed the New Deal, and who spent decades building institutions in opposition to it that bore fruit in the inequality to which we have returned—which some call the "New Gilded Age." NPA, says director George Goehl, did a kind of deep political analysis, something that community organizations like theirs had not really done before. It was a process, he says, of "moving from checkers to chess," from the short-term victories that wealthy philanthropists are willing to support to "next generation fights" that will advance the NPA's long-term goals: democratic control of the economy, racial justice, ecological sustainability, and real democracy. "Everybody knows that is not in our near future," he says, but the big ideas, the utopian end goals, are what make the smaller fights feel worth it.

Alexis Goldstein agrees, shrugging off the persistent calls for more "reasonable" demands from Occupy and the other movements, the demands that they limit themselves to voting for one of the two major parties. "I just don't think people are motivated to do something so extreme with such a mediocre platform of change," she says. To capture the attention of the people, these movements are intentionally thinking big and aiming high.

The next challenge for the movements will be creating organizations that last, that suit the needs of twenty-first-century troublemakers, that can be flexible and still enduring, that can overlap and connect up with one another and create more long-term plans for the future they want to see. "The reality is that we can't change the world without institutions that are democratically accountable to the movement and that have real power," Nick Espinosa says. "I think the challenge of our generation is to reinvent what institutions mean, and create new versions of institutions that have failed movements in the past, that are truly democratic, and that stick to our values, that fight for the things we believe in."

Alicia Garza, in addition to Black Lives Matter, helped found Left-Roots, an organization that she says originated in the realization that philanthropy and single-issue nonprofits were not going to create freedom. It was time, she said, to stop tinkering around the edges and propose something new.

To Espinosa and his Occupy Homes Minnesota collaborator Cat Salonek, the small individual victories—one home at a time, in some cases—serve as a way to bring people together, to expand the reaches of the movement. "Thinking about movement as a tidal wave, and we're the tidal pool, we hold that water," Salonek says. "After Occupy Wall Street or after Black Lives Matter, that tidal wave washes the nation and then goes back out and we try to contain as much of that as we can. We train and we develop, and when the next wave comes, we're that much bigger and that much stronger, and we can push it so much further and capture more as it washes back out."

It is the building from small demands to transformative demands that has become even more obvious after Occupy, which famously issued no demands. What many people missed was that the occupied spaces—from the Capitol in Wisconsin to Liberty Plaza and Oscar Grant Plaza to the Florida Capitol and beyond—brought people together and helped them to see that their problems were not personal, but political, an echo of the consciousness-raising groups of the feminist movement. Moving from the personal to the structural helped people move from frustration to action. Those spaces permitted the growth of many demands, from an end to stop-and-frisk to stronger bank regulation to stopping a foreclosure to envisioning a future beyond capitalism. The job of these movements going forward, Shabnam Bashiri says, will be to connect those pieces to one another, to make sure that movements that have built off of one another remain in solidarity with one another.

In the aftermath of Superstorm Sandy, Yotam Marom begins to put ideas about building institutions into action. In a moment when the country seems to be rocketing from one crisis to another, the organizations that he sees forming all seem to have certain things in common. "We have a big-picture vision, we want to have a real meaningful social transformation, we want to have an entirely new set of institutions that meet people's needs, we're going to move in that direction," he says. The Wildfire Project, which was founded in January 2013 in the Rockaways, was born out of that understanding and a desire to give these different groups, which were emerging from crisis moments—from Occupy Homes to the Dream Defenders—political and action training that would give them a shared language and understanding and create a network through which they could be in solidarity with one another. The training, he says, is designed to strengthen the groups to be as powerful as they can be, so that they will be able to last long enough to win their fights. But what's really exciting to him is that when they have meetings that bring different groups together, sparks fly. As he points out, when the energy is there, it doesn't take that many people to put together a massive action, especially if you're moving at the speed of social media.

The key to understanding how to make change is to understand how power operates. Being able to donate millions to a single candidate is power, but so is shutting down the busiest shopping district in Chicago on the busiest shopping day of the year, as activists did in 2015 to protest the police shooting of Laquan McDonald. The action is estimated to have cost retailers 25 to 50 percent of their sales that day. Refusing, collectively, to pay millions of dollars in debt, is also power, as is closing the schools in Detroit for days in "sick-out" protests in a kind of informal strike against abysmal conditions, as teachers did in early 2016 to force out the emergency manager appointed by the governor. Disruption is power when it is used strategically.[5]

This kind of power analysis is an awareness that used to be called "class-consciousness." It has become distinctly unfashionable to say such things, but that does not make it less true; in fact, in the twenty-first century of globalized inequality, it is perhaps more true than ever. Class is not simply one of a list of possible identity categories. It is a relation of power that is shaped in part by race; in part by gender, sexual orientation, and gender identity; and by immigration status, education, and even region. In the 1960s, centrifugal social forces pulled movements apart, largely on the basis of what gets derisively termed "identity politics," and movements splintered; in response, elites opened up a few spaces for people of color, for women, and for queer and transgender people at the same time as broader inequality spiraled out of control. Having a few representatives at the top was not enough; a few more women CEOs have not changed the fact that the face of poverty in

America is largely a woman's face. We elected the first black president, and got worse material conditions for the majority of black people.[6]

In this moment, the reverse is happening. Activists are reconnecting their struggles, thinking intersectionally about their problems, and understanding that they have much to learn from one another. BYP 100 puts out an economic justice "Agenda to Build Black Futures"; among other things, it calls for putting greater value on women's work. The Green Tea Coalition joins with the Sierra Club to fight for solar power. Barbara Smalley-McMahan goes to Ferguson to join a Moral Monday there. Housing activism in Buffalo turns into a challenge to the energy companies' wealth from fossil fuels.

It will be a struggle to maintain these coalitions. The easiest way to break up the momentum of the new movements will be to turn them against one another, to offer a victory for one group in order to demobilize them. Divide and conquer has worked to divide the labor movement from itself for decades, as the fight over the Keystone XL Pipeline reminded us. Some unions may continue to lobby for the short-term goal of jobs in today's crisis moment, while failing to push for the long-term goal of a livable planet for all. It is not surprising that the divide-and-conquer strategy often works, since short-term thinking has been the ruling ideology for so long, from "drill, baby, drill" to the logic of the credit default swap.

There will be a struggle, too, to avoid negative solidarity, the dark side of populism presented by Donald Trump, Scott Walker, and others who offer scapegoats to blame rather than real solutions. The backlash to Black Lives Matter has been instructive: pro-Confederate flag rallies, church burnings, and racist epithets abound, as does the more insidious murmur of "*all* lives matter," a quiet rebuke to the idea that any group of Americans might have anything in particular to be angry about.

The way to fight these inevitable divisions is twofold. First, it is important for activists to maintain that larger vision of a better world, one that is worth fighting for. Second, it is important to continue to point the finger at those who are responsible—the titans of finance and oil, and the budget-slashing politicians from both parties. Movements need not, as Stephen Lerner notes, worry about making themselves universally beloved—asking nicely is not the way to bring about change. There will inevitably be disagreements over tactics, but they should not be confused with disputes over goals. The diversity of what Yotam Marom and others simply call "the movement" is its strength. Its horizontal structures allow many people to be moving at once, in different directions—but all of their targets wind up being the same political and economic system that has disempowered them all for so long. There will be, inevitably, compromises, but they should be compromises that advance the movement rather than disband it. Perfection is not possible, although disingenuous critics will always demand it, but a clear vision is essential.

Horizontalism is itself a response to inequality: from Occupy's "leaderlessness" to what Alicia Garza calls the "leader-full" style of Black Lives Matter, the refusal to have a "movement elite" is a response to the deep desire for real democracy that so many Americans feel has been denied them. But those horizontal structures can mask power differentials and allow individuals to speak for a movement to which they are not accountable. The challenge for the troublemakers, as they create new institutions, will be to make sure they find ways to be accountable to one another, while preserving the flexibility and openness that have made their movement so big and so strong.

To Nick Espinosa, it is not a choice. "For people like me, people who are directly impacted by this financial crisis, whose families are one check away from foreclosure, maybe one check away from homelessness, there's a sense of urgency that hasn't gone away," he says. "And so to me the future of the hopes that were thrust onto our shoulders, whether or not we wanted them, is in those communities fighting for their basic human needs and being politicized around those needs. We can't afford to be cynical."

It has become a cliché to cite Frederick Douglass's famed speech—"Power concedes nothing without a demand"—but it remains true all the same. I have focused on the historical context for today's movements in this book in part to remind us that things were not always this way, and in part to provide a better understanding of just what today's movements are up against. From the early enslavers to the perpetrators of Naomi Klein's Shock Doctrine, there has been an incredible amount of power expended in order to consolidate power in a few hands. There is no "golden age" for us to return to, no period of American history to which a few tweaks and regulations will restore us. The wealthy never accepted the New Deal, but started moving to dismantle it nearly as soon as it passed. They have employed a broad range of strategies, from redlining to systematic union-busting to outsourcing to outright violence, to break any collective power that the majority of Americans ever possessed. To challenge them will take a broad range of tactics, which in turn will have to be adjusted and scrapped and revised as they are countered by those in power.[7]

All of this will have to happen in a changing world, where not only the energy sector, responding to climate change, is shifting, but the nature of work itself. The so-called "sharing economy," which has offloaded the costs of doing business onto the drivers of Uber cars, the owners of AirBNB homes, and the TaskRabbits who compile a living gig by gig, piece by piece, is one vision for the future. Another is a future where more of even those jobs are done by robots. As Peter Frase argues, the future of technology is not inevitable, but is itself a political question: what our future looks like depends on who has power in the present. It is why many of the troublemakers, from Saket Soni of the National Guestworker Alliance to NPA to BYP 100 to the occupiers, have turned themselves to the question of the future of work, and considered solutions ranging from worker cooperatives to shorter working hours to a universal basic income. The financial crisis moment may have passed, but changing technology affords new opportunities to put forth big ideas.

Instead of waiting for the world to change or being caught and shocked when it does, the troublemakers are hoping to shape that change. They are working not just to raise a minimum wage here, get a better contract there, and ban fracking somewhere else, but working to get at the root of the structures of our society. On the campaign trail in 2015 and 2016, Bernie Sanders called for a "political revolution," a movement that could take the country back from the billionaire class. But that revolution has been taking place—and will continue to take place, if it is to succeed—outside of a presidential election or any other election. It will take place in the streets and in homes and, yes, even on the Internet, where people are busy trying to figure out what a society that cares about people looks like. We have a world now that is structured around inequality—all different kinds of inequality—and changing it will require that we see each other differently. The best parts of today's movements, like the best parts of yesterday's, historian Robin D. G. Kelley notes, "find ways to love each other differently so that we eventually can transform the state into a structure that's in service of the people."

What, ask the new radicals, would that look like? If they get their way, there will be more public schools and universities, health care for all and infrastructure designed to withstand climate change, and jobs that pay a real living wage and that allow time off to spend with family and friends, or just relaxing. There will be housing that is accessible and affordable, and no one will lose their home for debts. Financiers, retail titans, and oil barons will no longer dictate policy. There will be no need for police.

It is toward that end that today's troublemakers are building and organizing. Sometimes they are doing so in front of the cameras—making headlines, shaping the conversation—and other times they are quieter, back in their tide pools, building something stronger, and waiting for the next wave. Over and over, as I interviewed people for this book, they told me, "We can't go back." Something had fundamentally changed for them, and it had made it impossible for them to imagine simply returning to their previous lives. And so they continue to build, and prepare, and expand.

Movements do not build in a straight line, climbing inevitably toward success. There are bursts of activity, and there are mistakes and moments when all seems quiet. Sitting in her office in Seattle's gleaming, modern City Hall last spring, Kshama Sawant told me, with a knowing smile, "If we miss the potential of a moment because we are not consciously recognizing it and building on it, there will be other moments, there's no question. But why lose the moment that's in front of us?"

It is up to those of us who have not yet taken action to decide if we want a more equal, a more just country. If we do, we may just have to make some trouble to bring it about.

ACKNOWLEDGMENTS

Without so very many people, this book quite literally would not exist. Writing a book is at once an incredibly solitary endeavor and a deeply collective one, as many writers have observed before me, and I have been lucky in being surrounded by people who illustrate what solidarity really means.

First and foremost, this book would be nothing without over a hundred people who took the time to talk to me about their decisions to cause trouble. That they were willing to entrust me with their stories is something for which I will always be grateful. I hope that I came close to doing them justice. They are the ones who will change the world. I'm just lucky enough to get to write about it.

Lydia Wills, gem among agents, friend and fighter, believed in this book even when I wasn't sure that I did.

My editor, Katy O'Donnell, understood immediately what I was trying to do and improved this book in countless ways with her sharp edits and wise guidance. Alessandra Bastagli, Kristina Fazzolaro, Lindsay Fradkoff, Clive Priddle, Sandra Beris, and the whole Nation Books and PublicAffairs team always made this first-time author feel like she had something important to say. Laura Feuillebois was always there when I needed her and transcribed so many of these interviews, and Kathy Streckfus did the necessary, hard, and often thankless work of copyediting—writers, thank your copyeditors! Also thanks to Daniel LoPreto, who acquired this book and gave me invaluable early advice that helped shape it. Taya Kitman, Roz Hunter, Annelise Whitley, and everyone at the Nation Institute gave this itinerant freelancer a journalistic home; I am grateful every day to be part of the Nation family. Thanks to everyone at the Lannan Foundation, whose generous support allowed me time and space to write.

I remain indebted to many wonderful people who shaped my writing and the way I see the world; to Melanie McKay, Shenid Bhayroo, Linn Washington, James Marra, Andrew Mendelson, Carolyn Kitch, Larry Stains, and the inimitable Edward Trayes, who all helped teach me to write and gave me confidence to enter the weird world of journalism in the first place.

Esther Kaplan has given me many wonderful pieces of advice over the past few years, but I am most thankful that she pointed me in the direction of Laura Flanders, who was the best mentor a young journalist could have had, whose insight, wit, generosity, and guidance made me a far better reporter. Working with Laura and with the whole GRITtv crew—including Danya Abt, Sam Alcoff, Gina Kim, Rebecca McDonald, David Rowley, Diane Shamis, Tami Woronoff, and Anna Lekas Miller, who I love to brag got her start as my intern—gave me the grounding that made this book and all the work I have done since possible.

I have had so many excellent colleagues over the years that this book spans. Tana Ganeva, Lauren Kelley, Sarah Seltzer, Julianne Escobedo Shepherd, Kristen Gwynne, Lynn Parramore, Adele Stan, and the rest of my former AlterNet colleagues remain friends and continue to turn out sharp and necessary work. Rebecca Burns, Sady Doyle, Miles Kampf-Lassin, and my *In These Times* comrades demonstrated real solidarity through our union campaign and beyond. As a freelancer, I have been blessed with incisive yet kind editors, who made me better and whose guidance made this book possible, among them Lizzy Ratner, Jessica Stites, Ruth Conniff, Richard Kim, Jessica Reed, Leslie Thatcher, Bhaskar Sunkara, Caroline Preston, Kera Bolonik, Akiba Solomon, Laura Marsh, Blake Zeff, Nico Lauricella, Ben Frumin, Jodi Jacobson, Jim Naureckas, Gabriel Arana, Peter Hogness, James Downie, and Alana Price. An extra note of gratitude to Sarah Leonard, as well as Natasha Lewis, Josh Eidelson, and Michelle Chen, for making my wild idea of a labor podcast come true and last for over three years. Thanks as well to Kaavya Asoka, Colin Kinniburgh, Michael Kazin, David Marcus, and everyone at *Dissent* for the editorial home, and to Steve Fraser for giving me the gift of "Under the Radar." Katrina vanden Heuvel took seriously my rants about social media and made me feel that I'd always be part of *The Nation.*

Jeremy Scahill, Matt Browner Hamlin, Max Fraser, Stephen Lerner, Ari Melber, and Anthony Arnove backed me early on when no one knew who I was. Without them, this book would not have been possible, because no one would care what I had to say.

An argument with Erik Loomis sparked the idea for this book, and something Rick Rowley said to me at a party crystallized it. Denise Scalfi first expressed interest in this book and confidence in my ability to write it, and Astra

Taylor gave me invaluable early advice that helped me understand how to make it happen. Max Berger, Yotam Marom, Molly Crabapple, Nick Espinosa, Manissa McCleave Maharawal, Kirin Kanakkanatt, Kenzo Shibata, Chris Maisano, Mariame Kaba, and Nastaran Mohit indulged me in long conversations about what is happening in the world and where we're going and why.

Cayden Mak, Yasmin Nair, Julia Carrie Wong, Anne Elizabeth Moore, Brett Banditelli, Mariya Strauss, Victoria Law, Kate Bahn, Sheila Bapat, Victoria Goff, Tressie McMillan Cottom, s. e. smith, Liliana Segura, Jamie Kilstein, Allison Kilkenny, Bryce Covert, Michelle Kinsey Bruns, Raven Rakia, Susie Cagle, Biola Jeje, Julieta Salgado, Laura Clawson, Sarah Nicole Prickett, Paul Mason, Deanna Zandt, Marcy Wheeler, Joanne McNeil, Liza Featherstone, Sarah McCarry, Helaine Olen, Joe Dinkin, Brenda Coughlin, and Travis Waldron are friends, teachers, and comrades-in-arms (or, well, words). Pat Blanchfield made the connection for one of the most interesting interviews in this book. Warren Ellis pointed Lydia Wills in my direction and made this whole process possible. David Kaib, Moe Tkacik, Dave Dayen, and Trish Kahle graciously answered my annoying questions time after time.

Rob Cruickshank, Shannon Duffy, Jeff Ordower, Alison Dreith, Nelini Stamp, Shabnam Bashiri, Jacob Lerner, Kirin Kanakkanatt, and Ivanna Gonzalez were my "fixers" who shared connections, insights, and understanding of the places they lived when I was parachuting in to report. Mike Konczal, Micah Uetricht, Meredith Clark, and Colin Kinniburgh read chapters, caught mistakes, and sharpened my understanding of key points. Sarah Feld read the whole thing and gave me important, generous, and clarifying feedback.

Thank you to my friends, without whose love and confidence I would not be here. To the GSC, all of you—you know who you are. Cortney Harding, for humor and rock 'n' roll; Kieron Gillen, who understands me at my strangest; Phillip Anderson, Passover host extraordinaire; Janelle Asselin, creative, fierce, and brilliant; Michael Whitney, there are no words. You know. And Melissa Gira Grant, for countless emails of support, humor, outrage, and inspiration, and a friendship that dates back to high school.

My sister, my brother-in-law, and my new niece, Agnes, for whom we're all trying to leave the world a little better. And Richard and Brigitte Frase, and Alex and Laura too, for accepting me into the family.

For my parents, who don't share my politics but who encouraged me to read, to learn, to argue, and to question. We may not agree, but I have never, ever doubted your faith in me.

Peter Frase feeds me, supports me, argues with me, and loves me even when I wonder if I deserve it. He has made me a kinder, smarter, better person in the years he's been in my life, and his influence is everywhere in my work.

NOTES

THE HEART OF THIS BOOK IS DRAWN FROM OVER ONE HUNDRED INTERVIEWS WITH activists, organizers, historians, political scientists, sociologists, and others over the course of two years of reporting. Unless otherwise cited, quotations are drawn from those interviews.

INTRODUCTION: NO FUTURE SHOCK

1. Christopher Hayes, *Twilight of the Elites: America After Meritocracy* (New York: Crown, 2012), 2–12; Matt O'Brien, "Economists Have Discovered How Bad the Economy Really Is," *Washington Post*, April 21, 2015, https://www.washingtonpost .com/news/wonk/wp/2015/04/21/economists-have-discovered-how-bad-the -economy-really-is; Matthew Yglesias, "American Democracy Is Doomed," Vox, October 8, 2015, www.vox.com/2015/3/2/8120063/american-democracy-doomed; Tom Jensen, "Americans Like Witches, the IRS, and Even Hemorrhoids Better Than Congress," Public Policy Polling, October 8, 2013, www.publicpolicypolling.com /main/2013/10/americans-like-witches-the-irs-and-even-hemorrhoids-better-than -congress.html.

2. John Nichols and Robert McChesney, *Dollarocracy: How the Money and Media Election Complex Is Destroying America* (New York: Nation Books, 2013), 8; Amie Parnes and Kevin Cirilli, "The $5 Billion Presidential Campaign?" The Hill, January 21, 2015, http://thehill.com/blogs/ballot-box/presidential-races/230318-the-5-billion -campaign; Helaine Olen, "Politics: You Lose, You Snooze," *The Baffler*, April 27, 2015, http://thebaffler.com/blog/lose-snooze.

3. Sarah Jaffe, "$230,000 for a Guard Dog: Why the Wealthy Are Afraid of Violence from Below," AlterNet, July 29, 2011, www.alternet.org/story/151837 /$230,000_for_a_guard_dog%3A_why_the_wealthy_are_afraid_of_violence_from _below; Lynn Parramore, "The Man Who Builds Luxury Bomb Shelters for Paranoid

One Percenters," Vice, October 11, 2015, www.vice.com/read/this-guy-is-building
-doomsday-shelters-for-billionaires-111.

4. Josh Sanburn, "The Witness: One Year After Filming Eric Garner's Fatal Confrontation with Police, Ramsey Orta's Life Has Been Upended," *Time*, July 2015,
http://time.com/ramsey-orta-eric-garner-video; Ian Murphy, "I Punk'd Scott Walker,"
Politico, November 18, 2013, www.politico.com/magazine/story/2013/11/i-punkd
-scott-walker-100033; Valerie Strauss, "Yes, Scott Walker Really Did Link Terrorists
with Protesting Teachers and Other Unionists," *Washington Post*, February 27, 2015,
https://www.washingtonpost.com/news/answer-sheet/wp/2015/02/27/yes-scott
-walker-really-did-link-terrorists-with-protesting-teachers-and-other-unionists.

5. Paul Mason, "Twenty Reasons Why It's Kicking Off Everywhere," BBC News,
February 5, 2011, www.bbc.co.uk/blogs/newsnight/paulmason/2011/02/twenty
_reasons_why_its_kicking.html.

6. Quoted in Charles E. Cobb Jr., *This Nonviolent Stuff'll Get You Killed* (New York:
Basic Books, 2014), Kindle edition, loc. 4565.

CHAPTER 1: BANKS GOT BAILED OUT, WE GOT SOLD OUT

1. Andrew Friend, "Workers' Republic," Vimeo, 2009, https://vimeo.com
/30882647.

2. Jerry Mead-Lucero, "Chicago Sitdown Strike Produces Win for Workers, Not
Banks," Labor Notes, December 22, 2008, http://labornotes.org/2008/12/chicago
-sitdown-strike-produces-win-workers-not-banks.

3. Monica Davey, "In Factory Sit-In, an Anger Spread Wide," *New York Times*, December 7, 2008, www.nytimes.com/2008/12/08/us/08chicago.html.

4. James Wilkowski is a bishop of the Evangelical Catholic Church, which is not
part of the Roman Catholic Church. It traces its heritage to splits in the church that
date back to the 1720s. See Patrick Butler, "Roamin' Catholics," *Chicago Reader*, May
28, 1998, www.chicagoreader.com/chicago/roamin-catholics/Content?oid=896402;
Davey, "In Factory Sit-In, an Anger Spread Wide."

5. Manny Fernandez, "For A.I.G. Executives, Here Comes the Tour Bus," *New
York Times*, March 21, 2009, www.nytimes.com/2009/03/22/nyregion/22cnd-tour
.html.

6. Chris Isidore, "Bailout Plan Rejected—Supporters Scramble," CNN Money,
September 29, 2008, http://money.cnn.com/2008/09/29/news/economy/bailout;
Matt Taibbi, "Secrets and Lies of the Bailout," *Rolling Stone*, January 4, 2013, www
.rollingstone.com/politics/news/secret-and-lies-of-the-bailout-20130104.

7. Fernandez, "For A.I.G. Executives"; Edmund L. Andrew and Peter Baker,
"A.I.G. Planning Huge Bonuses After $170 Billion Bailout," *New York Times*, March
14, 2009, www.nytimes.com/2009/03/15/business/15AIG.html.

8. Michael P. Mayko, "Activists Vent at AIG Executives," *Connecticut Post*,
March 22, 2009, www.ctpost.com/business/article/Activists-vent-at-AIG-executives
-1302788.php; Eric Gershon, "Driving It Home to AIG," *Hartford Courant*, March
22, 2009, http://articles.courant.com/2009-03-22/news/aig-tour-bus-0322_1_aig
-bonus-recipients-tour-taxpayer-aid.

9. James Barron and Russ Buettner, "Scorn Trails A.I.G. Executives, Even in

Their Driveways," *New York Times*, March 19, 2009, www.nytimes.com/2009/03/20 /nyregion/20siege.html; Mark Gongloff, "AIG CEO: Bonus Uproar 'Just as Bad' as Racist Lynch Mob," *Huffington Post*, September 24, 2013, www.huffingtonpost .com/2013/09/24/aig-bonuses-benmosche-deep-south_n_3981911.html.

10. Moe Tkacik, "Journals of the Crisis Year," *The Baffler*, February 1, 2010, www .daskrap.com/journals-crisis-year.

11. Bob Ivry, Bradley Keoun, and Phil Kuntz, "Secret Fed Loans Gave Banks $13 Billion Undisclosed to Congress," Bloomberg, November 27, 2011, www.bloomberg .com/news/articles/2011–11–28/secret-fed-loans-undisclosed-to-congress-gave -banks-13-billion-in-income; Dean Baker, *False Profits: Recovering from the Bubble Economy* (San Francisco: Berrett-Koehler, 2010), 83.

12. Baker, *False Profits*, 102.

13. "Chart Book: The Legacy of the Great Recession," Center on Budget and Policy Priorities, October 29, 2015, www.cbpp.org/research/chart-book-the-legacy -of-the-great-recession; Christopher J. Goodman and Steven M. Mance, "Employment Loss and the 2007–09 Recession: An Overview," *Monthly Labor Review*, Bureau of Labor Statistics, April 2011, www.bls.gov/mlr/2011/04/art1full.pdf; Matt Taibbi, *The Divide: American Injustice in the Age of the Wealth Gap* (New York: Spiegel and Grau, 2014), Kindle edition, loc. 3117–3121.

14. Sarah Jaffe, "6 Ways the Big Banks Are Getting Back-Door Bailouts and Making Big Money from Taxpayers," AlterNet, June 28, 2012, www.alternet .org/story/156005/6_ways_the_big_banks_are_getting_back-door_bailouts_and _making_big_money_from_taxpayers.

15. Jordan Weissman, "How Wall Street Devoured Corporate America," *The Atlantic*, March 5, 2013, www.theatlantic.com/business/archive/2013/03/how-wall -street-devoured-corporate-america/273732; Doug Henwood, *Wall Street: How It Works and for Whom* (New York: Verso, 1998), 13–14, 22; Zaid Jilani, "JP Morgan Investor Report: Huge Corporate Profits Resulted Directly from Reducing Wages and Benefits," ThinkProgress, July 14, 2011, http://thinkprogress.org/economy /2011/07/14/269213/report-corporate-profits-wage-cuts.

16. Philip Mirowski, *Never Let a Serious Crisis Go to Waste: How Neoliberalism Survived the Financial Meltdown* (New York: Verso, 2014), 319.

17. Henwood, *Wall Street*, 21.

18. Thomas Frank, *One Market Under God: Extreme Capitalism, Market Populism, and the End of Economic Democracy* (New York: Doubleday, 2000), xiv, 97–99; Timothy Noah, *The Great Divergence: America's Growing Inequality Crisis and What We Can Do About It* (New York: Bloomsbury, 2012), 178.

19. Mark Fisher, *Capitalist Realism* (Washington, DC: O Books, 2009).

20. "Capitalism at Bay," *The Economist*, October 16, 2008, www.economist.com/ node/12429544.

21. Eric Etheridge, "Rick Santelli: Tea Party Time," *New York Times*, February 20, 2009, http://opinionator.blogs.nytimes.com/2009/02/20/rick-santelli-tea-party-time.

22. Theda Skocpol and Vanessa Williamson, *The Tea Party and the Remaking of Republican Conservatism* (London: Oxford University Press, 2012), Kindle edition, loc. 3948.

23. Ibid., loc. 215.

24. Mark Lilla, "The Tea Party Jacobins," *New York Review of Books*, May 27, 2010, www.nybooks.com/articles/archives/2010/may/27/tea-party-jacobins.

25. Skocpol and Williamson, *Tea Party*, loc. 2579.

26. Ibid., loc. 607.

27. Barbara Ehrenreich, *Fear of Falling: The Inner Life of the Middle Class* (New York: Harper Perennial, 1990).

28. Michael Kazin, *The Populist Persuasion: An American History* (Ithaca, NY: Cornell University Press, 1998), 1; 2 Thessalonians 3:10.

29. Charles Postel, "Occupy: A Populist Response to the Crisis of Inequality," *Eurozine*, November 7, 2012, www.eurozine.com/articles/2012–11–07-postel -en.html; Charles Postel, *The Populist Vision* (Oxford: Oxford University Press, 2009), Kindle edition, loc. 17; Erik Loomis, "The Hidden Progressive History of the Income Tax," AlterNet, September 7, 2012, www.alternet.org/labor /hidden-progressive-history-income-tax.

30. Chip Berlet and Matthew Lyons, *Right-Wing Populism in America: Too Close for Comfort* (New York: Guilford Press, 2000), 5–6.

31. Kazin, *Populist Persuasion*, 263; Jefferson Cowie, *Stayin' Alive: The 1970s and the Last Days of the Working Class* (New York: New Press, 2010), Kindle edition, loc. 2469.

32. Ehrenreich, *Fear of Falling*, 251.

33. Frank, *One Market Under God*, xiv.

34. "Full Transcript of the Mitt Romney Secret Video," *Mother Jones*, September 19, 2012, www.motherjones.com/politics/2012/09/full-transcript-mitt-romney -secret-video.

35. Mirowski, *Never Let a Serious Crisis Go to Waste*, 130.

36. Ylan Q. Mui, "Americans Saw Wealth Plummet 40 Percent from 2007 to 2010, Federal Reserve Says," *Washington Post*, June 11, 2012, www.washingtonpost .com/business/economy/fed-americans-wealth-dropped-40-percent/2012/06/11 /gJQAlIsCVV_story.html.

37. Kelly Candaele, "The Year of the Organizer," *The American Prospect*, February 1, 2008, http://prospect.org/article/year-organizer; Marshall Ganz, "How Obama Lost His Voice, and How He Can Get It Back," *Los Angeles Times*, November 3, 2010 http:// articles.latimes.com/2010/nov/03/opinion/la-oe-1103-ganz-obama-20101103.

38. Matt Sledge, "March on Wall Street: Thousands of Teachers, Advocates Rally Against Bloomberg Cuts," *Huffington Post*, May 12, 2011, www.huffingtonpost .com/2011/05/12/wall-street-march-may-12_n_861367.html.

39. Doug Singsen and Sarita Flores, "What Bloombergville Achieved," *Socialist Worker*, July 25, 2011, http://socialistworker.org/2011/07/25/what-bloombergville -achieved; David W. Chen, "In 'Bloombergville,' Budget Protesters Sleep In," *New York Times*, CityRoom, June 15, 2011, http://cityroom.blogs.nytimes.com/2011/06/15 /in-bloombergville-budget-protesters-sleep-in.

40. Joan Walsh, *What's the Matter with White People? Why We Long for a Golden Age That Never Was* (Hoboken, NJ: John Wiley and Sons, 2012), 228; Thomas Piketty, *Capital in the Twenty-First Century*, trans. Arthur Goldhammer (Cambridge, MA: Belknap Press, 2014), Kindle edition, loc. 550–552.

41. "Public Views of Inequality, Fairness, and Wall Street," Pew Research Center,

January 5, 2012, www.pewresearch.org/daily-number/public-views-of-inequality-fairness-and-wall-street; Rich Morin, "Rising Share of Americans See Conflict Between Rich and Poor," Pew Research Center, January 11, 2012, www.pewsocialtrends.org/2012/01/11/rising-share-of-americans-see-conflict-between-rich-and-poor.

42. Manuel Castells, *Networks of Outrage and Hope: Social Movements in the Internet Age* (Malden, MA: Polity Press, 2012), 163.

43. Matt Stoller, "#OccupyWallStreet Is a Church of Dissent, Not a Protest," Naked Capitalism, September 29, 2011, www.nakedcapitalism.com/2011/09/matt-stoller-occupywallstreet-is-a-church-of-dissent-not-a-protest.html.

44. Castells, *Networks of Outrage and Hope*, 129.

45. Ibid., 171.

46. Paul Mason, *Why It's Kicking Off Everywhere: The New Global Revolutions* (New York: Verso, 2012), 80.

47. Manissa McCleave Maharawal, *"So Real It Hurts: Notes on Occupy Wall Street,"* Racialicious, October 3, 2011, www.racialicious.com/2011/10/03/so-real-it-hurts-notes-on-occupy-wall-street.

48. Richard Kim, Tweet, October 14, 2011, https://twitter.com/RichardKimNYC/status/124923212093071362.

49. Phillip Anderson, Tweet, October 14, 2011, https://twitter.com/phillipanderson/status/124793751687274498.

CHAPTER 2: MIDDLE-CLASS MELTDOWN AND THE DEBT TRAP

1. Zaid Jilani, "Occupy Atlanta Encamps in Neighborhood to Save Police Officer's Home from Foreclosure," ThinkProgress, November 8, 2011, http://thinkprogress.org/special/2011/11/08/363692/occupy-atlanta-encamps-in-neighborhood-to-save-police-officers-home-from-foreclosure; Jason Cherkis and Sara Kenigsburg, "Occupy Y'all Street: Occupy Atlanta Fights Foreclosure, Fannie Mae Demands Protesters' Emails," *Huffington Post*, December 2, 2011, www.huffingtonpost.com/2011/12/02/occupy-yall-street-ows-moves-into-atlanta-suburbs_n_1125645.html.

2. Interview with Nick Espinosa; Nick Espinosa, "11th Hour Victory! Citibank Cancels Foreclosure Auction of Minneapolis Mom's Home; Commits to Loan Modification with Reduced Payments," Occupy Homes Minnesota, June 12, 2012, www.occupyhomesmn.org/11th_hour_victory.

3. Ben Henry, Jill Reese, and Angel Torres, "Wasted Wealth: How the Wall Street Crash Continues to Stall Economic Recovery and Deepen Racial Inequity in America," Alliance for a Just Society, May 2013, http://allianceforajustsociety.org/wp-content/uploads/2013/05/Wasted.Wealth_NATIONAL.pdf.

4. "CoreLogic Reports 41,000 Completed Foreclosures in March 2015," CoreLogic, May 12, 2015, www.corelogic.com/about-us/news/corelogic-reports-41,000-completed-foreclosures-in-march-2015.aspx.

5. Dean Baker, *False Profits: Recovering from the Bubble Economy* (San Francisco: Berrett-Koehler, 2010), 19–20, 26–28.

6. Doug Henwood, "Leaking Bubble," *The Nation*, March 12, 2006, www.thenation.com/article/leaking-bubble; Baker, *False Profits*, 47.

7. Sarah Jaffe, "The Whistleblower's Tale: Countrywide Investigator Fired for

Doing Her Job While Rampant Fraud Was Concealed," AlterNet, July 19, 2012, www.alternet.org/story/156375/the_whistleblower%27s_tale%3A_countrywide _investigator_fired_for_doing_her_job_while_rampant_fraud%C2%A0was _concealed.

8. US Department of Labor, Occupational Safety and Health Administration, finding in the case of Eileen Foster, September 13, 2001, available at www .documentcloud.org/documents/250789-cwd-ef-final-osha-order.html.

9. Blake Ellis, "Countrywide's Mozilo to Pay $67.5 Million Settlement," CNN Money, October 15, 2010, http://money.cnn.com/2010/10/15/news/companies /mozilo_SEC/index.htm; Frank Ahrens, "Big Payday Awaits Chairman After Countrywide Sale," *Washington Post*, January 12, 2008, www.washingtonpost.com/wp-dyn /content/article/2008/01/11/AR2008011103673.html; Les Christie and Rebecca Stewart, "Countrywide Issued Hundreds of VIP Loans to Buy Influence, Report Says," CNN Money, July 5, 2012, http://money.cnn.com/2012/07/05/real_estate /countrywide-mortgage.

10. Pat Garofalo, "The Foreclosure Fraud Settlement, by the Numbers," Think-Progress, February 9, 2012, http://thinkprogress.org/economy/2012/02/09 /421865/foreclosure-fraud-settlement-numbers; Alan Pyke, "What the Government Won't Tell You About the Foreclosure Fraud Settlement," ThinkProgress, March 20, 2014, http://thinkprogress.org/economy/2014/03/20/3417092/foreclosure -fraud-settlement-complete.

11. Lynnley Browning, "Too Big to Tax: Settlements Are Tax Write-Offs for Banks," *Newsweek*, October 27, 2014, www.newsweek.com/2014/11/07/giant -penalties-are-giant-tax-write-offs-wall-street-279993.html.

12. Laura Gottesdiener, "Wall Street's Hot New Financial Product: Your Rent Check," *Mother Jones*, March/April 2014, www.motherjones.com/politics/2014/01 /blackstone-rental-homes-bundled-derivatives.

13. Rebecca Burns, "Wall Street's Teetering New Rental Empire," Al Jazeera America, September 13, 2014, http://america.aljazeera.com/opinions/2014/9 /wall-street-economyfinancialcrisisrentbackedsecurities.html; Diana Olick, "Housing's New Crisis: Half Your Income for Rent," CNBC, December 9, 2015, www.cnbc .com/2015/12/09/housings-new-crisis-half-your-income-for-rent.html.

14. Manuel Castells, *Networks of Outrage and Hope: Social Movements in the Internet Age* (Malden, MA: Polity Press, 2012), 11; Judith Stepan-Norris and Maurice Zeitlin, *Left Out: Reds and America's Industrial Unions* (New York: Cambridge University Press, 2002), Kindle edition, loc. 2686; Amy Sonnie and James Tracy, *Hillbilly Nationalists, Urban Race Rebels and Black Power: Community Organizing in Radical Times* (New York: Melville House, 2011), Kindle edition, loc. 878–891.

15. Andrew Ross, *Creditocracy and the Case for Debt Refusal* (New York: OR Books, 2014), 75–80.

16. *Time*, July 3, 1950, cover, available at http://content.time.com/time/covers /0,16641,1101500703,00.html.

17. Ross, *Creditocracy*, 80–82, 112–113; Ta-Nehisi Coates, "The Case for Reparations," *The Atlantic*, June 2014, www.theatlantic.com/magazine/archive/2014/06 /the-case-for-reparations/361631; Drew Desilver, "American Union Membership Declines as Public Support Fluctuates," Pew Research Center, February 20, 2014,

www.pewresearch.org/fact-tank/2014/02/20/for-american-unions-membership
-trails-far-behind-public-support; Andrew Cherlin, *Labor's Love Lost: The Rise and Fall of the Working-Class Family in America* (New York: Russell Sage Foundation, 2014), 192; Bethany Moreton, *To Serve God and Wal-Mart: The Making of Christian Free Enterprise* (Cambridge, MA: Harvard University Press, 2010), 135; "College Enrollment Hits All-Time High, Fueled by Community College Surge," Pew Research Center, October 29, 2009, www.pewsocialtrends.org/2009/10/29/college -enrollment-hits-all-time-high-fueled-by-community-college-surge.

18. Ross, *Creditocracy*, 114.

19. Ibid., 114–115.

20. Barbara Ehrenreich, *Fear of Falling: The Inner Life of the Middle Class* (New York: Harper Perennial, 1990), 200.

21. Timothy Noah, *The Great Divergence: America's Growing Inequality Crisis and What We Can Do About It* (New York: Bloomsbury, 2012), 76; Keith Miller and David Madland, "What the New Census Data Show About the Continuing Struggles of the Middle Class," Center for American Progress, September 16, 2014, https://www .americanprogress.org/issues/economy/news/2014/09/16/97203/what-the-new -census-data-show-about-the-continuing-struggles-of-the-middle-class; Dean Baker, "Median Wealth Is Down by 20 Percent Since 1984," Beat the Press, July 28, 2014, www .cepr.net/blogs/beat-the-press/median-wealth-is-down-by-20-percent-since-1984.

22. Frank Newport, "Fewer Americans Identify as Middle Class in Recent Years," Gallup, April 28, 2015, www.gallup.com/poll/182918/fewer-americans-identify -middle-class-recent-years.aspx; Shawn Fremstad, "America's Invisible—and Very Diverse—Working Class," CEPR Blog, February 21, 2014, www.cepr.net/blogs /cepr-blog/americas-invisibleand-very-diverseworking-class; Amy Chozick, "Middle Class Is Disappearing, at Least from Vocabulary of Possible 2016 Contenders," *New York Times*, May 11, 2015, www.nytimes.com/2015/05/12/us/politics/as-middle -class-fades-so-does-use-of-term-on-campaign-trail.html.

23. Cherlin, *Labor's Love Lost*, loc. 339, 2677; Catherine Rampell, "Majority of New Jobs Pay Low Wages, Study Finds," *New York Times*, August 30, 2012, www .nytimes.com/2012/08/31/business/majority-of-new-jobs-pay-low-wages-study- finds.html; Federal Reserve Board, "Household Debt Service and Financial Obligations Ratios," updated December 28, 2015, www.federalreserve.gov/releases /housedebt.

24. "'If You Owe the Bank $1 Trillion, You Own the Bank,' Say Student Debtors Who Are Fighting Back," PRI, The Takeaway, February 26, 2015, www.pri.org/stories /2015–02–26/if-you-owe-bank-1-trillion-you-own-bank-say-student-debtors-who-are -fighting-back.

25. Charles Postel, *The Populist Vision* (Oxford: Oxford University Press, 2009), 16.

26. Heidi Shierholz, Alyssa Davis, and Will Kimball, "The Class of 2014," Economic Policy Institute, May 1, 2014, www.epi.org/publication/class-of-2014; Kathryn Anne Edwards and Alexander Hertel-Fernandez, "The Kids Aren't Alright—A Labor Market Analysis of Young Workers," Economic Policy Institute, April 7, 2010, www.epi.org/publication/bp258; "Labor Force Statistics from the Current Population Survey," US Department of Labor, Bureau of Labor Statistics, November 6,

2015, http://data.bls.gov/timeseries/LNS14000000; "Employment and Unemployment Among Youth—Summer 2015," US Department of Labor, Bureau of Labor Statistics, August 18, 2015, www.bls.gov/news.release/youth.nr0.htm.

27. Will Stone, "A 'Lost Generation of Workers': The Cost of Youth Unemployment," National Public Radio, July 2, 2014, www.npr.org/2014/07/02/327058018/a-lost-generation-of-workers-the-cost-of-youth-unemployment; Jordan Weissman, "44% of Young College Grads Are Underemployed (and That's Good News)," *The Atlantic*, June 28, 2013, www.theatlantic.com/business/archive/2013/06/44-of-young-college-grads-are-underemployed-and-thats-good-news/277325; Lawrence Mishel, Elise Gould, and Josh Bivens, "Wage Stagnation in Nine Charts," Economic Policy Institute, January 6, 2015, www.epi.org/publication/charting-wage-stagnation.

28. Sarah Jaffe, "The Next Bubble Is About to Burst: College Grads Face Dwindling Jobs and Mounting Loans," AlterNet, May 31, 2011, www.alternet.org/story/151149/the_next_bubble_is_about_to_burst:_college_grads_face_dwindling_jobs_and_mounting_loans; Sarah Jaffe, "Is the Near-Trillion-Dollar Student Loan Bubble About to Pop?" AlterNet, September 21, 2011, www.alternet.org/story/152477/is_the_near-trillion-dollar_student_loan_bubble_about_to_pop; Robert Hiltonsmith and Tamara Draut, "The Great Cost Shift Continues: State Higher Education Funding After the Recession," Demos, March 21, 2014, www.demos.org/publication/great-cost-shift-continues-state-higher-education-funding-after-recession.

29. Daniel Indiviglio, "Chart of the Day: Student Loans Have Grown 511% Since 1999," *TheAtlantic*, August 18, 2011, www.theatlantic.com/business/archive/2011/08/chart-of-the-day-student-loans-have-grown-511-since-1999/243821.

30. Sarah Jaffe, "Wall Street–Inflated Student Debt Bubble Hits $1 Trillion, Debtors Rally for Relief," AlterNet, April 24, 2012, www.alternet.org/story/155133/wall_street-inflated_student_debt_bubble_hits_$1_trillion;_debtors_rally_for_relief.

31. Paul Mason, *Why It's Kicking Off Everywhere: The New Global Revolutions* (New York: Verso, 2012), 67; Sallie Mae Posts 1Q Profit of $47.7 Million, Result Tops Expectations," Associated Press, April 22, 2015, www.foxbusiness.com/markets/2015/04/22/sallie-mae-posts-1q-profit-477-million-result-tops-expectations; Shahien Nasiripour, "Student Loan Borrowers' Costs to Jump as Education Department Reaps Huge Profit," *Huffington Post*, April 14, 2014, www.huffingtonpost.com/2014/04/14/student-loan-profits_n_5149653.html.

32. Jeffrey Sparshott, "Congratulations, Class of 2015, You're the Most Indebted Ever (For Now)," *Wall Street Journal*, May 8, 2015, http://blogs.wsj.com/economics/2015/05/08/congratulations-class-of-2015-youre-the-most-indebted-ever-for-now; Allie Bidwell, "Average Student Loan Debt Approaches $30,000," *U.S. News and World Report*, November 13, 2014, www.usnews.com/news/articles/2014/11/13/average-student-loan-debt-hits-30–000; Robert Hiltonsmith, "At What Cost: How Student Debt Reduces Lifetime Wealth," Demos, August 2013, www.demos.org/what-cost-how-student-debt-reduces-lifetime-wealth; Ross, *Creditocracy*, 149.

33. "Sallie Mae Is Changing," Sallie Mae home page, https://www.salliemae.com/about/who-we-are/future.

34. Ross, *Creditocracy*, 117; Jaffe, "Wall Street–Inflated Student Debt Bubble."

35. Mike Konczal, "Student Loans, Social Security, and Debts You Carry for Life," Rortybomb, October 26, 2011, https://rortybomb.wordpress.com/2011/10

/26/student-loans-social-security-and-debts-you-carry-for-life; Mike Konczal, "Two Points on Reducing Student Loan Interest Rates, Featuring: Recoveries, Algebra, Arguments," February 24, 2012, https://rortybomb.wordpress.com/2012/02 /24/two-points-on-reducing-student-loan-interest-rates-featuring-recoveries -algebra-arguments; Rachel Rose Hartman, "Who Makes Money Off Your Student Loans? You Might Be Surprised," Yahoo News, May 23, 2013, http://news.yahoo .com/blogs/lookout/makes-money-off-student-loans-might-surprised-093332073 .html.

36. Jake New, "Not Worth It?" Inside Higher Ed, September 29, 2015, https:// www.insidehighered.com/news/2015/09/29/half-college-graduates-say-college -worth-cost-survey-finds.

37. Mason, *Why It's Kicking Off Everywhere*, 69.

38. Ross, *Creditocracy*, 119–122.

39. Kirk Carapezza and Mikaela Johnson, "For-Profit Colleges Continue to Cash In on Federal Dollars," WGBH, July 30, 2014, http://blogs.wgbh.org/on -campus/2014/7/30/corinthian-students-face-shutdown-consequences; Suevon Lee, "The For-Profit Higher Education Industry, By the Numbers," ProPublica, August 9, 2012, www.propublica.org/article/the-for-profit-higher-education-industry-by-the -numbers.

40. Jaffe, "Near-Trillion-Dollar Student Loan Bubble."

41. Jessica Glenza, "The Rise and Fall of Corinthian Colleges and the Wake of Debt It Left Behind," *The Guardian*, July 28, 2014, www.theguardian.com/education /2014/jul/28/corinthian-colleges-for-profit-education-debt-investigation; Sarah Jaffe, "'We Won't Pay': Students in Debt Take on For-Profit College Institution," *The Guardian*, February 23, 2015, www.theguardian.com/education/2015/feb/23/student -debt-for-profit-colleges.

42. Laura Mandaro, "Corinthian Colleges Shuts Remaining 28 Campuses," *USA Today*, April 27, 2015, www.usatoday.com/story/money/2015/04/27/corinthian- colleges/26437615.

CHAPTER 3: WALMART, WALMART, YOU CAN'T HIDE, WE CAN SEE YOUR GREEDY SIDE

1. Steven Greenhouse, "On Black Friday, Walmart Is Pressed for Wage Increases," *New York Times*, November 28, 2014, www.nytimes.com/2014/11/29 /business/on-black-friday-protesters-demand-wage-increases-and-schedule-changes -from-walmart.html; Josh Eidelson, "Exclusive: Wal-Mart Manager Speaks Out About His Store's Ugly Reality," Salon, March 25, 2014, www.salon.com/2014/03/25 /exclusive_wal_mart_manager_speaks_out_about_what_we%E2%80%99re _going_through.

2. "Occupations Projected to Add Most New Jobs," US Department of Labor, Bureau of Labor Statistics, January 27, 2014, www.bls.gov/opub/ted/2014 /ted_20140127.htm; Ruth Milkman, *Farewell to the Factory: Auto Workers in the Late Twentieth Century* (Oakland: University of California Press, 1997), 189.

3. "The Low-Wage Recovery and Growing Inequality," National Employment Law Project Fact Sheet, August 2012, https://www.nelp.org/content/uploads /2015/03/LowWageRecovery2012.pdf.

4. Sarah Jaffe, "Forever Temp?" *In These Times*, January 6, 2014, http://inthese times.com/article/15972/permatemps_in_manufacturing; Bethany Moreton and Pamela Voeckel, "Learning from the Right: A New Operation Dixie?" in *Labor Rising: The Past and Future of Working People in America*, ed. Daniel Katz and Richard A. Greenwald (New York: New Press, 2012), 28–29.

5. Erin Hatton, *The Temp Economy: From Kelly Girls to Permatemps in Postwar America* (Philadelphia: Temple University Press, 2011); Liza Featherstone, *Selling Women Short: The Landmark Battle for Women's Rights at Walmart* (New York: Basic Books, 2009), Kindle edition, loc. 237, 1441, 1556, 1575, 1648.

6. Bethany Moreton, *To Serve God and Wal-Mart: The Making of Christian Free Enterprise* (Cambridge, MA: Harvard University Press, 2010), 61.

7. Nelson Lichtenstein, *The Retail Revolution: How Wal-Mart Created a Brave New World of Business* (New York: Metropolitan Books, 2009), Kindle edition, loc. 1813.

8. Catherine Ruetschlin, "Retail's Hidden Potential: How Raising Wages Would Benefit Workers, the Industry, and the Overall Economy," Demos, November 19, 2012, www.demos.org/publication/retails-hidden-potential-how-raising-wages -would-benefit-workers-industry-and-overall-ec#liftfamilies.

9. Esther Kaplan, "The Spy Who Fired Me," *Harper's*, March 2015, http://harpers .org/archive/2015/03/the-spy-who-fired-me.

10. Jodi Kantor, "Starbucks to Revise Policies to End Irregular Schedules for Its 130,000 Baristas," *New York Times*, August 14, 2014, www.nytimes.com/2014/08/15 /us/starbucks-to-revise-work-scheduling-policies.html.

11. Stephanie Luce and Naoki Fujita, "Discounted Jobs: How Retailers Sell Workers Short," Retail Action Project and Murphy Institute, 2012, http://retailaction project.org/wp-content/uploads/2012/03/7–75_RAP+cover_lowres.pdf; Claire McKenna, "Data Points: A Look at Involuntary Part-Time Work in Retail," Raise the Minimum Wage at National Employment Law Project, March 3, 2015, www.raise theminimumwage.com/blog/entry/a-look-at-involuntary-part-time-work-in-retail.

12. Sarah Jaffe, "The Bad Boss Tax," *In These Times*, July 21, 2014, http://in thesetimes.com/article/16949/the_bad_boss_tax.

13. Ibid.; Featherstone, *Selling Women Short*, loc. 1832.

14. Bethany Moreton, "On Her Book, *To Serve God and Wal-Mart: The Making of Christian Free Enterprise*," Rorotoko, November 4, 2009, http://rorotoko.com /interview/20091104_moreton_bethany_serve_god_wal-mart_christian_free _enterprise.

15. Darren Dochuk, *From Bible Belt to Sunbelt: Plain-Folk Religion, Grassroots Politics, and the Rise of Evangelical Conservatism* (New York: W. W. Norton, 2012).

16. Ibid., loc. 104, 149, 187; Moreton, *To Serve God and Wal-Mart*, 50–110.

17. Moreton, *To Serve God and Wal-Mart*, 55, 78, 89, 253.

18. Lichtenstein, *The Retail Revolution*, loc. 182, 795, 804–818, 902.

19. Ibid., loc. 228, 894.

20. Steven Greenhouse, "As Firms Line Up on Factories, Wal-Mart Plans Solo Effort," *New York Times*, May 14, 2013, www.nytimes.com/2013/05/15/business /six-retailers-join-bangladesh-factory-pact.html; Lichtenstein, *The Retail Revolution*, loc. 2389, 2320; Susan Berfield, "How Walmart Keeps an Eye on Its Massive

Workforce," Bloomberg Businessweek, November 24, 2015, www.bloomberg.com /features/2015-walmart-union-surveillance.

21. Zachary R. Mider, "How Wal-Mart's Waltons Maintain Their Billionaire Fortune: Taxes," Bloomberg, September 12, 2013, www.bloomberg.com/news /articles/2013–09–12/how-wal-mart-s-waltons-maintain-their-billionaire-fortune -taxes; Tom Kertscher, "Just How Wealthy Is the Wal-Mart Walton Family?" Politi-fact, December 8, 2013, www.politifact.com/wisconsin/statements/2013/dec/08 /one-wisconsin-now/just-how-wealthy-wal-mart-walton-family; "Workers Gain Voice by Becoming Shareholders," *Dallas Morning News*, June 15, 2014, www.dallasnews .com/business/business-headlines/20140615-want-to-boss-your-boss.ece.

22. Lichtenstein, *The Retail Revolution*, loc. 1632–1671; Moreton, *To Serve God and Wal-Mart*, 176–211.

23. Featherstone, *Selling Women Short*, loc. 420–432.

24. Wal-Mart Stores, "Wal-Mart CEO Credits Consumers' 'Negotiating Power' in Creating Savings That Are Improving Lives," PR Newswire, February 23, 2005, www .prnewswire.com/news-releases/wal-mart-ceo-credits-consumers-negotiating -power-in-creating-savings-that-are-improving-lives-54133567.html.

25. Michael Kazin, *The Populist Persuasion: An American History* (Ithaca, NY: Cor-nell University Press, 1998), 145; Featherstone, *Selling Women Short*, loc. 2898–2913.

26. Featherstone, *Selling Women Short*.

27. Liza Featherstone, "'Dukes v. Wal-Mart' and the Limits of Legal Change," *The Nation*, June 21, 2011, www.thenation.com/article/161571/dukes -v-wal-mart-and-limits-legal-change.

28. Ashley Feinberg, "Walmart's Leaked Anti-Union Training Video: This Isn't About You," Gawker, May 19, 2015, http://gawker.com/walmarts-leaked -anti-union-training-video-this-isnt-ab-1705509442.

29. Al Norman, "Wal-Mart's 'Meat Wars' with Union Sizzles On," *Huffington Post*, March 16, 2008, www.huffingtonpost.com/al-norman/walmarts-meat-wars-with -u_b_91757.html.

30. Stephanie Marin, "Supreme Court of Canada: Wal-Mart Must Pay for Closing Unionized Store," *Huffington Post*, June 27, 2014, www.huffingtonpost .ca/2014/06/27/walmart-canada-supreme-court_n_5537051.html.

31. The C. J.'s Seafood case was covered widely in the news. See, for example, Steven Greenhouse, "Wal-Mart Suspends Supplier of Seafood," *New York Times*, June 29, 2012, www.nytimes.com/2012/07/09/opinion/forced-labor-on-american -shores.html; "Forced Labor on American Shores," *New York Times*, July 8, 2012, www .nytimes.com/2012/07/09/opinion/forced-labor-on-american-shores.html; Steven Greenhouse, "C. J.'s Seafood Fined for Labor Abuses," *New York Times*, July 24, 2012, www.nytimes.com/2012/07/25/business/cjs-seafood-fined-for-labor-abuses .html; Josh Eidelson, "Guest Workers as Bellwether," *Dissent*, Spring 2013, www .dissentmagazine.org/article/guest-workers-as-bellwether.

32. Alexandra Bradbury, "Walmart Warehouse Strikers Return to Work with Full Back Pay," Labor Notes, October 9, 2012, www.labornotes.org/2012/10 /walmart-warehouse-strikers-return-work-full-back-pay.

33. Bill Fletcher Jr., "Organized Labor: Declining Source of Hope?" in *Labor Rising*, 192–198.

34. Sarah Jaffe, "Wal-Mart Faces a New Round of Historic Strikes . . . But Why Now?" Religion Dispatches, December 4, 2012, http://religiondispatches.org /wal-mart-faces-a-new-round-of-historic-strikes-but-why-now.

35. Sarah Jaffe, "How Walmart Organizers Turned the Internet into a Shop Floor," *In These Times*, January 16, 2014, http://inthesetimes.com/article/16116 /how_walmart_organizers_turned_the_internet_into_a_shop_floor.

36. David Moberg, "The Union Behind the Biggest Campaign Against Walmart in History May Be Throwing in the Towel. Why?" *In These Times*, August 11, 2015, http://inthesetimes.com/article/18271/which-way-our-walmart.

37. Shan Li, "Wal-Mart Wrongly Fired Workers for Striking and Must Rehire Them, Labor Board Rules," *Los Angeles Times*, January 22, 2016, www.latimes.com /business/la-fi-walmart-labor-ruling-20160121-story.html.

38. "The Worker Adjustment and Retraining Notification Act" Fact Sheet, US Department of Labor, available at www.doleta.gov/programs/factsht/warn.htm; "Walmart Announces 2015 Annual Shareholders' Meeting Voting Results," Walmart Press Release, available at http://news.walmart.com/news-archive/2015/06/05 /walmart-announces-2015-annual-shareholders-meeting-voting-results.

39. Wayne F. Cascio, "The High Cost of Low Wages," *Harvard Business Review*, December 2006, https://hbr.org/2006/12/the-high-cost-of-low-wages; James Heskett, "Is Walmart Defying Economic Gravity?" *Forbes*, December 5, 2013, www.forbes .com/sites/hbsworkingknowledge/2013/12/05/is-walmart-defying-economic -gravity.

CHAPTER 4: CHALLENGING THE AUSTERITARIANS

1. Jason Stein, Patrick Marley, and Lee Bergquist, "Walker's Budget Cuts Would Touch Most Wisconsinites," *Milwaukee Journal-Sentinel*, March 1, 2011, www.jsonline .com/news/statepolitics/117154428.html.

2. Ryan Grim, "Why the Stimulus Is Too Small," *Huffington Post*, March 11, 2009, www.huffingtonpost.com/2009/02/09/is-stimulus-too-small_n_165076.html; Paul Krugman, "How Did We Know the Stimulus Was Too Small?" *New York Times*, July 28, 2010, http://krugman.blogs.nytimes.com/2010/07/28/how-did-we-know -the-stimulus-was-too-small.

3. Theda Skocpol and Vanessa Williamson, *The Tea Party and the Remaking of Republican Conservatism* (London: Oxford University Press, 2012), Kindle edition, loc. 1196, 1201, 1221–1248.

4. John Nichols, "Eric Cantor Defeated by a Conservative Who Rips Crony Capitalism," *The Nation*, June 11, 2014, www.thenation.com/article/eric-cantor-defeated -conservative-who-rips-crony-capitalism.

5. Matt Taibbi, *The Divide: American Injustice in the Age of the Wealth Gap* (New York: Spiegel and Grau, 2014), Kindle edition, loc. 5398.

6. Walter Dean Burnham and Thomas Ferguson, "Americans Are Sick to Death of Both Parties: Why Our Politics Is in Worse Shape Than We Thought," AlterNet, December 18, 2014, www.alternet.org/americans-are-sick-death-both-parties -why-our-politics-worse-shape-we-thought.

7. Dana Goldstein, *The Teacher Wars: A History of America's Most Embattled Profession* (New York: Anchor, 2014), Kindle edition, loc. 1265, 1303–1406, 1580.

8. "AFSCME: 75 Years of History," AFSCME, www.afscme.org/union/history /afscme-75-years-of-history; William P. Jones, interview with author, September 17, 2015.

9. William P. Jones, interview.

10. Jefferson Cowie, *Stayin' Alive: The 1970s and the Last Days of the Working Class* (New York: New Press, 2010), Kindle edition, loc. 1204–1238; William P. Jones, "Gutting Public Unions," *Dissent*, Fall 2015, https://www.dissentmagazine.org/article /daniel-disalvo-government-against-itself-review; Goldstein, *The Teacher Wars*, loc. 2461.

11. Cowie, *Stayin' Alive*, loc. 7062–7084; Joan Walsh, *What's the Matter with White People?: Why We Long for a Golden Age That Never Was* (Hoboken, NJ: John Wiley and Sons, 2012), 127–128; Sarah Jaffe, "Timothy Noah: Why the Rich Are Getting Richer and the Middle Class Is Disappearing," AlterNet, August 1, 2012, www.alternet.org /books/timothy-noah-why-rich-are-getting-richer-and-middle-class-disappearing.

12. Matt Stoller, "The Liquidation of Society vs. the Global Labor Revival," Naked Capitalism, February 24, 2011, www.nakedcapitalism.com/2011/02/matt -stoller-the-liquidation-of-society-versus-the-global-labor-revival.html; Timothy Noah, *The Great Divergence: America's Growing Inequality Crisis and What We Can Do About It* (New York: Bloomsbury, 2012), 128; US Department of Labor, Bureau of Labor Statistics, "Union Members—2014," www.bls.gov/news.release/union2.nr0.htm; Jones, "Gutting Public Unions."

13. Jones, "Gutting Public Unions."

14. Michael Kazin, *The Populist Persuasion: An American History* (Ithaca, NY: Cornell University Press, 1998), 137.

15. John Nichols, *Uprising: How Wisconsin Renewed the Politics of Protest, from Madison to Wall Street* (New York: Nation Books, 2012), 129–131.

16. Goldstein, *Teacher Wars*, loc. 402–463; Megan Erickson, *Class War: The Privatization of Childhood* (New York: Verso, 2015).

17. Stoller, "The Liquidation of Society."

18. Whet Moser, "Chicagoland Schools: For Blacks, the Most Segregated in the Country," *Chicago*, September 20, 2012, www.chicagomag.com/Chicago-Magazine /The-312/September-2012/Chicagoland-Schools-For-Blacks-the-Most-Segregated -in-the-Country; Jesse Sharkey, "Arne Duncan's Privatization Agenda," *Counter-Punch*, December 18, 2008, www.counterpunch.org/2008/12/18/arne-duncan-s -privatization-agenda.

19. Tony Arnold, "Why Don't Most Illinois Teachers Receive Social Security?" WBEZ, November 21, 2012, www.wbez.org/series/curious-city/why-don%E2%80 %99t-most-illinois-teachers-receive-social-security-103958.

20. "The Schools Chicago's Students Deserve," Chicago Teachers Union, 2012, www.ctunet.com/quest-center/research/the-schools-chicagos-students-deserve.

21. Micah Uetricht, "Strikebot Joins Striking Lane Tech Teachers on the Picket Line," YouTube, uploaded September 14, 2012, https://www.youtube.com /watch?v=LbzNJFsKECM.

22. Micah Uetricht, *Strike for America: Chicago Teachers Against Austerity* (New York: Verso, 2014), 66–68.

23. Melissa Harris, "Penny Pritzker Resigns from the School Board," *Chicago Tribune*, March 14, 2013, http://articles.chicagotribune.com/2013–03–14/business

/chi-penny-pritzker-resigns-from-the-school-board-20130314_1_penny-pritzker
-three-sentence-resignation-letter-school-board.

24. Micah Uetricht, "SEIU State Council Reverses Course, Endorses Jesus 'Chuy' Garcia's Run Against Rahm Emanuel," *In These Times*, March 14, 2015, http:// inthesetimes.com/working/entry/17747/seiu_state_council_reverses_course _endorses_jesus_chuy_garcias_run_against.

25. Jitu Brown and Bob Simpson, "The Fight for Dyett Will Go On," *Socialist Worker*, September 22, 2015, http://socialistworker.org/2015/09/22/the-fight -for-dyett-will-go-on.

26. Bill Ruthhart and Juan Perez Jr., "Teachers Union Has Triple the Public Support of Emanuel," *Chicago Tribune*, February 4, 2016, www.chicagotribune.com /news/local/politics/ct-rahm-emanuel-schools-poll-met-20160203-story.html; Sarah Jaffe, "Impending Chicago Teachers' Strike Adds Power to Nationwide Movements Against Inequality and Racism," Truthout, December 18, 2015, www .truth-out.org/news/item/34092-impending-teachers-strike-in-chicago-adds-power -to-nationwide-debates-on-inequality-and-racism.

27. Interview with Kenzo Shibata, May 5, 2016; Rebecca Burns and David Moberg, "Despite School District's Legal Threats, Chicago Teachers Stage One-Day Political Strike," *In These Times*, April 2, 2016, http://inthesetimes.com/working/entry /9013/despite_school_distrcits_legal_threats_Chicago_teachers_stage_one_day-polit.

CHAPTER 5: RACE TO THE BOTTOM

1. Paul Kane, "'Tea Party' Protesters Accused of Spitting on Lawmaker, Using Slurs," *Washington Post*, March 20, 2010, www.washingtonpost.com/wp-dyn/content /article/2010/03/20/AR2010032002556.html.

2. *White Power USA*, directed by Richard Rowley and Jacquie Soohen, 2010, Big Noise Films, www.bignoisefilms.com/videowire/38-latest/106-white.

3. Ibid.

4. Arian Campo-Flores, "Are Tea Partiers Racist?" *Newsweek*, April 25, 2010, www .newsweek.com/are-tea-partiers-racist-70695; Theda Skocpol and Vanessa Williamson, *The Tea Party and the Remaking of Republican Conservatism* (London: Oxford University Press, 2012), Kindle edition, loc. 1368.

5. Nathalie Baptiste, "Them That's Got Shall Get," *American Prospect*, October 13, 2014, http://prospect.org/article/staggering-loss-black-wealth-due-subprime -scandal-continues-unabated.

6. Elizabeth Weill-Greenberg, "From Troy Davis to Occupy Wall Street: How the Prison System Destroys the American Dream," Alternet, October 3, 2011, www .alternet.org/story/152607/from_troy_davis_to_occupy_wall_street%3A_how _the_prison_system_destroys_the_american_dream; Ryan Devereaux, "Troy Davis Protesters Occupy Wall Street," New America Media, September 24, 2011, http:// newamericamedia.org/2011/09/troy-davis-protesters-occupy-wall-street.php; Editors, "The Killing of Troy Davis," *The Nation*, September 21, 2011, www.thenation.com /article/killing-troy-davis.

7. Kimberlé Crenshaw, "Demarginalizing the Intersection of Race and Sex: A Black Feminist Critique of Antidiscrimination Doctrine, Feminist Theory and Antiracist Politics," *University of Chicago Legal Forum* 140 (1989): 139–167.

8. Hena Ashraf, "Brown Power at Occupy Wall Street!" Racialicious, October 3, 2011, www.racialicious.com/2011/10/03/brown-power-at-occupy-wall-street-92911; Manissa McCleave Maharawal, "What Makes Occupy Different: Inclusion," *The Guardian*, November 15, 2011, www.theguardian.com/commentisfree/cifamerica/2011/nov/15/occupy-wall-street-occupy-movement.

9. Joan Walsh, "The Man Who Blocked John Lewis Speaks," Salon, October 13, 2011, www.salon.com/2011/10/13/the_man_who_blocked_john_lewis_speaks.

10. Kristen Gwynne, "Is NYPD Running Wild? Patterns of Brutality Raise Questions About Mayor's Control of Police," Alternet, February 15, 2012, www.alternet.org/story/154161/is_nypd_running_wild_patterns_of_brutality_raise_questions_about_mayor's_control_of_police; Daniel Beekman, "500 Protest Cop Shooting of Ramarley Graham," *New York Daily News*, February 8, 2012, www.nydailynews.com/news/500-protest-shooting-ramarley-graham-article-1.1018297.

11. Edgar Sandoval and Helen Kennedy, "'Million Hoodie' March Takes Union Square in Protest of Trayvon Martin's Fatal Shooting," *New York Daily News*, March 21, 2012, www.nydailynews.com/new-york/million-hoodie-march-takes-union-square-protest-trayvon-martin-murder-article-1.1048522; Terrell Jermaine Starr, "'Million Hoody March' Organizer Says Trayvon's Murder 'Very Personal,'" Newsone, March 21, 2012; "Trayvon Martin Shooting Sparks Hoodie Movement," CBS News, www.cbsnews.com/pictures/trayvon-martin-shooting-sparks-hoodie-movement; "Celebrities Wear Hoodies in Support of Trayvon Martin," BET, www.bet.com celebrities/photos/2012/03/celebrities-wear-hoodies-in-support-of-trayvon-martin.html?ftcnt=HP_Celebrities#!032612-celebs-wear-hoodies-trayvon-nelly.

12. Terry Greene Sterling, "The Minuteman Vigilante's Arizona Murder Trial," *Daily Beast*, January 26, 2011, www.thedailybeast.com/articles/2011/01/26/minuteman-vigilantes-arizona-murder-trial-brisenia-flores-mother-testifies.html; US Department of Homeland Security, "Rightwing Extremism: Current Economic and Political Climate Fueling Resurgence in Radicalization and Recruitment," April 7, 2009, available at http://fas.org/irp/eprint/rightwing.pdf.

13. Andrea Kelly and Rhonda Bodfield, "Her Plot Will Unfold at Council Meetings," *Arizona Daily Star*, June 9, 2010, http://tucson.com/news/local/govt-and-politics/elections/article_349e18b8-ec64-5fd7-b347-afe7f1778a47.html; Adrian Chen, "Shot Congresswoman Was in Sarah Palin's 'Crosshairs,'" Gawker, January 8, 2011, http://gawker.com/5728545/shot-congresswoman-was-in-sarah-palins-crosshairs; Jeremy Diamond, "Trump Rally Attendee Charged with Assault," CNN, March 11, 2016, www.cnn.com/2016/03/10/politics/donald-trump-protestor-punch-face; Russ Choma, "A Journalist Was Just Manhandled and Detained at a Trump Rally," *Mother Jones*, February 29, 2016, www.motherjones.com/politics/2016/02/journalist-manhandled-and-arrested-trump-rally; Colin Dwyer, "Donald Trump: 'I Could . . . Shoot Somebody, and I Wouldn't Lose Any Voters,'" National Public Radio, January 25, 2016, www.npr.org/sections/thetwo-way/2016/01/23/464129029/donald-trump-i-could-shoot-somebody-and-i-wouldnt-lose-any-voters; Mary M. Chapman and Julie Bosman, "Detroit-Area Man Convicted of Murdering Teenager on His Porch," *New York Times*, August 7, 2014, www.nytimes.com/2014/08/08/us/detroit-area-man-convicted-of-murdering-woman-who-knocked-on-his-door.html.

14. Southern Poverty Law Center, "Gordon Baum," www.splcenter.org/get

-informed/intelligence-files/profiles/gordon-baum; Rowley and Soohen, *White Power USA.*

15. Charles Payne is quoted in Charles E. Cobb Jr., *This Nonviolent Stuff'll Get You Killed* (New York: Basic Books, 2014), Kindle edition, loc. 2518.

16. Laura Flanders, Rick Rowley, Chip Berlet, and J. D. Meadows, "White Power USA," in *At the Tea Party,* ed. Laura Flanders (New York: OR Books, 2010), 96–105.

17. Karen E. Fields and Barbara J. Fields, *Racecraft: The Soul of Inequality in American Life* (New York: Verso, 2014), Kindle edition.

18. W. E. B. Du Bois, "The Superior Race (An Essay)," first published in *The Smart Set: A Magazine of Cleverness,* 1923, available at www.webdubois.org/dbSuperior Race.html.

19. Fields and Fields, *Racecraft,* loc. 584; Dan Cantor, "The Civil Rights Movement Is Now," Working Families, n.d., http://workingfamilies.org/2015/07/the -civil-rights-movement-is-now.

20. David A. Graham, "The White Supremacist Group That Inspired a Racist Manifesto," *The Atlantic,* June 22, 2015, www.theatlantic.com/politics/archive/2015/06 /council-of-conservative-citizens-dylann-roof/396467.

21. Jon Swaine, "Leader of Group Cited in 'Dylann Roof Manifesto' Donated to Top Republicans," *The Guardian,* June 22, 2015, www.theguardian.com/us-news /2015/jun/21/dylann-roof-manifesto-charlston-shootings-republicans; Story of America, "Confederate Flag Honors My Ancestors—It Hurts My Feelings That People Are Against It," YouTube, posted by "StoryofAmerica," July 2, 2015, https:// www.youtube.com/watch?v=Nd4q6vGKJYw.

22. "South Carolina: Blacks and Traitors Attack Pro-Confederate Flag Protest," Occidental Dissent, June 30, 2015, www.occidentaldissent.com/2015/06/30/south -carolina-blacks-and-traitors-attack-pro-confederate-flag-protest; Brian Pace, "Your Opinion: Keep the Mississippi Flag for Our State's Traditions," *Daily Journal,* September 4, 2015, http://djournal.com/opinion/your-opinion-keep-the-mississippi -flag-for-our-states-traditions; Bruce Shapiro, "Don't Tell the Student Protesters at Yale to Grow Up," *The Nation,* November 13, 2015, www.thenation.com/article /dont-tell-the-student-protestors-at-yale-to-grow-up.

23. Thomas Piketty, *Capital in the Twenty-First Century,* trans. Arthur Goldhammer (Cambridge, MA: Belknap Press, 2014), Kindle edition, loc. 2703–2705.

24. Edward E. Baptist, *The Half Has Never Been Told: Slavery and the Making of American Capitalism* (New York: Basic Books, 2014), Kindle edition, loc. 5304, 7415.

25. Naomi Murakawa, *The First Civil Right: How Liberals Built Prison America* (Oxford: Oxford University Press, 2014), Kindle edition, loc. 161; Andrew Cherlin, *Labor's Love Lost: The Rise and Fall of the Working-Class Family in America* (New York: Russell Sage Foundation, 2014), Kindle edition, loc. 1206.

26. Angela Y. Davis, "From the Prison of Slavery to the Slavery of Prison: Frederick Douglass and the Convict Lease System," in *The Angela Y. Davis Reader,* ed. Joy James (Hoboken, NJ: Blackwell, 1998), 76.

27. Sheila Bapat, *Part of the Family?* (New York: IG Publishing, 2014).

28. Judith Stepan-Norris and Maurice Zeitlin, *Left Out: Reds and America's Industrial Unions* (New York: Cambridge University Press, 2002), Kindle edition, loc. 2607, 2776; Mark Ames, "You Hate 'Right to Work' Laws More Than You Know:

Here's Why," NSFWCorp, December 12, 2012, https://www.nsfwcorp.com/dispatch
/right-to-work.

29. Stepan-Norris and Zeitlin, *Left Out*, loc. 2915.

30. Justin Wm. Moyer, "Why South Carolina's Confederate Flag Isn't at Half-
Staff After Church Shooting," *Washington Post*, June 19, 2015, www.washington
post.com/news/morning-mix/wp/2015/06/19/why-south-carolinas-confederate
-flag-isnt-at-half-mast-after-church-shooting.

31. Jefferson Cowie, *Stayin' Alive: The 1970s and the Last Days of the Working Class*
(New York: New Press, 2010), Kindle edition, loc. 4728. I have written several articles
on the port trucking industry, deregulation, and labor. See Sarah Jaffe, "New Report: Port Trucking Companies Steal More Than $1 Billion in Wages from Drivers,"
In These Times, February 19, 2014, http://inthesetimes.com/working/entry/16312
/new_report_ports_steal_billions_from_truckers_through_misclassification.

32. Cowie, *Stayin' Alive*, loc. 5278.

33. This statement of Atwater's has been quoted in many places; I sourced it
from Bob Herbert, "Impossible, Ridiculous, Repugnant," *New York Times*, October 6, 2005, http://query.nytimes.com/gst/fullpage.html?res=9C04E6DF1E30F
935A35753C1A9639C8B63.

34. Paul Taylor et al., "Wealth Gaps Rise to Record Highs Between Whites, Blacks
and Hispanics," Pew Research Center, July 26, 2011, www.pewsocialtrends.org
/files/2011/07/SDT-Wealth-Report_7–26–11_FINAL.pdf; Michael Fletcher, "Study
Ties Black-White Wealth Gap to Stubborn Disparities in Real Estate," *Washington Post*,
February 26, 2013, www.washingtonpost.com/business/economy/study-ties-black
-white-wealth-gap-to-stubborn-disparities-in-real-estate/2013/02/26/8b4b3f50–
8035–11e2-b99e-6baf4ebe42df_story.html.

35. Ta-Nehisi Coates, "The Case for Reparations," *The Atlantic*, June 2014, www
.theatlantic.com/magazine/archive/2014/06/the-case-for-reparations/361631.

36. Fields and Fields, *Racecraft*, loc. 5015; Emily Badger, "Redlining: Still a
Thing," *Washington Post*, May 28, 2015, www.washingtonpost.com/blogs/wonkblog
/wp/2015/05/28/evidence-that-banks-still-deny-black-borrowers-just-as-they-did
-50-years-ago; Robert Gordon, "Did Liberals Cause the Sub-Prime Crisis?" *American Prospect*, April 7, 2008, http://prospect.org/article/did-liberals-cause-sub-prime-crisis.

37. Taylor et al., "Wealth Gaps"; Kai Wright, "The Subprime Swindle," in *Meltdown: How Greed and Corruption Shattered Our Financial System and How We Can Recover*,
ed. Katrina vanden Heuvel (New York: Nation Books, 2009), 140; GRITtv (*The Laura
Flanders Show*), "Kai Wright: Myth of Black Middle Class," YouTube, uploaded August 16, 2010, www.youtube.com/watch?v=oDK8536qOJk.

38. Fields and Fields, *Racecraft*, loc. 5015; Laura Shin, "The Racial Wealth
Gap: Why a Typical White Household Has 16 Times the Wealth of a Black One,"
Forbes, March 26, 2015, www.forbes.com/sites/laurashin/2015/03/26/the-racial
-wealth-gap-why-a-typical-white-household-has-16-times-the-wealth-of-a-black
-one; US Department of Justice, Office of Public Affairs, "Justice Department
Reaches Settlement with Wells Fargo Resulting in $175 Million in Relief for
Homeowners to Resolve Fair Lending Claims," July 12, 2012, www.justice.gov/opa
/pr/justice-department-reaches-settlement-wells-fargo-resulting-more-175-million
-relief.

39. Wright, "Subprime Swindle," 137; Bobbi Murray, "Hunting the Predators," in *Meltdown*, ed. vanden Heuvel, 44; Taylor et al., "Wealth Gaps"; Fletcher, "Black-White Wealth Gap."

40. Sylvia Allegretto and Steven Pitts, "The Great Recession, Jobless Recoveries and Black Workers," University of California at Berkeley, Center for Labor Research and Education, n.d., http://laborcenter.berkeley.edu/pdf/2010/the-great-recession.pdf; Christian E. Weller and Jaryn Fields, "The Black and White Labor Gap in America: Why African Americans Struggle to Find Jobs and Remain Employed Compared to Whites," Center for American Progress, July 25, 2011, https://www.americanprogress.org/issues/labor/report/2011/07/25/9992/the-black-and-white-labor-gap-in-america; Eileen Patten and Jens Manuel Krogstad, "Black Child Poverty Rate Holds Steady, Even as Other Groups See Declines," Pew Research Center, July 14, 2015, www.pewresearch.org/fact-tank/2015/07/14/black-child-poverty-rate-holds-steady-even-as-other-groups-see-declines.

41. Leon Neyfakh, "Freddie Gray's Broken Neighborhood," Slate, April 27, 2015, www.slate.com/articles/news_and_politics/crime/2015/04/freddie_gray_death_a_closer_look_at_the_tragically_impoverished_and_violent.html; Justin Fenton, "Autopsy of Freddie Gray Shows 'High Energy' Impact," *Baltimore Sun*, June 24, 2015, www.baltimoresun.com/news/maryland/freddie-gray/bs-md-ci-freddie-gray-autopsy-20150623-story.html; Matt Taibbi, *The Divide: American Injustice in the Age of the Wealth Gap* (New York: Spiegel and Grau, 2014), Kindle edition, loc. 1901.

42. Gordon, "Did Liberals Cause the Sub-Prime Crisis?"

43. A good example from George W. Bush's presidency is "Fact Sheet: America's Ownership Society: Expanding Opportunities," http://georgewbush-whitehouse.archives.gov/news/releases/2004/08/20040809–9.html.

44. Philip Mirowski, *Never Let a Serious Crisis Go to Waste: How Neoliberalism Survived the Financial Meltdown* (New York: Verso, 2014), 130.

45. Aidan Gardiner and Paul Lomas, "Silent March to Protest Stop-and-Frisks Takes over Upper East Side," DNAinfo, June 17, 2012, www.dnainfo.com/new-york/20120617/upper-east-side/silent-march-protest-stop-and-frisks-takes-over-upper-east-side; John Leland and Colin Moynihan, "Thousands March Silently to Protest Stop-and-Frisk Policies," *New York Times*, June 17, 2012, www.nytimes.com/2012/06/18/nyregion/thousands-march-silently-to-protest-stop-and-frisk-policies.html.

46. On Governor Scott's Confederate-flag boots, see Raillan Brooks, "Did You Know Protesters Have Been Occupying the Florida State Capitol for a Week? Yeah, Thought So," *Village Voice*, July 22, 2013, www.villagevoice.com/news/did-you-know-protesters-have-been-occupying-the-florida-state-capitol-for-a-week-yeah-thought-so-6713056. Governor Scott Tweeted a photo of his boots, and then deleted it a year later. It was archived by Politwoops, however, and is available at http://politwoops.sunlightfoundation.com/tweet/326790307524005888; Anthony Man, "Gov. Rick Scott Talks About Texting, Stand Your Ground and His Latest Boots," *Sun-Sentinel*, May 1, 2012, http://weblogs.sun-sentinel.com/news/politics/broward/blog/2012/05/gov_rick_scott_talks_about_tex_1.html.

47. BYP 100, "Agenda to Build Black Futures," http://agendatobuildblackfutures.org/our-agenda/solutions/#1.

48. Editorial Board, "Editorial: Rekia Boyd Shooting Was 'Beyond Reckless,' So Cop Got a Pass," *Chicago Tribune*, April 22, 2015, www.chicagotribune.com/news /opinion/editorials/ct-cop-verdict-servin-edit-0423–20150422-story.html; James C. McKinley Jr., "Manslaughter Charges in Beating Death of Transgender Woman in 2013," *New York Times*, March 3, 2015, www.nytimes.com/2015/03/04/nyregion/ manslaughter-charges-in-beating-death-of-transgender-woman-in-2013.html.

49. Goldie Taylor, "Exclusive: Bree Newsome Speaks for the First Time After Courageous Act of Civil Disobedience," *Blue Nation Review*, June 29, 2015, http:// bluenationreview.com/exclusive-bree-newsome-speaks-for-the-first-time-after -courageous-act-of-civil-disobedience.

CHAPTER 6: A MORAL MOVEMENT

1. Lynn Parramore, "A Holy War over Gay Marriage," Salon, April 28, 2012, www .salon.com/2012/04/28/a_holy_war_over_gay_marriage.

2. Christopher Ingraham, "America's Most Gerrymandered Congressional Districts," *Washington Post*, May 15, 2014, https://www.washingtonpost.com/news/wonk /wp/2014/05/15/americas-most-gerrymandered-congressional-districts.

3. Alex Kotch, "Inside Moral Mondays," Brooklyn Rail, October 3, 2013, http:// www.brooklynrail.org/2013/10/express/inside-moral-mondays.

4. Will Huntsberry, "Crowd Size and Arrest Totals Increase at Latest Moral Monday Protest," *Indyweek*, May 22, 2013, www.indyweek.com/indyweek/crowd -size-and-arrest-totals-increase-at-latest-moral-monday-protest/Content?oid=3641650.

5. Samantha Lachman, "Republican Mayor Partners with Moral Monday Movement, Walks 273 Miles for Health Care Access," *Huffington Post*, July 15, 2014, www .huffingtonpost.com/2014/07/15/moral-monday-health-care_n_5588211.html.

6. Lynn Parramore, "The Man Behind Moral Mondays," *American Prospect*, June 17, 2013, http://prospect.org/article/man-behind-moral-mondays.

7. Lindsay Wagner, "School Vouchers: A Pathway Toward Fraud and Abuse of Taxpayer Dollars," NC Policy Watch, April 24, 2013, www.ncpolicywatch.com /2013/04/24/school-vouchers-a-pathway-toward-fraud-and-abuse-of-taxpayer -dollars; Ari Berman, "North Carolina Is the New Wisconsin," *The Nation*, June 12, 2013, www.thenation.com/article/north-carolina-new-wisconsin.

8. Robin Marty, "North Carolina 'Motorcycle' Abortion Bill Passes House, Will Protect Women from 'Vaginal Organisms,' Says Supporter," RH Reality Check, July 12, 2013, http://rhrealitycheck.org/article/2013/07/12/north-carolina-motorcycle -abortion-bill-passes-house-will-protect-women-from-vaginal-organisms-says-supporter.

9. Igor Volsky, "Ohio Governor John Kasich Breaks Pledge, Excludes Gender Protections from Non-Discrimination Order," ThinkProgress, January 24, 2011, http:// thinkprogress.org/lgbt/2011/01/24/177230/kasich-eo; Tanya Somanader, "Scott Walker's Budget Limits Birth Control Coverage, Eliminates Access to Health Care Services for Women," ThinkProgress, March 3, 2011, http://thinkprogress.org /politics/2011/03/03/148048/walker-birth-control-women-health; Laura Bassett, "Scott Walker Signs 20-Week Abortion Ban into Law," *Huffington Post*, July 20, 2015, www.huffingtonpost.com/entry/scott-walker-abortion-ban_55ad0c69e4b065 dfe89ec3d8; Tanya Somanader, "House GOP Unanimously Passes Anti-Abortion Bill That Redefines Rape, Raises Taxes, and Creates Rape Audits," ThinkProgress,

May 4, 2011, http://thinkprogress.org/politics/2011/05/04/163656/house-gop-hr3; Sarah Jaffe, "Meet the HR3 Ten: Number One, Heath Shuler," RH Reality Check, February 8, 2011, http://rhrealitycheck.org/article/2011/02/08/meet-heath-shuler; Hayley Miller, "List of Anti-LGBT Legislation Across Nation Tops 100," Human Rights Campaign Blog, April 9, 2015, www.hrc.org/blog/entry/list-of-anti-lgbt-legislation-across-nation-tops-100.

10. Thomas Frank, *What's the Matter with Kansas?* (New York: Henry Holt, 2005).

11. Theda Skocpol and Vanessa Williamson, *The Tea Party and the Remaking of Republican Conservatism* (London: Oxford University Press, 2012), Kindle edition, loc. 753.

12. Corey Robin, *The Reactionary Mind: Conservatism from Edmund Burke to Sarah Palin* (Oxford: Oxford University Press, 2011), Kindle edition, loc. 3569.

13. Sarah Jaffe, "Can a Progressive Atheist Defeat the Democrats' 'Family' Man in NC?" Religion Dispatches, April 17, 2012, http://religiondispatches.org/can-a-progressive-atheist-defeat-the-democrats-family-man-in-nc; Lindsay Beyerstein, "Worse Than Fascists: Christian Political Group 'The Family' Openly Reveres Hitler," AlterNet, June 11, 2008, www.alternet.org/story/87665/worse_than_fascists%3A_christian_political_group_'the_family'_openly_reveres_hitler. For more on The Family, I recommend Jeff Sharlet, *The Family: The Secret Fundamentalism at the Heart of American Power* (New York: HarperCollins, 2008).

14. William Jennings Bryan's "Imperialism" speech, available at Voices of Democracy, http://voicesofdemocracy.umd.edu/william-jennings-bryan-imperialism-speech-text.

15. Michael Kazin, *The Populist Persuasion: An American History* (Ithaca, NY: Cornell University Press, 1998), 106.

16. Chip Berlet and Matthew Lyons, *Right-Wing Populism in America: Too Close for Comfort* (New York: Guilford Press, 2000), 159.

17. Andrew Hartman, *A War for the Soul of America: A History of the Culture* (Chicago: University of Chicago Press, 2015), Kindle edition, loc. 100.

18. Amy Sonnie and James Tracy, *Hillbilly Nationalists, Urban Race Rebels and Black Power: Community Organizing in Radical Times* (New York: Melville House, 2011), Kindle edition, loc. 235–282, 1266–1657.

19. "Amber Hollibaugh," Smith College Voices of Feminism Oral History Project, interviewed by Kelly Anderson December 15–16, 2003, and January 20, 2004, transcript available at https://www.smith.edu/library/libs/ssc/vof/transcripts/Hollibaugh.pdf.

20. Penny Lewis, *Hardhats, Hippies and Hawks: The Vietnam Antiwar Movement as Myth and Memory* (Ithaca, NY: ILR Press and Cornell University Press, 2013).

21. Jefferson Cowie, *Stayin' Alive: The 1970s and the Last Days of the Working Class* (New York: New Press, 2010), Kindle edition, loc. 4614–4618.

22. Kristin Luker, *Abortion and the Politics of Motherhood* (Berkeley: University of California Press, 1985), 123.

23. Robin, *Reactionary Mind,* loc. 785–791.

24. Kazin, *Populist Persuasion,* 262–263; Cowie, *Stayin' Alive,* loc. 5971.

25. David W. Moore, "Moral Values Important in the 2004 Exit Polls," Gallup, December 7, 2004, www.gallup.com/poll/14275/moral-values-important-2004

-exit-polls.aspx; "Religion and the Presidential Vote," Pew Research Center, December 6, 2004, www.people-press.org/2004/12/06/religion-and-the-presidential-vote.

26. Andrew Cherlin, *Labor's Love Lost: The Rise and Fall of the Working-Class Family in America* (New York: Russell Sage Foundation, 2014), Kindle edition, loc. 1109–1129.

27. Ibid., loc. 1158–1167, 2402; Luker, *Abortion*, 199–207.

28. Luker, *Abortion*, 8, 199–207.

29. Bethany Moreton, *To Serve God and Wal-Mart: The Making of Christian Free Enterprise* (Cambridge, MA: Harvard University Press, 2010), 5, 51–106; Bethany Moreton and Pamela Voeckel, "Learning from the Right," in *Labor Rising: The Past and Future of Working People in America*, ed. Daniel Katz and Richard A. Greenwald (New York: New Press, 2012), 28–36.

30. Moreton, *To Serve God and Wal-Mart*, 118–119.

31. M. E. Melody, "Acting Up Academically: AIDS and the Politics of Disempowerment," in *Global AIDS Policy*, ed. Douglas A. Feldman (Westport, CT: Bergin and Garvey, 1994), 176–177.

32. Premilla Nadasen, *Household Workers Unite: The Untold Story of African American Women Who Built a Movement* (Boston: Beacon Press, 2015), 20–32; Moreton and Voeckel, "Learning from the Right," 28–36.

33. "Republican Wave: Tillis Defeats Hagan, GOP Keeps Super Majority in N.C. Legislature," Voter Update, November 5, 2014, http://thevoterupdate.com/trail/?p=1923#.VeCmi9NViko.

34. Bob Hall, "Data Highlight: US Supreme Court Rejects Aggressive Segregation," Democracy North Carolina blog, April 21, 2015, http://nc-democracy.org/data-highlight-us-supreme-court-rejects-aggressive-segregation; Gary D. Robertson, "Judges Strike Down 2 North Carolina Congressional Districts," Associated Press, February 5, 2016, http://abcnews.go.com/US/wireStory/judges-strike-north-carolina-congressional-districts-36750506; Richard Fausset, "Supreme Court Won't Intervene in North Carolina Election Fight," *New York Times*, February 19, 2016, www.nytimes.com/2016/02/20/us/north-carolina-fights-over-its-election-rules.html.

35. Matthew Burns and Cullen Browder, "Wake DA Drops Charges Against Hundreds of Legislative Protesters," WRAL, September 19, 2014, www.wral.com/wake-da-drops-charges-against-hundreds-of-legislative-protesters/13996960.

36. Colin Campbell and Taylor Knopf, "Accusations Fly as NC House Changes Course on Greensboro Redistricting," *News & Observer*, July 2, 2015, www.newsobserver.com/news/politics-government/politics-columns-blogs/under-the-dome/article26047744.html.

37. Osagyefo Sekou, "The Liberation Theology of Ferguson," KineticsLive, April 8, 2015, http://kineticslive.com/2015/05/osagyefo-sekou-the-liberation-theology-of-ferguson.

CHAPTER 7: RED SCARES AND RADICAL IMAGINATION

1. "Kshama Sawant Victory Party 17nov2013," YouTube video, uploaded by "Todd Boyle," November 17, 2013, https://www.youtube.com/watch?v=xxmWhRiP8Zs&feature=youtu.be&t=18m5s.

2. Pat Garofalo, "Boeing's Corporate Tax Blackmail," *U.S. News & World Report*, November 13, 2013 www.usnews.com/opinion/blogs/pat-garofalo /2013/11/13/boeing-blackmails-washington-state-into-the-largest-corporate-tax -break-ever.

3. Rudolph Bell, "South Carolina Governor Says Ford, GM, Chrysler Union Jobs Not Welcome in State," *Detroit Free Press*, February 20, 2014 www.freep.com /article/20140220/BUSINESS01/302200065.

4. Anthony Rizutto, "City Council Socialism: An Interview with Ty Moore," *Jacobin*, December 5, 2013, https://www.jacobinmag.com/2013/12/city-council-socialism.

5. Hendrik Hertzberg, "Like, Socialism," *The New Yorker*, November 3, 2008, www.newyorker.com/magazine/2008/11/03/like-socialism; Scott Conroy, "Palin: Obama's Plan Is 'Experiment with Socialism,'" CBS News, October 19, 2008, www .cbsnews.com/news/palin-obamas-plan-is-experiment-with-socialism.

6. Kristen Schall, "Rasmussen Poll Indicates American Shift Toward Socialism," Common Dreams, April 11, 2009, www.commondreams.org/views/2009/04/11 /rasmussen-poll-indicates-american-shift-toward-socialism; "Glenn Beck—Ronald Reagan Warns About Socialized Health Care V2," YouTube video, uploaded by "americansunlight," August 28, 2009, https://www.youtube.com/watch?v=r4noO9 Wirps; "Glenn Beck . . . Rushing thru Socialized Medicine," YouTube video, uploaded by "SheepleNo," June 16, 2009, https://www.youtube.com/watch?v=jGkZA4NSF8o; Dianna Parker and Christine Schwen, "Media Infected with Conservatives' 'Socialized Medicine' Myth," Media Matters for America, April 30, 2009, http://media matters.org/research/2009/04/30/media-infected-with-conservatives-socialized -me/149717; John Nichols, "How Sarah Palin Renewed American Socialism," in *Going Rouge: Sarah Palin, An American Nightmare*, ed. Richard Kim and Betsy Reed (New York: OR Books, 2009).

7. Adele M. Stan, "Big Business's Hidden Hand in the Smear Job on Van Jones," AlterNet, September 7, 2009, www.alternet.org/story/142481/big_business %27s_hidden_hand_in_the_smear_job_on_van_jones.

8. Dahlia Lithwick, "Nuts About ACORN," Slate, October 16, 2008, www.slate. com/articles/news_and_politics/jurisprudence/2008/10/nuts_about_acorn .html; Aaron Sharockman, "Mickey Mouse Was Registered to Vote in Florida, Republican House Member Claims," Politifact, April 26, 2011, www.politifact.com /florida/statements/2011/apr/26/eric-eisnaugle/mickey-mouse-was-registered -vote-florida-republica.

9. T. Jefferson, "Glenn Beck: The Fight to Mainstream Socialism," GlennBeck. com, April 23, 2010, www.glennbeck.com/content/articles/article/198/39556; T. Jefferson, "Glenn Beck, Obama's #1," GlennBeck.com, October 3, 2008, www .glennbeck.com/content/articles/article/196/16130; "House Votes to Defund ACORN," CBS News, September 17, 2009, www.cbsnews.com/news/house-votes -to-defund-acorn; Rachel Slajda, "ACORN Files for Chapter 7 Bankruptcy," Talking Points Memo, November 2, 2010, http://talkingpointsmemo.com/muckraker /acorn-files-for-chapter-7-bankruptcy.

10. Jennifer Schuessler, "A Young Publisher Takes Marx into the Mainstream," *New York Times*, January 20, 2013, www.nytimes.com/2013/01/21/books/bhaskar

-sunkara-editor-of-jacobin-magazine.html; Ross Douthat, "How to Read in 2013," *New York Times*, December 29, 2012, www.nytimes.com/2012/12/30/opinion/sunday /douthat-how-to-read-in-2013.html.

11. Charles Postel, *The Populist Vision* (Oxford: Oxford University Press, 2009), Kindle edition, loc. 791–793.

12. Chip Berlet and Matthew Lyons, *Right-Wing Populism in America: Too Close for Comfort* (New York: Guilford Press, 2000), 88–89.

13. Judith Stepan-Norris and Maurice Zeitlin, *Left Out: Reds and America's Industrial Unions* (New York: Cambridge University Press, 2002), Kindle edition, loc. 3060, 3100.

14. Ibid., loc. 2951.

15. Victor Navasky, *Naming Names*, rev. ed. (New York: Open Road Media, 2013), Kindle edition, loc. 739; Stepan-Norris and Zeitlin, *Left Out*, loc. 3078.

16. Stepan-Norris and Zeitlin, *Left Out*, loc. 2776–2792; Robin D. G. Kelley, *Hammer and Hoe: Alabama Communists During the Great Depression*, 2nd ed. (Chapel Hill: University of North Carolina Press, 2015), Kindle edition, loc. 3067–3092.

17. Stepan-Norris and Zeitlin, *Left Out*, loc. 3048; Navasky, *Naming Names*, loc. 1878; Berlet and Lyons, *Right-Wing Populism*, 158.

18. Michael Kazin, *The Populist Persuasion: An American History* (Ithaca, NY: Cornell University Press, 1998), 184–190; Thomas Frank, *What's the Matter with Kansas?: How Conservatives Won the Heart of America* (New York: Henry Holt, 2005), 193.

19. Berlet and Lyons, *Right-Wing Populism*, 224–225; JoAnn Wypijewski, "Night Thoughts," *The Nation*, March 23, 2015, www.thenation.com/article/night-thoughts.

20. Trish Kahle, "Betting on Militancy," *Jacobin*, October 22, 2013, https://www .jacobinmag.com/2013/10/beyond-fast-food-strikes.

21. Candice Choi, "McDonald's Can Be Liable for Issues at Franchise-Owned Restaurants, NLRB Rules," Associated Press, July 29, 2014, www.huffington post.com/2014/07/29/mcdonalds-nlrb-joint-employer-ruling_n_5630902.html; Dave Jamieson, "The Labor Ruling McDonald's Has Been Dreading Just Became a Reality," *Huffington Post*, August 27, 2015, www.huffingtonpost.com/entry/the -federal-ruling-mcdonalds-has-dreaded-just-became-a-reality_us_55df39a1e4b 029b3f1b1db3b.

22. Eric M. Johnson, "Court Extends SeaTac's $15 Minimum Wage to Airport Workers," *Huffington Post*, August 21, 2015, www.huffingtonpost.com/entry /seatac-15-minimum-wage_us_55d74dcfe4b04ae49702fa99.

23. Dan Merica, "Windfall at Bernie's: Sanders Raises $1.5 Million in 24 Hours," CNN, May 1, 2015, www.cnn.com/2015/05/01/politics/bernie-sanders -fundraising; Clare Foran, "Bernie Sanders's Big Money," *The Atlantic*, March 1, 2016, www.theatlantic.com/politics/archive/2016/03/bernie-sanders-fund raising/471648; Aaron Blake, "74-Year-Old Bernie Sanders's Remarkable Dominance Among Young Voters, in 1 Chart," *Washington Post*, March 17, 2016, www .washingtonpost.com/news/the-fix/wp/2016/03/17/74-year-old-bernie -sanderss-amazing-dominance-among-young-voters-in-1-chart.

24. Gregory Krieg, "Hillary Clinton Just Set Herself Apart from Bernie Sanders on This One Critical Point," Mic.com, July 17, 2015, http://mic.com/articles /122461/hillary-clinton-declines-to-endorse-15-minimum-wage#.iZ8kaKYuv.

25. Ezra Klein, "Bernie Sanders and Hillary Clinton's Debate over Capitalism, Explained," Vox, October 14, 2015, www.vox.com/2015/10/14/9528873/bernie -sander-hillary-clinton-socialist-debate.

26. Real Clear Politics, "2016 Democratic Popular Vote," June 8, 2016, www .realclearpolitics.com/epolls/2016/president/democratic_vote_count.html; fund-raising total provided by Sanders campaign staff, June 8, 2016.

CHAPTER 8: THE MILITARIZATION OF EVERYTHING

1. "NYPD Police Pepper Spray Occupy Wall Street Protesters (Anthony Balogna)," YouTube video, uploaded by "USLAWdotcom," September 24, 2011, https://www.youtube.com/watch?v=TZ05rWx1pig; "Peaceful Female Protesters Penned in the Street and Maced! #OccupyWallStreet," YouTube video, uploaded by "TheOther99Percent's channel," September 24, 2011, https://www.youtube .com/watch?v=moD2JnGTToA.

2. Kristen Gwynne, "'This Is the Beginning of Something Big': Report from AlterNet Staffer Arrested on Brooklyn Bridge," AlterNet, October 3, 2011, www .alternet.org/newsandviews/article/674832/%22this_is_the_beginning_of_some thing_big%22%3A_report_from_alternet_staffer_arrested_on_brooklyn_bridge.

3. Wanda Johnson, "Oscar Grant's Mother: 'We Have to Be Relentless in the Vindication of Our Slain Sons,'" *Time*, August 26, 2014, http://time.com/3181736 /michael-brown-ferguson-oscar-grant; Michael McLaughlin, "Ex-Transit Officer Who Killed Oscar Grant, Unarmed Black Man, Wins Lawsuit," *Huffington Post*, July 1, 2014, www.huffingtonpost.com/2014/07/01/oscar-grant-lawsuit-bart-officer_n _5548719.html; Susie Cagle, "Police State in Oakland? Reporter's Arrest Contradicts Official Story," AlterNet, November 6, 2011, www.alternet.org/story/152990 /police_state_in_oakland_one_reporter%27s_arrest_contradicts_official_story; Susie Cagle, "Arrests 1am at Occupy Oakland," YouTube video, uploaded by Susie Cagle, November 4, 2011, https://www.youtube.com/watch?v=afcubFVMrMY.

4. Susie Cagle, "Police State in Oakland?"; Susie Cagle, "Arrests 1am at Occupy Oakland."

5. Ali Winston, "Oakland to Pay $4.5 Million to Iraq War Vet Scott Olsen," *East Bay Express*, March 21, 2014, www.eastbayexpress.com/SevenDays /archives/2014/03/21/oakland-to-pay-45-million-to-iraq-war-vet-scott-olsen; "Scott Olsen, U.S. Vet Nearly Killed by Police Beanbag at Occupy Oakland, Settles Lawsuit with City," *Democracy Now*, March 21, 2014, www.democracynow.org/2014/3/21 /scott_olsen_us_vet_nearly_killed.

6. Randy Erickson, "Two Years After Shooting at Occupy Oakland, OHS Grad Occupied with Healing, Lawsuit," *LaCrosse Tribune*, November 2, 2013, http:// lacrossetribune.com/news/local/two-years-after-shooting-at-occupy-oakland -ohs-grad-occupied/article_b4cf61b6–4377–11e3–8835–001a4bcf887a.html.

7. Jason Paladino and Jake Nicol, "Urban Shield Trains First Responders, Draws Fire over Weapons Show," OaklandNorth, October 30, 2013, https://oaklandnorth .net/2013/10/30/urban-shield-trains-first-responders-draws-fire-over-weapons-show.

8. Winston, "Oakland to Pay $4.5 Million."

9. "Los Angeles to Pay $2.45 Million to Settle Occupy LA Lawsuit," ABC 7, April

2, 2015, http://abc7.com/news/los-angeles-to-pay-$245-million-to-settle-occupy-la -lawsuit/611708.

10. Jason Leopold, "DHS Turns Over Occupy Wall Street Documents to Truthout," Truthout, March 20, 2012, www.truth-out.org/news/item/8012-dhs-turns-over -occupy-wall-street-documents-to-truthout; Michael S. Schmidt and Colin Moynihan, "F.B.I. Counterterrorism Agents Monitored Occupy Movement, Records Show," *New York Times*, December 24, 2012, www.nytimes.com/2012/12/25/nyregion /occupy-movement-was-investigated-by-fbi-counterterrorism-agents-records-show .html; "FBI Documents Reveal Secret Nationwide Occupy Monitoring," Partnership for Civil Justice Fund, December 21, 2012, www.justiceonline.org/fbi_files_ows.

11. Sarah Knuckey, Katherine Glenn, and Emi MacLean, et al., "Suppressing Protest: Human Rights Violations in the U.S. Response to Occupy Wall Street," Global Justice Clinic (NYU School of Law) and the Walter Leitner International Human Rights Clinic at the Leitner Center for International Law and Justice (Fordham Law School), available at Center for Human Rights and Global Justice, NYU School of Law, http://chrgj.org/wp-content/uploads/2012/10/suppressingprotest.pdf.

12. Ibid.

13. David Hunn and Kim Bell, "Why Was Michael Brown's Body Left There for Hours?" *St. Louis Post-Dispatch*, September 14, 2014, www.stltoday.com/news /local/crime-and-courts/why-was-michael-brown-s-body-left-there-for-hours/article _0b73ec58-c6a1–516e-882f-74d18a4246e0.html.

14. Rebecca Leber, "Ferguson's Police Force Is 94 Percent White, and That's Basically Normal in the U.S." *New Republic*, August 13, 2014, www.newrepublic.com /article/119070/michael-browns-death-leads-scrutiny-ferguson-white-police.

15. Barbara Starr and Wesley Bruer, "Missouri National Guard's Term for Ferguson Protesters: 'Enemy Forces,'" CNN, April 17, 2015, http://edition.cnn.com /2015/04/17/politics/missouri-national-guard-ferguson-protesters/index.html.

16. Tef Poe, "St. Louis Rapper Tef Poe Describes the Scene on the Ground in Ferguson, Missouri," *Vice*, August 14, 2014, http://noisey.vice.com/blog/st-louis -rapper-tef-poe-describes-the-scene-in-ferguson-missouri.

17. Lyle Jeremy Rubin, "A Former Marine Explains All the Weapons of War Being Used by Police in Ferguson," *The Nation*, August 20, 2014, www.thenation0 .com/article/181315/catalog-ferguson-police-weaponry; Joanne Stocker and Robin Jacks, "Police in Ferguson Are Firing Tear Gas Canisters Manufactured During the Cold War Era," Truthout, August 19, 2014, www.truth-out.org/news /item/25669-police-in-ferguson-are-firing-tear-gas-canisters-manufactured-during -the-cold-war-era; American Civil Liberties Union of Massachusetts, "Less Lethal Force: Proposed Standards for Massachusetts Law Enforcement Agencies," May 10, 2005, www.aclu.org/news/aclu-massachusetts-issues-recommendations -less-lethal-force-policies-police; Roberto Baldwin, "What Is the LRAD Sound Cannon?" Gizmodo, August 14, 2014, http://gizmodo.com/what-is-the-lrad-sound -cannon-5860592.

18. Mariah Stewart and Ryan J. Reilly, "Ferguson Protesters Outfitted in Orange Jumpsuits, Jailed with High Bail (Update)," *Huffington Post*, October 3, 2014, www .huffingtonpost.com/2014/10/03/ferguson-protesters-arrested_n_5929758.html.

19. Paul Szoldra, "This Is the Terrifying Result of the Militarization of Police," *Business Insider*, August 12, 2014, www.businessinsider.com/police-militarization -ferguson-2014–8#ixzz3AD9HMciA.

20. Jeremy Scahill, *Dirty Wars: The World Is a Battlefield* (New York: Nation Books, 2013), 65. Secretary of State Condoleezza Rice commented during the 2000 pres- idential election, "The United States has found it exceedingly difficult to define its 'national interest' in the absence of Soviet power." Corey Robin, *The Reaction- ary Mind: Conservatism from Edmund Burke to Sarah Palin* (Oxford: Oxford University Press, 2011), Kindle edition, loc. 2442.

21. Sarah Jaffe, "Scahill: Dirty Wars Institutionalized Despite Obama Promises," Truthout, May 28, 2013, http://truth-out.org/news/item/16627-scahill-expanded -executive-cia-and-pentagon-powers-institutionalize-dirty-wars-despite-obama-promises#.

22. Bob Moser, "Republican of the People," *Texas Observer*, February 18, 2010, www.texasobserver.org/republican-of-the-people; Sam Stein, "Sharron Angle Floated '2nd Amendment Remedies as "Cure" for 'The Harry Reid Problem,'" *Huff- ington Post*, June 16, 2010, www.huffingtonpost.com/2010/06/16/sharron-angle -floated-2nd_n_614003.html.

23. Theda Skocpol and Vanessa Williamson, *The Tea Party and the Remaking of Republican Conservatism* (London: Oxford University Press, 2012), Kindle edition, loc. 1279; Chip Berlet and Matthew Lyons, *Right-Wing Populism in America: Too Close for Comfort* (New York: Guilford Press, 2000), 289–303; Laura Flanders, Rick Rowley, Chip Berlet, and J. D. Meadows, "White Power USA," in *At The Tea Party*, ed. Laura Flanders (New York: OR Books, 2010); Justine Sharrock, "Oath Keepers and the Age of Treason," *Mother Jones*, March/April 2010, www.motherjones.com /politics/2010/03/oath-keepers.

24. Joel Currier, "About a Dozen Open-Carry Activists Gather in Ferguson," *St. Louis Post-Dispatch*, November 16, 2015, www.stltoday.com/news/local/crime-and -courts/about-a-dozen-open-carry-gun-rights-activists-gather-in/article_eaa0e41b -042f-58ff-a1ef-476898bf5de5.html.

25. Radley Balko, *The Rise of the Warrior Cop: The Militarization of America's Police Forces* (New York: PublicAffairs, 2014), Kindle edition, loc. 4875; population figures from 2010 US Census.

26. Taylor Wofford, "How America's Police Became an Army: The 1033 Pro- gram," *Newsweek*, August 13, 2014, www.newsweek.com/how-americas-police-became -army-1033-program-264537; Christian Sheckler, "Local Police Acquire More Fire- power," *South Bend Tribune*, July 21, 2014, www.southbendtribune.com/news/local /local-police-acquire-more-firepower/article_9d74c2aa-0ff4–11e4-ad41–001a4 bcf6878.html.

27. US Department of Homeland Security, "National Network of Fusion Centers Fact Sheet," www.dhs.gov/national-network-fusion-centers-fact-sheet.

28. Lily Hay Newman, "Border Patrol Drones Each Cost $12K an Hour to Fly, Don't Do Much," Slate, January 6, 2015, www.slate.com/blogs/future_tense/2015/01 /06/homeland_security_s_border_patrol_drones_cost_12k_an_hour_to_fly_and _don.html; "9 Things You Should Know About Border Militarization," United We Dream, 2013, http://unitedwedream.org/9-things-you-should-know-about-border -militarization; Balko, *Rise of the Warrior Cop*, loc. 3995; Lee Fang, "How Private

Prisons Game the Immigration System," *The Nation*, February 27, 2013, www
.thenation.com/article/173120/how-private-prisons-game-immigration-system;
"ACLU Factsheet: The NYPD Muslim Surveillance Program," https://www.aclu
.org/factsheet-nypd-muslim-surveillance-program; "ACLU: Surveillance by Other
Agencies," https://www.aclu.org/issues/national-security/privacy-and-surveillance
/surveillance-other-agencies.

29. Spencer Ackerman, "The Disappeared: Chicago Police Detain Americans at
Abuse-Laden 'Black Site,'" *The Guardian*, February 24, 2015, www.theguardian.com
/us-news/2015/feb/24/chicago-police-detain-americans-black-site.

30. Glenn Greenwald, "XKeyscore: NSA Tool Collects 'Nearly Everything a
User Does on the Internet,'" *The Guardian*, July 31, 2013, www.theguardian.com
/world/2013/jul/31/nsa-top-secret-program-online-data; Dustin Volz, "Everything
We Learned from Edward Snowden in 2013," *National Journal*, December 31, 2013,
www.nationaljournal.com/defense/everything-we-learned-from-edward-snowden
-in-2013–20131231; Ewen Macaskill and Gabriel Dance, "NSA Files Decoded:
What the Revelations Mean for You," *The Guardian*, November 1, 2013, www.the
guardian.com/world/interactive/2013/nov/01/snowden-nsa-files-surveillance
-revelations-decoded#section/1.

31. Craig Timberg, "FBI Gags State and Local Police on Capabilities of
Cellphone Spy Gear," *Washington Post*, September 23, 2014, https://www
.washingtonpost.com/news/the-switch/wp/2014/09/23/fbi-gags-state-and-local
-police-on-capabilities-of-cellphone-spy-gear.

32. Robin, *Reactionary Mind*, loc. 3085–3108.

33. Balko, *Rise of the Warrior Cop*, loc. 1344–1349.

34. Angela Davis, *Angela Davis: An Autobiography* (New York: Bantam, 1975),
226–227.

35. Balko, *Rise of the Warrior Cop*, loc. 1616–1688.

36. Gary Potter, "The History of Policing in the United States, Part 1," Eastern
Kentucky University, June 25, 2013, http://plsonline.eku.edu/insidelook/history
-policing-united-states-part-1; Balko, *Rise of the Warrior Cop*, loc. 718, 752–760.

37. Victor E. Kappeler, "A Brief History of Slavery and the Origins of American Policing," Eastern Kentucky University, January 7, 2014, http://plsonline.eku
.edu/insidelook/brief-history-slavery-and-origins-american-policing; Balko, *Rise of
the Warrior Cop*, loc. 644–647.

38. Tom McCarthy, "Police Killed More Than Twice as Many People as Reported by US Government," *The Guardian*, March 4, 2015, www.theguardian
.com/us-news/2015/mar/04/police-killed-people-fbi-data-justifiable-homicides;
"The Counted: People Killed by Police in the US," *The Guardian*, accessed January 29, 2016, www.theguardian.com/us-news/ng-interactive/2015/jun/01/the
-counted-police-killings-us-database.

39. Robin D. G. Kelley, *Hammer and Hoe: Alabama Communists During the Great
Depression*, 2nd ed. (Chapel Hill: University of North Carolina Press, 2015), Kindle
edition, loc. 1673, 3502–3507, 4538; Berlet and Lyons, *Right-Wing Populism*, 268.

40. Victor Navasky, *Naming Names*, rev. ed. (New York: Open Road Media,
2013), Kindle edition, loc. 321, 704; Berlet and Lyons, *Right-Wing Populism*, 153;
Amy Sonnie and James Tracy, *Hillbilly Nationalists, Urban Race Rebels and Black*

Power: Community Organizing in Radical Times (New York: Melville House, 2011), Kindle edition, loc. 1276, 1441, 1608–1625; Mike Konczal, "Mental Note: Link Black Panther Free Lunch Program, OWS Infrastructure," Rortybomb, January 19, 2012, https://rortybomb.wordpress.com/2012/01/19/mental-note-link-black -panther-free-lunch-program-ows-infrastructure; Jeffrey Haas, "Fred Hampton's Legacy," *The Nation*, November 24, 2009, www.thenation.com/article/fred-hamptons -legacy.

41. Berlet and Lyons, *Right-Wing Populism*, 290–291; Balko, *Rise of the Warrior Cop*, loc. 3902–3941.

42. Bob Young, "City to Pay $1 Million to Settle Lawsuit over WTO Arrests," *Seattle Times*, April 3, 2007, www.seattletimes.com/seattle-news/city-to-pay-1-million-to-settle-lawsuit-over-wto-arrests; "Seattle Settles WTO Protest Lawsuit," Associated Press, January 18, 2004, http://articles.latimes.com/2004/jan/18/nation/na-wto18.

43. Naomi Murakawa, *The First Civil Right: How Liberals Built Prison America* (Oxford: Oxford University Press, 2014), Kindle edition, loc. 1510–1516, 2461; Balko, *Rise of the Warrior Cop*, loc. 1490.

44. Murakawa, *First Civil Right*, loc. 663–667, 1496–1502, 1521–1532, 2334, 2607; Sonnie and Tracy, *Hillbilly Nationalists*, loc. 2828; Balko, *Rise of the Warrior Cop*, loc. 2795–2813, 2905.

45. Raven Rakia, "When People Are Property," Medium, July 22, 2014, https://medium.com/@aintacrow/when-people-are-property-296dfe5105b1; "Stop and Frisk Facts," New York Civil Liberties Union, 2010, www.nyclu.org/node/1598; "More Low-Level Arrests Under de Blasio Than Bloomberg," New School Center for New York City Affairs, September 19, 2014, www.centernyc.org/child-welfare -nyc/2014/09/more-low-level-arrests-under-de-blasio-than-bloomberg.

46. Robert Lewis, "When Broken Windows Leads to Busted Heads," WNYC, July 28, 2014, www.wnyc.org/story/when-broken-windows-leads-busted-heads.

47. Rakia, "When People Are Property."

48. Mariame Kaba and Tamara K. Nopper, "Itemizing Atrocity," *Jacobin*, August 15, 2014, https://www.jacobinmag.com/2014/08/itemizing-atrocity.

49. Samuel Bowles and Arjun Jayadev, "One Nation Under Guard," *New York Times*, Opinionator, February 15, 2014, http://opinionator.blogs.nytimes .com/2014/02/15/one-nation-under-guard/?smid=tw-share; Sarah Jaffe, "$230,000 for a Guard Dog: Why the Wealthy Are Afraid of Violence from Below," AlterNet, July 29, 2011, www.alternet.org/story/151837/$230,000_for_a_guard_dog%3A _why_the_wealthy_are_afraid_of_violence_from_below.

50. Kim Bell, "August Video: Man Justifies the Looting in Ferguson," *St. Louis Post-Dispatch*, August 11, 2014, www.stltoday.com/news/multimedia/video-man -justifies-the-looting-in-ferguson/html_7699be22-bb74–5d4f-aa49-fcc46f5cb025.html.

51. US Department of Justice, Civil Rights Division, Investigation of the Ferguson Police Department, available at *Washington Post*, http://apps.washingtonpost .com/g/documents/national/department-of-justice-report-on-the-ferguson-mo -police-department/1435.

52. Jeremy Kohler, Jennifer S. Mann, and Stephen Deere, "Municipal Courts Are Well-Oiled Money Machine," *St. Louis Post-Dispatch*, March 15, 2015, www .stltoday.com/news/local/crime-and-courts/municipal-courts-are-well-oiled-money

-machine/article_2f45bafb-6e0d-5e9e-8fe1–0ab9a794fcdc.html; Nicolas Medina Mora, "7 Curious Facts About the Ferguson Municipal Court Judge," Buzzfeed, March 6, 2015, www.buzzfeed.com/nicolasmedinamora/7-curious-facts-about-the -ferguson-municipal-judge#.ukR5yyE3Nx; Jeremy Kohler, Jennifer S. Mann, and Stephen Deere, "A Web of Lawyers Play Different Roles in Different Courts," *St. Louis Post-Dispatch*, March 29, 2015, www.stltoday.com/news/local/crime-and-courts /a-web-of-lawyers-play-different-roles-in-different-courts/article_b61728d1–09b0 –567f-9ff4–919cf4e34649.html.

53. Emily Badger, "Why Riots Erupted in One of the Most Segregated Metro Regions in the Country," *Washington Post*, August 11, 2014, www.washingtonpost .com/blogs/wonkblog/wp/2014/08/11/why-riots-erupted-in-one-of-the-most -segregated-metro-regions-in-the-country; Leber, "Ferguson's Police Force"; Judith Stepan-Norris and Maurice Zeitlin, *Left Out: Reds and America's Industrial Unions* (New York: Cambridge University Press, 2002), Kindle edition, loc. 2418–2421; Sarah Kendzior and Umar Lee, "'I Am Darren Wilson': St. Louis and the Geography of Fear," Quartz, October 21, 2014, http://qz.com/284383/i-am-darren -wilson-st-louis-and-the-geography-of-fear; Richard Rothstein, "The Making of Ferguson," Economic Policy Institute, October 15, 2014, www.epi.org/publication /making-ferguson/#urban-renewal-and-redevelopment-programs.

54. Todd Frankel, "50 Years Later, Jefferson Bank Protest Refuses to Fade Away," *St. Louis Post-Dispatch*, August 31, 2013, www.stltoday.com/news/local/metro/years -later-jefferson-bank-protest-refuses-to-fade-away/article_6419edb0-cfc9–5f17-bbe9 –2bd8598bf5cf.html.

55. Vesla M. Weaver, "The Only Government I Know," *Boston Review*, June 10, 2014, http://bostonreview.net/us/vesla-m-weaver-citizenship-custodial-state -incarceration.

56. Trymaine Lee, "Ferguson Protesters Win Injunction to Stop Cops Using Tear Gas," MSNBC, December 11, 2014, www.msnbc.com/msnbc/ferguson -protesters-win-injunction-stop-cops-using-tear-gas.

57. Niraj Chokshi, "Dozens of Ferguson-Related Reforms Were Proposed in Missouri. Just One Passed," *Washington Post*, May 16, 2015, www.washingtonpost .com/blogs/govbeat/wp/2015/05/15/the-missouri-legislature-is-about-to-end-its -session-having-passed-almost-none-of-the-dozens-of-ferguson-related-bills-proposed.

58. Radley Balko, "Obama Moves to Demilitarize America's Police," *Washington Post*, May 18, 2015, www.washingtonpost.com/news/the-watch/wp/2015/05/18 /obama-moves-to-demilitarize-americas-police; Congressman Jeff Duncan, Facebook post, https://www.facebook.com/RepJeffDuncan/posts/834018293282591.

CHAPTER 9: CHANGE IS GONNA COME

1. Andrew Freedman, "How Global Warming Made Sandy Worse," Climate Central, November 1, 2012, www.climatecentral.org/news/how-global-warming-made -hurricane-sandy-worse-15190.

2. Joe Romm, "How Does Climate Change Make Superstorms Like Sandy More Destructive?" ThinkProgress, October 31, 2012, http://thinkprogress.org/climate /2012/10/31/1117091/how-does-climate-change-make-hurricanes-like-sandy-more -destructive.

3. Justin Elliott, "Red Cross: How We Spent Sandy Money Is a Trade Secret," ProPublica, June 26, 2014, https://www.propublica.org/article/red-cross-how-we-spent-sandy-money-is-a-trade-secret.

4. "Hurricane Sandy's Impact, by the Numbers," *Huffington Post*, October 29, 2013, www.huffingtonpost.com/2013/10/29/hurricane-sandy-impact-infographic_n_4171243.html; Patrick McGeehan and Griff Palmer, "Displaced by Hurricane Sandy and Living in Limbo," *New York Times*, December 6, 2013, www.nytimes.com/2013/12/07/nyregion/displaced-by-hurricane-sandy-and-living-in-limbo-instead-of-at-home.html.

5. Corey Mitchell, "'Death of My Career': What Happened to New Orleans's Veteran Black Teachers?" *Education Week*, August 19, 2015, http://neworleans.edweek.org/veteran-black-female-teachers-fired; Richard A. Webster, "New Orleans Public Housing Remade After Katrina. Is It Working?" Nola.com, August 20, 2015, http://www.nola.com/katrina/index.ssf/2015/08/new_orleans_public_housing_dem.html; Wen Stephenson, *What We Are Fighting For Now Is Each Other: Dispatches from the Front Lines of Climate Justice* (Boston: Beacon Press, 2015), Kindle edition, loc. 1795.

6. The story of Malik Rahim and Common Ground is a long one and worth learning about. For a start, try Rahim's appearances on the show *Democracy Now*, available online at www.democracynow.org/appearances/malik_rahim, and Jake Olzen, "Repression Against Grassroots Hurricane Relief Lingers in New Orleans," Waging Nonviolence, November 9, 2012, http://wagingnonviolence.org/feature/repression-against-grassroots-hurricane-relief-lingers-in-new-orleans.

7. Erik Loomis, *Out of Sight: The Long and Disturbing History of Corporations Outsourcing Disaster* (New York: New Press, 2015), 138; Seth Motel, "5 Facts About the BP Oil Spill," Pew Research Center, FactTank, April 17, 2015, www.pewresearch.org/fact-tank/2015/04/17/5-facts-about-the-bp-oil-spill.

8. Loomis, *Out of Sight*, 138.

9. Howard Berkes, "Massey Mine Workers Disabled Safety Monitor," National Public Radio, July 15, 2010, http://www.npr.org/templates/story/story.php?storyId=128516777; Stephenson, *What We're Fighting For*, loc. 1770.

10. Howard Berkes, "Massey CEO's Pay Soared as Mine Concerns Grew," National Public Radio, April 17, 2010, www.npr.org/templates/story/story.php?storyId=126072828.

11. Christopher Hayes, "The New Abolitionism," *The Nation*, April 22, 2014, www.thenation.com/article/new-abolitionism; Naomi Klein, *This Changes Everything: Capitalism vs. the Climate* (New York: Simon and Schuster, 2014), 415–416.

12. Amanda Peterka, "Doing for Clean Energy What John Muir Did for Preservation," *Environment and Energy Daily*, December 9, 2013, www.eenews.net/special_reports/shades_green/stories/1059991472/print; Loomis, *Out of Sight*, 86.

13. Loomis, *Out of Sight*, 25, 87–91; Stephenson, *What We're Fighting For*, loc. 1973; David Biello, "Where Did the Carter White House's Solar Panels Go?" *Scientific American*, August 6, 2010, www.scientificamerican.com/article/carter-white-house-solar-panel-array; Joe Romm, "Who Got Us in This Energy Mess? Start with Ronald Reagan," ThinkProgress, July 8, 2008, http://thinkprogress.org/climate/2008/07/08/202854/who-got-us-in-this-energy-mess-start-with-ronald-reagan.

14. Trish Kahle, "Rank-and-File Environmentalism," *Jacobin*, June 11, 2014, https://www.jacobinmag.com/2014/06/rank-and-file-environmentalism; Loomis, *Out of Sight*, 57; Jefferson Cowie, *Stayin' Alive: The 1970s and the Last Days of the Working Class* (New York: New Press, 2010), Kindle edition, loc. 4934.

15. Robert D. Bullard, "Confronting Environmental Racism in the Twenty-First Century," *Global Dialogue* 4 (Winter 2002), www.worlddialogue.org/content .php?id=179; Stephenson, *What We're Fighting For*, loc. 1465.

16. Klein, *This Changes Everything*, 18–21, 79.

17. Andrew Ross, *Creditocracy and the Case for Debt Refusal* (New York: OR Books, 2014), 214–215; Steffen Böhm, "Why Are Carbon Markets Failing?" *The Guardian*, April 12, 2013, www.theguardian.com/sustainable-business/blog/why -are-carbon-markets-failing.

18. Van Jones, "Working Together for a Green New Deal," *The Nation*, October 28, 2008, www.thenation.com/article/working-together-green-new-deal; Klein, *This Changes Everything*, 17, 120–121; Seamus McGraw, *The End of Country: Dispatches from the Frack Zone* (New York: Random House, 2011), Kindle edition, loc. 2898–3059.

19. Hayes, "The New Abolitionism"; Loomis, *Out of Sight*, 142–143; Jane Mayer, "Taking It to the Streets," *The New Yorker*, November 28, 2011, www.newyorker.com /magazine/2011/11/28/taking-it-to-the-streets.

20. Klein, *This Changes Everything*, 11–12, 206–207; Stephenson, *What We're Fighting For*, loc. 235.

21. Klein, *This Changes Everything*, 44; Hayes, "The New Abolitionism."

22. Klein, *This Changes Everything*, 209, 215, 230–244.

23. The Strike Debt report is available at http://strikedebt.org/sandyreport; Ross, *Creditocracy*, 200–201.

24. Ross, *Creditocracy*, 182–189, 205–214.

25. Ibid., 205–214; Alyssa Battistoni, "Alive in the Sunshine," *Jacobin*, Winter 2014, www.jacobinmag.com/2014/01/alive-in-the-sunshine.

26. Sabrina Tavernise and Albert Sun, "Same City, but Very Different Life Spans," *New York Times*, April 28, 2015, www.nytimes.com/interactive/2015/04/29/health /life-expectancy-nyc-chi-atl-richmond.html

27. Associated Press, "Central Illinois County Turns Away Oil Drilling," November 19, 2014, www.dailyherald.com/article/20141119/news/141118218; McLean County Board, meeting audio, November 18, 2014, www.mcleancountyil.gov/index .aspx?NID=464.

28. Michael Brune, "From Walden to the White House," Sierra Club, January 22, 2013, www.sierraclub.org/michael-brune/2013/01/walden-white-house.

29. Terry Macalister, "Shell Abandons Alaska Arctic Drilling," *The Guardian*, September 28, 2015, www.theguardian.com/business/2015/sep/28/shell-ceases-alaska-arctic-drilling-exploratory-well-oil-gas-disappoints; Timothy Cama, "Obama Cancels Arctic Drilling Lease Sales," The Hill, October 16, 2015, http://thehill .com/policy/energy-environment/257191-obama-cancels-arctic-drilling-lease-sales.

CONCLUSION: OUR FUTURE IS NOT YOURS TO LEVERAGE

1. Yong Jung Cho, Waleed Shahid, Devontae Torriente, and Sara Blazevic, "Here's Why We're Committing Civil Disobedience: Young People Can No Longer

Be Silent About Our Broken System," Salon, November 2, 2015, www.salon.com /2015/11/02/heres_why_were_committing_civil_disobedience_millennials_can _no_longer_be_silent_about_our_broken_system.

2. Casey Quinlan, "What You Need to Know About the Huge Student Protest Sweeping the Country Today," ThinkProgress, November 12, 2015, http://think progress.org/education/2015/11/12/3721211/million-student-march.

3. Keith O'Brien, "Inside the Protest That Stopped the Trump Rally," Politico, March 13, 2016, www.politico.com/magazine/story/2016/03/donald-trump -chicago-protest-213728.

4. Michael Kazin, *The Populist Persuasion: An American History* (Ithaca, NY: Cornell University Press, 1998), 218; Leah Hope, "Republic Windows Ex-Workers to Get Back Pay 7 Years After Company Closed," ABC 7 News, January 21, 2016, http://abc7chicago.com/1168712.

5. Kim Janssen, "Michigan Avenue Black Friday Protests Cost Stores 25–50 Percent of Sales," *Chicago Tribune*, November 30, 2015, www.chicagotribune .com/business/ct-black-friday-mag-mile-fallout-1201-biz-20151130-story.html; Merrit Kennedy, "Controversial Emergency Manager of Detroit's Public Schools Resigns," National Public Radio, February 2, 2016.

6. Jefferson Cowie, *Stayin' Alive: The 1970s and the Last Days of the Working Class* (New York: New Press, 2010), Kindle edition, loc. 1416.

7. Mike Konczal, "Occupy Foreclosures and a Chart of Changing Tactical Innovations in Protest Movements," Rortybomb, December 5, 2011, https://rortybomb .wordpress.com/2011/12/05/occupy-foreclosures-and-a-chart-of-changing-tactical -innovations-in-protest-movements.

INDEX

Act 10 (WI), and union rights, 99–103
activism. *See* movements; protests
Adbusters, 35, 41
Agenda to Build Black Futures, 157
Agnew, Phillip (now umi selah), 134, 135, 154
Albany (New York), activism and protests, 185
Aldridge, Rasheen, 220–221, 235, 242, 244–246
American Bankers Association, 33
American International Group (AIG), 15, 16–17
American Recovery and Reinvestment Act (ARRA), 20
Andrews, Sam, 224–225, 228, 236
angry people and protests/activism, 3–7, 25, 277–279
anti-LGBT bills, 170
anticommunism and red-baiting, 194–195, 198–202
Association of Community Organizations for Reform Now (ACORN), 196
Atlanta (Georgia), foreclosures, 45–47, 50, 52
Atwater, Lee, 146
austeritarianism, 110–111, 112, 124

austerity
and Chicago schools, 119–124, 127
and natural disasters, 254
personal experiences, 99–102, 104–106
and protests, 112
strike of 2012 by Chicago teachers, 118
2008 financial crisis, 110
and union rights, 99–108, 110–111
and US politics, 109–110, 111–112
auto industry bailout, 20

bailouts
banks, 14, 15–16, 17–18, 19, 46
nonfinancial sector, 20
Baker, Dean, 19–20, 54
Baker, Ella, 10
Baltimore, 149
Banditelli, Brett, 102, 211
Bank of America, 13, 14–15, 46, 50
banks
anger at and protests, 32–34
bailout, 14, 15–16, 17–18, 19, 46
and foreclosures, 54, 55–56
and mortgages, 46, 49–50
mortgage fraud, 54–56
and 2008 financial crisis, 18, 19–20, 22
See also financial sector

Barber, William III, 167, 182
Barber, The Rev. William J. II
    advocacy and People's Assemblies,
        160–161, 166–167, 183, 187
    civil disobedience and arrest, 162,
        164–165
    on faith and sexual issues, 171–172
    as leader, 180, 181
Barlow, Lonnie, 270
Bartley, Aaron, 270
Bashiri, Shabnam, 46–47, 48, 49, 51,
    56, 282
Baum, Gordon, 138
Beck, Glenn, 23, 195, 196
Bentonville (Arkansas) Home Office,
    73, 93, 94–98
Black Lives Matter, 152, 157
Black Panthers and raid, 174, 229–230,
    231
black people
    activism and protests, 133–136,
        150–158
    civil rights movement, 144–145
    and court system, 234–235
    discrimination in labor and unions,
        143–144
    and economy, 131, 137, 138, 145–146
    homeownership, 57
    homes and wealth, 146–150
    mortgages, 147–148, 149
    and police, 132–134, 156, 232–237
    racism towards, 134–136, 139–140,
        146–150
    and redlined neighborhoods, 147
    segregation, 235–236
    shootings of, 133, 140, 147–148, 149,
        156
    and slavery, 139, 142–143
    2008 financial crisis, 146–148
    unemployment, 148
    voting, 168–169
    and white supremacy, 143, 156–157,
        246
Blackstone Group, 56
Bloomberg, Michael, 35, 44, 252
Bloombergville protest, 34–35

Boeing company and workers, 189–190
Bologna, Anthony, 215
borders, militarization, 227
Bowers, Ann, 65–67, 69, 70
Bridges, "Red Harry," 199–200
"broken windows" theory, 232–233
Brown, Michael, Jr., 186, 220–222, 238
Brown, Pam, 62–63
Brune, Michael, 97, 275
Bryan, William Jennings, 172
Burrus, Desean, 251
Bush, George W., 177, 195
Bush Administration, 19, 22–23
BYP 100, 150, 157

C. J.'s Seafood, 87
Cagle, Susie, 216, 217
capitalism
    alternative to, 193–194, 195, 197
    and climate, 263–264, 265–266, 267
    defense of, 23, 212
    and Democrats, 212
    environment and extractive
        industries, 260–261
    and Occupy Wall Street, 42
    and socialism, 190, 195, 196–197, 212
    and Tea Party, 25–26
    and 2008 financial crisis, 22, 195
car wash workers, 203
carbon trading and markets, 264
Carruthers, Charlene, 150, 155, 157
Caucus of Rank and File Educators
    (CORE), 120–121
Chambers, Sarah, 127–128
Chandler, Angel, 171, 183
change
    and action, 283–284
    demands and vision of activism and
        protests, 280–283
    and Ferguson events, 244–247
    and human-made disasters, 258–259
    impact of Superstorm Sandy, 255–257
    and labor unions, 120–121
    and movements, 286–287
    in people, 249–250
    and US politics, 210–211

Charleston (South Carolina) shooting, 140–141, 184
Chicago
  election of 2015, 124–127
  labor organization, 204
  police practices, 228
  strike of 2016, 126, 127–128
Chicago schools and teachers
  problems and reforms, 119–125
  strikes of 2012 and 2016, 118–119, 122–124, 127–128
Chicago Teachers Union, 118–119, 121–124, 127–128
Chopp, Frank, 191
Chow, Toby, 186
Church, Brian Jacob, 228
Citizens' Councils, 137
civil rights movement, 144–145, 173, 180–181
Clark, Cindy, 103, 117
Clarke, Angelica, 185
class, 58–59, 60, 283
  See also middle class, working class
climate and climate change
  activism and protests, 266, 268–270
  and capitalism, 263–264, 265–266, 267
  deniers, 265–266
  link to economy, 266–267
  and race, 268, 271–272
  responsibility for, 267
  solutions to, 265–266, 267–268
  and 2008 financial crisis, 264
climate debt, 267
Clinton, Bill, 80–81, 138, 263
Clinton, Hillary, 212, 278
Clinton, Mary, 34–35, 36, 38–42, 226–227
coal mining and burning, 260–261
collective bargaining, 100–101, 105, 110–111, 115, 117
colleges. *See* education
Common Ground Collective, 258
communism and red-baiting, 194–195, 198–202
Community Reinvestment Act (CRA), 147, 149

computerized scheduling, 79–80
Confederate flag and monuments, 141, 145, 184
consensus, at Occupy, 43
Consumer Financial Protection Bureau (CFPB), 52, 68
Cooper-Suggs, Malcolm, 208–209, 241
Corinthian Colleges, 66–67, 68–69
Cottom, Tressie McMillan, 62, 69, 70
Council of Conservative Citizens (CCC), 130, 137, 140–141
Countrywide Mortgage, 54–55
court system, and black people, 234–235
Crenshaw, Kimberlé, 8
Crockford, Kade, 226, 227, 228, 240
Cruickshank, Robert, 193, 212
Cuomo, Andrew, 208, 210, 272–273

Daniel, Nancy, 45–47, 52
Dannenbring, Dawn, 273–274
Davis, Angela, 229–230
Davis, Malaya, 153–154, 155–156, 157
Davis, Troy, 131
Dayen, David, 52–53
de Blasio, Bill, 233, 254–255
Debs, Eugene V., 198
debt, 19, 21, 46, 53–54, 60–61, 267
  See also climate debt, mortgages, student debt
Debt Collective, and student debt, 68, 69–70
debt for students. *See* student debt
democracy, 9, 270–271, 279
Democrats and Democratic Party
  abortion and anti-gay legislation, 171
  austerity and Act 10 (WI), 111
  and capitalism, 212
  in Chicago politics, 126–127
  as part of problem, 34
  response to activism and movements, 280–281
  and socialism, 212, 278
  2008 financial crisis and bailout, 17–18
Department of Education (federal) (DOE), student debt and for-profit colleges, 63, 66–70

Department of Homeland Security, 226, 227

Department of Justice, report on policing and court practices in Ferguson, 234–235

die-in, 241

Dinkin, Joe, 15–16, 17

disruption, as power, 10, 24, 43, 155, 241, 274, 283

Doctors Without Borders, 251–252

Donnelly, Ignatius, 28–29

Dooley, Debbie, 22–24, 25, 26–27, 265, 270–271

Dream Defenders, 150–151, 152–153, 154, 158

drug war, 232

Du Bois, W. E. B., 139–140, 143

Dukes v. Walmart, 78, 85

Duncan, Arne, 119

Dye, Jenni, 100, 101–102, 104–106, 107, 108, 112

ecological debt, 267

economy
  and black people, 131, 137, 138, 145–146
  link to climate change, 266–267
  and moral values, 173
  Red Scare and red-baiting, 199–200
  and sexual rights issues, 169–170, 171
  and US politics, 5, 6
  See also capitalism

education
  activism and protests, 278
  and austerity, 99–108, 110–111
  as commodity, 62–63
  and debt (*see* student debt)
  for-profit institutions, 64–67, 70–71
  importance, 61
  and job expectations, 61–62, 65, 67, 70
  loans and funding, 58, 62–64
  privatization and reforms, 119–120
  and securities, 63–64
  and union rights, 99–103

Educational Credit Management Corporation (ECMC), 66

elections in US
  activism and protests, 278–279
  and money, 5, 111–112
  and movements' work, 182–183
  outsider candidates, 209–212
  public participation, 32–33
  and socialism, 195
  young people in, 211

elite in US, 4–5, 25, 29, 30

Emanuel, Rahm, 121, 123–124, 125–127

employment and jobs, 20, 61–62, 148

energy democracy, 270–271

environment
  activism and protests, 270–275
  and capitalism, 260–261
  movement for, 261–262
  workers and labor movement, 262–263
  See also climate and climate change

environmental justice movement, 263

environmental racism, 268, 271–272

Epps-Addison, Jennifer, 108

Espinosa, Colleen McKee, 49

Espinosa, Nick, 49–50, 51, 281–282, 285

Everest College, 65–68

Everest College Avengers group, 67

extractive industries, 260–261, 262–265, 272–274
  See also fossil fuels

Facebook, 41, 47, 67–68, 91

Fairfield (Connecticut), 15, 16

faith, and social issues, 166, 171–173, 175–176

family and family values, 177–179

family wage, 177

Fannie Mae (Federal National Mortgage Association), 57

Fast Food Forward, 203

fast-food workers, 203–205

Faulkner, Tyfani, 92, 93, 95

FBI, 218, 231

Federal Family Education Loan (FFEL), 63

federal government
  militarization of police, 225–226, 227
  mortgages and foreclosures, 55–56
  programs for workers, 80
  response to 2008 financial crisis, 19–20
  student loans and college funding,
    58, 63
Federal Housing Administration
    (FHA), 146–147
Federal Reserve, 19
feminism, 147, 178
Ferguson, Thomas, 111, 112
Ferguson (Missouri)
  assembly and protests, 237–241, 246
  civil disobedience, 186
  importance to protest movement,
    240–241
  open carry rights, 225
  police force and militarization,
    219–223, 225, 226
  police practices, 234–235, 236, 239,
    240–241
  reforms and change, 244–247
$15 an hour wage. *See* Fight for $15
    campaign and Show Me $15
Fight for $15 campaign and Show Me $15
  connection with other protests, 241,
    277
  origins and early actions, 203–204
  and political debate, 210, 279
  Seattle elections and workers actions,
    189, 192–193, 205–208, 214
financial crisis of 2008
  and austerity, 110
  bailout for banks, 14, 15–16, 17–18,
    19, 46
  banks' reaction to, 18, 19, 22
  blame for, 266
  and capitalism, 22, 195
  and climate change, 264
  consequences for banks, 19–20, 22
  and employment, 148
  "end," 52
  and foreclosures, 15, 52–53
  homes and black people, 146–148
  and mortgages, 23

reaction to in US, 18–19
  response from US government, 19–20
  and socialism, 195, 197
  as spark for movements, 4–5, 25, 32
financial sector
  growth and wealth concentration,
    20–21
  houses as speculation, 53–54, 56
  and market populism, 30–31
  protests against, 33–35
  as target of Occupy Wall Street, 36–37
  See also banks
Flores, Brisenia, 137
Florida, 133–136, 152–153
for-profit educational institutions,
    64–67, 70–71
Foran, Greg, 96
Forbes, David, 187
foreclosures
  and banks, 54, 55–56
  blame on owners, 54
  extent and consequences, 52–53
  and legal battles, 49
  and mortgages, 49–51
  and Occupy, 47–51
  personal experiences, 46–47, 49–50
  "robosigning" practice, 55
  and 2008 financial crisis, 15, 52–53
  zombie foreclosures, 51, 53
fossil fuels
  and climate change, 264–266, 270
  disasters and protests, 258–260
Foster, Eileen, 54–55
Fox News, 23–24, 26
fracking, 264–265, 272–274
  See also hydraulic fracturing
franchises, and wages, 204–205
Freedom Side, 155
Fried, Leah, 13, 15, 88
fusion centers, and militarization of
    police, 227

Ganz, Marshall, 33
Garcia, Jesus "Chuy," 125–126
Garner, Eric, 233, 272
Garza, Alicia, 151, 153, 155, 157, 282

gay and LGBT rights, 170, 174, 179–180
  See also sexual rights issues
Gearhart, Jeff, 97
general strikes, 118, 127
  See also strikes
gerrymandering, 161, 182–183
Gerth, The Rev. David, 239, 246–247
GI Bill, 57–58
Global Justice Clinic, 218
Goehl, George, 17–18, 34, 266, 271,
  280, 281
Goldstein, Alexis
  on demands for change, 281
  on education as product, 65
  and mortgages and foreclosures, 53, 56
  and Occupy Wall Street, 18, 22, 31,
    39, 41
  on student debt and strike, 69
Goldstein, David, 190, 207–208,
  231–232
Gonzales, Ivanna, 161–164, 184
"good debt," 46, 61
Gough, Wooten, 167, 181
Graham, Ramarley, 133
Grant, Oscar and "Oscar Grant Plaza,"
  131, 216
Gwynne, Kristen, 216

Haley, Nikki, 190
Hamlin, Eileen, 272–273
Hanna, Alex, 99–101, 105, 107
Harris, Colby, 74–76, 90, 91, 92
health, and environment, 271–272
health care, after Superstorm Sandy,
  251–253
higher education, 69
  See also education
Higher Education Act, 58
Hoffman, Elle, 88
Hollywood, and Red Scare, 201
Holmes, Bene't, 80–81
homeownership, 57–58, 147
homes
  and black people, 57, 146–148
  and financial crisis (*see* foreclosures;
    mortgages)

and Occupy, 48–49, 50–51
and women's role, 177–179
homosexuality. *See* gay and gender
  rights
Hoopes, Alex, 192
Hoover, J. Edgar, 199, 231
horizontalism
  description, 8–9, 40
  and labor unions, 89–90
  and Occupy Wall Street, 40–41
  online organizing, 41
  and power, 9
  in social movements, 179–180, 285
Hornes, Natasha, 66, 67, 69
Hornes, Nathan, 66, 67, 69
housing, protests, 57
housing bubble, 53–54
human-made disasters, 258–259
Hurricane Katrina, 257–258
hydraulic fracturing, 264–265, 272–274
  See also fracking

identity politics and identity-based
  movements, 173–176
Illinois, 186, 273–274
Illinois People's Action (IPA), 273–274
immigrants in US, 227–228
Immigration and Customs
  Enforcement, 163–164
incomes, 53–54
inequality
  and Occupy Wall Street, 5–6, 35–37
  and police, 230, 234–235
  space for discussion of, 202–203
  as trigger of protests, 5–6
Internet, 2, 24–25, 41, 91, 242
  See also social media
intersectionality
  in activism and protests, 277–278,
    284–285
  and climate change, 268
  description, 8, 131
  and protesters, 164, 181, 243–244
  in racism and black people, 157

Jackson, Thomas, 244

Jacobin magazine, 197
jobs and employment, 20, 61–62, 148
  expectations from education, 61–62,
    65, 67, 70
Johnson, Jennifer, 121, 122
Johnson, Mychal, 271
Jones, Van, 195–196
judicial system, and black people,
  234–235
Justice to Justice, 51

Kahle, Trish, 204, 259, 262
Kanakkanatt, Kirin, 154, 155, 167–168,
  268
Kane, Pat, 252, 253
Kasich, John, 110, 153, 169
Kelley, Robin D. G., 11, 143, 146,
  156–157, 286–287
King, Justin, 225
Kinniburgh, Colin, 268, 269
Klein, Naomi, 120, 257, 267
Koch, Charles and David, 109, 196, 265

labor
  and communism, 199–200
  future of, 286
  laws, 72, 78–79, 143–144
  organization, 203–204
  racism in, 143–144
  See also workers
Labor Management Relations Act (or
  Taft-Hartley bill), 117, 199
labor unions
  and austerity, 99–108, 110–111
  Chicago strike of 2016, 126, 127
  decline, 115–116
  dues from workers, 86
  and extractive industries, 262–263
  minimum wage and $15 an hour,
    189, 192–193
  and minority unionism, 90
  and Occupy, 44, 89, 203
  and politics, 111–112, 116
  protests against banks, 33–34
  racial discrimination, 143–144
  rights and Act 10 (WI), 99–103

and service industry, 78
  shifts in models, 120–121
  as social movement, 117–118
  teachers and public workers, 112–116
  teaching assistants, 99–100
  Walmart, actions against, 71, 85–93
  Walmart, anti-unionism, 73, 74, 83,
    86–87
  workers in Seattle, 189, 192–193, 209
Larson, Ann, 68
Latchison, Diamond, 8, 219–222, 237,
  239, 242–244, 246
Latino people, 131, 232–233
Lerner, Jacob, 161–163, 164, 180, 184
Lerner, Stephen, 10, 18, 33–34, 37, 60,
  117, 202
Levitt, William, and Levittown, 57
Lewis, John, 10–11, 129, 131, 132, 153
Lewis, Karen, 118, 121, 123–125
Lewis, Penny, 36–37
liberals, 30, 201, 202
Liberty Plaza, and Occupy, 37–38, 39–40
  See also Zuccotti Park
"Lifestyles of the Rich and Shameless"
  tour, 16–17
loans
  for homes (*see* mortgages)
  for students and education, 58, 62–64
Loomis, Erik, 261–262
Luce, Stephanie, 36–37
Luna, Venanzi, 71–72, 73, 94–95, 97–98

Maharawal, Manissa McCleave, 43,
  131–132
manmade disasters, 258–259
Maree, Daniel, 134
market populism, 30–31, 84
Marom, Yotam, 256, 282–283
Martin, Trayvon, 133–134, 140,
  150–151, 152, 153
Mason, Paul, 42, 64
McCarthy, Joseph, 201, 202
McCrory, Pat, 161, 168, 169
McMillon, Doug, 94, 97
McNeill, Emily, 185
Meadows, J. D., 1–2, 3, 130

media, 23, 26, 42
medical care, after Superstorm Sandy, 251–253
middle class
  and debt, 60–61
  expansion and decline, 58–59, 60
  and homeownership, 57
  and identity, 58–59, 60
  and politics, 59
  producer ethic and populism, 30
  and Tea Party, 27–28
militarization of police
  extent of, 225–226, 227–228
  in Ferguson (Missouri), 219–223, 225, 226
  first event, 229–230
  origin and factors of, 223, 226–228
  people's reaction, 224–225
  and police abuses, 219
  reforms, 244
  and surveillance, 228–229
militias in US, 224, 231
Milkman, Ruth, 36–37, 41, 216
Miller, John Anthony, 141
Million Hoodies network and march, 134
minimum wage. See Fight for $15 campaign and Show Me $15; wage and minimum wage
Minnesota, foreclosures, 48–51
Missouri
  labor organization, 204
  police and court practices, 234–235
  protests, 186–187, 278
  segregation, 235–236
Mitchell, Mahlon, 106
Mohit, Nastaran, 251–252, 253, 254, 255, 256
Moore, Ty, 192
Moral Majority, 176–177
Moral Monday in St. Louis, 240
Moral Monday/Movement in NC
  activism, 182, 183–185, 187
  leadership and participants, 180–181
  principles and issues, 165–166, 172, 187

protests and arrests, 162–165, 166–168
Moral Mondays Illinois, 186
morality and moral values
  family and family values, 177–179
  1960s changes, 173–175, 179
  and religious right, 175–177
  and social issues, 166, 171–173, 175–176
  US politics and society, 172–173, 175–177
mortgages
  and banks, 46, 49–50
  and black people, 147–148, 149
  federal government actions, 55–56
  and foreclosures, 49–51
  fraud by banks, 54–56
  refinancing stories, 45–46, 52
  speculation by financial sector, 53–54
  subprime mortgages, 53–54, 148
  "underwater," 23
movements
  for angry people, 3–7, 25, 277–279
  and change, 286–287
  connections and links in, 8, 11, 241–242, 245
  demands and vision, 280–283, 284–285
  and foreclosures, 47, 49–50
  galvanization, 32–35
  history and rise in US, 7, 279–280
  horizontalism, 179–180, 285
  and media, 26
  and power, 283, 285–286
  resistance to and challenges, 280–281, 284–286
  and social media, 104–105
  types of people in, 7–8
  See also specific movements
Mozilo, Angelo, 55
Muñoz, Israel, 123–124
Murray, Cynthia, 72–73, 74, 97, 98
Muse, Vance, 144
Myers, Vonderrit, 239

NAACP, 161–162, 182, 187
National Defense Authorization Act, 226

National Defense Education Act, 58
National Fuel company, 270
National Guard, 221
National Labor Relations Act (NLRA, 1935), 144–145
National Labor Relations Board (NLRB), 72, 75, 86, 92, 205
National People's Action (NPA), 17–18, 33–34, 266, 271, 281
national security, and surveillance, 229
Nationstar, 46, 52
natural disasters, 254, 255–257, 258, 260, 266–267
Navient, 63
New Deal, discrimination in, 143–144
New Era Windows, 280
New Orleans, 257–258
New York City
    environmental racism, 271–272
    labor organization and $15 an hour, 203–204, 208
    misdemeanor arrests, 233
    outsider candidates, 209–210
    protests, 34–35, 268–269
    Superstorm Sandy, 249–255
    See also Occupy Wall Street
New York Communities for Change (NYCC), 203
New York Police Department (NYPD), 133, 215–216, 233
New York State, 185, 272–273
New York State Nurses Association (NYSNA), 251, 256–257
New Yorkers Against Budget Cuts, 34, 35
Newsome, Bree, 158
Nixon, Richard, 30
nonfinancial sector bailout, 20
North Carolina
    advocacy and People's Assemblies, 160–161
    civil disobedience and protests (*see* Moral Monday/Movement in NC)
    economic issues, 168, 169–170
    election of 2014, 182–183
    political power and legislative

measures, 159–162, 168–169, 183–184
    sexuality rights issues, 169–170
    voting, 168–169, 182, 183
nuclear family, 177–179

Oakland (CA), 216–218
Oath Keepers, 224–225
Obama, Barack
    militarization of police, 244
    racism towards, 129–130, 138
    and socialism, 195–196, 197
    and Tea Party, 25
    use of movements, 32–33
    workers' rights and pay, 14
Obama administration, 70, 224, 266
Obi, Mildred, 50
O'Brien, Mike, 193, 213, 274–275
Occupy
    "Declaration" and "blocks," 132
    foreclosures and homes, 47–51
    help for Superstorm Sandy, 249–251, 253–254
    and labor organization, 44, 89, 203
    mutual aid *vs.* charity, 255–256
    protesters and police, 38, 133–134, 215–219
    racial issues and color blindness, 131–133
    and student debt, 68
    and Walmart, 89
Occupy Atlanta, 47, 132
Occupy Oakland, 216–218
Occupy Our Homes / Occupy Homes, 46–49, 50–51
Occupy Sandy, 250–251, 253–254
Occupy Student Debt, 62
Occupy the SEC, 41–42
Occupy Wall Street
    beginning and spread, 2–3, 35, 38–42, 44
    and capitalism, 42
    demands, 43–44
    and financial sector, 36–37
    and horizontalism, 40–41
    and inequality, 5–6, 35–37

Occupy Wall Street *(continued)*
  personal experiences, 42
  practices and structures, 42–44
  protesters and police, 38, 215–216
  and social media, 2, 41–42
  See also Liberty Plaza
Ohio Student Association (OSA),
    153–154, 156
Olsen, Scott, 217–218
1-T Day, 62
online organizing. *See* Internet; social
    media
open carry rights, 225
Organization United for Respect at
    Walmart (OUR Walmart)
  aims and efforts, 85–86, 87, 89–92
  in Bentonville Home Office, 93, 94–98
  personal experiences, 71–72, 73, 75
"Oscar Grant Plaza," 131, 216
outsourcing, and workers, 77
Oxford, Robert, 63–64

Pace, Brian, 130, 141
Palin, Sarah, 137, 195
Pantaleo, Daniel, 233
Parikh, Sejal, 205, 206, 208–209
part-time work, 80
Patel, Amisha, 125, 127
Paulson, Henry, 15
People United for Sustainable Housing
    (PUSH), 269–270
People's Climate March, 268–270
"people's mic," 43
People's Movement Assembly, 237–238
Phelps, Martina, 206, 208–209
Poe, Tef, 221–222
police
  and black people, 132–134, 156,
    232–237
  "broken windows" theory, 232–233
  and drug war, 232
  equipment, 217–218
  history in US, 230–231
  and inequality, 230, 234–235
  militarization (*see* militarization of
    police)

and Occupy protesters, 38, 133–134,
    215–219
people's reaction to practices, 234,
    236–237
practices, 133, 228, 233, 234–236,
    239–241
and racism, 133–134, 233
reforms and civilian oversight, 244
revenue for, 234–235
targeted groups, 230–234
  See also Ferguson (MO)
Poling, Douglas L., 15, 16
politics in US
  anger with, 5
  and austerity, 109–110, 111–112
  change in, 210–211
  and Fight for $15 campaign, 210, 279
  and labor unions, 111–112, 116
  link to economy, 5, 6
  and middle class, 59
  money in, 111–112
  and movements, 9
  social and moral issues, 172–173,
    175–177
  See also elections in US
populism
  market populism, 30–31, 84
  and power, 29–30
  and producer ethic, 28–29
  in Tea Party, 28
  and victim-blaming, 31–32
  and Walmart, 84–85, 94
Populist movement of the late 1800s, 29
poverty and poor people, 31–32, 148–149
Powell, Denechia, 213
power, 9, 10, 29–30, 283, 285–286
producer ethic and producerism,
    28–29, 30–31, 59
Professional Air Traffic Controllers
    Organization (PATCO) strike, 115
protest movements. *See* movements
protests
  connections between, 241–242, 245
  importance of Ferguson events,
    240–241
  personal cost, 242–243

reforms and change from, 244–247
training for, 283
public spaces, occupation, 39–40
public workers, labor unions history,
112–116

quality-of-life policing, 232–233
Quebec, labor law, 87

race, as social construction, 139
racism and racial issues
activism and protests, 134–137,
150–158, 278
and black people, 134–136, 139–140,
146–150
civil rights movement, 144–145
and climate activism, 268, 271–272
communism and socialism, 200
Confederate flag in SC, 141, 145
and economy, 137, 138, 145–146
in homes and housing, 147–150
in labor and unions, 143–144
Occupy, 131–133
and police, 133–134, 233
reluctance to discuss in US, 138–139
segregation in US, 235–236
and shootings, 133, 137–138, 140
as systemic problem, 142–144, 145–146
and Tea Party, 129–131
violence in US history, 139–140,
141–143
violence since 2008 financial crisis,
137–139
radicalism and radicals, 5, 10, 198–202
Rahim, Malik, 258
Rakia, Raven, 233
Reagan, Ronald, 59, 115, 176, 232
red-baiting and anti-communism,
194–195, 198–202
Red Hook neighborhood (New York)
and Red Hook Initiative, 250
Red Scare, 199–201
redlined neighborhoods, and black
people, 147
religious right, 175–177
rentals of homes, 56

Republic Windows and Doors factory,
13–15, 280
Republicans and Republican Party,
23–24, 109–110, 111, 278–279
retail work in US, 76–77, 78–79
Ripley (MS), 1–2
Robin, Corey, 171, 229
"robosigning" in foreclosures, 55
Rockefeller, Nelson, 232
Roe v. Wade, 175–176, 178
Rolf, David, 193–194, 205–206, 213
Rolling Jubilee, 68
Romano, Tara, 166
Roof, Dylann, 140–141
Ross, Andrew, 58
Rowley, Rick, 2, 3

Salgado, Julieta, 250–251
Sallie Mae, and students loans, 63–64
Salonek, Cat, 48–49, 51, 282
Sanders, Bernie, 210–212, 278, 286
Santelli, Rick, 23, 31
Saunders, Jeremy, 255–256
Sawant, Kshama
on change and action, 287
criticism and success of, 212–213
minimum wage and $15 an hour,
189, 192–193, 205–207
as outsider candidate, 211, 213
socialism and Seattle elections,
189–192, 194, 212–213
support for socialism in US, 197
Scahill, Jeremy, 223
scheduling of work, 79–80
Schlademan, Dan, 85, 86–87, 89, 91, 92
Schlafly, Phyllis, 176
Scott, H. Lee, 84
Scott, Patricia, 94
Scott, Ray, 93, 96
Scott, Rick, 152
Seattle-Tacoma International Airport
workers, and SeaTac 192–193, 206,
209
Seattle
actions and strikes by workers,
205–207

Seattle *(continued)*
  election of 2013 and socialism,
    189–192, 194
  environmental activism, 274–275
  Fight for $15 campaign and $15 an
    hour, 189, 192–193, 205–208, 214
  as role model, 207–208
  workers union, 209
  WTO protests and police, 231–232
securities, 18, 21, 53, 63–64
Securities and Exchange Commission,
  42, 55
segregation in US, 235–236
Sekou, Osagyefo, 186–187
selah, umi selah (was Agnew, Phillip),
  134, 135, 154
Serious Materials, 15
Service Employees International Union
  (SEIU) Local 775, 189–190
service jobs and industry, 76–79, 81–82, 86
severance pay, 14
sexual rights issues, 169–172, 174, 179–180
Shenker-Osorio, Anat, 36, 58, 59
Sheridan-Gonzalez, Judy, 251, 252, 253,
  257
Shibata, Kenzo
  Chicago schools and unions,
    119–121, 122, 123, 124–125
  election of 2015, 125, 126
Show Me $15. *See* Fight for $15
  campaign and Show Me $15
"Showdown in America" campaign, 33
Shuler, Heath, 171, 182–183
Silberman-Gorn, Isaac, 272, 273
Simmons, Montague, 238, 243, 244
slavery in US, 139, 142–143
Slay, Francis G., 240
Smalley-McMahan, Barbara, 159–160,
  165, 172, 182, 186–187
Smith, Andy, 255, 256
Smith, DeAndre, 234
social media
  and help in crises, 249–250
  and Occupy Wall Street, 2, 41–42
  in protests and strikes, 91, 104–105,
    123, 216, 242

  union rights and Act 10, 100–101
  See also Internet
socialism
  acceptance in US, 195, 196–197
  and capitalism, 190, 195, 196–197,
    212
  fight against in US, 195–196
  in political debate and elections, 195,
    210–212, 213–214, 278
  and 2008 financial crisis, 195, 197
  workers and labor unions, 189–190
Socialist Alternative group, 190,
  191–192, 194, 206–207
solidarity, 9, 255–257, 258–259
Soni, Saket, 87–88
South Carolina, 140–141, 145
"Special Weapons and Tactics" (SWAT),
  229–230
St. Louis (MO), 235–236, 240
Stamp, Nelini
  activism and protests, 151, 153, 155,
    156
  and Occupy, 36, 38–39, 43–44
  and police, 132–133, 135, 136
Stan, Adele, 175, 176, 180
Stand Your Ground law, 133, 136
Stoller, Matt, 118–119
"stop-and frisk" tactics, 133, 233
The Stranger (newspaper), 191
Strike Debt, 68
strikes
  Chicago schools and teachers,
    118–119, 122–124, 127–128
  fossil fuel industry, 259–260
  general strikes, 118, 127
  goals, 260
  PATCO, 115
  purposes and success factors, 118–119
  Seattle workers, 205–207
  at Walmart, 71, 73, 74, 87–89, 122–123
student debt
  actions and strike against, 67–70
  bubble, 61–62
  defaults, 64
  and education, 61–65
  forgiveness, 65, 69

personal experiences, 65–67
and wealth, 60–61
Student Loan Asset Backed Securities
(SLABs), 63
students
loans, 58, 62–64
union in Chicago, 123–124
See also education
subprime mortgages, 53–54, 148
Superstorm Sandy
help initiatives, 249–255
impact on social change groups,
255–257
surveillance, and militarization of
police, 228–229
Szoldra, Paul, 223

Taft-Hartley bill (Labor Management
Relations Act), 117, 199
Tahrir Square protests, 101
Taylor, Ciara, 134–136, 150–151, 152, 158
Tea Party
on abortion and sexual identity,
170–171
and austerity, 109, 110
and capitalism, 25–26
and climate change, 265
influence on protest, 26–27
members and middle class, 27–28
and online tools, 25
as protest movement, 24–25
racism in, 129–131
rise and expansion, 1–2, 22–24, 26
slogan and populism, 28
and socialism, 196–197
teachers
and austerity, 118
in Chicago (*see* Chicago schools and
teachers)
labor unions history, 113–116
Teaching Assistants Association (TAA),
99–101, 106
technology, 8
See also social media
terrorism, impact on policing, 223–224
Tifft, Mary Pat, 97

Tillis, Thom, 182
transformative demands, 156–157, 282
trauma and PTSD, for protesters, 243
Troubled Asset Relief Program (TARP),
19–20, 21, 195
troublemaking, as power, 10
Trump, Donald, 137, 279
Twitter and Tweets, 42, 104, 219–220, 242
2008 financial crisis. *See* financial crisis
of 2008

unionization, legislation, 86
unions. *See* labor unions
United Food and Commercial Workers
(UFCW), 71, 86–87, 91–92
United Public Workers of America, 114
US government. *See* federal government

victim-blaming, 31–32
voting and voters, 151, 168–169, 182,
183, 196

Waco (Texas), 231
wage and minimum wage
fast-food industry and franchises,
204–205
Seattle workers, 189, 192–193
service and retail jobs, 78–79, 81
at Walmart, 81–82, 84, 90, 92, 94–95, 97
and women, 113, 177–179
See also Fight for $15 campaign and
Show Me $15
Walker, Scott, 99–100, 103, 105–108,
110–111, 169–170
Wall Street. *See* banks; financial sector
Walmart
anti-union stance and efforts, 73, 74,
83, 86–87
beginnings, 81–82
in Bentonville (Arkansas), 93–94
business model and free enterprise,
83–85
change towards workers' demands,
88–89
Christian affiliation, 81–82, 90
distribution and logistics, 82, 88

Walmart *(continued)*
    gender discrimination, 78, 85
    and government assistance for
        workers, 80–81
    labor organization, 71–76, 85–93
    labor organizers at Home Office,
        73–74, 93, 94–98
    Occupy and activism, 89
    online organizing, 91
    personal experiences, 71–76
    and populism, 84–85, 94
    prices *vs.* wages, 81–82, 84, 90
    shareholders meeting and
        resolutions, 94–98
    stock option program, 83
    strikes, 71, 73, 74, 87–89, 122–123
    supply chain, 87–89
    wages, 81–82, 84, 90, 92, 94–95, 97
    and women, 78, 81–82, 85
    working conditions, 75, 82–83
    See also Organization United for
        Respect at Walmart (OUR Walmart)
Walmart Museum, 94
Walter Leitner International Human
    Rights Clinic, 218
Walton, H. Rob, 96
Walton, Sam, and heirs, 81, 82, 83,
    94, 96
War on Drugs, 232
War on Terror, and militarization of
    police, 223, 228
Way, Jamie, 91
"We are the 99 percent," success as
    message, 35–37
wealth concentration, 21
Weiner, Heather, 192–193, 206
white supremacy, 143, 156–157, 246
Williams, Kennard, 222–223, 226,
    240–241, 242, 245
Wilson, Darren, 220, 240
Wisconsin
    protests and Act 10, 99–105, 107–108,
        111, 117–118
    recalls from office, 105–107
    unions and collective bargaining, 115

Wolff, Richard D., 196–197
women
    austerity and Act 10, 103
    at home, 177–179
    liberation movement, 174
    support between, 243–244
    and wage, 113, 177–179
    and Walmart, 78, 81–82, 85
    as workers and in unions, 78, 113
Worker Adjustment and Retraining
    Notification (WARN) Act, 14
workers
    and communism, 199–200
    and extractive industries, 260–261,
        262–263
    fight for rights and severance pay,
        13–15
    financial sector, 21
    and government assistance, 80–81
    and outsourcing, 77
    part-time work, 80
    salaries and conditions, 189–190, 192
    scheduling of work, 79–80
    service and retail industries, 76–79
    and socialism, 189–190
    wage and minimum wage, 78–79,
        189, 192–193
    women as, 78, 113
    See also Fight for $15 campaign and
        Show Me $15
working class, 21, 35, 60, 76–77, 143,
    174–175,
Working Families Party (WFP), 15–17,
    209–210
WTO protests, 231–232
Wurf, Jerry, 115

You Are Never Alone (YANA), 252
young people, 32, 34, 41, 211

Zimmerman, George, 133–134, 136,
    140, 150–151
zombie foreclosures, 51, 53
Zuccotti Park, 2, 37, 40, 44
    See also Liberty Plaza

JULIETA SALGADO

SARAH JAFFE is an independent journalist and a reporting fellow at the Nation Institute. She is the cohost of *Dissent* magazine's Belabored podcast, as well as an editorial board member at *Dissent* and a columnist at *New Labor Forum*. Her work has appeared in *The Nation, Salon, The Week, The American Prospect,* the *Washington Post, The Atlantic,* and many other publications. *Necessary Trouble: America's New Radicals* is her first book. She lives in Newburgh, New York. For more information, follow her on Twitter @sarahljaffe or head to necessarytrouble.org.

The Nation Institute

Founded in 2000, **Nation Books** has become a leading voice in American independent publishing. The imprint's mission is to tell stories that inform and empower just as they inspire or entertain readers. We publish award-winning and bestselling journalists, thought leaders, whistleblowers, and truthtellers, and we are also committed to seeking out a new generation of emerging writers, particularly voices from underrepresented communities and writers from diverse backgrounds. As a publisher with a focused list, we work closely with all our authors to ensure that their books have broad and lasting impact. With each of our books we aim to constructively affect and amplify cultural and political discourse and to engender positive social change.

Nation Books is a project of The Nation Institute, a nonprofit media center established to extend the reach of democratic ideals and strengthen the independent press. The Nation Institute is home to a dynamic range of programs: the award-winning Investigative Fund, which supports groundbreaking investigative journalism; the widely read and syndicated website TomDispatch; journalism fellowships that support and cultivate over twenty-five emerging and high-profile reporters each year; and the Victor S. Navasky Internship Program.

For more information on Nation Books and The Nation Institute, please visit:

www.nationbooks.org
www.nationinstitute.org
www.facebook.com/nationbooks.ny
Twitter: @nationbooks